LOOSE WOMEN, LECHEROUS MEN

A Feminist Philosophy of Sex

LINDA LeMONCHECK

New York   Oxford   •   Oxford University Press   1997

Oxford University Press

Oxford   New York

Athens   Auckland   Bangkok   Bogota   Bombay   Buenos Aires
Calcutta   Cape Town   Dar es Salaam   Delhi   Florence   Hong Kong
Istanbul   Karachi   Kuala Lumpur   Madras   Madrid   Melbourne
Mexico City   Nairobi   Paris   Singapore   Taipei   Tokyo   Toronto   Warsaw

and associated companies in
Berlin   Ibadan

Copyright © 1997 by Linda LeMoncheck

Published by Oxford University Press, Inc.
198 Madison Avenue, New York, New York 10016

Oxford is a registered trademark of Oxford University Press

Library of Congress Cataloging-in-Publication Data
LeMoncheck, Linda.
Loose women, lecherous men : a feminist philosophy of sex / Linda
LeMoncheck.
p.   cm.
Includes bibliographical references and index.
ISBN 0-19-510555-9; ISBN 0-19-510556-7 (pbk.)
1. Sex—Philosophy.   2. Sexual ethics.   3. Feminist theory.
I. Title.
HQ12.L398   1997
306.7'01—dc20   96-34477

1 3 5 7 9 8 6 4 2

Printed in the United States of America
on acid-free paper

Preface

Contemporary feminism has the potential to be the defining political movement for women coming of age in the twenty-first century. However, nowhere is feminism more controversial among women than in its role as a sexually liberating force in women's lives. Indeed, feminist politics, once regarded as synonymous with women's sexual liberation, is now perceived by many women to be its antithesis. Despite their support for women's rights, many women reject feminism in the belief that feminists are antimale, antisex moralists who define men's violence against, and victimization of, women as pervasive features of modern sexual life. Many heterosexual women enjoy sex and value their femininity but complain that feminists make them feel guilty about it. Some women define their sexual liberation in terms of the freedom to be sexually promiscuous or in finding partners whose dominance or control is sexually exciting. Yet many feminists have equated both promiscuity and sexual submission with the oppression of women. Some feminists fight male oppression by choosing other women as lovers. Other women whose sex partners have always been women wonder why their sex should be a matter of feminist politics at all.

I believe that feminism can provide all women with an informative, wide-ranging, and practical politics for investigating the meaning and value of women's sexuality, now and in the future. If it is to do so, however, the philosophical foundations of feminism must be structured to embrace the complexity and diversity of individual women's sexual lives. Therefore, the feminist philosophy of sex introduced in the pages that follow offers a framework for thinking and talking about women's sexuality that can negotiate the tensions and advance the dialogue among a wide array of perspectives on women's sexual liberation. I am deeply concerned that the absence of such a framework, particularly in light of renewed attacks on feminism from the political right, has the potential to splinter feminist ranks, thus weakening feminism's efforts to promote the sexual agency and self-definition of all women. Therefore, this book is designed to appeal not only to those already committed to feminism but also to those who are skeptical of feminism's place in their sexual lives or uncertain of whether feminism can survive internal debates among competing feminist constituencies. The book is also written for those who would like to know more about how feminism and women's sexuality can be integrated into a framework for philosophizing about sex—a framework designed to encourage respect for sexual diversity in a caring community of socially responsible women and men.

Several colleagues, friends, and family members have made the writing of this enormously challenging project worth every frustrating moment. First, I wish to extend my sincere appreciation to Al Spangler and Jed Shafer, both of whom read the first long draft of this book from start to finish and took the time to offer their constructive criticisms throughout. To Robin Parks, Julie Van Camp, and Laurie Shrage, who read significant portions of the manuscript, I attribute many of the important feminist philosophical insights that would otherwise have escaped me. Robin has taught me more about the creativity and complexity of women than I ever thought possible. Alan Soble and John Miller shared their observations on feminist sexual politics with me in detailed correspondence. Carol Caraway, president of the Society for the Philosophy of Sex and Love, generously gave me the opportunity to read a portion of the manuscript at the Eastern Division meeting of the American Philosophical Association in Atlanta in 1993, where I received valuable feedback. The Philosophy Department at California State University, Long Beach, also organized and advertised two colloquia in which I presented papers on sexual promiscuity and the commercial sex industry, both of which became part of the current book.

To Ann Garry, Sandra Bartky, and Rosemarie Tong, I offer my thanks for their willingness to read the manuscript for Oxford University Press should they be asked. I would like to express a particularly heartfelt thank-you to Rosie, who has given me endless encouragement to pursue what for me is one of the most difficult and elusive disciplines I have ever encountered. Ann and Sandra generously contributed incisive commentary on the manuscript at a special session of the Pacific Division meeting of the American Philosophical Association in Berkeley, March 1997. I also wish to extend my appreciation to Julie Van Camp for initiating this panel discussion and organizing it in her consistently efficient and responsible way. Without the support and confidence of Robert Stewart, I would never have considered my work in feminist philosophy of interest to Oxford University Press. Rob also agreed to chair the Berkeley APA special session where my work in the feminist philosophy of sex was discussed. I also wish to thank philosophy advisers Philip Kitcher and Barry Stroud and editors Angela Blackburn, Robert Miller, and Cynthia Read at Oxford University Press for their encouragement and constructive commentary on my work. Cynthia was especially helpful in negotiating and generating the finished product. Production editor Paula Wald was instrumental in bringing the manuscript to print on schedule.

I commend my entire family for seeing me through the inevitable agony and un-certainty associated with this project without disowning me outright. I would also like to acknowledge the many wonderful friends who have consistently and conscientiously asked after the manuscript ("So Linda, how's the book!?") and supported me through the many months, now years, of its gestation. I dedicate this book to my husband Jed, whose generosity, good humor, and equanimity under stress are the envy of his wife. To all, I encourage your reflections and feedback on the discussion that follows.

Seal Beach, California   L. L.
June 1997

CONTENTS

LOOSE WOMEN, LECHEROUS MEN

Introduction

Loose women and lecherous men have been gloriously depicted throughout history in painting, prose, poetry, and song celebrating the passions and pleasures of unbridled sexuality. Nevertheless, conservative responses to sexual permissiveness are becoming more commonplace in the industrialized West, where anxieties over teenage pregnancy, sexually transmitted diseases, sexual deviance, and sexual violence have prompted a call for the revalorization of monogamy, loving commitment, and heterosexual stability.

Feminists are also deeply troubled by the escalation of sexual violence both at home and abroad, and the feminist demand for better health care and sex education for women is designed to help young people avoid unwanted pregnancy and debilitating disease. However, many feminists have long been suspicious that moralistic rejections of sexual license in the name of restoring social harmony merely reflect a sexual double standard of male lechery and female chastity, by which dutiful women are paradoxically required to be both whore and virgin to men's promiscuous heterosexual desire. Such feminists have thus encouraged women to defy traditional norms of feminine sexuality in an effort to hasten the sexual liberation of women. Expressions of such defiance may include women's safe and consensual explorations of sexual promiscuity, bisexuality, lesbianism, transsexualism and transvestism, sadomasochism, erotic dancing and other forms of public sexual performance, pornographic posing or acting, and prostitution. All such sexual practices are self-consciously defiant of the so-called traditional family values of moral conservatives because the sex need not be monogamous, heterosexual, stable, intimate, private, or loving and may involve graphic displays of nudity, bondage and discipline, group sex, sex with objects, or some other "perverse" sex. Feminists who advocate women's experimentation with such practices believe that a heterosexual and male-dominated society has a vested interest in confining women to sexual attitudes and practices that maintain the status quo of female heterosexual subordination. Therefore, one way to undermine such oppressive politics is to subvert precisely those sexual practices that reinforce male-identified sexual norms. Indeed, many feminists who adopt this perspective believe that the oppression of sexual diversity, not the oppression of women per se, should be feminism's primary enemy since both men's and women's challenges to the sexual status quo help subvert the sexual dominance of women circumscribed by heterosexual monogamy.[1]

However, other feminists are equally convinced that the appropriate expression of women's sexual liberation is the participation in caring and committed lesbian or heterosexual relationships in which the sexual politics of dominance and submission is self-consciously avoided. Feminists who would advocate more intimate and egalitarian relationships either with other women or with men are at odds with their more sexually radical sisters since they regard the practices of sex radicals as precisely the behavior most identified with men's sexual objectification and exploitation of women. From this view, promiscuity, sadomasochism, and commercial sex work are pervasively patriarchal forms of sexuality specifically designed to subordinate women to men, and feminists therefore cannot adopt them without also adopting the sexual politics of dominance and submission that accompanies them. Indeed, some feminists point out that the public display of radical feminist sexuality invites the sexual harassment, rape, and abuse of women by men who use women's consent to such displays as justifications for men's assaultive behavior. It is argued that male-dominated societies establish and perpetuate themselves by legitimizing the sexual intimidation of women in order to keep women in a state of dependency, wariness, and fear. Many feminists note that women will hesitate to take advantage of economic and social opportunities if men's sexual harassment of women is perceived as the cost of doing business. Women are also intimidated into remaining in physically abusive relationships upon which they are emotionally or financially dependent.[2]

Many women who consider themselves political liberals, if not sexual liberals, counter that feminism's emphasis on men's sexual intimidation of women reflects an antimale and antisex bias that equates all heterosexual sex with violence against women. They argue that although some men are abusive, the notion that men as a group conspire in smoke-filled rooms to oppress all women through sex promotes a form of sexism against men that should be anathema to any feminist pursuing sex equality. Some women regard feminist sexual harassment policies, rape brochures, and sexual abuse therapy as discouraging women from free, open, and responsible expression of their sexuality, bombarding women with an onslaught of oppressive propaganda that only undermines women's successful pursuit of sexual liberation. These women acknowledge the disturbingly high incidence of men's sexual violence against women, including men's sexual harassment, exploitation, and abuse of women. Nevertheless, they enjoy heterosexual sex and see themselves as the subjects of moralizing lectures by feminists interested in forcing all of the power dynamics—and so all of the realism, risk, and exhilaration—out of sex.[3]

Other more sexually conservative women simply want to feel comfortable being both feminine and feminist. They are in favor of equal opportunity for women under the law but find that some feminists' emphasis on men's sexual oppression of women limits the free expression of their femininity. Like their sexually more liberal counterparts, they understand how sexual violence against women threatens women's physical and emotional well-being, but they enjoy the company of men who respond to their efforts to look attractive. Such women will hesitate to discuss pay equity or reproductive rights in ways that risk identifying them with abrasive male-bashing.[4]

Indeed, many women whose sexuality ranges from the radical to the traditional find no place for feminist politics in their sexual lives. Some prostitutes' idea of sexual liberation is to be free of feminists picketing their street corners so that sex workers can get on with their work. Some lesbians whose homosexuality is a way of life and not a political choice say they pursue the sex that feels good to them whether or not it is "politically correct." Many promiscuous teenage girls simply want to be attractive to the most popular or best-looking boys despite the boys' mistreatment of them. Other women, from working-class mothers to society matrons, do not have the time, resources, energy, or interest to infuse their sex lives with feminist politics, and some women are not interested in having a sex life at all.

This book introduces a feminist philosophy of sex whose express purpose is to advance the dialogue among the competing viewpoints on women's sexual liberation typified in the preceding paragraphs. These sexual debates are philosophical as well as feminist, insofar as they raise not only questions about the nature and extent of the sexual oppression of women but also questions of conceptual clarification (What does it mean to be promiscuous? What is presupposed by the claim that pornography is degrading to women?) and normative evaluation (Is there anything wrong with sadomasochistic sex between consenting adults? Is men's sexual harassment of women ever morally justified?) that are the contemporary moral philosopher's stock-in-trade. Such debates also raise epistemological questions about how much women can know about their own sexual desires under conditions of sexual oppression and whether such knowledge is essential to women's sexual liberation. Concomitant metaphysical questions arise about the possibility of women's sexual agency under conditions of oppression and the likelihood of an enduring self whose sexual self-definition changes over time. Can philosophy help feminists negotiate the conceptual and normative tensions among our often disparate views of women's sexuality? Can feminists help philosophers understand how male dominance and control of women figure in some of the most fundamental questions philosophers raise about women's sexual preferences and sexual desires? Can women and men unfamiliar with either feminism or philosophy gain some insight into the variety and complexity of feminists' debates over women's sexuality in ways that will help them understand their own sexual needs and experiences?

My thesis is that a philosophical and feminist dialogue on women's sexual liberation is possible if women's sexuality—the erotic passions, pleasures, and preferences that circumscribe women as sexually desiring and desirable beings—is examined from two equally compelling perspectives: (1) the perspective of women's sexual oppression under conditions of individual and institutionalized male dominance; and

(2) the perspective of women's sexual liberation, identified both in terms of each woman's personal pursuit of sexual agency and self-definition and in terms of the sexual liberation of women as a class. This approach to women's sexuality posits that individual women's sexual lives are variously oppressive or liberating, and sometimes both at once; they are seldom static over time or identical to one another, and they are often complex and contradictory. Indeed, there may be as many different kinds of women's sexuality as there are women. As a feminist philosopher, I believe that a caring as well as critical understanding of this variety is essential to a feminism committed to cultural pluralism and social equity. The aim of this book is to develop a philosophical framework, which I call the "view from somewhere different," to recognize and celebrate the different ways that women find meaning and value in their sexual lives.

Underlying my arguments for this approach is my belief that feminist discussions of women's sexuality have bogged down in recent years. Feminists from a variety of theoretical perspectives have staked out apparently unwavering and unilateral positions on women's sexuality despite disagreement among ourselves as to the aims or values of those positions. This multitude of voices has been significant in establishing the importance of feminism in discussions of sex and sexuality, but it has also encouraged a backlash that paints feminism as either dangerously extremist or hopelessly divided. As a result, feminists of different backgrounds have appeared to each other, and to other women, to approach issues of women's sexuality in one of two exclusive ways: either by perpetuating the notion of women as sexual victims with an emphasis on the ways in which men dominate women through heterosexual sex or by downplaying the ways in which gender politics figures in the construction of women's sexuality, demanding instead that women be identified as self-determining sexual agents who freely choose the nature and value of our erotic lives.

My sense is that neither women's sexual oppression nor women's sexual liberation alone is the dominant thread in the tapestry of women's sexuality; my nascent postmodern sensibilities tell me that such discrete and oppositional thinking hinders our understanding of the complexity, ambiguity, and variety of sex and sexuality. My goal is to further a philosophical dialogue about sex among feminists and traditionalists alike through an exploration of the variety of ways in which a woman's risk of sexual victimization by men and her potential for sexual self-determination, despite conditions of institutionalized male dominance, influence the construction of her sexual identity. My fear is that without such a dialogue, feminism will become the very thing its detractors now claim: a fragmented and narrow-minded political movement whose members are unwilling to recognize and listen carefully to the concerns of women with different views than our own. Therefore, this book is designed both to help feminists frame the dialogue on women's sexuality in realistic and nondoctrinaire language and to help those wary of feminism to see the value of approaching issues in women's sexuality in the context of the larger political and cultural institutions from which they spring.

Chapter 1 introduces an epistemological framework for thinking and talking about the different ways that women living under conditions of gender inequality ascribe meaning and value to our sexual lives. In chapter 2 I argue that this framework can advance the feminist dialogue on the nature and value of sexual promiscuity in women's lives, by conceptualizing promiscuity as one of many avenues for expressing sexual intimacy, exploring sexual pleasure, and encouraging women's sexual empowerment. This chapter also introduces a sexual ethic that values both care and respect for persons in ways that can provide a place for sexual exclusivity and sexual promiscuity in women's lives. In chapter 3 I develop a concept of sexual difference that accommodates both so-called normal and perverse sexual practices within a larger schema for valuing diversity in human sexual experience. I use this schema to flesh out the sexual ethic introduced in chapter 2, which recommends locating all sexual practice within an actively caring community of women and men sensitive to the ways that gender oppression, sexual exploration, and the eroticization of power figure in the construction of human sexuality.

Chapter 4 examines the feminist claim that commercial sex work is degrading to women. I argue that strippers, prostitutes, pornography models, and other sex workers can be understood as both the defining subjects of their sexual experience and the commodified objects of oppressive and institutionalized male dominance. I then use this subject/object dialectic to offer some of the ways in which feminists who debate the nature and value of sex work can begin a constructive dialogue that recognizes both the patriarchal politics of the sex industry and the sexually liberating possibilities for the women who work within it. In chapter 5 I discuss how feminists from different theoretical backgrounds approach the subject of men's sexual intimidation of women—specifically, men's sexual harassment, rape, battering, and abuse of women and girls. I use the subject/object dialectic introduced in chapter 4 to describe women as survivors of a system of institutionalized sexual intimidation that neither determines women as sexual victims nor frees women fully to pursue our own passions and pleasures. I then examine how a sexual ethic incorporating both care and respect can help women and men better understand each other's sexual experience and promote supportive sexual relationships in which sexual intimidation is absent. I emphasize by way of conclusion the importance of engaging incommensurable political views despite any apparent commonality or consensus and suggest how the framework for thinking and talking about women's sexuality described in this book can be used as a model for doing so.

Many people who associate philosophy with the logic of Aristotle and the rationality of eighteenth-century Enlightenment do not find the passion, eccentricity, and ambivalence of sex conducive to philosophical investigation. From this perspective, sex doesn't seem to be *sex* anymore, once philosophers get their intellectual or analytical hands on it. I share this concern, since I found some of my own philosophizing about women's sexuality frustrating in its inability to express what I believe to be the profoundly complex and contradictory nature of sex. Philosophy and sex do not enjoy an easy or exact fit, nor do I expect or want them to do so. One of the pleasures that I derive from sexual arousal is the extent to which I can completely lose all sense of myself as a philosopher and simply enjoy the sensuousness of the moment. As I have said elsewhere, I do not want to discuss Cartesian dualism in bed; I want to have sex.[5] On the other hand, perhaps some of my frustration with trying to use philosophy to speak a kind of sexually informative feminist language reflects the aptness of the postmodern injunction to abandon the differentiation and oppositional valuation of terms like "intellectual" and "sexual." Indeed, my philosophical writing about sex may be overly intellectualized or humorless for some, too politically contentious for others. This problem may only be exacerbated by my determination to give the reader some sense of the emotional turmoil and psychic tension that many women living under both individual and institutionalized heterosexual intimidation confront on a daily basis. Under such constraints, I am convinced that what counts as reason in Western culture must accommodate the experiences of real women living the real contradiction of being both the sexual objects of men's gaze and the defining subjects of our sexual experience as women.

In short, writing this book has taught me that there is much concerning traditional analytic philosophizing about sex that needs reevaluation and rejuvenation. I believe that contemporary feminist philosophical investigation can bring a unique and valuable perspective to discussions of sex and sexuality. My own recommendations for advancing the dialogue on women's sexuality are admittedly not free of bias toward my own race, class, sexual preference, age, marital status, physical ability, or gender. One of the claims of this book is that each of us is partial to our own social perspective but that such partiality can be a source for recognizing and celebrating the differences among all of us. What I hope is that the combination of political, sociological, historical, and philosophical commentaries that have provided the resources for this book will help the reader make some positive sense out of the partiality that each of us brings to our own, and others', sexual lives.

Yet I also believe that cohesion and cooperation, not deconstruction and dismemberment, is what gives contemporary feminism its strength to foment change. Thus, I will remain loyal to those philosophical schemas that aim at combining, without universalizing, women's efforts from disparate quarters to effect liberation and transformation for all women. At the same time, my enterprise is profoundly postmodern in its refusal to authorize the framework I set forth as *the* feminist philosophy of sex but merely as one possible framework among many that can encourage ongoing conversation about women's sexuality.

1

What Is a Feminist Philosophy of Sex?

Overview

Feminist philosophy is a discipline rich in its diversity of speculative argument and practical politics. Despite our differences, feminist philosophers are united in the vision of a philosophy free of the misogyny and male bias that have characterized so much of Western philosophical tradition. Feminist philosophy's challenge to this tradition has been the challenge of repairing the distortions, centering the marginalizations, and valorizing what were once considered the trivial, if not invisible, facets of *woman's* nature, *woman's* knowledge, and *woman's* happiness.[1]

However, contemporary feminists also agree that unless feminist philosophers attend to women's diversity, women will remain stereotyped by the same kinds of restrictive and ahistorical paradigms as those advanced by traditional philosophy. Therefore, many feminist philosophers have advocated the exploration of the complexity and variety of women's experience. Such an exploration has been recommended as a way of learning about women by listening to our individual voices, differentiated by such features as race, class, and sexual preference. In so doing, feminists hope to avoid the essentialism of claiming some single, immutable, and universal nature of "Woman."[2]

A feminist philosophy of sex reflects these feminist philosophical values. Both ancient and contemporary traditions in the philosophy of sex can be characterized by speculative and critical inquiry into the nature, meaning, and value of sex and sexuality.[3] A specifically feminist philosophy of sex can be characterized as one that regards speculative and critical inquiry into the nature, meaning, and value of women's sexuality as philosophically valuable and as one whose express purpose is *not* to trivialize, distort, or ignore the variety and complexity of women's sexuality in any discussions of human sexuality. A feminist philosophy of sex acknowledges that women compose a diverse group whose members vary by such features as race, class, ethnicity, nationality, religion, sexual preference, age, and physical ability. To avoid the ontological myopia of traditional essentialist claims about women, a feminist philosophy of sex acknowledges the diversity of women's sexual experience, and values, for their own sake, the voices that give testimony to that diversity.

From more traditional philosophical discussions of sex, we might learn that the term "sex" has several meanings: an essential and biological maleness or femaleness; a culturally relative and socially constructed masculinity or femininity, usually referred to by the term "gender"; the activity constitutive of the arousal and pursuit of erotic passion and pleasure; the capacity for reproducing the species; and the expression of spiritual communion and love. Normative evaluations accompanying such conceptual clarification might focus on what constitutes good versus bad sex and the role of good sex in a life well lived. However, many feminists have been critical of traditional philosophical analyses of sex and sexuality for the ways in which such approaches fail to situate men and women within a context that is sensitive to what feminists refer to as the politics of gender. From this perspective, all human interaction is gendered, such that any understanding of sex, as well as art, science, law, education, and the family requires an analysis of the way such institutions are influenced by cultural conceptions of masculinity and femininity. Moreover, it is argued that such conceptions of gender delineate relations of status and power between men and women. Therefore, women's and men's sexuality examined through the gendered lens of contemporary Western culture requires an examination of the ways in which individuals' sexual preferences and desires—the how, when, where, and with whom of erotic arousal and satisfaction—are influenced by the relations of dominance and submission that characterize the traditional gender roles of Western culture.[4] The assertion that some societies do not regard men as the dominant gender or that gender relations are only contingently oppressive is nevertheless consistent with the claim that an understanding of the culture in which women and men live requires an understanding of the gender relations of that culture. The feminist philosophy of sex introduced in this chapter provides a framework for thinking and talking about women's sexuality within a gendered context of contemporary Western norms, in which the diversity of women's voices, often silenced or marginalized by traditional philosophical approaches to women's sexuality, can be heard.

The strength and unifying vision of this feminist framework is its recognition that women's sexuality can be exploited as a powerful tool for the social, economic, and political subordination of women. Many feminists point to the pervasive sexual harassment, rape, prostitution, pornographic degradation, and spousal abuse of women as strong evidence of the prevalence of powerful social institutions supporting men's subordination of women through heterosexual sex.[5] According to this view, women's sexual desires and preferences are carefully circumscribed and controlled by cultural sanctions aimed at maintaining heterosexual male power, status, and privilege. Such sanctions are patriarchal, according to Marilyn Frye, when they form part of "institutions, relationships, roles, and activities which are male-defined, male-dominated and operating for the benefit of males and the maintenance of male privilege."[6] Many feminists claim that when a woman lives in a patriarchal society, her sexual exploration, pleasure, and agency become targets for her sexual restriction, repression, and violation.[7] A feminist philosophy of sex explores the nature and extent of this oppressive environment and seeks to expose women's sexual subordination in an effort to promote change. Thus, philosophy of sex is uniquely positioned to benefit from a feminist analysis, since philosophy of sex examines those very relations in which women's autonomous voices are often submerged, if not silenced altogether.

However, I believe it is a mistake for a feminist philosophy of sex to define women's sexuality solely, or even primarily, in terms of men's sexual subordination of women. In so doing, feminists run the risk of recreating and reinforcing the very victimization from which we would extricate ourselves. Feminists must expose the often brutal, coercive, and humiliating nature of women's heterosexual experience if we wish to garner women's support and justify an activist feminist agenda for change in women's sexual lives. On the other hand, women's sexuality is also the source for women's pursuit of erotic pleasure, our creation of erotic fantasy, and our expression of erotic communion. The experience of this aspect of a woman's sexuality encourages her to view herself as a sexual agent and sexual subject, not merely as the sexual object of male heterosexual subordination. Indeed, women's sexual agency is essential, if women living under conditions of gender inequality can be ascribed the power to mitigate, if not eliminate, our oppression. Yet women as well as men can be both ignorant and fearful of this dimension of women's erotic lives. A feminist philosophy of sex must encourage safe, honest, and open discussions of both the dangers and pleasures of women's sexuality, if this philosophy seeks to facilitate each woman's discovery of the meaning and value of the erotic in her own life.[8]

The Dialectical and Contextual Relationship between Gender and Sexuality

The role of sexual agency and self-definition in a caring and cooperative community and the extent of women's sexual freedom within oppressive social institutions continue to be debated among feminists and traditionalists alike. The introduction to this book outlines some of the controversies over how women's discovery of their sexuality should be realized: examples include choosing promiscuous experimentation over monogamous commitment, traditional femininity over radical sexuality, feminist partnerships over depoliticized sex. Indeed, many women do not regard their sexual preferences as choices at all but simply as ways of living out their sexual lives. To promote constructive dialogue and negotiate tensions among conflicting views, we need an epistemological framework for thinking and talking about a wide variety of perspectives on women's sexuality. The framework that I will outline in this chapter and that will inform the remainder of the book describes women's sexuality both as a function of women's sexual oppression under conditions of individual and institutionalized male dominance and as a function of women's sexual liberation under those same conditions. Such a framework defines a dialectical and variable relationship between the politics of gender and the erotic possibilities of sex: a woman's gender circumscribes her sexuality within the framework of dominance and sub-mission constitutive of Western cultural conceptions of masculinity and femininity; in opposition to sexual oppression, sexuality informs gender with potentially liberat-ing strategies for transforming women's sexual exploration, pleasure, and agency.

Conceived as a fluid, variable, and often unstable relationship between her sex-ual oppression and her liberation, a woman's sexuality may be both oppressive and liberating over the course of her life, often simultaneously so. A disaffected wife grown tired of her sexual relations with a domineering husband may find care and consideration in a lesbian lover. Women who have found a sexual community in which to live out their sadomasochistic fantasies may feel the constant anxiety of be-ing "found out" by more conservative family and coworkers. An actress who regards her pornographic performance art as an expression of sexual liberation may also be a woman whose audience interprets her display as her consent to be the sexual sub-ordinate of men. The sexually harassed employee may be motivated by her harass-ment to organize her company's first formal grievance procedures. All such exam-ples suggest that women's sexual lives are dialectically situated within a culture that circumscribes women both as the subordinated objects of an oppressive heterosexu-ality and as the defining subjects of our sexual experience as women. Because women live in such a culture, each woman's knowledge of her own "true" sexual needs and desires is constrained and complicated by the contradiction of living as both object and subject of her sexuality. Such contradictions play themselves out in ways unique to the character and history of each woman.

Given the variety and complexity in women's sexuality, I take seriously the post-modern feminist injunction to be wary of universalizing prescriptions of sexual norms. Postmodern feminists would argue that any feminist philosophy of sex is mis-guided if it aims to reveal "the truth" about women's erotic lives. The dialectical framework I have introduced for understanding women's sexuality suggests that women's sexual lives are misrepresented by perspectives that do not appreciate the intersection of gender, sexuality, and male heterosexual domination. However, many postmodern feminists would claim that a gendered perspective of this type is no more universalizable than the stories traditional Western philosophy has told about women's sexuality. Competing feminist theories of women's sexual subordination, like all theories, become texts to be interpreted, stories to be told about the way the world appears from the perspective of the storyteller. According to many postmod-ern feminists, we can hardly expect feminism in general, or any feminist theory in particular, to tell us how women as a class *ought* to understand women's sexuality, when feminists have faulted the whole of Western philosophy for doing the very same thing.[9]

The feminist philosophy of sex described thus far has challenged the position of power and authority of those who traditionally ask the questions of philosophy by challenging the legitimacy of sociopolitical and intellectual hierarchies that have historically stifled the philosophical voice of women. It is a challenge that reminds us that those who ask the questions in philosophy determine what the questions are, how they are formulated, what methods are used to answer them (including who is consulted as an expert in the field), and the answers that are ultimately given. If the theoretical foundation for any feminist philosophy of sex *requires* us to appreciate a dialectical relation between gender and sexuality in women's lives, then a feminist philosophy of sex appears to advocate exactly the kind of epistemological authoritarianism and moral elitism that oppresses dissent and difference.

It would appear, therefore, that a feminist philosophy of sex cannot, without hypocrisy, advance the "true" story of women's sexuality if its own agenda is one of challenging the philosophical canon's assumed monopoly on truth. Indeed, the very presumption of a theoretical foundation in feminist philosophy of sex would seem to be no more than a thinly veiled attempt to offer an ahistorical, univocal, and universalizable definition of *the* feminist philosophy of sex from what is more accurately described as a historically situated, culturally loaded perspective of a female author. Furthermore, if a feminist philosophy of sex is being constructed within a patriarchal context, how free of male bias and female misrepresentation can it be?

What these questions imply is that both the nature and evaluation of women's sexuality are social constructions arising out of the particular culture, history, and context in which claims to women's sexuality are made. The assertion that there exists a dialectical relation between gender and sexuality is simply an instantiation of the more general assertion that human practice is socially situated. As Linda Alcoff points out, "Gender is not a point to start out from in the sense of being a given thing but is, instead, a posit or construct, formalizable in a nonarbitrary way through a matrix of habits, practices, and discourses."[10] According to this view, theories of women's sexuality that are gender-sensitive are more representative of the complex and diverse group that makes up the class "woman" than those that are not because they are theories that acknowledge the bias of social location. Because feminist theory is itself socially situated, what we cannot say is that feminism presents an undistorted or "true" vision of women's sexuality.[11]

If we adopt Alcoff's relational matrix, then it also appears that a woman's gender cannot be discretely separated from such features as her race, class, or sexual preference. Being the woman who is Linda LeMoncheck *means* being a white, middleclass, heterosexual female, not someone who is a woman *and* white *and* middle-class. Such features of human being are relational and interlocking, such that "one cannot dislodge one piece without disturbing the others."[12] The affinity many feminists feel for the struggle against racism, classism, heterosexism, and imperialism is a function of our belief that interlocking social relations will generate interlocking social oppressions as well. However, the insidious and complex nature of the interlocking of social oppressions has the unfortunate consequence that many women, including feminists, do not recognize our complicity in our own and others' victimization.[13]

How can these observations be used to flesh out a dialectic between gender and sexuality that is sensitive to the sexual experiences, preferences, and desires of a wide variety of women? I have already argued that such a dialectic acknowledges both the potential for individual women's sexual subordination by men and by maledominated institutions, and women's capacity to liberate themselves from such subordination to define their sexuality in their own terms. Moreover, if gender is but one of many interlocking social relations, then when we investigate the relation between gender and women's sexuality, we will be embarking on a complex contextual study of the ways in which all such social relations as race, gender, class, ethnicity, sexual preference, nationality, religion, age, and physical ability inform, and are informed by, women's sexuality. I will refer to this composite of interlocking social relations as a person's "social location" or as the "contextual relations" in a person's life. Third, such a study will also ask us to pay careful attention to the unique as well as the unifying details of the lives of the individual women whose erotic preferences are under investigation. From this perspective, women are understood both in terms of their sexual specialness and in the ways they may share sexual anxieties, needs, or interests with other women. And finally, because we are adopting the perspective that the philosophy of sex is socially constructed, any philosophizing about the nature and value of women's sexuality will be informed by a dialectic between the philosopher and her subject, which will affect the social locations of each. Not only is the subject socially situated in the complex ways I just described; the philosopher is socially situated as well.[14]

The existence of such bias in the philosopher of sex can be a source for either exclusionary or visionary practice. The remainder of this chapter discusses three ways in which the bias of social location figures in traditional philosophizing about sex and sexuality. My claim is that the contextual and dialectical investigation just outlined offers a more representative vision of women's sexuality than any of the three philosophical perspectives I will describe later. The chapter concludes with an elaboration of this alternative perspective, whose appreciation of sexual diversity within a caring community can provide us with the feminist philosophy of sex that informs the remainder of the book.

The "View from Somewhere Better"

One perspective in philosophy of sex is a perspective familiar to feminist philosophers; I shall call it the "view from somewhere better." The "view from somewhere better" is a perspective in which a philosopher's social location becomes social prejudice due to a belief in the superiority of his social location. This view informs the work of some of the ancient philosophers, such as Aristotle, and medieval scholars, such as Thomas Aquinas, both of whom believed that because men's rational faculties are superior to women's, a husband should act as his wife's governor in marriage. By adopting the "view from somewhere better," Arthur Schopenhauer could assert that a woman's primary purpose is to act as the inferior but necessary procreative instrument by which a man reproduces other men. This same perspective prompts Friedrich Nietzsche to claim, "When a woman has scholarly inclinations, there is generally something wrong with her sexual nature; . . . man, if I may say so, is the barren animal."[15]

These philosophers perceived themselves as having an intellectually privileged place from which to expound on human nature because they were men purportedly endowed with superior rational faculties to those of women. It is the sort of socially located bias in which little, if any, attempt is made to understand or empathize with the view of "others" (in this case, women) because others are believed to be inferior to "us" (in this case, men). It is a perspective that acknowledges social location yet fails to acknowledge the social bias inherent in that location. To use María Lugones's terminology, this prejudice is the result of an absence of "'world'-traveling," in which the philosopher not only acknowledges the partiality of her own location but also makes an effort to understand the location of others. An absence of "world"-traveling indicates that one has not attempted to "understand what it is to be them and what it is to be ourselves in their eyes."[16] Because the "view from somewhere better" in much of traditional philosophy greatly distorts the lives and experiences of women, it is a perspective many feminist philosophers have sought to avoid.

Therefore, it is ironic to discover in at least some feminist theorizing about women's sexuality that it too assumes a "view from somewhere better." This bias is revealed when feminists replace an "androcentric" or "masculinist" vision of women's sexual life, in which women's sexuality is defined exclusively in men's terms, with an equally gynocentric vision (from the Greek "gyne" or "female"). From such a perspective, being a woman somehow privileges, not just opens, the discourse. In a gynocentric world, women can give not simply a better account of their own sexuality but the best account of it.[17] If all philosophers of sex are socially located, however, such feminist discourse is merely one socially located vision among many and so subject to the same kind of distorting prism as traditional philosophy of sex.

As I have noted, this does not mean that all social locations are equally biased, only that all social locations are biased in some way or other. Feminists have sometimes argued that without identifying women's perspective as the right or true perspective, feminists can offer no formal justification for change in women's sexual lives. However, I have argued in favor of situating less biased, but not unbiased, theories of women's sexuality within a composite of interlocking social relations that circumscribe both women's sexual oppression and women's sexual liberation. Such a framework suggests that feminists can offer an agenda for women's sexuality that recommends listening to the diverse voices of women. Such an agenda is simply not *the* agenda for securing women's sexual agency and self-definition, nor can such an agenda promise to be representative of all women in all times and places. Furthermore, the perception that some feminists are promoting an oppressive gynocentrism has only succeeded in dividing feminist ranks, producing a sizable group of women suspicious of the essentialism that often hides behind an appeal to "the woman's voice."[18]

The "View from Nowhere"

One way to avoid the prejudice of gynocentrism is to advocate what I will call, borrowing an expression from Thomas Nagel, the "view from nowhere."[19] Someone who adopts the "view from nowhere" claims that there is an ideal or privileged position from which one can ascertain indubitable truths about oneself and the world. This privileged position is purportedly devoid of the particularity and partiality of any more personal perspective. In this way, the "view from nowhere" differs from the "view from somewhere better" in that the "view from nowhere" is intended as a perspective of objectivity and emotional distance whose ideal observer avoids the prejudices of the "view from somewhere better" by being removed from any position of bias. Thus, one who adopts the "view from nowhere" claims the epistemological advantage over the advocate of the "view from somewhere better" through the ability to make claims about the world that are true for all persons in all times and places. Those who would advocate adopting the "view from nowhere" would argue that particularly in such areas as mathematics and the physical sciences, an objective and impartial perspective is essential for formulating theorems, completing proofs, and constructing empirical hypotheses whose confirmation can be validated by any observer.

Contrary to such views, some feminist philosophers have underscored how a "view from nowhere" in the sciences is in fact socially and historically biased by the particular scientific methodology, subject matter, and investigator chosen to perform the research. Feminism's contribution to philosophical questions about scientific objectivity is the recognition that science is a gendered discipline whose standards and methods may be partial not only to time and place but also to the gender of the scientist, whose traditionally male-identified research practices marginalize, ignore, or silence the scientific contributions of women. Moreover, because so-called impartial research often yields results that unjustly discriminate against women in favor of men, feminists argue that the modern notion of "objective" science must be seriously reconsidered.[20]

In virtue of its purportedly unbiased stance, the "view from nowhere" also lays claim to making normative judgments without unfairly favoring one person or opinion over another. From this perspective, impartiality and objectivity are essential to making fair judgments, justifying right behavior, and condemning what is wrong. However, feminist theorists in epistemology, ethics, and aesthetics have joined feminist philosophers of science to contest the claim that men in historically and culturally situated contexts can successfully or noncontroversially determine one reality that is valid for all persons.[21] Feminists interested in epistemology and value theory have argued that in the name of objectivity and impartiality, traditional philosophy's assessment of what human beings can know and how we evaluate our world has misrepresented women's voices or excluded them altogether. Feminists contend that such misrepresentation occurs because the male philosopher who adopts the "view from nowhere" does not recognize that his sense of what counts as objectivity will reflect the partiality of his gendered location. In this sense, he differs from someone who adopts the "view from somewhere better," who recognizes his own difference but simply believes that his location is the superior one. Nevertheless, the perspective of the purportedly ideal observer from the "view from nowhere" is like the perspective of the observer of the "view from somewhere better," because the "view from nowhere" is ideal only with reference to some favored way of viewing the world. Absent any recognition that his perspective is only one of many partial perspectives, the philosopher who adopts the "view from nowhere" assumes that *his* ideal perspective is *everyone's* perspective.

The "view from nowhere" inspired Immanuel Kant to assert that sex outside of marriage is a degradation of human nature. David Hume adopted this perspective when he claimed that marriage is an institution entered into by mutual consent and has for its end the propagation of the species.[22] It is the perspective to which the "view from somewhere better" inevitably shifts when the bias of superior location must be claimed as universal truth. Postmodernists have challenged much of Western philosophy for assuming that there can be one correct use of the human faculties which will reveal truths about the world that are valid for all. A feminist philosophy of sex that is gender-sensitive to the partiality of social location takes great pains to be critical of such universalizing perspectives and to avoid them as much as possible.

Moreover, I would argue that the "view from nowhere" may be a more distorted and insidious perspective than the "view from somewhere better," precisely because the "view from nowhere" assumes that an unbiased, ahistorical, and universalizable vision of the world is both possible and desirable. No one knows the pain of prejudice better than women who struggle to form an identity of their own in a misogynistic and androcentric society. Feminists' advocacy for equal rights is in part an advocacy for fair and impartial treatment under the law. Nevertheless, I would argue that the "view from nowhere" too often disguises the very prejudices it is designed to mitigate by presupposing a "truth" about the world that in fact favors a particular social location.

For example, the feminist theoretical perspective often called "liberal feminism" contends that gender blindness in the law encourages gender-blind social attitudes which, it is argued, will ultimately result in a more democratic and fully human community. It is claimed that as soon as men and women are given equal protection under the law, such crimes against women as men's sexual assault and sexual intimidation will be indefensible in principle and punishable in fact. From a liberal feminist's perspective, sex equality requires that pay equity and political parity be the rule and not the exception. I interpret this position as advocating the adoption of the "view from nowhere" in pursuit of sex equality for women, since a liberal feminist advocates gender-blind legal statutes not out of a recognition of the bias of her particular social location but because she believes that gender does not and should not matter in the distribution of social goods.[23]

The attraction of this "view from nowhere" is that unlike the "view from somewhere better," it eschews gender prejudice in the name of social equality. Reference to human beings or persons is preferred over references to women or men, because speech and action in human terms is believed to be objective, neutral, or impartial—the only perspective, a liberal feminist would argue, that can guarantee social justice for all.

A prevailing problem with liberal feminism's "view from nowhere," however, is that it fails to acknowledge the bias of social location. Subjectivity and partiality cloaked in the morally superior guise of objectivity and neutrality is no guarantee that justice for all will be served, when justice itself is circumscribed by the social location of those who judge. Many feminists point out that questions about human nature, human knowledge, and human happiness are questions that are asked by *someone or other* who is socially situated by race, gender, and class, among many other things. To ignore or deny the claim that gender matters in determinations of social justice is to assume that women's interests are the same as men's, when they may not be. The failure in the "view from nowhere" to acknowledge the bias of every social location is the failure to acknowledge that one observer cannot speak for all. Susan Bordo writes:

> Professional women saw in the "neutral" standards of objectivity and excellence the means of being accepted as "humans," not women. . . . In a culture that is *in fact* constructed by gender duality, however, one *cannot* simply be "human." This is no more possible than it is possible that we can "just be people" in a racist culture. . . . Our lan-

guage, intellectual history, and social forms are "gendered"; there is no escape from this fact and from its consequences on our lives.[24]

Bordo's philosophizing about "this fact" of social location may come dangerously close to the kind of epistemological authoritarianism I have sought to avoid. What feminists can say is that in theorizing about women's sexuality, one must appreciate gender because one paints a more representative picture of women's sexuality with gender than without it.

By assuming that a universal epistemological ideal is possible, liberals and conservatives alike who adopt the "view from nowhere" fail to recognize that individuals from other travelable "worlds" may not share the same observations. Furthermore, if, by adopting the "view from nowhere," I ignore or deny that gender matters in determinations of social practice, I will have no incentive for the empathic understanding recommended by María Lugones's "world"-traveling. Even the "view from somewhere better" must ultimately devolve into a denial of its own socially located bias, if its advocates make claims about human nature and human happiness that are purported to be true

The "View from Everywhere"

A postmodern response to both the "view from somewhere better" and the "view from nowhere" is to replace the *mis*location of gender prejudice and the *non*location of gender blindness with the *dis*location of gender deconstruction. In their pursuit of a philosophy that explodes the notion of a single, unifying reality, postmodern feminist philosophers celebrate diversity by celebrating the multiple possibilities of social location. We can call this third perspective, the "view from everywhere," since a postmodernist believes that in order to avoid the oppressive biases of either an assumption of superiority or the presumption of universal truth, we must embrace the multiplicity of *every* social voice.[25]

Postmodernism has a strong appeal for feminists who perceive women's voices to be misunderstood by the commitment to rationality, objectivity, and truth of the "view from nowhere." In an era marked by a strong advocacy for multiculturalism within the academy as well as outside it, a postmodern vision holds out the promise of an inclusive global perspective that many feminists regard as crucial to their political vision of respect for diversity and difference.[26] A postmodern celebration of diversity in sexual preference has particular resonance for a feminist philosopher of sex interested in exploring the depth and complexity of women's sexual experience and desire. It is only through such an exploration, many feminists believe, that a woman can escape her identity as sexual victim of a misogynous and heterosexist patriarchy and begin to pursue a self-determined sexual identity.[27]

However, if both the "view from somewhere better" and the "view from nowhere" suffer from appreciating too little about social location in assessments of women's sexuality, a postmodern vision suffers from the determination to appreciate too much. My contention that the human condition is socially situated implies that the human condition is a partial and incomplete condition of being and knowing. Therefore, no matter how much we learn about human diversity or no matter how much of an effort we make at "world"-traveling, as socially situated human beings living in a finite place and time, we cannot, at any one moment, travel to all worlds at once. Feminist progress can be made by moving away from the "view from somewhere better" or the "view from nowhere" to less partial ways of knowing; the non-partiality of total knowledge is beyond us.

By regarding any partiality of location as necessarily prejudiced, postmodernists drive us to an impossible dislocation where no one can conceivably go. In celebration of the multiple possibilities of social location, postmodernism seems to require an impossible omniscience. Yet a postmodern philosophical claim is that we must dislocate ourselves, if we are to be free of the oppression of located knowledge. Ironically, by advocating what Susan Bordo refers to as a relentless heterogeneity,[28] postmodern feminists advocate an epistemological ubiquity that is not only impossible to achieve but is no less demanding of conformity than their modern Enlightenment counterparts.

Furthermore, by diffusing women's voices amid a sea of multiplicity, this postmodern view deprives feminism not only of a coherent political agenda but also of any identifiably gendered voice that could call for liberation and change for the speakers with that voice. Many postmodern feminists would contend that until we make the hierarchical and value-laden opposition of "man" versus "woman" incoherent, the inferiority and otherness ascribed to women will remain intact.[29] However, I would argue that it is impossible to condemn the patriarchal oppression of women without giving meaning and value to the injustice of hierarchical gender categories; and the apparent absence of any unifying postmodern vision of gender or sexuality makes a foundational framework for advancing a feminist dialogue in women's sexuality superfluous. Thus, the *deconstruction* of gender seems to make the *destruction* of a specifically feminist agenda inevitable.

The "View from Somewhere Different"

I have contended that a postmodernist incorrectly believes that any partiality of location requires deconstruction. Indeed, it is through the perception of the partiality of our own location that we perceive ourselves as different from others. Without this perception, as I noted in my critique of the "view from nowhere," there is no incentive for the empathic understanding of another's location, which is the essence of María Lugones's "world"-traveling. Yet I have also noted in my critique of the "view from somewhere better" that the mere perception of partiality or difference is not enough to keep from misunderstanding women's sexuality. A conscientious attempt at an empathic understanding of women's sexuality is also required. Social location becomes social prejudice when, in María Lugones's words, we "arrogantly" fail to recognize the existence of other social locations or when we refuse to "world"-travel in deference to a perceived superiority.[30] Yet "world"-traveling becomes impossible from a postmodern philosopher's "view from everywhere," since those who adopt this view are required to be in all places at once.

If none of these three epistemological perspectives can properly capture the importance of social location for a feminist philosophy of sex, what are the alternatives?

The perception that my worldview is neither better, nor nowhere, nor everywhere, but simply *somewhere different* is the perception that (1) my "world" is not the only social location worth knowing; (2) no matter how much or how often I "world"-travel, my "world" will always be partial, because I am always *somewhere*; and (3) there are other "worlds" whose members may wish to travel to my own. For women and men engaged in the practice of philosophy, what I shall call the "view from somewhere different" is a celebration of the social location—the partiality, particularity, and contextuality—of all philosophical investigation. From this perspective, a philosopher of sex can locate both the subject and the investigator of her philosophical enterprise and begin to appreciate the complex and variable dialectic between them. The "view from somewhere different" also acknowledges that "world"-traveling will be intrusive if visits are involuntary. The "view from somewhere different" advocates not epistemological imperialism but a sharing of "world"-views in a collaborative and empathic effort of being and knowing.

If the "view from somewhere different" can acknowledge difference without presuming superiority and without devolving into dislocation, then such a perspective can offer philosophy of sex a more representative vision of women's sexual experiences, preferences, and desires than any of the other three perspectives discussed. Such a perspective will also recognize that different women will have very different experiences of sexual subordination by men and that some women may be more empowered to determine the course of their sexual lives than others. It will acknowledge that any one woman's life is a unique, complex, and variable mix of sexual subordination and empowerment under institutional and ideological constraints that limit the sexual choices she makes. Thus, the "view from somewhere different" incorporates the dialectic between gender and sexuality introduced earlier in the chapter—a dialectic that understands individual women's sexuality as the contextual interplay between the gender politics of sexual subordination and the sexual politics of women's liberation. If one of the aims of a feminist philosophy of sex is to repair the distortions of patriarchal visions of women's sexuality, then the "view from somewhere different" seems tailor-made to a feminist philosophy of sex.

However, a counterargument could be made that the "view from somewhere different" only succeeds in oppressing women, not liberating them. This argument claims that for centuries, being a woman has meant being other to man's self, object to his subject, inferior to his superior. Woman has been marginal to man's centrality, trivial to his importance, somewhere to his everywhere. Indeed, it is the term "man" which is used to mean "human"; woman is someone *different*. In short, in a culture in which not only the social power and prestige but also the ascription of meaning and value is controlled by men, to be different from men means to be *inferior* to them. Therefore, it can be argued that by adopting the "view from somewhere different" within a patriarchal context, the feminist philosophy of sex advocated here only reinforces the notion that women are inferior to men.

This counterargument further suggests that by requiring all locations to be in some way biased or partial, the "view from somewhere different" condemns us to a world of racism, sexism, classism, heterosexism, and imperialism. According to this line of reasoning, it is only by overcoming, not celebrating, our partiality that social prejudice will be eliminated. Instead of liberating women from the sexual subordination of men, a feminist philosophy of sex that adopts the "view from somewhere different" only succeeds in keeping woman "in her place."

The success of this counterargument, however, relies on retaining the patriarchal notion that "different" means "inferior," "wrong," or "bad." One's pointing out my difference from men is indeed oppressive when it is used to make me feel inferior or less valuable. Yet feminist philosophers have often pointed out that we need not adopt the view that difference is bad. Indeed, when all selves are "others," the notion that one self is better than another cannot be justified by appeal to difference alone. When *everyone* is different, the value of difference is an open question.

Indeed, racism, sexism, classism, heterosexism, and imperialism are the result of either believing we are superior to others who are different from us or believing there is no difference among persons when there *is* difference. Yet these are precisely the prejudices of the "view from somewhere better" and the "view from nowhere," respectively. On the contrary, the "view from somewhere different" recognizes difference without a presumption of superiority, thus avoiding the prejudice of both of the other perspectives. Furthermore, this recognition explodes any attempts to equate the polarities of superior/inferior, right/wrong, or good/bad with those of man/woman or male/female, without denying that there are differences between each pole. In so doing, the "view from somewhere different" avoids making the postmodern mistake of exploding the polarities themselves and deconstructing the notion of difference in a way that forces us to be all things to all people.

The "view from somewhere different" recommends that we perceive partiality and difference in all of us. A feminist philosophy of sex can justifiably adopt this view, because the "view from somewhere different" better represents the sexual experience of individual women than does ignoring or denying our partiality. This is not a claim that difference is good where once it was bad or that to adopt the "view from somewhere different" is to adopt the correct perspective, since to do so would be to recreate the prejudice that many feminists find so oppressive in the "view from somewhere better" and the "view from nowhere." Demands for so-called politically correct speech have made many people uneasy, precisely because those demands appear to be replacing one set of oppressive values with another. What the feminist philosopher of sex can argue is that the "view from somewhere different" provides more representative visions of women's sexuality, because this perspective suggests that no location has a lock on the truth about women's sexuality and that dislocation is impossible. From this perspective, we cannot please all of the people all of the time. As my critique of a postmodern epistemology suggests, we cannot even please all of the people *some* of the time. However, because difference from the perspective of the "view from somewhere different" no longer means inferiority or invisibility, a feminist philosopher of sex who adopts this perspective can encourage "world"-traveling as a way of sensitizing women and men to the diverse sexual experiences, preferences, and desires of individual women, *some* of whom we can please *some* of the time. Thus, the "view from somewhere different" promotes a woman-centered philosophy of sex that is less essentialist and less biased, thus more representative of women's sexual lives, than perspectives that fail to acknowledge the ubiquity of partiality. Indeed, it is this perspective that makes both women and men individual and visible members of the human community.

Toward a Framework for a Feminist Philosophy of Sex

By adopting the perspective of the "view from somewhere different," a feminist philosopher of sex can understand her speculative and critical investigations into the nature, meaning, and value of women's sexuality as investigations into the contextual and dialectical relations between gender and sexuality. Her investigations are contextual when she perceives that gender is but one of many interlocking social relations informing women's sexuality. A feminist philosopher of sex who adopts this perspective believes that women's sexuality will mean different things to different women of different races, classes, and sexual preferences. Furthermore, this perspective asks a feminist philosopher of sex to investigate not only the network of social relations that situate the subject of her philosophical investigations but also those social relations that situate the philosopher herself. A feminist philosopher of sex will ask both (1) what is the subject context in which claims about women's sexuality are made? and (2) what is the investigative context in which such claims are evaluated? It is a perspective that asks a feminist philosopher of sex to attempt to gain an empathic understanding of others from whose sexual experience, preference, and desire her own location differs ("What is it like to be them?") and to acknowledge the partiality of all such locations ("What is it like to be myself in their eyes?").[31] Therefore, such investigations are also dialectical because they will engage a feminist philosopher of sex in a relationship with her subject whose interplay reflects the dynamic nature of that relationship.

As I argued earlier in this chapter, this dialectic also expresses itself in the interplay between a woman's sexual subordination and her sexual liberation under institutional and ideological conditions that constrain the sexual decisions she makes. Adopting this perspective asks us to notice that sex can be a source of victimization for individual women as well as a source for their resistance to, and transcendence of, that victimization. I remarked earlier in this chapter that heterosexual sex can take a variety of forms that are humiliating, if not brutal, to women: sexual harassment, rape, battering, and abuse, including degrading or abusive commercial sex work. On the other hand, feminists have also pointed out that to dwell exclusively or even primarily on the sexual victimization of women only serves to reinforce, if not confirm, women's identification as the dehumanized and exploited sexual objects of men. Therefore, a feminist philosophy of sex from the perspective of the "view from somewhere different" also needs a recognition of those aspects of women's erotic lives in which women identify and pursue what is erotically pleasurable *for them*.

This perspective acknowledges women as subjects with individual sexual histories to be celebrated and explored; women are properly seen as agents, many of whom create and prescribe their own sexual play. For some women, this means that sexual promiscuity becomes a safe and positive alternative for their active pursuit of sexual pleasure instead of the slur on women's sexuality that contemporary connotations of "slut" or "whore" suggest. For others, it means debunking the argument that sado-masochism is anathema to women because it re-creates the dominant/submissive gender roles of patriarchy. For still other women, it means creating woman-identified pornography and sex toys to open new avenues for women's sexual stimulation. Indeed, some women's idea of sexual liberation is in recognizing that men are little more than sexual predators whom heterosexual women should approach boldly, responsibly, and at their own risk.[32] In short, investigating the context of individual women's erotic lives from the "view from somewhere different" asks us to recognize as well as reconsider patriarchy's oppressive claim on women's sexuality. In subsequent chapters I will continue to explore the dialectical relationship between women's sexual oppression and our liberation by pursuing the kinds of issues in women's sexuality raised above.

Despite any one woman's capacity for sexual agency, the current context for renaming and revalorizing women's sexuality is still one of patriarchy. This context is inscribed by androcentric concepts and norms for women, many of whom remain far from sexual liberation. Therefore, feminists must be as location-sensitive to, and as philosophically demanding of, our new ways of thinking and acting as of our old ones. Some feminists have argued that to do any theorizing about women's sexuality at all requires the use of a fundamentally new language in order to reflect more accurately the nature of female eroticism.[33] Yet we must be just as wary of our *recon*ceptualizations as our *pre*conceptualizations, since they will inevitably draw on the very social location from which we would liberate ourselves. This caveat is by no means an argument for delegitimizing the feminist enterprise. It is a strong recommendation for continuing to localize the discourse and particularize the context in women's efforts to effect change in our sexual lives.

Indeed, the many contextual differences in women's sexual experience remind us that a feminist philosophy of sex that adopts the "view from somewhere different" is woman-centered without being "Woman"-centered: such a philosophy can investigate the complexity and diversity of individual women's sexual lives without devolving into the essentializing prescriptions that have misrepresented women's sexuality using more traditional models. A feminist philosophy of sex from the "view from somewhere different" also recognizes the common ideological and institutional constraints under which women live and our shared capacity to resist and transform conditions oppressive to us. In this way feminists may simultaneously acknowledge the diversity of sexual experience among women and establish our common gender identity as women.

Moreover, a feminist philosophy of sex from the "view from somewhere different" recognizes that one woman's sexual experience can vary widely in different contexts; her sexual experience may also vary greatly over the course of her life. Sex can be scary, passionate, funny, unsuccessful, unsafe, painful, boring, publicly humiliating, privately beautiful, extremely personal, consciously political, cheerfully avoided, or regrettably absent, each in a different woman's life, or all in a single life. Gayle Rubin describes contemporary sexual norms as differentiating so-called good sex from bad: "good" sex is heterosexual, marital, monogamous, reproductive, and noncommercial sex, coupled, relational, within the same generation, and occurring at home; "bad" sex is practiced by the homosexual, the unmarried, the promiscuous, the nonprocreative, or the commercial sex worker, any of whom may masturbate, engage in orgies, have sex across generational lines, or have casual or public sex with or without the use of pornography, sex toys, or sadomasochistic sex roles.[34] A feminist philosophy of sex from the "view from somewhere different" questions the value of universal prescriptions of sexual norms without deconstructing the norms themselves, so that they can be identified and constructively critiqued. Moreover, this perspective not only acknowledges the sexual diversity among women but also recognizes, to use Teresa de Lauretis's term, the diversity "within" women,[35] since one story from one woman may not be all there is to tell about her.

On the other hand, not every, if any, story of her sexual life will be one that a woman will want to tell. A feminist philosophy of sex from the "view from somewhere different" also recognizes that sex means discrete and very private conduct for many women who would reject the feminist assertion that the personal is political. Some women who subscribe to the feminist claim that pornography and prostitution are patriarchal institutions in the business of subordinating women to men may still wish to make their own sexual activity a nonpolitical event. In addition, a feminist philosophy of sex from the "view from somewhere different" should remind us that both distinct and overlapping boundaries exist in our descriptions and evaluations of sex. When does sexual pleasure stop and pain begin? Is consensual sadomasochistic sex between husband and wife "good" sex or "bad"? In a patriarchal society in which heterosexual sex is commonly used to dominate women, does the very personal nature of any sex require a political interpretation? With help from the "view from somewhere different," the chapters that follow will allow us to examine these types of questions in more detail.

In the beginning of this section I noted that the subject investigated by a feminist philosopher both influences and is influenced by the particular sexual experience, preference, and desires of the philosopher herself. Specifically, the social location that informs my own feminist philosophical inquiry into women's sexuality is that of a white, middle-class, married, educated, forty-something, heterosexual woman; and I live in a Western industrialized culture inhabited by women whose gender is still a barrier to equitable employment and political power. The dialectical nature of the relation between gender and sexuality often translates being a woman into being the victim of both violent and subtle forms of sexual intimidation—intimidation that is a systemic and structural feature of the patriarchal world in which women live. A feminist philosopher of sex who is located in such a culture and who subscribes to the "view from somewhere different" recognizes that she is the member of a gendered class which is often identified primarily, if not solely, by women's sexual accessibility to men and for which that very identification is often a central vehicle for the exploitation, harassment, and abuse of women.

Under these constraints, racism, classism, and homophobia are real and compelling concerns for women who are already gender-oppressed. Indeed, many women of color argue that feminism will never be a priority for them if related social oppressions are not addressed with the same energy and commitment as that given to feminism. Some women of color eschew feminist activism altogether because they believe that other social oppressions take priority and because they believe that feminist gains are gains for white, middle-class women, not women of color. A feminist philosopher of sex must address the question of whether developing new ways for thinking and talking about sex is relevant to liberating women oppressed by overwhelming poverty or racial prejudice.[36] Yet no matter what our race or ethnicity, women in Western culture are bombarded by feminine images defined by an extremely narrow range of acceptable criteria of beauty. It is a culture where a woman's sexual allure is typically equated with physical beauty, the commercial imagery of which is defined by Naomi Wolf as "beauty porn." Because being openly sexy is often interpreted in such a culture as a woman's consent to men's sexual aggression against her, women who want to be physically attractive to men run the risk of being blamed for their own sexual abuse.[37]

A feminist philosopher of sex who adopts the "view from somewhere different" recognizes this oppressive environment and seeks to expose its injustices in an effort to effect change. At the same time, a feminist philosopher of sex who adopts the "view from somewhere different" acknowledges that progress toward sexual self-definition and sexual agency is as much a feminist goal as progress away from sexual victimization. Thus, from this perspective it is understood that there are many women for whom the equation of beauty with sex appears to open doors to personal liberation instead of closing them or for whom the concept of an institutionalized patriarchy mistakes individual injustices perpetrated by men for a universal male conspiracy.[38] A feminist philosopher who adopts the "view from somewhere different" recognizes that feminist theorizing comes in many forms, each of which has a part to play in the lives of women for whom that theory resonates. She also remembers that theory cannot take the place of listening to individual women's socially situated stories as a means of helping each woman discover the meaning and value of the erotic in her life. How to respond in a caring and constructive way to so many voices with such different erotic needs is one of the challenges explored in this book.

In summary, a feminist philosophy of sex that adopts the "view from somewhere different" is a philosophy of sex that locates a framework for understanding women's sexuality within a contextual and dialectical relation between gender and sexuality. The context of investigation is dependent on the social relations that locate the subjects investigated. The context of the investigator is discovered through her particular social location. To say that a woman's social location situates the discourse is to say that the injustices I have described are historical, contextual, and particular to individual women. However, to say that a woman's sexual subordination is relative to time and place is not to suggest that the demand for her sexual liberation has no moral or political force. To situate injustice within the particular social relations that constitute women's oppression is nonarbitrary in the same way that situating gender is nonarbitrary within Alcoff's matrix of practices, habits, and discourses. One can argue for better treatment of women within the specific context of a patriarchy that distorts, marginalizes, or appropriates women's sexuality, by detailing the individual misrepresentations within that context and composing strategies that can be used to enhance each woman's sexual experience. A feminist philosophy of sex that adopts the "view from somewhere different" asks new questions about women's sexuality and answers many of the old questions in new ways. But feminists cannot argue that the results of their research are "true." To quote Linda Alcoff,

> [B]eing a "woman" is to take up a position within a moving historical context and to be able to choose what we make of this position and how we alter this context. From the perspective of that fairly determinate though fluid and mutable position, women can themselves articulate a set of interests and ground a feminist politics. [However], [t]he concept and the position of women is not ultimately undecidable or arbitrary. It is simply not possible to interpret our society in such a way that women have more power or

equal power relative to men. The conception of woman that I have outlined limits the constructions of woman we can offer by defining subjectivity as positionality within a context.[39]

A feminist philosopher of sex who adopts the "view from somewhere different" can argue that achieving sexual agency and self-definition for women requires freeing women from their social location within a sexually oppressive context, Alcoff's "positionality within a context," by *re*positioning women within a context that is more representative of their conceptions of themselves as sexual beings. This repositioning requires a safe place where women can tell the varied stories of their sexual lives, and it requires others who are willing to listen and share their stories. The repositioning of women's sexuality requires us to be critical of both our own and others' quick condemnations of alternative sexual preferences and wary of easy solutions to the problem of women's sexual subordination. It requires us to recognize that sex is a topic that many people, including philosophers of sex, approach with ignorance, anxiety, and fear.[40] Such an approach will tend to cloud the advantages of the relatively destabilizing "view from somewhere different," enticing us with the secure moral platitudes of the "view from somewhere better" or the "view from nowhere." Echoing Sandra Harding's feminist destabilization in philosophy of science, we must remain confident that the destabilization in our thinking about women's sexuality will advance our understanding more effectively than restabilizations of it.[41] The following chapters explore what it means to destabilize prevailing claims about women's sexuality.

2

In Hot Pursuit of Sexual Liberation

Should a Woman Be Promiscuous?

Overview

In a contemporary era dominated by fears of debilitating and often deadly sexually transmitted diseases, it is not uncommon to regard promiscuous sex as dangerous sex. Promiscuous sex evokes visions of sex with many different partners, and sex with many different partners in an era of AIDS is believed to be incautious at best, morally reprehensible at worst, since the virus that causes Acquired Immunodeficiency Syndrome can be transmitted undetected and so passed from partner to partner unnoticed. This condemnation of sexual promiscuity ironically comes at a time when the use of available and effective contraception can mitigate the once onerous fear of pregnancy, and when Western society as a whole has become more accepting than it was fifty years ago, if only grudgingly so, of premarital sex, with its potential for multiple, uncommitted partners. Yet despite these changes in our sexual attitudes, in an era of AIDS, promiscuous sex continues to be regarded as dangerous sex, to be approached, regardless of differences of opinion on sexual liberation, with an obvious and natural caution.

For women, the pleasures of promiscuity promised by the postwar sexual revolution have been complicated by much more than the fear of AIDS. While their increased economic independence and reproductive choice have given many middle-class women the freedom to pursue sex outside of marriage, this freedom has not come without its price. In a society that has increasingly liberated men as well as women from the confines of marital sex, many men have less incentive to take re-

sponsibility for family planning or family support. Without the promise of sex in exchange for the financial security and social status of marriage, single women often
complain that they have had to throw away one of their few remaining bargaining
chips for physical and emotional well-being. ("Why buy the milk when you can get
the cow for free?")[1] Furthermore, living in an economic climate that continues to
undervalue women's labor, many divorced or deserted women left with children to
support are often relegated to a life of financial struggle. It is ironic that in an era
promising women's sexual liberation, the prostitution that Kathleen Barry refers to
as "female sexual slavery" is often the only avenue of gainful employment available
to unskilled or underemployed women worldwide who are the sole providers for
themselves or their families.[2]

In addition, women still live in a world where many believe that something is
wrong with a woman who does not have "a (one) man in her life," a belief especially
disturbing to lesbians, whose daily confrontations with heterosexism make being a
monogamous couple no protection against social stigma.[3] Aging single women become sexually less desirable in a culture that defines a woman's sexual attractiveness
in terms of her youth and beauty, a fact that puts older, heterosexually active women
in fierce competition with their younger counterparts for still sexually attractive older
men. For women who do choose marriage, the specter of a multitude of heterosexually active single women often represents not only a real threat to any hope of an
emotionally stable and financially secure domestic life but also the threat of contracting their husband's sexually transmitted diseases. A single woman, not an errant
husband, is most likely to be singled out for censure or abuse, since it is she who has
historically been described as tempting men into sin.[4] In this patriarchal climate, a
sexually promiscuous woman is regarded derogatorily by both other women and men
as nothing more than a "slut."

At a time of often brutal and unpredictable sexual violence against women, the
spontaneous or casual sex associated with promiscuity has made many women eschew sex with multiple partners as too risky to be worth any anticipated pleasure. The
alarming frequency of acquaintance rape, in which the victim knows her assailant,
has left many single women with little prospect of a safe sexual life. Yet many women,
especially teenagers, feel tremendous peer pressure to have sex, in a post-Victorian
society that still marks sexually reticent women as "frigid." Such pressure can lead to
psychological turmoil when the emotional investment a woman may have made in
her sexual relationship is not reciprocated. At its worst, resistance to such pressure
can lead to rape. Combine such concerns with the fear of AIDS, which has everyone from sex educators to political pundits advocating abstinence as the only safe sex
outside of marriage, and it is no wonder that promiscuity is regarded by many women
as the pursuit of personal danger and sexual anxiety, not sexual pleasure and psychological well-being.[5]

The issue of a woman's control over her own body has been one of the most important political platforms of the women's movement. To tell a woman that she cannot or should not be promiscuous seems to run counter to the feminist effort to secure sexual agency and self-definition for all women. Many feminists regard the
sexual liberation movement of the 1960s and 1970s, as well as its contemporary vestiges, as serving primarily the interests of men precisely because the movement made

more women sexually available to men without affording enough women the economic and political tools to escape being sexually subordinated by them. According to this view, sexual liberation convinced women that sex without love or marriage was a good thing without giving women the opportunity to define what good sex is *for women.* Heterosexual and lesbian feminists alike have argued that truly liberating sex for women requires a fundamental reconceptualization and reevaluation of women's sexual exploration, pleasure, and agency.[6]

Such reframing raises difficult questions, however: Should a feminist reconceptualization of women's sexual desire include a sexually promiscuous lifestyle? Or are promiscuous women simply appropriating a masculine sexual value that is ill-suited to our temperament as women? What exactly counts as promiscuous sex, and what, if anything, can promiscuity contribute to women's control over our bodies in an environment increasingly characterized by sexual violence, disease, and death? This chapter explores these questions from the "view from somewhere different" introduced in chapter 1, which characterizes women's sexual promiscuity as a contextual and dialectical function of both women's sexual oppression and our sexual liberation. From such a perspective, a woman's promiscuity is understood contextually, in terms of her particular social location ("What is it like to be her?") and in terms of how those who would question her behavior are perceived by her ("What is it like to be us in her eyes?") From the "view from somewhere different," a woman's promiscuity is also understood dialectically, as both encouraging her subordination by men ready to exploit her sexuality and facilitating her exploration of one among many different ways that she may give meaning and value to her erotic life.

The next section of this chapter explores the variety of meanings that are given to the terms "promiscuous" and "promiscuity." I argue that many of the difficulties in sorting out some of the complaints against sexual promiscuity may be attributed to this semantic variety. I also show how a patriarchy that has an investment in women's sexual monogamy also has an investment in convincing women that monogamy is the only safe haven for intimate and satisfying sex. Further discussion examines some of the specific complaints that feminists have against women's adopting a promiscuous lifestyle. I argue that because a woman's promiscuous sex can be, although it need not be, sex that respects and nurtures the particular sexual needs of her partners, feminists who object to sex that is impersonal and objectifying cannot reject women's promiscuity out of hand. I then address some of the arguments offered in favor of women's sexual promiscuity, particularly the argument that a woman's promiscuity promotes her sexual satisfaction and growth by encouraging her to explore her own sexual needs. I argue that the "view from somewhere different" can empower women to negotiate the tensions among conflicting moral views on promiscuity by describing promiscuous sex as dialectically situated in a world in which women are both the subordinated objects and active subjects of our sexual lives. I also examine some of the special complaints reserved for a sexually promiscuous woman that do not apply to her male counterpart and explore some of the stereotypes of promiscuous sexual behavior that circumscribe women and men of color. I contend that the denigration of a woman's promiscuity acts as a way of limiting her capacity to act as a self-determining sexual subject. The closing discussion examines the argument that promiscuous sex is lethal in an era of AIDS and so objectionable on those grounds alone. My claim is that AIDS is reason for caution regarding our sexual behavior, but the danger of AIDS is not sufficient reason for condemning all promiscuous sexual exploration, nor is it sufficient to support an argument for abstinence. On the contrary, because AIDS has been used to heap renewed abuse on a homosexual community struggling to define a sexual lifestyle that does not simply mirror traditional heterosexual norms, I argue that we should be wary of any arguments that treat the medical crisis of AIDS as a social commentary on the dangers of sexual liberation.

Only a Numbers Game?

In the conceptual analysis that comprises much of the traditional literature on the philosophy of sex, very little has been written on the meaning of sexual promiscuity.[7] However, what is traditionally meant by the term "promiscuity" is vital philosophical information if we are to examine any feminist attempts at its *reconceptualization*. For example, if promiscuity is only a numbers game, then why did polygamous Mormon men at the turn of this century, men with six or more wives, each of whom received weekly conjugal visits, rail against the evils of promiscuity? To cite hypocrisy or self-deception is too facile. If we resolve the Mormon case by claiming that promiscuity must also constitute a failure to promise a lifelong sexual commitment, then the unmarried woman, widowed three times, whose current sexual experience consists of her exclusive two-year romance with her childhood sweetheart must be considered promiscuous.[8] Compare this sexually faithful woman to her sister, a barhopper who goes home with a different man every night, and the behavior suggests a difference in kind, not just degree. Furthermore, if the dangers of pregnancy or sexually transmitted diseases explain our contemporary disapproval of promiscuity, then why is the disease-free woman who uses effective contraception, sleeps only with AIDS-tested disease-free men, and, like our barhopper, sleeps with a different man every night derisively considered by many people to be a "slut"?

What these cases suggest is that exactly what we mean by sexual promiscuity will depend on the identity and context of the subject "we." What I intend to show is that it is a philosophical mistake to try to offer a single *definition* of sexual promiscuity, one with necessary and sufficient conditions that are designed to cover all possible contexts of its use. Rather, I will take the approach that the term "promiscuity," like so many expressions in the English language, is used in a variety of contexts with meanings related to, but not identical with, one another. Instead of *the* meaning of promiscuity, I will uncover a wide variety of meanings for the term derived from the particular social location of each speaker and the social context of the speaker's sexual behavior.[9] Like the "view from somewhere different" introduced in chapter 1, this approach eschews the universal analytic categories typical of the "view from nowhere" in favor of assigning meaning on the case-by-case basis of social location. This approach is consistent with a feminist philosophy of sex that appreciates the context-specific dialectic between gender and sexuality.[10]

Consider the following propositions:

1. Distributing condoms to high school students only encourages them to be promiscuous.

2. If Magic Johnson hadn't been so promiscuous, he never would have contracted HIV, the virus that can cause AIDS.
3. A promiscuous woman is a loose woman.

Note that in all three propositions, the reference is to *sexual* promiscuity. High school distribution of devices designed to inhibit the exchange of bodily fluids *during sex* makes many parents fear that their children are being given tacit permission to be *sexually* promiscuous. Many people believe that Magic Johnson's *sexual* promiscuity resulted in his contracting a virus typically, but not necessarily, caused by the exchange of bodily fluids *during sex*; and it is the *sexually* promiscuous woman who is the *sexually* loose woman.

However, not all contexts in which speakers use the token terms "promiscuous" or "promiscuity" prompt us to identify the type as sexual. Promiscuity also has a non-sexual sense that connotes merely indiscriminate or careless behavior. Suppose a sexually promiscuous bank executive is our proverbial "loose woman." We may know this much about her yet still know nothing about the way she spends her bank's money. On the other hand, the bank executive who is promiscuous with her bank's money is an incautious financier whatever her sexual habits. Furthermore, promiscuity can connote an abundance, excess, or profusion with or without sexual overtones. The sight of a promiscuous display of bougainvillea is the sight of vibrant color, while the sight of a promiscuous display of Chihuahuas is the sight of dogs in heat.

In addition, a sexually promiscuous person is a sexually active person. A teenager who fantasizes about sex after acquiring a condom but never acts out those fantasies is not a sexually promiscuous teenager; and no matter how strong Magic Johnson's intentions to be sexually active may have been, if none of those intentions had been fulfilled, he would not be accused of sexual promiscuity. A sexually active person need not be promiscuous, however, as many faithful and happily married couples will attest. Moreover, former president Jimmy Carter could admit to "lusting in his heart" after women other than his wife Rosalyn without being accused of sexual promiscuity because while he and his wife may have had a great sex life together, he was not sexually active with the women about whom he fantasized. A loose woman doesn't just think about sleeping around; she sleeps around.

A commonly held view of the sexually promiscuous person is that she is sexually active in an uncoerced or voluntary way. When a single woman is raped by a coworker whom she accompanies home after a cocktail party, she is often accused of sexual promiscuity by those who think she was "asking for it" or "really wanted it," not because she is perceived as the victim of coercive or involuntary sex. Sexually molested girls are sometimes considered promiscuous when there is some question as to their seductiveness or sexual precocity, suggesting their willing cooperation in their sexual molestation. When a victim of sexual abuse can convince her skeptics of her coerced participation in sex, her molestation becomes a form of assault perpetrated against the innocent, not a form of promiscuous sexual activity voluntarily pursued.

The freedom to be sexually active, however, involves more than freedom from physical coercion. As Kathryn Pauly Morgan points out in her discussion of women and romantic love, a genuine choice must include both knowledge of, and access to, real alternatives.[11] The woman who "chooses" to earn money as a prostitute is an especially complex and controversial case of genuine choice. Homeless women and teenage runaways have been forced into the sex trade by abusive traffickers whose sexual coercion relies on a combination of economic blackmail, psychological manipulation, and threats of physical violence. Pimps often threaten runaways with the specter of jail sentences or with their return to the abusive familial or institutional settings from which they have fled. Some pimps regularly beat their prostitutes or abuse one as an example to the rest. Moreover, none of this treatment indicates the level of emotional blackmail involved in making a vulnerable young girl feel wanted and needed by an apparently powerful male. Poor families have sold their children into sexual service. Children have been kidnapped, chained, or imprisoned in brothels. If a woman is promiscuous only if her sex is noncoercive, then women who are the literal sex slaves of men cannot be called promiscuous solely in virtue of the number of their sexual partners.

However, being forced into prostitution can take much subtler forms. Many poor women inexperienced in the job market report feeling forced *by their circumstances* into prostitution because they perceive no alternative to support themselves and their families. In cultures where an infertile woman may be ostracized from her family of origin or where there are simply too many mouths to feed and too little paid work for men, women may regard prostitution as their sole source of survival. In an environment that restricts women's economic opportunities and defines women in terms of their sexual availability to men, prostitution is often the only means women have of earning a living, whether they prefer prostitution or not. While some prostitutes report that they choose their work for the money, flexibility, and independence sex work affords them, others report finding the stigma, exploitation, and abuse in an illegal (and, some would say, immoral) line of work impossible to avoid. The stereotype of the drugged-out prostitute is often a startlingly real picture of a woman using the mind-numbing effect of narcotics to blot out the emotional and physical pain of her work. Many erstwhile prostitutes liken their experience to rape.[12]

Under such conditions, describing all prostitutes as "choosing" their line of work ignores the complexity of women's cultural, economic, and sexual oppression under patriarchy. The epithets "slut" and "whore" are commonly used to denigrate promiscuous women who are perceived as freely pursuing an immoral sex life. Such epithets reveal the socially degrading stigma of sex work, but they also reveal how little is understood about the nature of many prostitutes' "choice" of work. This is not to deny that many of us feel social and economic pressures to work for a living or that many individuals have jobs that they do not particularly enjoy. What I am suggesting is that many prostitutes in particular, and many women in general, may be under the kinds of social constraints that are not simply influential but, rather, coercive. If the victim of rape is not considered sexually promiscuous because her sex is performed under circumstances for which there is no real alternative and for which she cannot determine the conditions of her consent, then we must seriously question the ascription of promiscuity to those women whose variously oppressive conditions compel them to become prostitutes.

My conceptual analysis of promiscuity also suggests that the sexual partners of the promiscuous person are typically *other people*, although special cases of sexual activity with animals may variously be described as promiscuous. A compulsive and solitary masturbator is not usually described as promiscuous when there is no sexual partner present to share or encourage sexual stimulation, even if such stimulation is achieved with a wide variety of objects in a wide variety of ways. Popular disdain of masturbation might label such behavior neurotic or oversexed, even promiscuously perverse, but not promiscuous *simpliciter*. Make this same masturbator into a frequent exhibitionist whose sexual stimulation is, in part, his public display to a wide audience, and the behavior begins to look more like promiscuity. What this example suggests is that some so-called perverse sexual behavior may be considered promiscuous when that behavior engages other persons for sexual satisfaction; but other forms of sexual perversity may not be promiscuous because of the lack of that engagement. An especially interesting case is the husband who is sexually faithful to his wife except for his occasional and private indulgence in bestiality. I suspect that if she were to discover him, his wife would brand him sexually perverse before she accused him of promiscuity, although a person with a favorite pet sheep has a decidedly different sort of sex life than someone who takes on the whole flock. Is the latter sort of person "promiscuously perverse," "perversely promiscuous," or something else entirely? A promiscuously perverse man sounds like someone who practices a wide variety of perversions alone or with partners, or, like the bougainvillea, exhibits an abundance or profusion of one kind of activity. On the other hand, a perversely promiscuous man sounds more like someone in active pursuit of several sexual partners, where the pursuit is itself somehow perverse or where each of his many partners can indulge his perverse sexual tastes.

Frederick Elliston has written one of the few sustained, albeit dated, accounts of promiscuity in the philosophical literature. In that account, he attempts to justify a set of individually necessary and jointly sufficient conditions for sexual promiscuity. For example, Elliston implicitly acknowledges my claim that the promiscuous person is a sexually active person when he says that the telos, or goal, of promiscuity is sexual intercourse.[13] For Elliston, this telos is not an incidental or inconstant feature of sexual promiscuity. He stipulates that a *necessary condition* of sexual promiscuity is sexual intercourse or "copulation." While copulation can be described as oral or anal, Elliston appears to have only vaginal penetration by the penis in mind: he states that while not every seduction succeeds, "the intention to *consummate the relation* must be present on all occasions and realized on some" (my italics).[14]

A suspiciously convenient consequence of this requirement is that married men can rationalize that they have not been promiscuous because they have "only" engaged with other partners in oral or anal sex, sex with dildos or vibrators, or any other sex not requiring the vaginal penetration by the penis of "consummated" sexual intercourse.[15] Moreover, in the contemporary language of feminism, to require of promiscuity the intention to consummate heterosexual relations betrays a kind of heterosexism: some lesbians are sexually promiscuous but have no intention of engaging in the penile penetration that Elliston implies is necessary for promiscuous sex; and promiscuous gay men eschew the heterosexual penetration typified by "consummated" sexual intercourse. Moreover, the gay or heterosexual promiscuous pedophile need not "intend to consummate the relation" with the children he fondles in order to be sexually promiscuous with them; and certainly we can imagine the promiscuous heterosexual who, out of fear of AIDS, *never* "copulates" with his sexual partner, oral, anal, or otherwise, but strokes and caresses a different woman every night because it turns him on. What will become even clearer as we examine more of Elliston's analysis is that Elliston's insistence on a single and comprehensive definition of sexual promiscuity invites a host of counterexamples. Such an insistence obscures any legitimate distinctions he wishes to make, as in his distinction between unfulfilled sexual intentions and promiscuous sex. In many cases Elliston simply misses important features that a feminist appreciation of the dialectic between gender and sexuality would not ignore, such as the absence of voluntary sex involving rape victims and women compelled into prostitution or the promiscuous nature of some gay sex. Elliston's apparent "view from nowhere," which does not countenance the bias of social location, will become especially noticeable when I describe, later in this section, the investment that a patriarchal society has in conjoining intimacy with women's heterosexual exclusivity.

Elliston also argues that *"both* partners must be *adults"*[16] (Elliston's and my italics). A cavil, perhaps, but sexually promiscuous people have been known to have sex with more than one person at one time, so the "both" in Elliston's phrase seems too conservative. I would also take exception to the claim that the partners of a sexually promiscuous person must be adults: the pedophile who repeatedly fondles a variety of children is a *sexually promiscuous* pedophile, in contrast to one whose sexual gratification comes from fondling children but who has little opportunity to satisfy the desire. In fact, nowhere in Elliston's analysis is there any indication that the so-called sexual perversions—bestiality, pedophilia, incest, and the like—are sexual preoccupations of persons to which the term "promiscuous" can be applied.[17]

Elliston also stipulates that promiscuous sex is necessarily repetitive: "[T]he pursuit of a new partner *must* recur" (my italics).[18] I agree that someone like the sexually faithful lesbian in a monogamous relationship is not promiscuous, nor is the man whose one sexual experiment consists of an ill-conceived one-night stand; and I agree with Elliston that to stipulate the precise number of partners required for promiscuous sex would be an arbitrary judgment that creates more problems that it solves by limiting the contexts in which the term is actually used. But is repetition an *essential* feature of promiscuity for all speakers who refer to promiscuous sex?

Let us return to my first proposition about condom distribution. Many (though certainly not all) parents who believe that distributing condoms to high school students encourages them to be promiscuous are not simply or even primarily worried about their children pursuing new and different sexual partners from the ones their children already have. These parents are worried about their children's having *premarital sex.* Condom distribution, many parents fear, will give their children *the license to have sex* when those children would otherwise abstain. Are such parents misusing the word "promiscuous"? Is the proposition only referring to those parents who fear that their already sexually active children, now with steady sexual partners, will be encouraged to "play the field"? Or has Elliston misidentified a necessary condition of sexual promiscuity?

To answer these questions, we must discover why someone might think that even one instance of premarital sex is promiscuous sex. Ironically, it is Elliston, convinced as he is of the necessity of repetition, who provides us with the answer. It is not only the specter of a series of different sexual partners that a concerned parent contemplates when she worries about her child's promiscuity. It is the *noncommittal* nature of the sex. As Elliston states, "Promiscuity asserts a freedom from the obligation within or without marriage to 'love, honor, and obey' and a freedom to engage in sex with any peer who agrees. These refusals to issue promissory notes for affection and support throughout an indefinite future and to issue a guarantee of sexual exclusivity are promiscuity's most significant departures from the traditional sexual norm."[19] For many parents, premarital sex is necessarily noncommittal sex, since it lacks the requisite "promissory note" of sexual and emotional commitment that the traditional Judeo-Christian marriage offers. For these parents, promiscuity is eradicated not through sexual exclusivity alone but through the sexual commitment inherent in traditional heterosexual marriage. A father who holds such views may accuse his teenage daughter of immaturity or foolishness if she marries her high school classmate, but when she marries, he will no longer consider her promiscuous.

The belief that the sexual commitment of traditional marriage is the antithesis of promiscuity is given further credence by many speakers who accuse the *adulterous* spouse of promiscuity. However, equating adultery with promiscuity obscures some compelling alternative uses of the term "promiscuous." Suppose George marries Sarah, his first and only sexual partner, and stays married and sexually faithful to her for twenty years. However, he suddenly finds himself extremely attracted to one of his newer professional colleagues, so taken, in fact, that he carefully and successfully executes a steamy night with her in a convention hotel room. Has George committed adultery? Yes. But is he promiscuous? If you use the term "promiscuous" based on the belief that promiscuity is the opposite of marital commitment, then your answer will be "yes." But if you use the term believing that promiscuity is the voluntary and *repetitious* pursuit of *different* sexual partners, then your answer must be "no." George's adultery consists of a single affair; and until we have more information about his disposition to repeat such an affair with a different colleague, George's adultery does not constitute promiscuity for all speakers who use the term. Even if George feels terrific after his affair, pursuing his relationship with the same colleague for three more years with no intention of telling his sexually available and doting wife, we can call George a "sneak," a "rat," an "ingrate," "insensitive and self-serving," but we cannot call him "promiscuous" when the term "promiscuity" is used to refer to the repetitious pursuit of different sexual partners. This is why a woman who is unmarried throughout her life, but who in her mature years carries on a sexually exclusive relationship with a man she met in her square-dancing class, can describe herself as promiscuous only in her youth. If promiscuous sex is not pre-or extramarital sex but merely the repetitious pursuit of different sexual partners, then when one stops this repetition, one stops being promiscuous.

If parents complain that their already sexually active teens will be further induced to engage in the pursuit of different sexual partners, then their worry is one of promiscuity characterized this way. But if parents are concerned that condom distribution will encourage their teens to try sex out when they otherwise would abstain, then these parents' use of the term "promiscuity" may well be linked to their concern over the absence of their children's marital commitment, or some equally binding sexual and emotional commitment, to their sexual partners. For many parents, since formally sanctioned, committed, and exclusive sex is the only sex that they will condone for their children, the term "promiscuous" often reduces to a moral condemnation of sex outside of marriage.

Promiscuity's absence of marital commitment can also help us understand the objection of the polygamous Mormon man mentioned at the beginning of this section. In marriages where sex is both possible and desirable, marriage typically serves as a socially sanctioned restriction on one's choice of sexual partner.[20] In Judeo-Christian communities in which marriage is defined by monogamy, sexual exclusivity means sex *with this (one) partner and no others.* In those communities where marriage to more than one person at a time is both an accepted and common practice, sexual choice for one marital partner is restricted by marriage to some *multiple* of spouses. Thus, sexual exclusivity still has meaning for the polygamous spouse, even though, like his promiscuous counterpart, he engages in the pursuit of different sexual partners. Sexual exclusivity in a polygamous community simply means sex *with these (several) people and no others.* His pursuit of new and different sexual partners is restricted, not repeated. Thus, promiscuous sex for the Mormon man is objectionable because it is simple fornication, sex outside of marriage, sex *without commitment.* (Many feminists would also contend that within a patriarchal tradition that defines marriage as man's acquisition of a wife, polygamous spouses will always be men.) When a devout Muslim woman, raped by Serbian soldiers, is derisively called a "whore" by her husband, it is because she has engaged in what he perceives as promiscuous (extramarital) sex that defiles her in his eyes. The irony is that rape victims and prostitutes are often mistakenly regarded as "asking for" the abuse they receive. Many feminists contend that such explanations serve the interests of patriarchy by blaming women, not men, for men's sexual violation of women.[21]

One affair, a single one-night stand, or the victimization of rape, however, is not promiscuity for those who associate the term with the voluntary and repetitious pursuit of different sexual partners. The previous description of George's adultery shows that some speakers will describe George's adultery as promiscuous while others will not. Furthermore, if George does decide to "play the field" with a series of different lovers, his promiscuous peccadillos do not *erase* his original marital commitment to his wife. He has simply failed to live up to that commitment. Therefore, it is not only the *absence* of commitment, as in premarital sex, that marks the presence of promiscuity, but also the failure to live up to commitments already made. It is the latter sense of promiscuity that characterizes adultery.

In addition, it is far from clear that unmarried promiscuous sex partners cannot or do not issue their lovers "promissory notes for affection and support throughout an indefinite future," as Elliston maintains. Suppose Joan has sex with several men on a regular basis. Joan enjoys the company of men and finds sex the perfect vehicle for establishing intimacy with them. We can suppose that Joan travels frequently and has different lovers in different cities. Some of Joan's lovers are men whom she has known for months; others are fairly new acquaintances. Thus, we can imagine that her lovers may also have their own interests and interconnecting but not identical circle of lovers and acquaintances, so that none of Joan's lovers feels unattended or unloved by Joan. In this scenario, Joan is promiscuous insofar as she is actively and voluntarily engaged in the repetitious pursuit of different sexual partners. Does this mean that she cannot offer any of her current lovers, or indeed any of her future lovers, a "commitment" of sex, affection, and moral or even financial support? Why can't a promiscuous Joan maintain sexual relationships with several men at the same time, even *promise* them she will love them "in sickness and in health," knowing full well that since her lovers have other lovers who attend to them as well, this will not be asking too much of her?

A common complaint against promiscuous sex is that it lacks intimacy—that it lacks the personal attentiveness and commitment of time and emotional energy that one can more easily give to just one person. But why should sexual intimacy demand sexual exclusivity? I would argue that while it may be true of many or even most of us that we cannot maintain several intimate sexual relationships at one time, there is nothing logically, or even practically, impossible about doing so. Joan's sexual history may be rare, especially in a patriarchal culture in which a tradition of regarding women as property and regarding masculinity in terms of sexual power and control prompts strong feelings of sexual competition and propriety among men; in such a culture, women's monogamy is also reinforced by socialization that teaches women to desire and preserve exclusive heterosexual relationships. Nevertheless, Joan's sexual life is not nonsensical or contradictory or beyond every person's sexual or emotional energies. It depends on the people involved and the commitments made. Of course, women can be jealous of their sexual partners as well, as I will later discuss in more detail. However, I believe that jealous heterosexual women do not act to defend their property as much as they defend their social status and security. When women are status objects for men, the status comes from the *possession* of a prized object, not the mere *association* with it. Jealous lesbians can be expected to base their jealousies on the particular gendered roles, if any, they adopt in their sexual relationships.[22]

What Joan's case also suggests is that the closer her sexual commitment comes to a formal, ritualized, publicly sanctioned contract, the more her commitment will resemble marriage. Suppose Joan has standing dates to spend her evenings as follows: Monday nights are spent with Ron, Wednesdays with Hamilton, Fridays with Ken, and Sundays with Bruce. While Joan may have committed herself to sleep with each of her partners on specific days, she has not committed herself to sleeping with these partners *and no others*. In other words, Joan may still be called "promiscuous," because her standing agreement with her lovers lacks the commitment to sexual exclusivity of either monogamy or polygamy. Joan is still contractually free to have sex with partners other than those with whom she currently has sex. However, the more Joan yields to the demands of her original lovers that she refrain from pursuing new partners, the more exclusive her relationships with them become. Indeed, in such an event her relationships take on the sexual restrictiveness associated with polygamy and lose the sexual permissiveness of promiscuity. Given my claim that what separates polygamy from promiscuity is the restriction on the former's choice of sexual partner, committed promiscuous sex appears to differ from at least certain forms of marital sex only in degree of exclusivity, not in the quantity of partners or the quality of the sexual exchange.

One reason why many people believe that sexual intimacy must and should be shared with only one person is that partners get jealous or proprietary. They want more from their lovers than they are getting and think that others will take away sexual attention that should be paid to them. Another reason people believe sexual intimacy requires monogamy is that they believe sexual intimacy requires one to share with one's sexual partner information about oneself that is not shared with anyone else.[23] From this view, sexual intimates have a unique relationship with one another in virtue of their exclusive knowledge of each other. If nothing else, sex reveals visual and tactile information about one's body. Some people claim that to give any portion of this information to anyone else would necessarily lessen the intimacy. However, these reasons imply that sexual relations are merely quantitative—that we have only so much of our sexuality to spend before it is used up. Such reasons ignore a qualitative dimension to sexual intimacy, the *how* as opposed to the *how much* of what is actually expressed, shared, and felt, which is not necessarily reduced by the quantity of sexual encounters.

Furthermore, Paul Gregory has suggested that placing too great a value on the scarcity of sexual intimacy encourages sexual frustration, jealousy, loneliness, and possessiveness.[24] Single women and men who believe that intimacy can only be found in monogamous heterosexuality become desperate to "pair up" instead of spending their sexual time and energy exploring what kinds of relationships might truly satisfy their sexual needs. Men become possessive of women when men define their sexual power in terms of the women they can keep from other men. As a result, men often feel emasculated by promiscuous women, whose behavior signifies to men that such women cannot be controlled. In a society in which power and prestige reside largely in the hands of men, many heterosexual women become defensive of the status and security men provide them; such defensiveness often results in deep jealousies and unwarranted fear or hatred of other women. Overvaluing sexual exclusivity can also make financially independent women unwilling to leave a disastrous sexual relationship when the alternatives of loneliness and social alienation loom large. Each of these cases suggests that when the scarcity of sexual intimacy is a cultural value, promiscuity inevitably undermines the sexual happiness of both women and men. If promiscuity is to have any credibility, then requiring sexual exclusivity for sexual intimacy must be questioned.

Many feminists have been particularly concerned about the oppressive nature of heterosexual, monogamous marriage for women. In the absence of economic independence from men, women are often left to languish in loveless and abusive marriages in which they are their husband's sexual and domestic subordinates. Even those who have gained some share of economic independence are often made unhappy by a sexual freedom that turns them into nothing more than the impersonal and replaceable sexual objects of male lust. Under such circumstances, women become easily convinced that the only means to sexual intimacy is sexual exclusivity. This conviction is tailor-made for men whose sexual status lies, in part, in the women they can keep other men from acquiring. Therefore, according to this view, in a culture that sanctions sexual exclusivity only through the historically unequal distribution of power and status of monogamous, heterosexual marriage, a woman will feel compelled to choose a type of sexual relationship that invests her sexual subordination with patriarchal legitimacy. Shulamith Firestone laments that while we may have recently loosened the tie between sexual exclusivity and monogamous marriage, we have replaced it with a vision of romantic love that is equally confining to women. Monogamous *marriage* may not be required for sexual intimacy, but a monogamous *relationship* still is.[25]

However, some feminists would point out that not all good sex is sex with partners to whom we have either personal or emotional ties.[26] Many people find sex with relative strangers to be exciting in its novelty. The psychiatrist Robert Stoller suggests that the more emotionally secure we feel around our sexual partners, the less exciting sex with that partner becomes.[27] Lack of intimacy with one's sexual partner does not mean that one will disrespect, exploit, or fail to satisfy one's partner sexually, nor that one will be disrespected, exploited, or sexually unfulfilled by one's partner. According to some feminists, women have been sold a bill of goods by men who promise satisfying sex only through the intimacy of sexual exclusivity. Men denigrate promiscuous women in order to convince women that promiscuous sex is unsatisfying sex. What these feminists remind us is that some people value intimacy in sex and others do not, and that both kinds of sex can be promiscuous. Thus, women should not feel compelled to pursue monogamy, especially if it is true that the promise of intimacy has been used by men to restrict women's sexual behavior.

On the other hand, many people would offer the case of Magic Johnson as proof that *knowing* your sexual partner constitutes the only safe sex outside of no sex. Their claim would be that Magic Johnson's mistake was not that he had sex with lots of different people but that he was *indiscriminate* about it, analogous to the way in which our bank executive was *indiscriminate* with her bank's money. According to this line of reasoning, if Johnson had been more cautious or careful in his choice of sexual partners, taking the time to learn more about his partners' sexual habits and histories, he would have greatly reduced the risk of contracting HIV. Persons arguing in this way conclude that promiscuous sex is dangerous sex because it is indiscriminate sex.

Yet here again we can describe cases of what would count for many speakers as "promiscuous" behavior that is not careless, incautious, or random. We can imagine the adulterous George deciding to have several affairs in a row, satisfying the characterization of promiscuity as the repetitious pursuit of different sexual partners, but we can also describe him as demanding that each partner take an AIDS test; or we can imagine that in addition to this demand, he prefers only his professional colleagues as bed partners, because the conventions they attend together provide him with the perfect hotel accommodations. Even Magic Johnson was very probably not *completely* indiscriminate in his choice of sexual partner. Each of us has particular preferences about our sexual partners, concerning their appearance, age, ethnicity, race, gender, or sexual style, such that we "discriminate" in favor of some partners over others in virtue of those preferences.

My claim is not that it is wrong or incorrect to think of promiscuous sex as indiscriminate sex or incautious sex or simply sex with anyone who agrees. Certainly some heterosexual men are promiscuous precisely because they are more interested in the sexual conquest than they are in the particular woman they are having sex with — the classic complaint of the sexually objectified woman[28] — but not all cases of promiscuity are cases of a lack of care, caution, or deliberation in one's choice of partner. My claim is that the indiscrimination in some cases of promiscuous sex merely reflects one of many uses of the term "promiscuity." In my estimation, Elliston too handily dismisses the indiscrimination issue on the grounds that no promiscuous person is "completely indiscriminate"[29] in the ways I have mentioned. Indeed, if your goal is to specify the necessary and sufficient conditions for promiscuous sex, as Elliston's is, indiscriminate sex will fail to appear in your definition at all, since faithful spouses can be careless in their choice of mate and promiscuous spouses can be discriminating in their choice of affairs. But this sexual variety is precisely what we lose when we look for a single and comprehensive definition of sexual promiscuity. Failing to notice that some promiscuous sex is indiscriminate, and that this feature is what some or even many people complain about when they talk about promiscuity, obscures an important context of its use: a context in which we may wish to draw a distinction between a careful and deliberate choice of sexual partner and one in which the primary aim is simply sexual satisfaction, not satisfaction from *this person*.

Similarly, promiscuous sex is not necessarily *casual* sex, characterized by A. Ellis as "sex between partners who have no deep or substantial relationships of which sex is a component." Anonymous sex between strangers and sex between people who are only recently acquainted are typical cases of casual sex, although Ellis (I think correctly) notes that close friends can have casual sex when "sex is no part of what makes it the relationship that it is."[30] If promiscuous sex can be committed and intimate sex, as in the case of Joan, then promiscuous sex need not be casual sex in the way described by Ellis; nor need it be "recreational" as opposed to "serious" sex, as if sexual exclusivity were real work and promiscuity were perfunctory or immature play. If nothing else, such epithets doom monogamy to the struggle and effort to which the notion of "play" is typically opposed.

I have been arguing that if we demand a single and comprehensive definition to suit all contexts of its use, we deprive the expression "sexual promiscuity" of the kind of philosophical analysis that can help speakers understand its subtlety and variety in the language. Recognizing this variety is essential if we want to use the "view from somewhere different" to uncover the social contexts in which individuals are promiscuous, or in which they evaluate the promiscuity of others, and to identify any patriarchal climate that defines women's sexuality in men's terms. My claim has been that because the words "promiscuous" and "promiscuity" are members of a family of terms we use to talk about sex, their meaning will change depending on the speakers and the contexts in which such terms are used. When promiscuous sex is primarily identified with noncommittal sex, it is commonly identified with nonmarital and premarital sex. When promiscuous sex is identified with the failure to live up to commitments already made, it is commonly identified with adultery.

On the other hand, when promiscuous sex is identified primarily as a numbers game, where the repetitious pursuit of different sexual partners plays a central role, the otherwise loyal husband whose adultery consists of one affair or the unmarried woman whose square-dancing partner is also her exclusive sexual partner is not considered promiscuous. Promiscuous sex can be indiscriminate, although almost never completely so. It can also be, although it need not be, defined by feelings of intimacy or the strong emotional bonds of affection and support that many people regard as the sole province of sexual exclusivity. Lesbians, gay men, heterosexuals who engage in genital intercourse as well as heterosexuals who do not, can all be sexually promiscuous. Pedophiles and others engaged in so-called perverse sex with other people can be, but need not be, promiscuous. In addition, victims of rape and sexual abuse are not promiscuous in virtue of their unwitting or unwilling participation in such activity. All such cases are of vital interest if we are to understand why people object to sexual promiscuity when they do. We are now in the requisite philosophical position to investigate some of the specific complaints that feminists have lodged against promiscuity.

Feminist Objections to Promiscuity

Feminists have argued that sexual liberation can never be *women's* liberation if the terms and conditions of sexual freedom are determined by men. Promiscuous sex with strangers, sex often associated with cruising bars and nightclubs, came under especially heavy fire by some feminists in the late 1970s as antithetical to women's true sexual needs. Such sex, along with sadomasochistic sex, cross-generational sex between adults and young children, and lesbian butch/femme sexual role-playing, was believed to constitute patriarchal relations of dominance and submission that were profoundly antifeminist and antiwoman. Women, it was claimed, value the sexual intimacy and tenderness of romance, not the emotional distance and sexual objectification of a one-night stand. From this perspective, good sex for a woman should make her feel safe about exposing her sexual vulnerability, not fearful of her sexual abuse or exploitation. Good sex should make a woman feel comfortable and cared for, not content with being one in a series of sexual romps. It was concluded, therefore, that for a woman, truly satisfying sex is monogamous sex with a single, loving, committed partner.

From this point of view, good sex for men cannot be good sex for women, since men prefer the *divorce* of eros from romance. Some feminists would refer to the feelings of loneliness, guilt, and alienation many women experienced during the postwar sexual revolution (and ever since) as confirming evidence that sex without love, tenderness, or commitment serves men's needs for unencumbered heterosexual sex, not women's. According to feminists of this perspective, the sex that men prefer is casual, performance-oriented, and objectifying. Male sex victimizes women by making them replaceable and expendable sexual objects of male fantasy and desire. Male sex is body-centered without being person-centered. The sex men prefer is power-motivated, dominating, "scoring" sex that is inherently promiscuous and profoundly unromantic.[31]

While appearing to reinvigorate the 1950s stereotype of the docile, nurturing, and sexually monogamous female, which feminists of varied theoretical backgrounds have long claimed subordinates women to men,[32] some feminists see in a uniquely female sexual nature a way to celebrate and value individual women for their own sake. Alice Echols and others refer to such feminists as "cultural feminists" for their insistence on essential gender differences to discover a separable and valuable female identity. Echols also uses this specific feminist nomenclature to distinguish cultural feminists from other feminists who also regard a hierarchical heterosexuality as essential to patriarchal stability but who neither require sexual intimacy as insurance against women's sexual victimization nor characterize women as the sexual objects of male subordination in the absence of such intimacy.[33] While many cultural feminists prefer women as sexual partners, most would advocate the rejection of contemporary male-identified sexual values and not the rejection of heterosexual eroticism per se. Adrienne Rich has argued that the "woman-identified woman" is on what she calls a "lesbian continuum" that can accommodate heterosexual and homosexual women alike.[34]

On the other hand, self-styled sex radical feminists, often referred to as "sexual libertarian feminists" or as "sexual liberals" by their critics, see cultural feminism as a reaction to the pleasure, variety, self-expression, and adventure that sex radicals believe are women's right as sexually autonomous beings. Such feminists claim that by confining women to an essentialist stereotype, cultural feminism misrepresents the plurality of women's erotic needs and reinforces the oppression of alternative sexual preferences. For a sex radical, the role of feminism is to identify patriarchal stereotypes of women in order to transcend them and move toward a new vision of women's sexuality constructed by individual women to suit their individual erotic needs. For sex radical feminists, the sexual intimacy required by cultural feminists is only one of many ways a woman can discover what good sex means to her. According to this view, under conditions of mutual consent, individual women can explore with their partners the breadth and depth of their erotic preferences, whether tame or taboo. Sex radical feminists contend that to regard sex as completely determined by gender is to play right into the hands of patriarchy by reaffirming the feminine archetype definitive of women's oppression. From a sex radical's perspective, feminism's role is to show women not only how gender informs sex but how sex can inform gender.

Cultural feminists respond that women continue to be sexually victimized by a patriarchy that defines women's sexual lives in men's terms. From this view, women must separately identify our own sexual needs *as women* in order to discover those needs, cherish them, and pursue them. Cultural feminists remind us that too many women are dissatisfied with a promiscuous sex life whose casual nature quickly becomes perfunctory, shallow, and boring. Sex lacking in intimacy leaves many women feeling empty and alone. According to cultural feminists, this dissatisfaction is because women are seeking sexual pleasure that is male-defined, not female-defined. From this view, women who say they find butch/femme sex or sadomasochistic sex to be erotic have been coopted by a patriarchal sexual value system that encourages the degradation of women as the sexual slaves of men. At the very least, according to a cultural feminist, women must equalize the heterosexual power dynamics conducive to patriarchy in order to realize our sexual potential as women. For a cultural feminist, citing mutual consent is no guarantee of mutual respect for each sexual partner in a society that continues to deprive women of access to real sexual alternatives by labeling women "frigid" or "slut" when we do not live up to the male sexual ideal. Furthermore, it is argued that the so-called adventure that sex radicals advocate can lead to unwanted pregnancy, sexual violence, disease, and death.[35] Ignoring these facts about women's sexual lives only reinforces women's invisibility as sexually autonomous beings with our own sexual agenda. According to cultural feminism, unless we put the spiritual and personal elements back into sex, women will continue to lead lives of sexual fear, frustration, and dissatisfaction.

The controversy between cultural and sex radical feminists outlined here took shape in the aftermath of the sexual revolution of the 1960s and early 1970s. While it is too generalized a description of the debate to capture some of the more subtle distinctions among various radical factions, it nevertheless captures some of the deeper rifts that continue to divide feminist approaches to women's sexuality as we enter the twenty-first century: does identifying male heterosexual sex as essentially dehumanizing to women liberate women to demand our own sexual needs, or does it reinforce women's identity as the sexual victims of men? Just how important is the oppression of *women* to women's sexuality, and how important is the oppression of *sexuality* to women's sexuality? Can women define sexuality in our own terms when what we have learned about our sexuality is itself a function of its social location under patriarchy?[36] Suppose we could show that promiscuous "cruising" sex *could be*, although it need not be, the kind of intimate, caring, and emotionally satisfying sex that a cultural feminist values. If we can loosen sexual exclusivity's stranglehold on care and respect in sex, then the promiscuity option that sex radical feminists want can satisfy the cultural feminist's requirement that good sex for women be sex that treats women as the subjects, not the objects, of our sexual experience. We would then have satisfied the desire of both groups that women's sex be defined in women's terms. In so doing, we can lay the foundation for a sexual ethic from the "view from somewhere different," an ethic that would encourage a sex radical's pursuit of sexual exploration without mirroring the heterosexual subordination of women by men that cultural feminism's demand for sexual intimacy is meant to preclude. Such an ethic could thus unify, not divide, the feminist vision of women as the agents and self-defining subjects of our sexual lives.

When cultural feminists say they value sexual intimacy, they seem to have at least three values in mind: (1) the *private* nature of the sex; (2) the *personal* nature of the sex; and (3) the *comfort through trust* in one's sexual partner. Can promiscuous "cruising" sex be any or all of these things? The conceptual analysis of promiscuity in the previous section can help us explore this question.

A cultural feminist is not accusing men of having all of their sex *in public*. What she is looking for in the privacy of sexual intimacy is to share with her lover what she would not wish to share or be shared with anyone else. A single act of premarital sex or fornication (with the appropriate caring attitudes) is no problem for a cultural feminist in search of a private relationship, since such sex is monogamous sex. On the other hand, single acts of adultery and the repetitious pursuit of different sexual partners are troublesome precisely because a promiscuous lover characterized in these ways is in a position to give both physical and emotional access to several partners. In the previous section, however, I argued that to require a limit to the sexual *quantity* in a relationship was unnecessary to provide that relationship with good *quality* sex.

Furthermore, I argued that the demand for sexual scarcity was very often detrimental to healthy, long-term sexual relationships. Both women and men often become jealously possessive of partners with whom they have shared sexual secrets that they believe no one else should know. Simone de Beauvoir points out that women who do not feel free to experiment under the restriction of sexual scarcity but whose identity in a male-dominated society rests in their associations with, and approval by, men often become desperate to "find a man" before discovering what they really want in a sexual partner. Such women compete fiercely with other women for the best "catch," only to languish in loveless relationships whose sexual exclusivity has become a curse instead of a blessing.[37] A woman's desire to submerge her identity in such relationships makes promiscuity unthinkable, since a woman has only one identity to offer. Robert Nozick believes that sexual love demands exclusivity precisely because such love requires us to "share an identity," of which each of us has only one. What he fails to recognize is that in a society in which sex is a vehicle for men's sexual subordination of women, women *lose* their identity in romance as often as they share it.[38]

Shulamith Firestone suggests that women's "sex privatization" by men under patriarchal conditions is nothing more than a ruse to convince women that they are each man's one and only when women are in reality generically dehumanized, stripped of any semblance of individuality. Men devalue all women but idealize the women they fall in love with to "justify [their] descent to a lower caste."[39] Combine these concerns with the suggestion that one person may simply not be able to satisfy any one person's sexual needs, and it would appear that the private nature of sexual intimacy, far from being a requirement for female sexual satisfaction, is antithetical to a cultural feminist program for women's sexual fulfillment.

When a cultural feminist claims that good sex for women is *personal* sex, she is claiming that women's sex is person-centered, individuated, and personalized in the way she believes that the body-centered, performance-oriented, and dehumanizing sex of men is not. Men's sex, in Susan Minot's words, makes a woman "begin to feel like a piece of pounded veal."[40] The sex that a cultural feminist values is sex defined by what Robin Dillon calls "care respect." This respect includes (1) responding to others as "the particular individuals they are" instead of merely generalizing over persons in search of some abstract capacity that all persons share; (2) understanding others by trying to see the world from their point of view; and (3) actively caring about the well-being of others by helping them pursue their own wants and needs.[41] To help a self-centered pleasure seeker pursue his own wants and needs would be precluded because to do so would be to encourage a disregard for the care respect of others.

The high incidence of wife battering around the world is evidence enough that monogamy does not have a lock on the personal side of sex defined in terms of Dillon's care respect. Indeed, the sexual frustration that often accompanies sexual scarcity is one of many factors contributing to unhappy monogamous marriages. Could we expect promiscuous "cruising" relationships to fare any better? Premarital sex and fornication with a single partner can certainly be as particularizing, understanding, and caring as a loving monogamous marriage. But what about the repetitious pursuit of different sexual partners who become no more than scores for the confident Don Juan, or adultery whose stereotype is the errant husband sneaking off for a tryst that his doting wife knows nothing about?

While it is true that like monogamy, promiscuous relationships can lack care respect, the case of Joan in the previous section tells us that promiscuity can also be defined by care respect. We described Joan as having lovers none of whom feels unattended or unloved by Joan. Suppose, for the purposes of this argument, that none of Joan's lovers are longtime acquaintances, but different men she has met in singles' bars and dance clubs that she frequents during various business trips. (Joan need not be affluent: we can imagine her going to the same club in her hometown on week-days when the bar and entry prices are lowest.) If cultural feminists require that good sex for women involve *long-term* emotional commitment, then such relationships will fail by definition. But the time frame appears to be less important to cultural feminists than the quality of the relationship itself. My contention is that we can well imagine that Joan responds to her one-time lovers as "the particular individuals they are" by trying to discern what kind of sex they like instead of assuming that one man's sexual needs, interests, or style will be just like any other's. Indeed, this individuation can help facilitate an open discussion of safe and satisfying sex in terms of the par-ticular sexual experience of each person, instead of Joan's perfunctorily passing each partner a condom "just like all the rest." She may also know that being sensitive to the needs of each one of her lovers individually means that she will have a more sat-isfying sexual experience herself. Indeed, Joan may be promiscuous precisely be-cause sex with different partners on a regular basis gives her the opportunity to dis-cover and experience a wide variety of sexual styles and tastes and so come to know what she likes best in sex. Even if each of Joan's lovers is a one-night stand, she can communicate to all of them that she regards them as special, that she is interested in what they want out of sex as they can best express it, and that she is interested in sex that fulfills her partner's needs as well as her own. Such efforts on Joan's part take a personal commitment of time and emotional energy, energy that perhaps the typical "cruiser" does not have any interest in expending. Indeed, there is good reason for thinking that much, if not most, "cruising" sex is much less personal than Joan's, be-cause straightforwardly pleasure-seeking, self-gratifying, and anonymous sex is a large part of what attracts many people to cruising. Moreover, it might be objected that Joan's affluence, education, and mobility afford her the opportunity and self-confidence to initiate successful sexual encounters and request sexual feedback that many women from more humble circumstances may lack. However, as I argued in the previous section, none of these caveats makes it a conceptual mistake to describe some cases of promiscuous sex in terms of care respect. It simply means that as in monogamy, some promiscuous lovers will treat their partners with care respect and some will not.

Likewise, whether adultery can be defined in terms of care respect will depend on the context of its occurrence. Extramarital sex can be the sex of the gay and les-bian couple who are married in order to raise their children from previous marriages or from their own marriage. Their affairs are understood to be a part of their sexual fulfillment as homosexuals. Extramarital sex can be the sex of a woman who marries an American man to establish her U.S. citizenship, both of whom care deeply for one another and who have an active sex life together but who did not marry with the intention of restricting each other's sexual choices. Even the adultery of deceit can be particularizing, understanding, and caring of the partner outside of the marriage. Trying to make adultery wrong by defining marriage as a commitment to sexual ex-clusivity ignores these special cases. Even if we were to define marriage in these terms, as Michael Wreen does in his article "What's Really Wrong with Adultery?,"[42] the Kantian imperative that Wreen invokes (that we must be able to universalize right conduct without logical contradiction) has no *moral* force beyond Kant's insistence that reason direct right action. In matters of sex and love in particular, Kant has been taken to task by feminist and nonfeminist moral philosophers alike for refusing to give the partiality of one's emotions a place in moral decision-making.[43] Our stereotypes of adultery and the repetitive pursuit of different sexual partners may be that they involve callous and dehumanizing sex, but this may be as much a function of the failure of monogamy as the failure of promiscuity.

We can offer similar arguments concerning a cultural feminist's desire for comfort and trust. Monogamy is no guarantee of sexual security or honesty. Promiscuous Joan, on the other hand, is characterized in previous examples specifically as someone who makes every effort *not* to make her partners feel either insecure or anxious. Whether or not her lovers have other lovers of their own, her expression of emotional support and understanding is one that she has personalized so as to make each of her partners trust their physical exposure and emotional access to her.

Even so, can any of Joan's relationships properly be called "romantic"? Paradigms of romance in Anglo-American culture are Romeo and Juliet or Rhett Butler and Scarlett O'Hara, lovers who believe of their partners that this partner is the one and only person in the world who will love them forever. Indeed, romantic love is based on the notion that one's lover is extraordinary, ideal, perfect in every way, such that slander directed against such a person is intolerable and unbelievable. In Robert Solomon's words, "It is the elevation of *one* otherwise ordinary person to extraordinary heights with extraordinary privileges" (my italics).[44] Even if Joan is an emotionally understanding and caring lover, if Joan's promiscuity is the repetitive pursuit of *different* sexual partners, her sex cannot consistently be called the *romantic* sex characterized here.

According to Shulamith Firestone, however, Joan should be thankful that her relationships with her lovers are *not* romantic, if by being romantic they instantiate the possessiveness and sexual subordination of patriarchy. For Firestone, romance under such conditions includes not only the deceitful sex privatization that I mentioned earlier but also a man's possession of a single woman under the auspices of true love for the sole purpose of making her his sexual subordinate. According to Firestone, the availability and social sanction of birth control combined with the influx of large numbers of women into the labor market decrease a woman's dependence on any one man for economic support and sexual security. From her view, the sexual domination of women under the pretense of romance serves the needs of a patriarchy weakened by women's increasing economic and social status. For Firestone, there can be no heterosexual sex other than male-dominated sex, when men's economic power and social privilege under patriarchy are threatened without it. The mutuality, vulnerability, and interdependency that Firestone believes is essential to sexual love simply do not exist, she contends, amid relations of inequality.[45]

Furthermore, according to Firestone, the idealization of each partner, particularly of women, only dooms the partners' sexual relationships to failure, as each partner inevitably fails to live up to the other's romantic ideal. According to Firestone, women *must* fail to match this ideal, since their sexual access symbolizes their inferiority to a sexually inaccessible, idealized Freudian mother.[46] Firestone contends that a woman's fall from the pedestal is particularly painful, as she often becomes economically and emotionally dependent on the man whom she regards as the love of her life, with few of the same economic and social resources to recoup her losses when the relationship flounders. In an article where she argues for a necessary relationship between love and monogamous (not polygamous) sexual exclusivity, Bonnie Steinbock dooms monogamy from the start by admitting that after "the first throes of romantic love[,] it is precisely because this stage does *not* last that we must promise to be faithful through the notoriously unromantic realities of married life."[47] Were Steinbock to appreciate the ways gender informs sexuality, she, like Firestone, might regard this fact as good reason for *not* entering into a relationship of sexual exclusivity.

The Don Juan who obsesses over, pursues, and ultimately possesses each of his lovers is an impersonal lover precisely because he does not love each of his partners for her own sake as a unique and particular individual but regards each one as a means to sexual conquest, to add to his list of conquests. He pretends to love them for themselves alone, detailing each perfection that he attests is theirs, promising an indefinite future of affection and attention. In other words, he *pretends* to be romantic, luring women with the bait of true love. Once lured to his bed, his partners become interchangeable, and so expendable, sexual objects. Here I disagree with Søren Kierkegaard, who says that the Don Juan is not deceiving his lovers; he is only fickle and truly believes, in his momentary sexual frenzy, that he will marry each one of them. This way of describing the Don Juan makes his peccadillos purely aesthetic, quite distinct from the ethical stage to which, according to Kierkegaard, he must ultimately aspire, if he does not wish to become bored. My point is that the Don Juan is a cad and a bounder precisely because his sexual behavior is intentionally deceptive, and to regard his behavior as purely aesthetic is to excuse an immoral promiscuity. (I wonder, would Kierkegaard have given solely aesthetic content to an equally promiscuous *woman's* behavior?)[48] The promiscuous man cannot flaunt his promiscuity among women for fear of being rejected as a profoundly unromantic gigolo by the very women he has convinced of the value of monogamy and whom he wishes to possess. On the other hand, sexual conquests are the stuff of serious conversation among many men ready to snicker and boast of a promiscuity encouraged in their peer group. Such conversation has historically been the type that so-called ladies are too delicate to hear, when women's discovery of the pretense, obfuscated by a compliment to our femininity, would ruin the game. Ever in search of new women to conquer, the promiscuous man must *appear* to be romantic even while he "plays around."

According to Firestone, romantic love is a male invention designed to make women into men's legitimate sexual property. If a woman can be convinced that romance is her only source for sexual intimacy, she will avoid promiscuous affairs for fear of losing access to that intimacy. Ironically, the supposed depersonalization of promiscuity that cultural feminists seek to avoid directs them toward a vision of romantic love that is often neither personal nor affectionate. On the other hand, women's promiscuity, according to Firestone, is typically no more than a false imitation of patriarchal power and another instance of women's co-optation by a system of sexual subordination. Under such circumstances, women are confronted with "less-than-love or daily agony." For all of these reasons, Firestone condemns contemporary romance while applauding what would be fulfilling sex for both partners *under different social conditions.*[49]

Therefore, I believe that it is a mistake to charge, as Robert Solomon does, that Firestone represents the feminist position that *requires* heterosexual love to be unfulfilling for women.[50] Solomon's claim is that only by regarding sexual roles as "fundamentally sex-neutral" and by presupposing "a significant degree of equality" between the sexes can we keep from condemning romantic love and restore its moral virtue. Solomon is convinced that if we use gender politics to describe the nature of romance, we will necessarily limit love to gender stereotypes. True romance for Solomon requires the kind of autonomous choice between sexual partners that is unavailable to women in Firestone's patriarchy, where sex is, according to Solomon, "often used to reinforce submissive and subservient female roles."[51]

Solomon perceptively describes the insidious nature of gender hierarchy under patriarchy only to dismiss such a hierarchy as having no bearing on "romantic love as such."[52] According to Solomon, a romantic consciousness simply does not make a political issue out of social differences. Romeo's and Juliet's love for one another would not have been romantic, for example, if they had been preoccupied with the political consequences of their union. However, suppose Romeo's idea of romance is regular sex, and Juliet's version is much less physical, more a function of loving intimacy and affection. Furthermore, suppose Juliet is feeling some pressure from Romeo to "put out," since he has been paying for their clandestine rendezvous at the cafe outside of town. In such a case, to view the couple's romance as a relationship between autonomous equals is to ignore the sexual and gender politics of their relationship and to misrepresent each partner's very different conceptions of romantic love. If, according to Solomon, "[o]ur roles in romance are in every case personally determined,"[53] then the "view from somewhere different," not the "view from nowhere," is vital to understanding the very political nature of "personally determined" romance in gendered, hierarchical contexts. By defining such contexts as deterministic and monolithic instead of viewing a gendered perspective as offering a more representative picture of sexual relationships, Solomon rejects the point of view from which he could identify the complex social location of each couple's romance.

Even if Romeo's and Juliet's conceptions of romance are the same, their romance need not be dissipated by an appreciation of social politics. Romeo could fully recognize the devastating political consequences of his pursuit of Juliet and make a "romantic" effort to accompany her to a more egalitarian society where family name or position is of no consequence to personal relationships. In such an environment, Solomon's romantic "sex-neutral" relationships might indeed be possible in virtue of the enlightened political context in which such relationships would take place; indeed, the elimination of gender and class hierarchies is the ideal context that Firestone believes is necessary for constructing positive human relationships. However, I have argued that within a patriarchal context, we cannot ignore social location without misrepresenting the sexual experiences, preferences, and desires of individual women.

Solomon's belief that romance must be defined as a relation among equals, despite the political context in which such romance exists, reflects the perspective of the "view from nowhere" described in chapter 1, since he maintains that "[t]he equality that is the precondition for love only consists in the demand that social differences do not matter."[54] No wonder he is convinced of Firestone's universal condemnation of romance, since her analysis is based on the fact that social differences *always* matter under hierarchical social conditions; what Firestone advocates is a rejection of the sex/class system that drives such hierarchies, so that the oppressive nature of romantic love under such a system will collapse. Solomon goes so far as to suggest that a "quasi-political self-consciousness . . . undermines the intimacy of love"; yet without such a consciousness, "the intimacy of love" for many heterosexual women will be nothing over and above acquiescing to domination and control. Solomon's feminism consists of such things as equal pay for equal work and equal access to jobs and careers; according to him, to drag a personal and private affair like romance into the public arena of gender politics might undermine "the very different strategies that are required to encounter each of them."[55] I argued in chapter 1 that this type of liberal feminism advocates a kind of gender blindness that is typical of the "view from nowhere." Solomon's insistence that we discover the true nature of romance divorced from its social location is consistent with a liberal feminism whose public/private dualism offers sanctuary from the politics of sexuality. Indeed, only by making feminism into liberal feminism can Solomon hope to argue that current gender roles are generally unfavorable to women *and* that gender equality requires gender blindness. Feminists of a more radical perspective would argue that gender blindness fails to recognize that romantic love sterilized of its gender politics entices women to enter into personal relationships that may be oppressive to them.

Both Solomon and Robert Nozick argue in favor of the sexual exclusivity of romantic lovers, because they believe romance requires the partners to share an identity designed to create what Solomon calls a kind of "ontological dependency" by which the lover is always present or "in mind" of the beloved.[56] This premise, however, ignores Beauvoir's insight that many women's perceived inferiority to and high valuation of men, combined with men's desire to assert their superiority, will compel women to submerge rather than share their identities with men, leaving women anonymous and invisible (the proverbial "woman *behind* the man"). As I argued earlier in this chapter concerning prostitution, to imply that all women are in a position to make autonomous choices with regard to their sexuality or that they value the "affective individualism" upon which Solomon's autonomy is based is to ignore the very real social subordination of many women that Solomon himself describes. In order to remain true to a feminist vision of sex equality yet advance an agenda for the intrinsic virtue of romance, Solomon dismisses the radical feminist agenda out of hand by dismissing the dialectic between gender and sexuality. Indeed, one of Beauvoir's paradoxes of romantic love reflects what I have contended is the dialectical complexity and contradiction in women's sexuality: Women who are able to assert their own needs in heterosexual relationships may remain dissatisfied, questioning whether their more agreeable partners are "real men," while women who feel incapable of asserting their own needs in their heterosexual relationships must confront their own powerlessness.[57]

Solomon admits that romance is "sometimes ontologically vicious" and by definition a struggle "for control over shared and reciprocal self-images."[58] If this is part of the intrinsic nature of romance, then Firestone is right that romance is no place for women in a society where such struggles are biased in favor of men. A cultural feminist would not want the romantic love Firestone describes, with only its pretense of care respect. I have quoted Firestone and others to suggest that the sexual exclusivity required by romance is circumscribed by a historical possessiveness and subjugation of women that makes its adoption as a feminist value extremely suspect. I have also argued that sexual exclusivity is no guarantee either of serious sexual commitment or of the warmth and affection cultural feminists value.

My intention is not to confirm cultural feminism's sexual values for women by detailing the intimate and affectionate landscape of at least some forms of promiscuity. Because human beings are socially situated, any attempt to determine an intrinsic female nature faces the postmodern challenge of nonarbitrarily differentiating those aspects of our sexuality that are nurtured from those that are natural. Furthermore, recent sociological evidence suggests that women and men have as many similar sexual needs as dissimilar ones, however they are to be accounted for.[59] My claim is that *even if* good sex for women amounts to intimate, sensitive, and affectionate sex, promiscuous "cruising" sex is as likely a candidate in the prevailing Western social climate as sexual exclusivity. Therefore, promiscuous sex can satisfy a sex radical feminist's desire for sexual exploration, while providing a cultural feminist with the sexual care and respect she demands for good sex. In the following section, I examine some of the arguments in favor of promiscuity that do not rely on its compatibility with intimacy.

Sexual Satisfaction, Sexual Growth, and Sexual Empowerment

The foregoing arguments in favor of promiscuity serve those who value personal and loving sex. A sex radical feminist, however, argues that the sexual exploration promised by promiscuity is not, and should not be, limited to intimate sex alone. I will investigate the anonymity of commercial sex work in chapter 4. Are there any reasons to recommend noncommercial promiscuous, casual, or recreational sex that divorces eros from romance?

I suggested in my discussion of sexual privacy that sexual exclusivity places a tremendous burden on one person alone to satisfy the diverse sexual needs of another, in all times and places, throughout the course of a single life. One of the arguments frequently offered in favor of promiscuity regarded as either the repetitious pursuit of different sexual partners or as adultery is that promiscuity eases the pressure on any one person to provide for all of a partner's sexual needs. The pursuit of a number of different partners can drastically reduce the sexual dissatisfaction and sexual frustration that can result from the failure to fulfill the diverse sexual demands of any one person.[60] A sex radical feminist would argue that our expectation that one person should carry such profound weight in our sexual lives results from a belief that the social construct of monogamy is, in reality, a natural fact. The documented sexual habits and customs of diverse cultures, however, reveal otherwise.[61] A sex radical would add that the sexual apathy and emotional distance from one's sexual partner that often accompany the sexual frustration of monogamy would be minimized if one had many different sexual partners. Furthermore, sex radical feminists claim that any sexual harassment of women and the violence committed against them that can be attributed to monogamous, unfulfilled heterosexual desire would be eliminated by lifting the sanctions against promiscuity.

Freudians would respond that the price we pay for civilization is a fairly large dose of sexual frustration. The more sex is repressed into the narrow range offered by heterosexual monogamy, the more human energies will redirect themselves to the pursuit of business, science, and the arts.[62] Moreover, sexual frustration is tremendously profitable for businesses who convince consumers to purchase their wares with the promise of otherwise scarce sexual satisfaction. Sexually provocative advertising whose success depends on sexual scarcity offers much less temptation to the person afforded socially sanctioned access to sex in the open market.

Furthermore, it could be argued that even promiscuity is no *guarantee* of sexual satisfaction. This is precisely the complaint of many women whose "liberated" sex life has made them feel shallow, objectified, and alone. Sexual satisfaction for many people would seem to require the time and emotional energy spent with just one person in order to discover and pursue their own sexual needs. Promiscuous teenage girls are especially vulnerable to the epithet of "slut," censure that makes otherwise pleasurable sex a blow to their self-image.

In addition, some feminists might contend that violence against women is a product of misogyny, not sexual frustration. Promiscuity will only make life more difficult and dangerous for women as we seek out partners who may wish to do no more than abuse or dominate women in bed. From this view, if we really want to rid our society of its sexual subordination of women, then we need to change men's attitudes toward women, not give them sexual license to reinforce patriarchal behavior.

A sex radical feminist challenges the sexual psychologism that says a free libido would mean chaos, monstrosity, or debility. As Gayle Rubin points out, "[S]exuality is impervious to political analysis as long as it is primarily conceived as a biological phenomenon or an aspect of individual psychology."[63] An alternative way of understanding promiscuity would be to imagine how creative, productive, and supportive we would be *in the absence* of the sexual repression bound up in sexual exclusivity. According to this view, regarding sex as an evil to be repressed instead of a blessing to be celebrated is a culturally loaded, medieval prejudice that contemporary Western society has made into debilitating neuroses for men as well as women.

For sex radicals, the belief held by some feminists that freedom from women's heterosexual subordination requires the dissociation of women from sex is yet another sign of the Western presumption that sex is bad. A sex radical feminist points out that once we situate sex in a Judeo-Christian context, sex is something to be repressed because sex is something evil. Therefore, women become repressed, marginalized, and dissipated by their association with sex. Rather than dissociate women from sex, the sex radical challenges us to celebrate women's association with sex *by liberating sex from evil*—specifically, from the evils implicit in nonmonogamous, nonprocreative, nonintimate sex acts that run contrary to the prescribed Western norm.[64] Promiscuous sex then becomes a source for sexual satisfaction for women free of the fear of social stigma.

Furthermore, sex radical feminists point out that women's complaints against heterosexual promiscuity as well as those against monogamy are the result of oppressive social conditions under which women's sexuality is currently constructed. To finger promiscuity as the culprit in women's sexual dissatisfaction is to ignore the sexual oppression that overlays men's subordination of women and to victimize women for their sexual choice. A sex radical feminist would remove women's sexual oppression, so that women were not punished for promiscuity; only then would individual women be in a position to decide for themselves whether or how promiscuity figured in their lives. Sex radicals would contend that from the "view from nowhere," it is easy to ignore Western sexual prejudices that both eschew and punish those who would stray from the prevailing sexual norms.

With regard to sexual violence against women, a sex radical feminist would argue that sexual liberation from the constraints of sexual exclusivity does not imply that any sex goes. As a radical feminist, she balks at any sex that subordinates women to the unwelcome demands of men. As a sex radical, she rejects any attempt to oppress sexual preferences solely because they fail to match the cultural norm; yet she disdains alternative sexualities that fail to meet minimum requirements of consent. Thus Gayle Rubin asserts both that "[a] radical theory of sex must identify, describe, explain, and denounce erotic injustice and sexual oppression" and that "[i]n the long run, feminism's critique of gender hierarchy must be incorporated into a radical theory of sex, and the critique of sexual oppression should enrich feminism." [65] Under such conditions, a sex radical feminist sees nothing wrong with promiscuous sex that is recreational or anonymous, nor with the frequent use of dominant/submissive roles in sex such as lesbian butch/femme sex or sadomasochistic sex. As long as each partners' sexual needs are accorded the kind of care respect (neither "forced [n]or fooled" to use Rubin's phrase) that appreciates the particular desires of one's partner and assures a context of mutual consent, sexual variety and experimentation are both permissible and encouraged.[66] Furthermore, according to sex radicals, sex liberated in this way would create new markets for erotica that would more than offset any commercial loss due to the release of sexual frustration. In short, promiscuous sex is part of sex radical feminism's positive program for women's sexual pleasure, agency, and self-definition.

Another kind of argument offered in favor of promiscuous sex has to do with the advantage in the *variety* of sexual partners. According to this line of reasoning, the sexual variety available through promiscuous sex increases the likelihood that a person will discover what kind of sex suits her individual needs. Sex never becomes boring or routine, since a person has the freedom not only to change partners but also to change his own sexual style. Adopting a sexual ethic of care respect, sexual partners can remain sensitive to the particular sexual needs of diverse others and encourage experimentation and change if desired. Frederick Elliston remarks that this variety gives us a "repertoire of gestures" that can "facilitate the mastery of one kind of body language." He suggests that such a repertoire can afford the promiscuous person a kind of sexual growth and creativity that sexually exclusive relationships cannot.[67]

However, Elliston gives away the game by concluding that ultimately, "the good sex life cannot be achieved through physical gratification alone. . . . [H]aving talked with many, we may discover that our most meaningful dialogue can be carried on with one." His claim is that a "principled life represented by the traditional commitment 'to love, honor, and obey' signifies a higher mode of existence" than that of a promiscuous life, which ultimately succumbs to the aesthetic boredom of Kierkegaard's Don Juan complex.[68]

I have argued, however, that promiscuous sex need not lack the principled ethical stage of love and commitment that Elliston requires. Furthermore, sex radicals challenge the notion that there is anything *wrong* with "physical gratification alone." Indeed, "having talked with so many," we may equally be assured that *one* would be boring. Elliston adopts the less radical alternative that promiscuous sex is justified as long as it is a means to the discovery of a person's most compatible, monogamous sexual partner.[69] Premarital sex is often justified in just this fashion: premarital sex increases the likelihood that an otherwise uncommitted person will find a partner *with whom she would wish to share the rest of her life.* When two people have had sex, they can better decide whether to pursue the relationship further, both physically and emotionally.

Implicit in such arguments, however, is the assumption that a sexually exclusive relationship, of a serial if not permanent sort, is the requisite sexual ideal. For many people, mastering their sexual body language may actually be easier and more efficient with just one person; and certainly there are lots of sexually creative, monogamous couples who do not need a promiscuous life for sexual satisfaction or growth. But Elliston's claim that promiscuity is somehow lower than monogamy on the moral totem pole only acknowledges his own adherence to a sexual norm that I claim is not more "principled" in its particular social context just because it is the norm. Only by deriving such principles from the "view from nowhere" can Elliston disguise socially situated sexual values as true ones.

Robert Solomon's virtues of romantic love also appear to suffer from a moral presumption of monogamy, since it could be argued that those same virtues may also be a part of promiscuous sex: Solomon states that romantic love promotes self-awareness, a healthy outlook on the world, inspiration and creativity, and excitement.[70] However, if such virtues are the result of sex with only *one* person, then sex with *more than one* person could be at least as virtuous, perhaps even more so. There is no fallacy of composition here. A variety of partners are often more capable of promoting self-awareness in one person than any one of them alone. Bruce shows Joan how much Joan likes to be stroked on her back. Hamilton reveals to her how many ways there are to be orgasmic. Ron reminds Joan of how hungry she is after really good sex. Furthermore, Joan's outlook on the world may be especially enhanced by the knowledge that she can satisfy and care for several men. Joan might easily be more inspired in her work or more creative in her sex play because of the variety of her sexual partners. Certainly the opportunity for new levels of sexual excitement are present that might be absent for Joan in a more exclusive relationship. My point is that Solomon invests in sexual exclusivity virtues that do not justify the value he places in romantic love. The "view from somewhere different" reveals that sexuality is much too contextual a feature of human relationships to exclude promiscuity from the sphere of the sexually valuable.

Moreover, Solomon says that "the aim of [romantic] love is to *make* a single person extraordinary and to reconceptualize oneself in his or her terms, to *create* an escape from the anonymity of the Kantian moral world and thrive in a world *à deux* of one's own" (Solomon's italics).[71] I have already argued that romantic love can be much less satisfying for women than Solomon makes out simply because he personalizes sexual exclusivity without gendering it. In addition, the obsessive (and possessive) implications of *making* someone extraordinary combined with Solomon's suggestion that lovers remain content in a self-contained moral universe would not appeal to many feminists interested in promoting loving sex within caring communities.

Feminists have often argued that women's freedom from their sexual subordination by men is directly proportional to the amount of control women have over our bodies. The exercise of such control is often interpreted in terms of a woman's right to make sexual and reproductive decisions for herself without undue interference from others. In the language of an ethic of care, such control can be interpreted as creating opportunities for individual women to choose sexual and reproductive lives that allow them to care for themselves and others. Marjorie Weinzweig has combined the language of individual autonomy with the language of care to develop the notion of "autonomous relating to others," by which a woman is able to choose her sexual and reproductive roles amid a community of others and out of a concern for others in a way that does not hinder her self-development.[72] Each interpretation describes a kind of empowerment that would enable individual women to direct the course of their own sexual and reproductive destinies. I have suggested that sexual liberation is women's liberation when women can define its terms and conditions. Is promiscuity consistent with women's sexual empowerment? Could a promiscuous lifestyle promote such empowerment?

The answer lies in a promiscuous woman's knowledge of her own social location. The "view from somewhere different" requires an appreciation of the dialectic between gender and sexuality. A woman who adopts this perspective understands that men who promise true love have little incentive to be faithful under a patriarchal system that rewards men for "scoring." When men do "settle down," they often do so only in exchange for the sexual and domestic subordination of their wives, a subordination with no guarantee of emotional or financial payoff.[73] A woman who adopts the "view from somewhere different" is situated to recognize that her own casual or recreational promiscuity bears little resemblance to men's, when a promiscuous woman's score makes her a "slut" but her sexual reticence makes her "frigid." She recognizes that her own domestic and child-care responsibilities can make an adulterous affair look especially appealing, while those very responsibilities, often shouldered alone in addition to salaried work, make finding the time and energy for extramarital sex a near impossibility. In a society that makes women the keepers of monogamy and the family, her awareness of the dialectic between gender and sexuality reveals that promiscuous married women symbolize the breakdown of the very foundation of social life.[74] Such a society will be loath to free women from our domestic chores once we enter the workforce: with access to an array of new potential sexual partners while on the job, women must be dissuaded from promiscuous pursuits at all costs. Husbands, on the other hand, often have more social and domestic freedom to play the field. Furthermore, despite her lopsided domestic responsibilities, a woman is typically marked insensitive to her children's needs when her marriage falls apart due to her infidelity. From the recognition of her own social location, a woman can begin to understand how her economic and monogamous dependence on men has made it easy to be co-opted by a system that has made sexual liberation a synonym for women's derogation and sexual subordination.

If the "view from somewhere different" acknowledges difference without presuming superiority and without devolving into dislocation, then women who adopt such a perspective will (1) recognize their sexual partners as "the particular individuals they are" and not treat them solely in terms of some general capacity they share with other human beings; and (2) try to see the world from their point of view. Because such a perspective acknowledges that sexual partners have sexual needs of their own, the "view from somewhere different" encourages its adopters to (3) care about their sexual partners' well-being by helping them pursue their own wants and needs. This is precisely the ethic of care respect that both describes the intimate sex of cultural feminists and affords sex radical feminists the respectful regard between persons that is definitive of mutually consenting sex.

From such a perspective, promiscuity can empower those women who would choose it over monogamy by encouraging the sexual autonomy characterized by Weinzweig's "autonomous relating to others." With no illusions about the advantages of marriage, monogamous relationships, or romance, a woman who chooses promiscuity from the "view from somewhere different" knows that she is asserting her own sexual agenda in a world ready to denigrate her or dismiss her for failing to act in a sexually subordinate role. At the same time, by acknowledging her potential as a self-defining sexual subject acting contrary to monogamous norms, she can begin to forge a sexual identity of her own. Acting under an ethic of care respect, however, such a woman will not become so absorbed in the pursuit of her own sexual needs that she is blind to those of others. She will acknowledge that promiscuity may not be for everyone. She will recognize that some sexual partners prefer intimacy and others prefer anonymity. She will be less inclined to regard any promiscuous man's insensitive treatment of women as her model for promiscuous sex, since she will recognize that such a model is inconsistent with care respect and only reinforces the belief that monogamy is really better for women after all. When a woman chooses sexual exclusivity, she will have done so knowing that as with promiscuity, there are benefits as well as risks.

A woman whose sex life is understood from the "view from somewhere different" also recognizes that in many women's lives there is a place for celibacy, when freedom from an active sexual life is a source of comfort or relief. Women who would rather be sexually active than celibate may be frustrated by the "view from somewhere different" for encouraging them to perceive themselves as sexual agents when there is simply no safe or satisfying sex to be had. However, the "view from somewhere different" would recommend that such women see their celibacy dialectically as both misfortune and opportunity; as I will argue in the following section, in a culture where a woman's sexual assertiveness can make her a "good" girl, a "bad" girl, or both, rejecting celibacy will mean embarking on a complex and often contradictory quest for sexual satisfaction. No one feminist sexual framework can *promise* satisfying sex for women, but the "view from somewhere different" can give individual women the epistemological and moral tools to begin making, even demanding, the kinds of changes in their sexual lives that will give meaning and value to them.

Indeed, as Simone de Beauvoir would remind us, promiscuous sex alone empowers no one under conditions of women's economic disenfranchisement. More women are talking about their affairs, and more women are having affairs, as more women gain the economic clout to be able to survive independently of heterosexual monogamy. But the sexual empowerment of a handful of promiscuous career women will have little or no practical meaning for those millions of women whose livelihoods continue to depend on the sexual and domestic demands of men. Many women struggling to defend themselves against men's sexual violence in the absence of the economic and legal means to prevent it will find feminists' claims that sexual promiscuity promotes women's liberation insensitive at best, classist and racist at worst; nor will it do to encourage teenage girls to be promiscuous without teaching them about the responsibilities that accompany women's sexual agency and about the contradictory and oppressive patriarchal climate in which their sexual choices are evaluated. Nevertheless, the mere fact that some women are beginning to take control of their own sexual destinies and are choosing to do so *by choosing to be promiscuous* cannot be underestimated in a society whose social voices are women's voices only when women *act* on the belief that we will be heard. The following section details some of the specific ways in which patriarchy thwarts the sexual empowerment of promiscuous white women and women of color and the ways in which sexual stereotypes are used to favor heterosexual white men over homosexual white men and men of color.

Good Girls and Bad Girls

> In a way, my life has been an upside-down experience. I never made love to the men I married, and I did not marry the men I loved. I do not know if that makes me a good girl gone bad, or a bad girl gone good.
>
> —Beatrice Wood, *I Shock Myself: The Autobiography of Beatrice Wood*

Women's heterosexual subordination by men is a subordination of *identity*. In a patriarchal society, women are defined in terms of our heterosexuality and reproductivity in order to serve the needs and maintain the privileges of men. Therefore, women's sexuality under patriarchy must be very carefully circumscribed lest it gain an independent credibility and power of its own. Men's ideal of women is that we be sexual only *in a certain way*.

America's good girl/bad girl stereotype defines the parameters of acceptable sexual behavior for women, circumscribing our identity as women under conditions of male status and privilege. Sheila Ruth calls this stereotype one of the heterosexual "serviceability" of women to emphasize how much a woman's identity is defined by her sexual access to men:[75] the sexually "serviceable" woman is a heterosexually available mistress or lover, sensuous, responsive, and receptive. Wives sometimes fit this stereotype, but only when their husbands have not grown sexually bored with them. The sexually serviceable woman is a sexually "good" woman, playful yet submissive, eager, perhaps slightly mysterious. As a playmate fantasy, she can be even more independent, experienced, exotic, or dangerous. She is to be distinguished from the nonsexual "good" woman/mother/wife, who is nurturing where the sexually serviceable woman will be challenging, virginal where the sexually serviceable woman will be carnal. The sexually "nonserviceable" woman is a bitch-temptress, immodest, coarse, and demanding. She is a promiscuous woman who is "nonserviceable" despite her availability to men because she is ungovernable, indiscriminate, and selfish. The seductive lustiness of a serviceable woman becomes salacious, lewd, and uncomfortably lascivious in a nonserviceable woman. Her nonsexual counterpart is cloying, manipulative, and catty. A nonserviceable woman is "bad."

The irony in these distinctions is that they are arbitrarily and ambiguously applied. Feminists not only object to the content and restrictiveness of the stereotypes; we also object to the fickle, tenuous, and often contradictory ways in which women are asked to instantiate them. A wife may be congratulated by an ambitious husband for the way she successfully flirts with his boss at a company cocktail party. Having lost his chance at promotion, he may regard her identical flirtation as an insensitive assault on his masculinity or as an irritating habit of "the bitch who can't shut her mouth." If her clothes are not sexy enough, she is "frumpy." When in those very same clothes she seduces the wrong man, she is "sleazy." Many husbands want a wife who is simultaneously sexually available and chaste, the virgin who is a whore in bed. A woman is "bad" whether she strays on purpose or by accident because, like a servant, she is supposed to know what is expected of her.

What these examples suggest is that a woman is "good" only by being *both* an experienced sexual seductress and a nonsexual maternal caretaker with the capacity to know not only which role suits which occasion for which man but also how to play both roles at once. Success in one social setting is no guarantee of future success even in the very same setting. The feminine stereotype of an anxious woman fussing over her appearance, caring more about her hair than her opinions, is testimony to the insecurity of her position, not merely personal vanity. By being required to fill contradictory social roles whose demands women cannot confidently predict, women must inevitably fail to be "good." The quote from Beatrice Wood at the beginning of this section represents the feelings of many women who get the mixed message that the good girl is bad and the bad girl is good. What difference does it make, when no matter what she does, she doesn't get it right?

Commonly used sexual terms to describe women are terms used to describe the promiscuous woman: trollop, vamp, slut, hussy, whore, pickup, Jezebel, tart, bawd, vixen, floozy.[76] Such a woman is loose, easy, and indiscriminate—a "nonserviceable" woman for men, to use Ruth's phrase. Not surprisingly, these terms are used by men primarily to insult or denigrate women, since a woman who is promiscuous is "bad." Women are so closely identified with these terms that they are used by both men and women to insult women outside of any explicitly sexual context ("Who does that hussy think she is, humiliating me like that?," or "The slut brought me ham when I ordered sausage.") Sexualized terms for women like "broad," "skirt," and "tail" do not necessarily connote promiscuity, so they are often used to refer to "serviceable" women, as in "That's a nice piece of tail," or "Now that's a broad!" If women who are feminists object to these forms of address, men often react in disbelief, as if women were taking offense at a compliment.

Still, women can never be certain of our serviceability, given women's denigration in such phrases as "Who let this broad on the highway?!" When men use the term "bitch" to refer to particular women, the intent is to slur, degrade, vilify, since it refers to an animal in heat, an animal that indiscriminately and promiscuously copulates. Certainly the word implies "nonserviceable" when applied to women: "I can't stand taking direct orders from that bitch!" Not only are women being male-identified sexually by such terms, but we are being identified with a sexuality that demeans us. Women might object less to an externally imposed identity if the value of that identity were positive. But women's promiscuity has become so imbued with negativity and our sexuality so filled with contradiction that it is no wonder Beatrice Wood regards her sex life as "an upside-down experience."

I am not arguing that words used to describe the sexually active man—"lecher," "old goat," "roué," "gigolo," "rake," and the like—cannot be offensive, even humiliating. My claim is that in a heterosexually dominated culture whose male advantage rests in pressing women's sexuality to the service of individual men, women will be judged "bad" when they fail to live up to particular men's sexual expectations of them, no matter how eccentric or contradictory. Furthermore, because women's identity is a function of our sexuality, such condemnation strikes at the very core of our self-image as women. Some men are lechers *and* overbearing; women are broads *because* they are overbearing.

In addition, special condemnation is reserved for the sexually promiscuous woman that is not matched by terms used to describe promiscuous men. A promiscuous woman is referred to as "dirt" in virtue of her sexual profligacy alone. "My girlfriend? You mean that whore? She's a piece of dirt." A promiscuous man is "dirt" when, in the course of being promiscuous, he has been sexually deceptive, disrespectful, exploitative, or mean. His promiscuity is primarily a function of what he *does*, not a function of who he *is*. Thus, a man who was promiscuous in his youth may, with an appropriate show of repentance, come to his marriage with his community's (and wife's) expectation that he will be faithful, while a woman with a similar history may still be regarded as suspiciously adulterous. A "dirty old man" who does no more than leer at young women is reviled not because he is promiscuous (although he would like to be) but because elderly men are ironically committed to a stereotypical asexuality that precludes the very sexual objectification of women encouraged in younger men.

Indeed, a dirty old man wishes he were a roué, and for good reason. A promiscuous man is often called a "stud," a "stallion," a "man of the world," a "man of experience." A young promiscuous man may be a "hot rod" or "sowing his wild oats." He is not identified with "used goods" or described as "loose" the way a promiscuous woman often is. Contemporary women who refer to their errant boyfriends as sluts complain, at least in part, because *their boyfriends are getting away with being sluts* no matter what their girlfriends think; but once a woman is heterosexually promiscuous, she must justify her behavior as in some way serviceable to men or be identified as a slut. (Thus, promiscuous women do not *get away with* being sluts; promiscuous women *are* sluts.) Feminists like Mary Daly believe that the only way for women to empower ourselves sexually is to reconceptualize and reevaluate women's sexuality, with new terminology, if necessary, so that women's "pure lust" has meaning for women. Clarissa Pinkola Estes believes that there are "wild woman archetypes" throughout history that women need to regain access to in order to fulfill our sexual destinies as women.[77] In both cases, sexual empowerment for women is a function of eschewing patriarchal definitions of our sexuality in order to redefine it in women's terms. Absent a tendency toward gynocentrism, this approach is consistent with the perspective of the "view from somewhere different" since it encourages women to understand our social location in order to facilitate women's sexual agency and self-definition.

Yet here we confront a fascinating paradox: if women are *sexually* identified by heterosexual society, why are we *condemned* for promiscuous sex? Shouldn't the heterosexually identified female be encouraged to do what her male-identified culture expects of her—namely, have as much sex with as many men as possible?

The characterization of promiscuous sex in the first section of this chapter can provide the resolution to this paradox: recall that an important condition for at least some kinds of promiscuous sex is that it be the active and repetitious pursuit of different sexual partners. The promiscuous person, if nothing else, is the *agent* of her sexual desire. But in a patriarchal society, this is precisely the role reserved for the heterosexually active *male*. In such a society, women are sex *objects*, not sex subjects. Women are to be dominated and controlled through sex, not free to pursue an unabashed love of sex untainted by degradation or shame. If sexual promiscuity is sexual agency, that is, the active pursuit of sex by an autonomous subject, then the sexually promiscuous woman is regarded as attempting to take control of her sexual life. But this is anathema to a system of power in which the oppression of women through sex is a primary means of establishing and maintaining dominance over women. Thus, the harsher criticism that a patriarchal society lodges against the sexually promiscuous woman can be understood as intended to inhibit her pursuit of the kind of sexual activity which has long been the exclusive preserve of men and which signals rebellion against her oppressor. It is a striking feminist irony that the expression "loose woman" is both a symbol of women's degradation and profound evidence of women's attempts to liberate ourselves from the sexual dominance of men.

What these uses of language suggest is that in a culture whose power and status lie in the hands of men, sex is a badge of honor for men, a sign of power, dominance, and possession. However, race, class, and sexual preference intersect with gender in the social construction of promiscuity to narrow the range of this dominance. Sex is a badge of honor for *white, affluent, heterosexual* men. African American men are often sexually stereotyped by Anglos as primitive and dangerous sexual animals with enlarged penises, a sexuality threatening to many white men, commonly used by them to denigrate and straitjacket blacks. When a black man marries a white woman, he is often regarded by the black community as a traitor to his race and by whites as appropriating and defiling one of a white man's own.[78] When a black man pursues a woman of his own race, he may be regarded by whites as typical of an oversexed primitive in search of an equally lusty partner. If an African American man is homosexual, he may well be burdened with the additional heterosexist presumption that given his sexual profligacy, he is a rabid transmitter of AIDS. Sexual conservatives and liberals alike have singled out gay men of all races and ethnicities as paradigmatic performance-oriented, promiscuous sex seekers whose lifestyle of casual or anonymous sex is regarded as the primary cause of AIDS.

Latinos are frequently categorized in sexual terms as passionate but ultimately self-serving Don Juans who display a machismo that defines their masculinity in terms of their sexual prowess. However, Anglos' class stereotype of Latinos as coarse and uneducated often makes these very same macho men sexually unappealing to middle-class white women determined to find a man who will maintain, if not enhance, their social status. Many middle-class white men see large Latino families as no more than welfare recipients.[79]

The way sex guarantees authority for the Asian or Asian American man depends largely on his class: the working-class Vietnamese immigrant cannot afford to entertain a blond American girlfriend in the way his rich Japanese counterpart can. On the other hand, despite the commonly held Anglo stereotype of the sexually restrained Asian, Asian cultures are notorious for a socially sanctioned sexual freedom which Asian men enjoy regardless of class but which Asian women do not.[80]

All of these stereotypes derive their pervasiveness and staying power from the social status and authority conferred on white, affluent, heterosexual males in patriarchy. The sexual stereotype of the uptight and ineffectual lover, which the black man may have of his white counterpart, will be of little consequence to the wealthy white man whose institutionalized power gives him a sexuality all his own: "He's so rich! Isn't he sexy?" Unlike white women and people of color, such men represent success objects who have become sex objects without becoming sexually subordinated or vilified. A rich man of color may also be made sexy by his money, but his stereotyping by whites has notoriously restricted his social stature to that of the successful drug dealer, pimp, or professional athlete. Such restrictions are only exacerbated by the fact that successful African American corporate businessmen or academics are often accused by members of their own race as "selling out" to white culture. Even less well-to-do white men can ignore blacks' stereotypes of them simply in virtue of an entrenched racist social standard that marginalizes the perspectives of people of color of all classes. Sexual stereotypes exist both within and across social categories, but the prevalence of any one stereotype is determined by the power of the stereotyper to define the parameters of the category.

Women of color are multiply oppressed, both by the appropriation of their sexuality by men and by the particular sexual stereotypes associated with their race or ethnicity. Many women of color are sexually stereotyped as promiscuous in virtue of their race or ethnicity in addition to being heterosexually identified. If they are lesbians or poor, they are further victimized in virtue of their sexual preference or class. Black women are frequently stereotyped by whites as wild and untamed sensualists who can offer white men a kind of exotic sexual thrill that white women cannot. When a black woman chooses a white lover, she is often considered by both black men and black women as a traitor to her race, someone trading on her stereotype to increase her social status. To white women, she is often a threatening sexual competitor taking unfair advantage of her color.[81]

Latina and American Indian women are stereotyped by many Anglos as poor, illiterate, and eternally pregnant. Single, young Latinas are often categorized as promiscuous despite the acknowledged sanctions of the Catholic Church, to which many Latinas belong, but especially when those same sanctions discourage contraception or family planning. Middle-class white men attracted to the sexual fecundity of the Latina stereotype also often expect a feistiness they associate with a fiery Latin spirit that may be a particular turn-on. Ironically, many modern Latino households maintain a traditional double standard whereby husbands may have affairs, but wives should be virgins prior to marriage and faithful afterward. On the other hand, the machismo image of the Latina's peers makes it especially difficult for Latina teenagers to say no to sex when young Latino men buy into their own stereotype.[82]

Asian and Asian American women are commonly typed outside their cultural community as docile, submissive, and restrained sexually, making them tempting targets for many Anglo men grown bored with more assertive or demanding playmates. A frequent assumption is that Asian women eschew promiscuity, only tolerating sex because it is required of married women or forced on them by unscrupulous mercenaries in the commerce of prostitution known as "sex tourism." Geisha girls do not dispel this assumption, since they are typically regarded as women for whom sex is a job, not a joy, and whose promiscuity is tightly circumscribed by their male clients. In addition, the extremely strong prohibition against women's adultery in most Asian cultures reinforces the presupposition that Asian women much prefer monogamy or no sex at all.[83]

Promiscuous lesbians are marked as heterosexually frigid, unattractive dykes who couldn't land a man if they tried. When model-beautiful, they are propositioned incessantly by men who cannot understand why they are "wasting their looks" on other women. Poverty makes white women and women of color especially vulnerable to men who appear to promise financial security in exchange for sex. Because each woman has a social location defined by her race, class, and sexual preference in addition to her gender, her oppressions multiply when she is *not* white, *not* affluent, or *not* heterosexual. Her age, her physical ability or attractiveness, even her willingness to wear makeup may also work against her if she does not accommodate the sexual expectations of her culture. Men and women both suffer from strict sexual stereotyping, but the cultural expectation that women be sexually subordinate to men undermines many women's self-respect in a way that expectations for men to live up to the sexual dominance and agency definitive of the masculine ideal do not. Multiple oppressions will be particularly painful for women who are already sexually oppressed by a society that makes much of monogamy into domestic and sexual servitude for women but often makes promiscuity a degrading, if not dangerous, undertaking. In the final section I examine some of the arguments offered against promiscuity amid a growing AIDS epidemic.

Pregnancy and Sexually Transmitted Diseases

Before modern scientific research developed popular and reliable birth control methods and prior to the introduction of antibiotics, pregnancy and sexually transmitted diseases were commonly offered as reasons against promiscuity. If women chose to avoid painful and dangerous abortions, they faced the prospect of unwanted or stigmatized children, or lives alone without the financial or emotional support of the fathers of their offspring. Men faced the moral and legal responsibilities of paternity. Sexually transmitted diseases were often difficult for sexual partners to detect and were notoriously painful once contracted. Some, if left untreated, were lethal.

A counterclaim of the pre-AIDS sexual revolution was that with the advent of modern technology, including modern birth control drugs and devices, safer and eas- ier access to abortions, and medications to ease the pain of venereal disease, promis- cuity was a safe, sane, and even recommended way to enjoy sex. Women could at last taste the pleasures of sex free from the fear or guilt of pregnancy, and men could indulge their fantasies fully liberated from the Victorian banes of enforced marriage or debilitating disease. Despite the conservative moral lament that sex was appropri- ate only within the confines of marriage, the practical arguments discouraging a va- riety of sexual partners seemed to be dispelled once and for all by modern science.

Decades after the flowering of the 1960s sexual revolution, however, American middle-class access to abortion and birth control still does not include the millions of poor or working-class single women with or without children, who have no health insurance or benefits to cover the costs of family planning. Women of color are par- ticularly affected, since they rank extremely low in average income relative to single white women or white men. For poor married women, men at home are no guar- antee of a steady paycheck or emotional support for birth control. Furthermore, de- spite the 1973 U.S. Supreme Court ruling of *Roe v. Wade* establishing a woman's le- gal right to abortion, many states still make abortions psychologically and practically difficult for women of all classes.[84] Thus, marriage provides no guarantee of ready solutions to unwanted pregnancies, nor is it a bulwark against the venereal disease that errant husbands may bring home with them. Many teenage girls are not allowed by their parents or physicians to use birth control, yet they continue to have sex with boyfriends who find condoms uncomfortable or inhibiting. The sexual revolution not only appears to cater to the interests of men over women in the ways discussed in the preceding sections; it also appears to cater to an adult, white, and middle-class bias as well.

The politically liberal solution has been to advocate for state and federal monies for education and access to contraception and abortion. The conservative moral so- lution has been to continue to argue against the morality of promiscuity, calling for a reinstatement of the intimacy, emotional commitment, and strong "family values" that monogamous marriage promises. The emergence of AIDS in the late 1970s seemed made to order for a sexual counterrevolution aimed to strike a fatal blow against promiscuous sex. For many conservatives, AIDS symbolizes the inevitable de- cline of a sexually permissive society, a society that condones a gay lifestyle that con- servatives believe is disgusting or perverse. AIDS is regarded by many such conserv- atives as just punishment for an unnatural sex life irresponsibly lived. Intravenous drug users who contract AIDS are denigrated not for their sexual habits but for their immoral lifestyle. By the mid-1980s, when the sexual transmission of AIDS came to be regarded as a serious threat to the heterosexual community, AIDS became a rallying cry for conservatives eager to use the fatality of AIDS to redouble social support for monogamous marriage over promiscuity.[85]

Even those who do not blame the gay population for the AIDS crisis typically give considerable weight to the admonition to avoid promiscuous sex. Condoms are no guarantee of protection. One can test negative for HIV—the Human Immunodeficiency Virus, which has been regarded as the primary cause of AIDS—but, due to the virus's dormancy, test positive in subsequent trials. How reliable are the tests? Since the virus has no apparent history in the United States prior to 1978, many believe that any sexual partner since that time must be considered suspect.[86] Wishing to avoid the politics of repression against the gay community that AIDS has been used to exacerbate, many political liberals lobby for a return to monogamy for homosexuals and heterosexuals alike. There has also been a strong faction of the gay community that has begun advocating a monogamous lifestyle in apparent imitation of the heterosexual norms many gay men have long rejected. Many in the gay community regard this trend as internalized homophobia that blames AIDS on a promiscuous gay lifestyle. Alternatively, some gay men advocate a pluralistic gay sexuality designed around safe-sex guidelines and defined in gay terms.[87]

The following argument emerges: promiscuity puts people at high risk of contracting HIV. HIV causes AIDS. AIDS is fatal. Therefore, promiscuity puts people at unnecessarily high risk of death. The correlative normative conclusion asserts that promiscuity should be avoided. A second set of what I call "Russian roulette" arguments asserts that promiscuity is wrong, since single instances of HIV testing cannot test for all future contractions of the virus; hence, one cannot know whether or not one is infecting (or being infected by) multiple partners over time. Because this knowledge is vital to a safe sex life for all parties, any one partner's promiscuity is immoral. The premises of the first argument bear examining, as does the validity of both the first and second sets of arguments.

First, why would someone think that *promiscuity* puts one at high risk of contracting HIV? This premise implies that promiscuous sex is sex with someone whose infection with the virus one is unsure about. Uncertainty typically accompanies indiscriminate or anonymous sex (indeed, the risks of such sex can be a large part of its allure); however, uncertainty need not be a factor in all promiscuous relationships. A gay or heterosexual man can be on such intimate terms with each of his sexual partners that he knows their sexual histories well enough to be at low risk. The terms may not even be intimate, just reliable, as when a man has sex with recent divorcées whose long prior marriages are known by many to have been faithful ones. Promiscuous women who have been lesbians for several decades or who have never had heterosexual sex, and have always practiced safe sex with women with similar sexual histories, are similarly at low risk.[88] Many heterosexual women buy their own condoms because they want some control over the condom's reliability and want to make sure that all of their sexual partners use them. Discriminating George from a previous example required each of his partners to be tested for AIDS; promiscuous Joan could require each of her regular sexual partners to take frequent AIDS tests. If the *test* is the reason for the uncertainty, then this is an argument for abstinence from sexual partners who have had sex with anyone since 1978, not an argument against promiscuity in favor of monogamy or romance.

People can of course lie, withhold information, not know they are infected, or simply be careless. But these factors are as much a feature of monogamous relationships as promiscuous ones: one act of sexual penetration is sufficient to contract the disease, an act consistent with sexual exclusivity. Furthermore, someone with a monogamous partner of several years' duration can still pass the disease on from a previous partner who was an unknown carrier. HIV has come under critical scrutiny of late, since its latency in some carriers and dormancy in others makes its causal link to AIDS subject to question. AIDS is still a much-misunderstood medical problem that cannot convincingly be used to argue for what feminists have claimed is an already suspect sexual traditionalism.[89]

Furthermore, HIV is also contracted through the infected blood of blood transfusions as well as infected needles. Yet the argument offered in response is not that blood transfusions are wrong or objectionable, only that we should take extra precautions to insure the use of untainted blood. Similar notes of caution are offered to those of us who drive Los Angeles freeways. Such freeways can be lethal. Such freeways are *often* lethal, such that driving them puts people at high risk. Yet the watchword for California drivers is caution, reduced speeds, sobriety, and attentiveness behind the wheel, not *absence* from behind the wheel. The fact that promiscuous sex is high-risk sex in an era of AIDS is insufficient reason to conclude that promiscuous sex should be avoided or that promiscuous sex is wrong. It is an argument for precautionary measures with regard to promiscuous sex that may not have been taken at a different point in our sexual history. Compare Laurie Shrage's comments about the role of commercial sex in the spread of AIDS: "To blame commercial sex providers for the spread of AIDS is like blaming commercial airline companies for the spread of terrorism. Instead, we need to respond by requiring that the industry take extraordinary precautions to abate this epidemic, just as we require commercial airline companies to take extreme precautions to abate terrorism; we do not shut them down."[90]

This is not to argue that condoms or AIDS tests constitute safe sex for the promiscuous. Without a reliable and detailed sexual history on every sexual partner, there is no foolproof way to avoid contracting HIV and also have promiscuous frontal or anal intercourse. Feminists have long claimed that heterosexual sex has seldom been safe for women in a world of frequently unaffordable antibiotics or reliable but expensive contraception, inaccessible abortion, rape, dishonest sex partners, and violent or errant husbands. With the advent of AIDS, men are just beginning to feel a sexual threat whose generalized angst has been felt by women for centuries. One of the ironies of the AIDS crisis is that men's condom use in response to AIDS has encouraged men to share in both contraceptive responsibility and sexual safety, a responsibility men have often sought to avoid. Yet feminists have often argued that unless women take full responsibility for our contraception and sexual safety, we will be denied the full control over our bodies that sexual autonomy requires. On the other hand, others question why we should equate sexual safety with sexual desirability, when part of the eroticism of sex for at least some people is sex that is dangerous, mysterious, or taboo.[91] In any case, the requirement of safety in sex is an unrealistic and androcentric basis for objecting to promiscuous sex, particularly when contemporary monogamy can be so cruel to women.

Many writers have suggested that AIDS has been exploited by those who would condemn alternative sexual preferences in favor of sexual intimacy, commitment, and monogamy.[92] Fear and uncertainty about AIDS has made already marginalized groups—gay men, IV drug users, and prostitutes—into easy scapegoats for a disease that both scientists and the general public still do not fully understand. While many women and men choose monogamy, even celibacy, amid such fears, I have argued that these fears should caution us about promiscuity but should not cause women or men to dismiss promiscuity as a real alternative for sexual pleasure, agency, and self-definition.

Conclusion

In a society in which monogamous marriage is both the common and accepted norm of sexual partnership, promiscuity will have derogatory meaning. (Compare "My congratulations on your marriage!" to "My congratulations on your promiscuity!") Nevertheless, in that same society, promiscuity is many things to many people. It can be premarital or extramarital sex, simple fornication, or the repetitious pursuit of several partners. In its repetition it is unlike monogamous sex, in which sexual activity is exclusive to one partner. Like monogamy, however, promiscuity can be loving or cruel, intimate or exploitative, committed or callous. Thus, if care respect is a woman's requirement for pleasurable sex, she can look for it promiscuously and in her promiscuous lovers if she does not find it monogamously. Furthermore, because care respect is flexible enough in its acknowledgment of particularity to accommodate the minimum of mutual consent required by sex radical feminists and the maximum of sexual intimacy required by cultural feminists, the ethic has value for uniting the otherwise disparate sexual ideologies of each.

From the "view from somewhere different," promiscuous sex can also bring sexual satisfaction, sexual growth, and sexual empowerment to women who would otherwise feel physically and emotionally trapped by the constraints of monogamy. From this perspective, women can begin to develop a contextual and dialectical understanding, indeed, a realistic understanding of the pleasures and risks involved in pursuing a promiscuous lifestyle. This understanding, I have argued, is an important first step in liberating individual women to determine for themselves the place of promiscuity in their lives. However, unless women can gain economic independence from men so that they are not confined to heterosexual monogamy for their very survival, the promiscuity of other women will remain a burden or a threat, or both.

Free of economic dependence on men, women who appreciate the dialectic between gender and sexuality can begin to unravel the complex dynamic of women's sexual oppression under patriarchy, an unraveling that is necessary if individual women wish to define their sexuality in their own terms. The existence of AIDS would appear to demand that all women be cautious in our choice of sexual partners. Yet women under patriarchy have never been promised that sex would be a safe and straightforward affair, nor has sex been easily defined in women's terms. Indeed, many feminists wish women would *stop* worrying about safety (its promise, they maintain, is a myth) and *start* exploring those alternative sexual preferences that make the dangerous or the taboo into the supremely erotic. My claim is that promiscuity pursued from the "view from somewhere different" provides one way for individual women to begin reclaiming and reevaluating their own sexual pleasure. The extent to which the ethic of care respect derived from this perspective can accommodate both the socially acceptable and the taboo in sex is the subject of the next chapter.

3

Challenging the Normal and the Perverse

Feminist Speculations on Sexual Preference

Overview

The "loose women" described thus far pose a threat to patriarchy by challenging the constraints of monogamy imposed on women by an androcentric heterosexuality. However, women in search of sexual liberation may also challenge patriarchal appropriations of women's sexuality by challenging traditional heterosexuality's dominance over what constitutes "normal" sex. Along these lines, a feminist reclamation of sex for women would mean redefining and rediscovering so-called deviant or perverted sex as a way to subvert the patriarchal subordination of women that "normal" heterosexuality reinforces.

Such a reclamation of women's sexuality is not without its feminist critics, however, since feminists past and present have had a love/hate relationship with sexual deviance. On the one hand, feminist consciousness-raising has been instrumental in revealing to women the extent to which we have unquestioningly accepted patriarchal norms that fail to address women's sexual pleasure, agency, and self-definition. Feminists' recognition of the importance of clitoral orgasm, masturbation, and fantasy for women's sexual pleasure is in large part due to feminists' determination to secure sexual agency for women as the defining subjects of our own erotic needs.[1] Therefore, one would expect feminists to tolerate a fair amount of the sexual deviance traditionally referred to as sexual perversion—for example, homosexuality, consensual sadomasochism, or the pederasty commonly known in the gay community as man/boy love—if only because the stigmatization of such sexual minorities can be considered yet another example of the patriarchal oppression of alternative sexual expression that many feminists have sought for themselves.

On the contrary, social purity feminists of the late nineteenth century sought to "protect" women in the sex trade from the apparent male tyranny of prostitution by condemning women's promiscuity and masturbation as sinful, with the goal of encouraging all women to adopt the highly stratified social roles defined by traditional heterosexual marriage. In doing so, they only succeeded in replacing one kind of repressive sexual compliance with another.[2] Between 1969 and 1971, the National Organization for Women (NOW) attempted to purge its membership of lesbians, seeing in what Betty Friedan had called the "lavender menace" a retreat to a male-identified sexuality that was regarded as antithetical to feminism and disruptive of the movement.[3] Yet in the following decade, lesbianism was to become a defining political statement for many erstwhile heterosexual feminists discouraged by the seemingly inevitable power dynamics of compulsory heterosexuality. This merging of the politics of feminism with the sexual preference of lesbianism was captured by Ti-Grace Atkinson's pronouncement that "feminism is the theory; but lesbianism is the practice." However, since many lesbian feminists (like most heterosexuals) regard their sexuality not as a conscious political choice but as a sexual orientation or way of life, such a merger has continued to be a source of controversy among lesbian as well as heterosexual feminists.[4]

Many lesbian feminists who reject heterosexual sex as dehumanizing to women continue to separate themselves from a gay male community that they regard as perpetuating an oppressive sexuality: performance-oriented, casually (if not anonymously) promiscuous, objectifying, and misogynistic. Yet other lesbians and gay men who favor traditional, if not closeted, versions of heterosexual family roles and non-sadomasochistic "vanilla" sex join forces to divorce themselves from political efforts at legitimizing the consensual bondage and discipline of gay and lesbian sado-masochism or the moral acceptability of pederasty. Their belief is that such "'queer' queers" conform to the very stereotypes of grossly perverted sexualities that the status quo exploits to insure the marginality of the homosexual community. Many heterosexual and lesbian feminists reject all practitioners of sadomasochistic sex for their apparent internalization of the sexual dominance and submission paradigmatic of patriarchal power.[5]

By 1980, NOW had come out against sadomasochism as well as the pederasty and pedophilia referred to by the sex radical community as cross-generational sex for precisely the same reasons the organization had rejected lesbianism a decade earlier: sexual preferences that replicated the oppressive power relations of patriarchy were anathema to feminism. Moreover, sadomasochism was regarded as encouraging violence against women, pornographically depicted as bondage and discipline that women both need and want.[6] The feminist rejection of alternative sexualities found another public outlet in the disruption by some feminists of the 1982 Barnard College Scholar and the Feminist IX conference on sexuality. Objections by such groups as Women Against Pornography, Women Against Violence Against Women, and New York Radical Feminists that conference leaders and seminars were exploring sado-masochism and cross-generational sex resulted in confiscation of the conference diary, accusations of sexually perverse practices, and the cancellation by a major corporation of funding for any future conferences.[7]

Conflict over the acceptability of sexual deviance within the feminist community continues to the present day. In addition to their concerns regarding sadomasochistic and cross-generational sex, many feminists reject the cross-gender dressing of transvestism or the overt gender dressing of drag, both of which may be exemplified by lesbians exhibiting the masculine and feminine sexual roles of "butch" and "femme." From this view, such behavior only mirrors the oppressive male-identified gender roles from which many feminists seek to liberate themselves. Transsexualism has been touted by some sex radicals as a reclamation of a self-identified sexuality in a world where biology is mistakenly regarded as destiny, while other feminists believe that biological sex changes represent the misplaced efforts of people deluded by rigidly constructed patriarchal sex roles into trying to get their bodies "right."[8]

Many feminists have long regarded pedophilic incest between parent and child as a viciously convenient vehicle for the victimization of women, since the incest is often repeated over many years and commonly initiated by an adult male relation toward his preteen female charge whose emotional and material dependence is exploited by a powerful patriarch.[9] Mothers of incest victims are often unjustly accused of either insidiously encouraging the incest or "looking the other way"; conversely, they may be vilified for depriving an abusive husband of his legal visitation. Their husbands, on the other hand, are often perceived as needing no more than family therapy when incest cannot be legally proved. Yet other feminists have argued that to describe women primarily as victims of male lust is to play right into the hands of a patriarchy determined to define women's sexuality in men's terms and that men who love boys or women who love girls are much less likely to recreate the patriarchal power dynamics of adult male heterosexual pedophilia.[10]

Feminism's conflict over the meaning and morality of sexual deviance can be represented by the two factions of feminism introduced in chapter 2: cultural feminism and sex radical feminism. Cultural feminists characterize heterosexual relations that are not self-consciously feminist in terms of the sexual objectification of women, which is in turn regarded as paradigmatic of the dominant/submissive power dynamic definitive of patriarchy. According to cultural feminism, any replication of this power polarization in social institutions such as pornography or prostitution, or in sexual relations such as man/boy love, butch/femme sexual role-playing, or sadomasochism, must be rejected as antifeminist. Cultural feminists contend that women's sexual needs and values are those of fully consenting and self-determining moral agents whose desire for intimacy and affection is inconsistent with the dominance and submission of polarized sexual roles. Indeed, for cultural feminists, sadomasochism is the essence of a patriarchal ideology that empowers some to compel others to do their bidding. From this view, women's liberation is a liberation from male heterosexual victimization in pursuit of a reclaimed, unifying, female sexuality of care, sensitivity, and intimacy.

Sex radical feminists regard both women's and men's sexuality under patriarchy as controlled and repressed by a heterosexist status quo, in which acceptance of the sexual norm is insidiously accomplished through individual and institutional social stigmatization and marginalization of sexual deviance. According to sex radicals, sexual minorities need to reclaim their sexual freedom to pursue what is erotically pleasurable for them. Therefore, a sex radical feminist claims that feminism should actively promote the kind of sexual agency and self-definition for women that will maximize women's sexual pleasure and satisfaction, especially when women's sexuality deviates from the acceptable norm. It is contended that radical feminism is properly placed to challenge socially respectable categories of sexuality as a means of transforming the repressive sexual climate of patriarchy. This is one reason that some sex radicals describe themselves as "sex positive" feminists and regard feminists suspicious of women's sexual exploration as "sex negative" feminists who would ironically join more conservative moralists in condemning all but the most narrow band of sexual behavior. From a sex radical perspective, feminists should demand that fully consenting partners whose sex is neither exploitative nor abusive have the opportunity to practice whatever gives them sexual satisfaction. From this view, women's liberation is liberation toward a plurality of sexual pleasure, exploration, and agency, limited by the requirements of mutual desire within the relationship and of respect for the sexual preferences of others.[11]

Many feminists have avoided using expressions such as "sex positive" to refer to feminists debating women's sexual liberation, since cultural feminists would regard themselves as "sex positive" feminists in virtue of their insistence that women's sexuality not be infused with the oppressive power dynamics of patriarchy. Chris Straayer reminds us that the sex radical's "sex positivity" was built on a (sex positive) feminist platform shared by cultural feminists, a platform of sexual agency and self-definition for all women. Thus, Straayer contends that "the current ['sex positive'] sexual rebellion . . . is a *feminist* sexual rebellion of benefit to and properly credited to 'both sides'" (Straayer's italics).[12] Indeed, both cultural and sex radical feminists would agree that behavioral norms in patriarchal society serve to reinforce the male power and privilege of the status quo. Feminists of both groups would also contend that since such privilege is in large part determined by men's sexual access to women, any deviation from the sexual norms specified by a patriarchal ideology will be particularly threatening to the stability of social institutions dependent on women's sexual compliance. The relevant questions for a feminist philosophy of sex that explores issues of sexual deviance can be summarized as follows: is sexual deviance yet another instance of the physical and psychic corruption of an oppressive patriarchy? Or does conceiving of sexual deviance as patriarchal victimization itself constitute the persecution of an oppressed minority, no less repressive than the patriarchy from which feminists would liberate ourselves? Is power so male-identified as the "power-over" of dominance and submission that its manifestation in sex always constitutes an abuse of women? Or can power in sexual relations be a positive and pleasurable "power-with" sexuality that can liberate eroticism for both women and men under patriarchy?

This chapter pursues the strategy begun in chapter 2, a strategy in which I use the dialectical and contextual perspective of the "view from somewhere different" to negotiate the tensions between conflicting feminist perspectives. In what follows, I offer a conceptual analysis of the expression "sexual perversion" by contrasting the "normal" with the "perverse" in a variety of contexts. This variety suggests that the expression "sexual perversion" is heavily weighted with negative normative content, such that questions of whether and how to value sexual perversion become moot. Such questions are essential, however, if we are to take seriously the sex radical's claims that at least certain forms of cross-generational and sadomasochistic sex are not only aesthetically pleasurable but also morally unobjectionable and profeminist. Instead of attempting to define necessary and sufficient conditions for sexual perversion, an approach found in much of the contemporary philosophical literature on the subject, I propose to replace expressions such as "sexual perversion" and "sexual norm" with the less evaluatively charged expression of "sexual difference," consistent with the perspective of the "view from somewhere different" in chapter 1; we can then "world"-travel to both a cultural feminist's and a sex radical feminist's social location without the bias of superiority or the assumption of absolute truth, in order to investigate their claims about the pursuit of sexual pleasure.

Proceeding from this analysis, I describe and evaluate the debate over three types of sexual difference of particular concern to both cultural feminists and sex radical feminists: man/boy love, butch/femme sexual role-playing, and lesbian sadomasochism. This exploration reveals some fascinating similarities between the two feminisms concerning the goals of a feminist sexuality. I also contend that their ideological differences can be used to expand our understanding of the complexity of women's sexuality only if we dispense with the oppositional character of the debates in favor of reading them in terms of the dialectical relation between gender and sexuality described in the previous chapters. The discussion then expands on the feminist sexual ethic of care respect introduced in chapter 2, an ethic that can accommodate both cultural and sex radical feminists' concerns about sexual difference in women's lives and that reflects the advantages of regarding a feminist philosophy of sex from the "view from somewhere different." This feminist sexual ethic can then be used throughout the remainder of the book to identify and explore further controversial issues in women's sexuality.

Deviance, Difference, and Otherness

The typical conceptual analysis of sexual perversion in the contemporary philosophical literature defines perversion as that which sexual desire or sexual relations are *not*: if sexual desire is the desire for interpersonal or reciprocal sex, perverse sex is *truncated* or *incomplete* sex. If sexual desire is the desire for successful communication, perverse sex is a *breakdown* of such communication. If sexual relations are reproductive relations, then perverse sex is a *failure* of reproduction.[13] Philosophers tend to justify and distinguish such analyses by what they capture about sexual perversion that alternative definitions do not. I shall argue, however, that each such analysis tends to repeat the error of its rivals by delineating some set of necessary and sufficient conditions for sexual perversion that inevitably fail to capture the variety of its uses. Furthermore, making perverse sexual desire the *contradiction* of sexual desire (complete/incomplete, successful communication/unsuccessful communication, reproductive/not reproductive, p/not p) only makes sense if perversion is opposed to the *norm* or the *natural* in sex, as in normal sex/not normal sex—otherwise *perverse* sexual desire is simply *not* sexual desire.

My claim is that while philosophers have argued that norms can be merely statistical and that what is natural is not necessarily what is good, the concept of perversion is, to use Mortimer Kadish's phrase, "invincibly pejorative."[14] For this reason its use is charged with negativity despite attempts either to remove its normative content altogether or to enhance its value over the normal. The former strategy is reminiscent of the "view from nowhere," in which conceptual analysis is blind to the bias of social location, while the latter reflects the "view from somewhere better," which replaces one oppressive normative framework with another. I shall argue that those philosophers who contend that they do not equate the natural with the good in their conceptual analyses of perversion either fail to provide a substantive account of sexual perversion or fail to undermine the notion that natural or normal sex is in some way better than perverse sex. I claim instead that the concept of perversion understood from the "view from somewhere different" is a socially situated concept designed to stigmatize and marginalize those who do not practice the sex deemed normal by the status quo. As such, perversion constitutes a devalued form of sexuality produced, according to such writers as Michel Foucault, by the power of those who define the norms of sexual behavior for the institutional regulation and social control of sexuality.[15] However, rather than redefining what counts as normal sex by replacing one power structure with another, I would replace the notions of sexual normality and perversity altogether with a notion more consistent with a dialectical and contextual relationship between gender and sexuality, since this relationship, I have argued, better represents the sexual complexity and diversity in women's lives. This reading will allow me to develop a concept of sexual difference that incorporates both so-called normal and perverse sexuality into a larger schema for valuing the diversity of human sexuality.

By suggesting that the concept of sexual perversion is weighted with negative normative content, I am not suggesting that perverse sex is in fact bad sex. Such a suggestion would limit any discussion of sexual perversion to the perspective of the "view from somewhere better," whose perception of superior location makes all others inferior, or to the "view from nowhere," whose truths are unequivocal and universal. My point is that if we want to investigate the normative value of sexual perversion from the "view from somewhere different," we cannot beg the question of *whether* sexual perversion is negative by being required to assume that such sex *is* somehow negative. Yet in a patriarchal culture whose sexual norms are designed to reinforce a heterosexist status quo, the concept of sexual perversion is necessarily Other to man's Self: not merely different but *deviant*, not merely an alternative but an *aberration*. How, then, are we to understand the claims of a sex radical feminist that certain so-called sexual perversions—man/boy love, butch/femme sexual role-playing, and consensual lesbian sadomasochism—are not only pleasurable for those who choose to engage in them but are consistent with, even promote, feminist values? My solution is to jettison the notion of perversion in favor of a notion of sexual difference that respects the bias of social location without assuming the superiority of the normal.

My strategy in this section is threefold: first, I will contrast linguistic uses of the term "normal" with that of the term "perverse" to reveal the variety of its uses in the language. This variety will help us name some of the sexual preferences or lifestyles commonly referred to as perverse and suggest a way of thinking about sexual perversion that explains its derogatory use in the language. Second, I will show how several philosophers' normatively negative definitions of sexual perversion are troublesome because they presume too much about how to evaluate sexual perversion; or when philosophers offer normatively neutral definitions, I will show how their definitions fail to distinguish particular forms of sexual perversion from normal sex. Third, I will replace the expressions "sexual perversion" and "sexual normality" with the expression "sexual difference"; this replacement is consistent with the "view from somewhere different," which eschews the normative superiority of the "view from somewhere better" as well as the normative universality of the "view from nowhere" in favor of a dialectical and contextual understanding of sexual preference. This understanding is one that appreciates both the oppressive and liberating ways that women may explore their sexuality; and it promotes an empathic reading of the particular social locations of persons from whose sexual preferences uniquely located but equally partial observers may differ. From this perspective, we can then explore some of the feminist debates over ways of practicing sexual difference.

What Does "Normal" Mean?

Consider the following uses of the term "normal":

1. Normal teenagers like rock 'n' roll.
2. It is normal for a married couple to value each other's companionship even after their sexual intimacy wanes.
3. Children have a normal curiosity about their bodies.
4. The bearded lady at the circus always draws a large crowd because everyone seems to be curious about people who are not normal.
5. I am back to normal after three days of fever.

Sentence 1 describes typical, average, or representative teenagers. This sense of "normal" is in contrast to the deviant, aberrant, odd, queer, weird, peculiar, eccentric, strange, or kinky. ("My fourteen-year-old brother only listens to classical music stations. He's *weird*!") Sentence 2 refers to an acceptable, unobjectionable, or tolerable marriage. Contrasted with this sense of "normal" is the unacceptable, objectionable, intolerable, abhorrent, disgusting, revolting, repugnant, or taboo. ("It would be intolerable for my husband to demand more sex than I wanted to give him.") Sentence 3 refers to pure, innocent, or untainted children. Such normality is in stark contrast to the corrupt, vile, degenerate, dirty, depraved, or defiled. Such depravity is often associated, again, with the abhorrence, disgust, and repugnance of the objectionable. ("Children who are victims of incest sometimes regard their own sexuality as dirty or defiled.") Sentence 4 describes an absence of the natural, the biological, or that which is definitive of the species. The bearded woman might be called "freakish," "monstrous," "grotesque," "twisted," "subversive," "unspeakable," or "unnatural." ("This circus spectacle is nothing but a freak show.") Similar reactions of horror and disgust that accompany the defiled also accompany the unnatural, inviting speculation that what persons regard as monstrous is also that which they regard as in some way tainted or corrupt. Sentence 5 refers to that which is in good health, physically well, psychologically stable, or sane. Such notions are contrasted with the sick, unhealthy, mentally ill, unstable, disordered, or pathological.

("Her condition became so unstable that we had to take her to the emergency room.")

The term "perverse" is the contrary but not the contradiction of the term "normal." Perversity does not refer to everything that the normal lacks, since a teenager who does not like rock 'n' roll is not typically considered perverse, even if normal teenagers like this kind of music. The term "perverse" can be used to describe the teenager who is obstinate in the face of efforts to change his mind over the question of musical taste, but obstinacy is hardly the odd or the unusual. Similarly, marital sex on demand might be considered intolerable or abhorrent to a woman, but she need not consider such abnormal sex to be a "perverse" feature of her marriage; and the woman with a three-day fever is not a "perverse" sufferer simply because she is not well.

Furthermore, perversity is not equivalent to the exceptionally odd or the very eccentric, the extremely objectionable or the seriously ill. Otherwise, people with no eyelashes or twenty manicured French poodles, no manners or terminal cancer would all be considered perverse. So, too, sexual eccentricity or sexual unacceptability is insufficient to characterize sexual perversion. Painting my toenails purple before sex may be eccentric, and insulting my lover when he doesn't perform may be unacceptable, but neither is commonly considered perverse.

Yet when people confront the bestiality, necrophilia, or pedophilia commonly considered to be sexual perversions, a typical response is indeed a kind of objection in extremis: such perversions are abhorrent, disgusting, revolting, vile, not merely eccentric or unacceptable. I suggest that such responses are themselves derivative of a more basic revulsion. An individual's fear or horror at perversion is the fear of the subversive, the twisted, the unnatural—that which, according to Michael Slote, could not possibly be a part of us (the "normal" ones).[16] Sexual perversion challenges the nature and value of sex prescribed by the status quo by transforming the personal and social meaning of sexuality. Mortimer Kadish suggests that while sexual deviance is an offense *within* the system, sexual perversion is an offense *against* the system.[17]

Such a view of sexual perversion is consistent with the claim that the moral deviance of adultery or the statistical deviance of twelve-hour continuous sex is not considered sexually perverse, even though each is contrary to a sexual norm. Nor is it surprising that category 4 in the earlier discussion of deviance—the category in which the term "subversive" appears—is also the category of the "unnatural," since the unnatural is a common synonym for sexual perversion.[18] What is often fundamental to an individual's conception of sexuality is that which is essential to human nature; anything else is freakish, monstrous, grotesque, or twisted. Indeed, such terms are commonly used to describe bestiality, necrophilia, and coprophilia. Sexual perversion that is subversive by defiling what it touches is labeled corrupt, vile, degenerate, dirty, or depraved. Homosexuality, pedophilia, sodomy, exhibitionism, voyeurism, and sadomasochism are often described in just this way. By all but the highly trained specialist, an incomprehensible psychopathology is typically ascribed to the transsexual, the transvestite, or the fetishist; such "perverts" betray to many people a mental instability that challenges the very foundations of what is meant by human nature and "normal" sex.

The claim that sexual perversion is a reconceptualization of the sexual is consistent with the view that sexual perversions are not occasional dalliances or infrequent fantasies. Persons, acts, or states of mind may be sexually perverted, but persons are referred to as perverse in virtue of a disposition or inclination toward entertaining perverse desires. If perversion is defined as a psychological state, acts are perverse only in virtue of the perverse desires that motivate them. Moreover, a person's sexual self-identification may not match that person's actual sexual practices, as when a married man who has frequent affairs with gay men continues to regard himself as heterosexual. In this way he can reassure himself, and reinforce in others, that he is "normal." This way of thinking about perversion accommodates both perversions that are deep-seated sexual orientations and those that are consciously chosen preferences. However, choosing to practice sexual perversion as a substitute for the normal sex that one in fact desires does not make one a pervert. Perversion is subversive in its total annihilation of "normal" desire.[19]

This conception of sexual perversion is at odds with Sara Ketchum's claim that sexually perverse preferences constitute the *reverse* of a sexual ideal.[20] I suggest that sexual perversion is more than a reversal of an ideal, since one's failure to live up to a sexual ideal can simply result in wrongful or unpleasant behavior that is socially deviant but not sexually perverse. Adultery is the "reverse" of the cultural ideal of marital sex but does not thereby constitute a perversion. Indeed, Ketchum's criterion for perversity is its lack of reciprocity or mutuality—a moral failure perhaps, but not a necessary feature of perversion. The sadist who returns the masochist's requests for the whip with lashes timed in synchronicity to her partner's orgasms is not clearly in violation of a reciprocal or mutual relationship, yet such sadomasochism is still regarded by many as perverse.

Furthermore, understanding perversion as subversive offers some insight into those perversions that are not sexual. Perversions of the law, medicine, and morals are called perverse because they challenge the way such institutions are conceived by the status quo. For example, some antiabortion activists believe it is a perversion of the law to think that a constitutional right to privacy authorizes the right to kill an unborn child. Certainly it is a perverse surgical doctor who cuts into his patients simply to see how much they will bleed. Such examples suggest why the connotations of perversion, particularly sexual perversion, are, according to Gayle Rubin, "uniformly bad."[21] If perversion challenges the ideological stability of the status quo, then the social institutions that represent and reinforce that ideology cannot afford to invest perversion with the moral complexity that would recommend or excuse some perversions and condemn others. The unremitting derogation of perversion is much like a taboo that, in Jerome Neu's words, "puts the demand for reasons out of place[,] . . . imposes strict liability and so puts the offering of excuses out of place as well."[22] Therefore, medical, legal, psychoanalytic, and educational institutions conforming to the status quo can be expected to act so that sexual perversion is perceived as a menace to social security and public health. According to such institutions, sexual perversion, quoting Michael Slote, "involves at least the idea of deviation from some favored, explanatorily rich, ideal-typic causal model of the development of human sexual motivation."[23]

This is not to suggest that particular individuals always agree on what constitutes sexual perversion. As Michael Ruse points out, the incomprehensibility of perversion is as much a function of individual ways of understanding sex as it is a function of the larger society.[24] Rape has been variously regarded by feminists as the essence of heterosexual sex, a sadistic sexual perversion, and a crime of violence, not one of sex.[25] Thus, one person's sexual norm may be another's perversion. Indeed, sexual perversions appear to be limited in form and content only by the imagination and needs of the practitioner. (A man might expose himself while fondling a favorite shoe; another might have continuous sex with three dead sheep.) What cultural norms succeed in doing is establishing the negative evaluative content of sexual perversion by stigmatizing those individuals whose sexual habits or opinions fall outside an acceptable sexual range.

Feminists who are sensitive to the ways in which patriarchal social institutions have disguised androcentric cultural norms as natural and inevitable are particularly wary of normative evaluations of deviations from those norms. Indeed, some lesbian feminists have argued that it should be heterosexuality that ought to be questioned, since patriarchal institutions offer us so little information about, and access to, sexual alternatives.[26] Especially for sex radicals in search of sexual freedom from sexually repressive norms, what began as Freud's natural polymorphous perversity appears to have become an unnatural sexual deviance in the service of patriarchal stability.

Indeed, it might be argued that while the normative connotations of the term "subversive" may be negative for members of the status quo threatened with the overthrow of treasured norms, the term has often signified to oppressed minorities a positive liberation from those norms. Thus, the political aims of both cultural and sex radical feminism could be construed as the attempt to *subvert* patriarchal sexual norms in the pursuit of a woman-identified sexual autonomy. On this interpretation, to accept the "invincibly pejorative" nature of sexual perversion would be to accept the negative connotations of the term "subversive" that the status quo uses to marginalize and silence dissidence. According to this line of reasoning, a truly subversive and liberating feminist approach to women's sexuality would involve reclaiming the subversive element of perversion by retaining the use of the term "perversion" in the language but ascribing to it a positive normative content.[27]

My concern with such an approach is with the insular nature of the "liberation." The preceding argument makes no claims that a reappropriation by the feminist community of the normative content of sexual perversion will ultimately result in a patriarchal or nonfeminist change in normative usage as well. The primary aim is for individual women to be able to value and make central to their lives that which has been on the periphery. However, I would argue that unless feminist activism aims at fundamental change in the status quo, normative changes that remain within the women's community run the risk of reifying and marginalizing already marginalized groups.

Lesbian separatists argue that the only way for women to escape patriarchal oppression is to divest themselves of male-identified ideology and institutions altogether. On the contrary, I believe that such separatism only reinforces the separate but unequal status that women already have; and many women want to rid themselves of oppression but not rid themselves of men. While many lesbians argue for the importance of appropriating androcentric language in order to give women a sense of being centered where once marginalized, I would still respond that without continuing activism outside the women's community, women's sense of our own centrality will remain illusory. [28] I agree that feminism is in an important sense subversive in its challenge to patriarchal norms, but I disagree that the best way to subvert the status quo is to redefine terminology for a limited audience. The tradition of institutionalized heterosexuality associates perversion with revulsion, corruption, and mental illness for good reason: to compel compliance by stigmatizing those who would do otherwise. Revalorizing perversion requires more than reclaiming its norm for the needs of a feminist community, since a heterosexist and patriarchal community need only ignore or misunderstand the reclamation.

Furthermore, it is unclear just how much can be gained by using patriarchal language for feminist purposes, since linguistic intentionality and use are easily confused by those whose ear is accustomed to the semantics of the status quo. Accusations of identifying with the aggressor or internalizing oppressive norms are common among feminist groups whose attempts at changing patriarchal norms appear co-optive to other feminists. Indeed, many members of the feminist community will not construe the practice of sexual perversion as liberating to any woman, and this situation can result in a feminist divisiveness that gives patriarchal power the upper hand. If we wish to include all members of the feminist community in the pursuit of women's sexual agency *and* change the sexual ideology of patriarchal institutions, my contention is that we must jettison the notion of perversion entirely so that it can no longer be used to reinforce the status quo. As I shall argue in the following pages, by replacing the notion of sexual perversion with the notion of sexual difference, we can allow for a wide variety of sexual practices without the pejorative stigma that is such a powerful tool of sexual oppression.

Philosophically Misleading Conceptions of Perversion

Several philosophers have concluded that sexual perversion is in some important sense morally *wrong*. Their conclusions are misleading, however, for two reasons: (1) when moral wrong becomes a criterion of perversion, investigations into controversial cases become irrelevant; and (2) the moral wrong indicated does not require that perverse sexual behavior be in any sense *subversive* or *incomprehensible* sex as I have described it. Sara Ketchum's characterization of perversion as the failure to live up to an ideal in sex—specifically, as a lack of sexual reciprocity—is one example, since reciprocity in sex appears to be compatible with some perverse sexual behavior, and adultery is not perverse at all. Another example is Donald Levy's claim that "*[p]erversion degrades* is a necessary truth" (Levy's italics). Levy's view is that the pervert denies himself or others some "basic human good" purely for the pleasure of perverse sex, rejecting the good life that other sorts of behavior could afford.[29] Yet certainly sexual pleasure is a basic good for some people, and some sexual perverts practice the mutually enjoyable and consensual sex that affords them more of what they need for a good life *in their terms* than if they were not doing so. Indeed, this is one of the arguments that a sex radical feminist uses against those who would claim that her sex life is immoral. Levy's analysis seems to rely on the perspective from the "view from nowhere," in which *Levy's* sense of a basic human good is *everyone's* sense of a basic human good.

Roger Scruton also appears to adopt the "view from nowhere" when he argues that sexual perversion is wrong because it is a violation of a person's "sexual integrity." From this view, sexual perversion is sex that divorces lust from love, flesh from the spirit, the animal from the personal.[30] Bestiality, masturbation, and fetishism are examples of perversion, in that they concentrate either totally on the body or part of a body or not on a live human body at all, missing the personal element that, for Scruton, elevates human sexuality above that of the other animals.

Scruton is a good example of a philosopher whom feminists would take to task for assuming that sex for pleasure alone is somehow evil in the absence of a higher goal. Scruton assumes not only that all perverted sex is degrading in its abolition or diminishment of the other but also that there is a clear conceptual and moral demarcation between the flesh and the spirit. Scruton does make an important normative distinction between two forms of sadomasochism (s/m), which those who object to this form of perversion often miss: s/m as the sexual embodiment of an immoral slavery and s/m as the sexual embodiment of mutual recognition of each partner's embodied desires. However, given his claims about the necessarily degrading nature of perversion, Scruton cannot recognize the latter case as an example of perversion.[31] On the contrary, some sex radical feminists would argue that both cases reveal important moral distinctions between different sorts of perversions. Moreover, Scruton's normative characterization of perversion does not capture all that feminists object to in perverse sex, since a cultural feminist's objection is precisely that no matter how consensual or reciprocal the s/m sex, there is still something degrading about it.

While Scruton's analysis may not go far enough in one direction, his analysis goes too far in another by compelling us to regard any sex that is dehumanizing as perverse. People who treat others as mere sexual objects include the intimidating or abusive spouse, the sexually harassing employer, or the leering passerby; yet their behavior is not perverse simply because it is dehumanizing. Even if Scruton can somehow distinguish these cases from sexual perversion, his morally biased analysis leaves no room for questioning whether, as opposed to how, any of the perversions that are exclusively bodily or immediately sensual are objectionable.[32]

Thomas Nagel and Robert Solomon both offer conceptual analyses of perversion that profess moral neutrality and confine perversion to the failure to conform to a sexual ideal. Nagel defines sexual perversion in terms of the unnatural, and the unnatural in terms of the failure of a reciprocal interpersonal sexual awareness; such an awareness implies that each partner is aroused not only by the other but by each partner's awareness of the other's arousal. Like Scruton, Nagel sees sexual perversion as a truncation or incompleteness in an otherwise natural process of flirtation and seduction. Robert Solomon regards sexual perversion as a breakdown in communication of the body language that is the essence of sex.[33]

Both philosophers contend that sexual perversion need not be immoral sex, although Nagel admits that his concept of completeness makes perversion (by definition) the failure to conform to an ideal in sex, giving the concept of perversion negative evaluative meaning. He comments that perverse sex will be more pleasurable sex for some people than his reciprocally aware complete sex and that, other things being equal, perverse sex is probably better for such people than no sex at all.[34]

However, if perverse sex can be made better by being made pleasurable, then it would appear that its characteristic of incompleteness does not condemn it to the wholly bad. Indeed, if incompleteness is a sign of inferior sex (as Nagel's original analysis implies), but pleasurable sex is prima facie good, then perversion, by being pleasurable, could theoretically offset its failure of completeness. If completeness is an ideal in virtue of the sexual satisfaction that results from it, then sexual perversion, when sexually satisfying, need not be bad at all. Indeed, unless Nagel is willing to say that perverse sex can never be pleasurable, perverse sex will conform to at least *some persons'* ideals of sex, although not everyone's. Thus, *whose* ideal perverse sex fails to conform to remains the crucial question; Nagel's assertion that perversion is a *failure* to live up to (someone's) sexual ideal is no more compelling than perversion construed as *success* in living up to the sexual ideal of a practitioner of perversion.

In his article "Sexual Paradigms," Solomon contends that perverse sex need not be either bad or immoral sex;[35] yet his analysis of perversion as a failure of communication is no less a socially located evaluation than Nagel's, since it is unclear whose sexual communication is failing or whether all practitioners of perverse sex would describe their sex as a failure of anything. In another article offering the same body-language analysis of sex, Solomon refers to perversion as an *"abuse* of an established function, a corruption, not simply a diversion or a deviation" (Solomon's italics).[36] Such normative bias is complicated by the fact that Solomon's and Nagel's analyses are both too broad and too narrow: intimidating or abusive sex can be incomplete or noncommunicative, as can unrequited love or sex between partners who enjoy pleasure through fantasy; yet such sex need not be perverse. In addition, pedophilia, group sex, sadomasochism, homosexuality, and sodomy are often regarded as unnatural or perverse, yet each can be complete sex and communicative of intense personal feelings. Janice Moulton has pointed out that Nagel's complex system of arousal through flirtation and seduction does not often fit long-standing, familiar partners, whose arousal may be a function of their understanding of what each partner wants out of sex. Therefore, Nagel's and Solomon's psychological analyses of perversion in terms of interpersonal communication can neither justify the negative normative status they give to sexual perversion nor capture distinctions typically made between perverse and normal sex.[37]

Alan Goldman and Robert Gray claim that the least problematic way to conceptualize sexual perversion is to describe it without any normative content at all. Goldman suggests that while perversion is a deviation from a norm, that norm is purely statistical, not evaluative. Gray contends that a description of sexual perversion is merely an empirical description of those sexual activities that are "not consonant with the natural adaptive function(s) of sexual activity," whatever these turn out to be.[38]

The difficulty with both of these analyses is that while they leave open the question of whether sexual perversion is bad or immoral sex, they fail to provide the concept of perversion with any substantive content. For example, while Goldman acknowledges that not all deviations from a sexual norm constitute perversions, he never goes beyond specific examples of perversion to tell us what kinds of deviations count. Investigating what he calls "the form of the desire" to identify instances of perversion is meaningless if we have no theoretical understanding of *what* form particular types of perversion take.

Gray's analysis does not fare much better, as he is unwilling to specify exactly what the natural adaptive function of human sexuality is. Without knowing this, we have no way of distinguishing sexual perversions from sexual activities that are not perverse. Furthermore, Gray suggests that such adaptation might be culturally relative, such that homosexuality might be adaptive in a society with a higher population of males than in one where the female population is higher. However, this line of reasoning suggests that Gray's "natural" adaptation is really non-essential and relative after all. Indeed, it could turn out that sexual activities like homosexuality, bestiality, necrophilia, and coprophilia contribute to population control, in which case none of them could correctly be called perversions on Gray's model.[39] As Donald Levy remarks, if it turns out that artificial insemination is more adaptive to the survival of the species than heterosexual sex, then we will have to start calling straight sex perverted.[40] Gray laments that the expression "sexual perversion" has become so morally loaded that we should consider dropping it from the language: "Other clearer and less emotive terms may just as easily be substituted for it."[41] Given the difficulties associated with refining a working concept of perversion, this is just the strategy I plan to pursue.

Michael Slote comes closer to my own perspective on sexual perversion by calling it an "inapplicable concept," although his reasons differ from my own. Slote contends that the notion of sexual perversion is made nonsensical by its synonymy with the term "unnatural." Since the unnatural is not of this world, according to Slote, and sexual perversion clearly *is* of this world, as much as we would repress or deny it, the term has no applicability as a description of abnormal sexual preference.[42]

However, rejecting the semantic applicability of perversion in this way requires that we accept (1) Slote's equation of the perverse with the unnatural and (2) his definition of the unnatural. If sexual perversion is subversive of normal sexuality in the ways I have suggested, then according to Slote, the subversive becomes the unnatural. Yet subversive sex may be no less "natural" for the practitioner of perversion (and very much "of this world"). Even if we equate perversion with the unnatural, Slote's definition of unnatural appears to be both too narrow (Why should something not of this world be *unnatural?*) and too vague (What is to constitute "this world"?). Slote has rejected the term "nonprocreative" outright as failing to specify all and only those activities that are sexually perverse; yet his own characterization of perversion as unnatural sex is subject to the same criticism, particularly if from the "view from somewhere different," we recognize that equally partial but differently situated subjects will have different conceptions of perversion.[43]

Even if we reject the concept of perversion, as Slote recommends, he has given us no replacement for identifying that which fills so many people, Slote readily admits, with both horror and fear.[44] The concept of perversion may be inapplicable as typically understood, but I contend that its controversial meaning and value require that we look for an alternative means of talking about it.

Mortimer Kadish compares what I have called the subversiveness of perversion to the violation of the deep structural grammar of a language. According to Kadish, sexual perversion is like unintelligible talk that we vaguely recognize as language but that we ultimately do not understand. Thus, sexual perversion constitutes an offense to the deep structure of society's sexual institutions and ideology, "an assault on [society's] identity rather than a possible variation."[45] Michael Ruse also suggests that perversion is not merely the different or the deviant but something personally incomprehensible. According to Ruse, sexual perversion is "something we could not imagine wanting to do."[46]

But who is this "we" exactly? The practitioner of sexual perversion may sensibly refer to herself as a pervert, if only because this is how she has been taught to refer to her sexuality; yet at the same time, she may not only "imagine" her sexual practice but also engage in it, relish it, and, in a deeply personal sense, understand its role in her life. While I agree with Kadish's and Ruse's sense of the profoundly subversive nature of perversion, I suspect that their "view from nowhere" ignores the differently situated perspectives of those who practice perversion.

I have also argued in the preceding pages that the dominant perception of perversion as a threat to the status quo gives the concept of perversion compellingly negative normative weight. The two authors seem to share this view, albeit from the "view from nowhere": Ruse believes that we [sic] call something perverse that repels us but that its negative normative weight need not be a moral one. Kadish goes further by describing sexual perversion as a "spiritual malaise, a malaise in the consciousness of self," where the pervert "feels pain when he ought to feel pleasure."[47] It is my contention that because negative normative weight, moral or otherwise, biases any investigations we may wish to conduct concerning the value of sexual perversion, the concept of perversion must be replaced with a more representative one that can describe sexual difference without presuming its devaluation. I believe that Kadish and Ruse are on the right phenomenological track in their explorations into sexual perversion but that they err in retaining conceptions of sexual difference that overdetermine any normative evaluations of it.

Sara Ruddick and Janice Moulton come closest to voicing my own concern that one should socially locate individual cases of sexual perversion in order to evaluate perversion with a minimum of misrepresentation. Ruddick rejects the equation of the natural with the good, contending instead that "[t]he social desirability of types of sexual acts depends on particular social conditions and independent criteria of social desirability." Janice Moulton echoes this view when she states, "I believe that sexual behavior will not fit any single characterization."[48]

However, Ruddick offers a definition of perversion that makes her claims about the importance of social location in evaluating sexual behavior less convincing. Ruddick suggests that the sexually perverse desire is an unnatural sexual desire that "could [not] lead to reproduction in normal physiological circumstances."[49] Yet this characterization misleadingly implies that the desire to have sex after menopause is sexually perverse and that perverse sex includes sex that is not hetero-genital. (Does kissing count? Fondling without intercourse?) In addition, Ruddick's characterization makes the pedophilic desire to make a twelve-year-old pregnant perfectly natural. Moulton, on the other hand, believes that the only thing we can really say about sexual perversion is that it "makes people frightened or uncomfortable by its bizarreness."[50]

Sexual Preference from the "View from Somewhere Different"

Since the reaction Moulton refers to is itself a socially located reaction based on a perception of the incomprehensibility of sexual perversion, I suggest that the concept of sexual perversion be replaced with the concept of sexual *difference*. This replacement has the advantage of making all sexual behavior different, not just perverse behavior, since by jettisoning the notion of sexual perversion, we jettison the concept of the normal as well. In this sense, the concept of sexual difference is a deconstructive concept designed to explode the polarity of normal/perverse that equates the perverse with the unacceptable, corrupt, sick, bad, and the normal with the acceptable, innocent, healthy, good. The concept of sexual difference avoids the pejorative connotations of being on the "wrong" side of the polarity of the normal yet does not deconstruct the concept of difference itself that allows us to locate, particularize, and evaluate worldviews. In so doing we can reconstitute sexuality as a differentiated category of nonstigmatized sexual variation. When all sexual behavior is "other" than some "other" behavior, the value of otherness remains an open question.[51]

What my critique of the philosophical literature on sexual perversion suggests is that when perversion is regarded as subversive or in some other way bad, we close the question as to whether some sexual perversion may be unobjectionable. Yet when we retain the concept of sexual perversion but ascribe it normative neutrality, sexual perversion becomes empty of meaning or inadequate as a way of distinguishing sexually perverse behavior from the normal. I have suggested that this is because the concept of sexual perversion only makes sense when polarized against a norm of behavior that is preferred to the perverse in order to encourage social compliance with the norm. Once we deconstruct that polarity, we can make room for an exploration of difference that does not presuppose that some sexual behavior ("ours") is better than others ("theirs").

For those who bristle at compulsory sexual normality but find marginalization equally oppressive, such deconstruction can create new ways of thinking and talking about sex that makes marginality and centrality equally valuable in their difference. Indeed, many contemporary philosophers and social critics argue that gender constitutes a broad spectrum of socially constructed behaviors, revealing the lability and complexity of gender in such phenomena as the inventive cross-gender performance of drag queens, the sadomasochistic sex play of lace and leather-clad dominatrixes, the gender fascination and sex transformation of transsexuals, and the dynamic and conflicting uses of the term "queer."[52] Moreover, if we continue to treat the perverse as the bad, we repeat the mistake of the "view from nowhere" by refusing to countenance alternative points of view; or we reiterate the "view from somewhere better" by acknowledging alternatives but refusing to question the superiority of our own location. If thinking and talking about sexual perversion in terms of sexual difference can create new avenues for sexual understanding, then we may well question Freud's contention that heterosexual norms are the necessary price of civilization.

The notion of sexual difference derives its significance from the "view from somewhere different," which eschews assumptions of superiority in the name of recognizing, understanding, and promoting worldviews from which one's own views differ. While such a perspective encourages a respect for what Jeffrey Weeks calls a "radical pluralism" of diverse sexual behaviors,[53] this perspective does not require that every behavior be accepted as equally valid. The feminist philosophy of sex described thus far is grounded in the belief that patriarchal institutions and ideology are sexually oppressive to women. The "view from somewhere different" recommends characterizing human sexual behavior in terms of the individual social location that gives such behavior meaning and value. From within that context we can articulate a feminist ethics and politics of sex that affords individual women better treatment than one that would harm, marginalize, or exclude them.

In fact, the "view from somewhere different" acknowledges that there will be those whose sexual stimulation derives in large part from the association of their sexual behavior with what is immoral, unspeakable, forbidden, or taboo.[54] As I have already argued, jettisoning the polarity of normal/perverse does not also mean that we must jettison the categories of sexual difference that allow us to call some sex good and some sex bad. It simply means that no one will be compelled by social stigmatization of sexual deviance to perceive difference as bad. The appreciation from the "view from somewhere different" of the dialectic between gender and sexuality also means that a woman's pursuit of passion and pleasure becomes as pressing an issue for a feminist philosophy of sex as her sexual violation and victimization. While such a philosophy cannot promise undistorted investigations into the meaning and value of sexual difference, my contention is that the "view from somewhere different" offers us a more representative picture than philosophies of sex that would determine difference from the beginning.

Politically Correct Sexuality

> The problem with correct ideas is that they can all too readily become correctional ideals.
>
> —Jeffrey Weeks, *Sexuality and Its Discontents:*
> *Meanings, Myths, and Modern Sexualities*

The feminist movement is driven by an activism aimed at reclaiming women's power over the content and direction of our lives. As such, it is a political movement with inevitable tendencies toward defining "politically correct" behavior in terms of its consistency with feminist values. Indeed, since many members of the feminist community condemn sexual experiences, preferences, or desires that either replicate or reinforce the institutional and ideological patterns of male dominance, such sex might arguably be called "politically incorrect" sex from a feminist point of view. Such sex is criticized by feminists for being both oppressive and androcentric since it is sex that unjustly subordinates women to men by defining women's sexual needs and interests in men's terms.[55]

The immediate danger with any form of political correctness, however, is that in its demands for strict compliance with purportedly less oppressive forms of behavior, it tends to replace one oppressive regime with another. Thus, feminists must take care that an androcentric vision of women's sexuality is not replaced with an equally narrow gynocentric vision that, as I pointed out in chapter 1, risks allegiance to the "view from somewhere better." Even if appeals to a superior perspective are avoided, proponents of political correctness will tend to adopt a "view from nowhere" that is averse to considering alternative points of view if they adhere to a universal truth about what is best about human behavior. Neither cultural nor sex radical feminists consider themselves advocates of politically correct sex, since this would imply, as Jeffrey Weeks warns above, a dogmatism and special interest that would preclude valuing alternative points of view. Yet feminism is often maligned for expressing an unequivocal political bias that many women and men regard as totally foreign to their own life experience. I have argued in this and other chapters that the advantage of understanding women's sexuality from the "view from somewhere different" is that of embracing disparate views of women's sexual experience, so that no one sexuality is perceived as right for all women or right for any one woman in all areas of her sexual life. Thus, the conflict between cultural and sex radical feminists over sexual preference can be viewed not as an unbridgeable rift between mutually inconsistent perspectives but as a disagreement within a continuing dialogue over the meaning and value of sexual difference.

An Outline of the Debate

For cultural feminists, a truly woman-identified sexuality is one that eschews defining women's sexual experiences, preferences, and desires in terms of *power*: while male-identified sex is constructed in terms of dominance and submission, a cultural feminist's woman-identified sex consists of a relationship among moral equals whose partners share a care and respect for one another's sexual needs. Such mutuality is regarded as impossible when one partner alone controls the when, where, and how of sex. According to cultural feminism, the sex that women prefer is egalitarian sex, where the power to determine the terms and conditions of sexual experience is either equally shared or eliminated altogether; the sex that men typically prefer is characterized by a power *im*balance in which those who do not control the action are coerced into sex that they do not really want. From this view, women's consent to such sex only signifies the depth of the oppression that they experience under patriarchy, since women, if given a real choice, would choose nonpolarized roles over polarized ones.

Three forms of sexuality are particular targets for cultural feminists who condone gay and lesbian sex but not their so-called perverse variations: cross-generational sex between men and boys, sex between lesbians adopting butch/femme roles, and gay and lesbian sadomasochistic sex. All three are oppressive forms of sexuality from a cultural feminist perspective, since they are believed to replicate the oppressive hierarchical relations of male dominance that cultural feminists actively resist. From this view, man/boy love is exploitative of young boys not emotionally or sexually mature enough to decide for themselves whether their lovers are right for them. It is argued that unlike lesbian cross-generational sex, man/boy love exemplifies the patriarchal dominance and control of an adult male over his young sexual charge. Butch/femme sexual roles and lesbian sadomasochism are regarded as nothing more than corrupt manifestations of women consenting to sex that is oppressive in its form and often violent in its content. Gay male sadomasochism is regarded as an ironic reconstruction of the most harmful and exploitative aspects of heterosexuality. Many feminists who do not advocate cultural feminism's strong adherence to a specific set of woman-identified values have nevertheless joined cultural feminists in condemning women's sexuality that appears to do no more than re-create oppressive, male-dominated sexual hierarchies.[56]

A sex radical feminist's response is that cultural feminists are mistaken in thinking that all man/boy love, butch/femme sexual role-playing, or gay and lesbian sadomasochism are mere replications of the dominance and submission of patriarchy. From this point of view, the relations between butch and femme or lesbian sado-masochists express feminist values because such relations enhance each partner's ability to recreate power in sexual relationships *in women's terms*, not in men's. According to a sex radical perspective, such relations are consensual relations constitutive of the sexual ethic of care respect described in the previous chapter, the same ethic that a cultural feminist demands of her "vanilla" sex. Indeed, sex radicals contend that butch/femme sexual role-playing or lesbian sadomasochistic sex can liberate individual women to explore their sexuality in positive and creative ways. From this point of view, such sex is predictably vilified by a patriarchal society whose sexual norms are designed to favor an oppressive male-identified heterosexuality, referred to by Julia Penelope as "hetero-patriarchy."[57] Sex radical feminists further contend that the sexual relations between a man and his young gay lover or between two gay men engaged in sadomasochistic sex should be equally judged, not by what they appear to imitate but by their real concern for understanding and promoting one another's sexual needs as revealed by the partners themselves. From a sex radical point of view, cultural feminists create an oppressive sexual environment equal to, if not greater than, that of the status quo by refusing to allow either women or men their full range of passion and pleasure.[58]

In what follows I will explore the debate over sexual difference between cultural feminism and sex radical feminism, first by looking more closely at what cultural feminists mean by "egalitarian" sex in two distinct types of arguments. I will give primary attention to the complaints lodged against man/boy love, butch/femme sexual role-playing, and lesbian sadomasochism; the issue of reinforcing patriarchal dominance, exploitation, and abuse that arises in feminist complaints against gay male sado-masochism will be subsumed for my purposes under these three types of sexual difference. This is not to suggest that gay male sadomasochism exactly parallels lesbian sadomasochism or that there are no features of gay male sadomasochism that are worthy of separate investigation. I simply wish to focus my attention on some of the complex ways that women in sadomasochistic relationships with other women may reinforce men's sexual subordination of women.[59] I will then investigate the variety of responses sex radicals can offer to cultural feminists' complaints as well as arguments in favor of a sex radical feminist approach to sexual difference made on her own and others' behalf. While I will refer to feminists from a variety of theoretical backgrounds in my discussion of the issues on both sides, I have intentionally situated cultural feminism in diametric opposition to sex radical feminism to emphasize the kind of polarization that has occurred within feminism generally over issues of freedom of sexual expression for women. In the last part of this section I will argue that the "view from somewhere different" can negotiate the tensions between the two sides of the debate and provide a framework for understanding some of the conflict and contradiction in women's and men's conceptions of sexual deviance. In this way, individuals from a variety of social locations may begin to explore how different, not deviant, sexualities may figure in their own conceptions of sexual preference.

Antifeminist or Profeminist? Coercive or Consensual?

A cultural feminist's complaints against the adoption or advocacy of dominant/submissive sexual roles take two basic forms. One type of argument condemns man/boy love, butch/femme sexual role-playing, and lesbian sadomasochism for being antifeminist. This argument asserts that sex replicating the oppressive power relations of patriarchy is antifeminist and that these three types of sexual practice replicate just those relations. Those who argue in this manner tend to balk at condemning a sex radical's private sexual habits but object to the claim by some radicals that their sexual behavior is not only unobjectionable but also profeminist.[60] Thus, even apparently consensual dominant/submissive sex is not sex that cultural feminists can conscientiously promote or advocate.

A second type of argument suggests that just because patriarchal power relations are replicated in the privacy of the bedroom is no reason for thinking that those relations are unobjectionable. From this view, since the personal is political, one's "private" consent to dominant/submissive sex has public ramifications. Indeed, according to this line of reasoning, it is a mistake to think that such sex is not openly political: practitioners wear distinctive dress; advertise their services and needs in newsletters and magazines; plan festivals and parades; associate in public parks, bars, and bathhouses; and attend academic conferences where their sexual lives are openly discussed. From this perspective, the public approval and encouragement of dominant/submissive sex by even the smallest feminist subgroup validates men's sexual intimidation, humiliation, or violation of women. Worse, this validation comes out of the very community that is designed to protect women from such abuse. Therefore, according to this view, no matter how much personal sexual pleasure or satisfaction may be gained through man/boy love, butch/femme sexual role-playing, or lesbian sadomasochism, their practice encourages men's violence against women—indeed, constitutes violence against those who submit to it—and so is morally wrong.[61]

In the first argument, cultural feminists are claiming that since a sex radical's dominant/submissive sex is not sex *between equals*, such sex is antifeminist. In the second argument, cultural feminists claim that since a sex radical's dominant/submissive sex is not sex *between equals*, such sex is not only antifeminist but also morally wrong. In both arguments, cultural feminists assert that appropriate sex for feminists is *egalitarian* sex.

What does it mean to say that feminist sexual practice should be egalitarian sex? "Terry is the equal of Alex" means not that "Terry is the same person as Alex" but that Terry and Alex are equal in some specified respect(s). Not just any respects will do for a cultural feminist, however, since Terry and Alex could both be African

American, middle-class, and gay but still be in a relationship between adult and child that constitutes man/boy love. In fact, they could be "equal" in their mutual enjoyment of every type of dominant/submissive sex that a cultural feminist rejects.

Furthermore, cultural feminists would not want to deny that egalitarian sex can exist between individuals of widely different races, classes, religions, physical abilities, personal interests, or age. The equality in which a cultural feminist is primarily interested is that relation in which each partner is equally cared for and respected by the other. However, since each partner could equally respect the other's desire for dominant/submissive sex, we still need to specify in what respects a cultural feminist wishes sexual partners to be cared for and respected. In chapter 2 I suggested that such respect implied acknowledging, understanding, and promoting one's partner's interests as she would define them; but if such interests include a sex radical's desire for sadomasochistic sex, then a cultural feminist will simply dismiss this desire as one she could not possibly respect.[62] Furthermore, if one of the complaints about man/boy love is that no matter how caring his sexual partner, a very young boy is simply not capable of making reasoned judgments with regard to his sexuality, then more than acknowledging, understanding, and promoting the expressed desires of at least some sexual partners will be required of a cultural feminist's sexual ethic. I suggest that before we can specify a sexual ethic that is flexible enough to explore the tensions between a cultural feminist and a sex radical feminist, we must look at three respects in which equality in sex is an issue for both feminists: equality of *power*, equality of *attention*, and equality of *affection*.

Cultural Feminism's Egalitarian Sex   For a cultural feminist, equality of power in sexual relations means that each partner has both the capacity and the opportunity to participate in the decisions that determine the nature and purpose of the sex act. Equality of power in sex means that at no time does only one partner dictate the content, timing, or technique of sex, creating a power imbalance in which only one person is in control. Some feminists refer to this kind of equality in sex as a sharing of power, as opposed to an exchange of power; others advocate the elimination of power dynamics in sex altogether.[63] According to either view, equality of power in sex means the absence of dominant and submissive sexual roles whose essentially oppressive nature under hetero-patriarchy turns a woman's willingness to dominate or her consent to submit into reconstructions of antifeminist sexual norms. From this perspective, when individual women "choose" to play either dominant or submissive roles in sex, they simply reflect the internalization of patriarchal values that are so strong and so insidious that women have unwittingly adopted them as their own. Dominant/submissive sex is perceived as a male invention promoting male sexual values that are coercive and ubiquitous—values of physical force, psychological intimidation, and hierarchical privilege. From a cultural feminist's perspective, choosing or consenting to dominant/submissive sex simply makes no sense in a society in which heterosexual dominance is forced on women, sexual submission is required of women, and power is defined exclusively by men to eroticize the victimization of women.[64]

According to cultural feminists, given women's inability in principle to define sexually polarizing roles in our own terms, women are doing nothing but hurting ourselves politically by not actively resisting patriarchal sexual models. Many feminists believe that sex radicals are hurting themselves morally and physically as well. Sarah Lucia Hoagland asserts that "it is not OK for a woman to consent to her own humiliation" because this humiliation constitutes "[t]he erasure of [he]r autonomy, integrity and humor" (Hoagland's spelling). In Valerie Heller's words, "Sadomasochism is nothing less than assault and battery."[65] Some feminists also point out that when women practice, write, and talk about butch/femme sexual roles or lesbian sadomasochism, they glamorize the violence and abuse of women and so reinforce the male belief that women are only turned on by violent, coercive, or abusive sex.[66] This reinforcement only encourages men to rape, harass, and humiliate women. Thus, from this perspective, sex that is polarized by power dynamics or power that is eroticized for its own sake not only constitutes harm to women but also has political ramifications that reinforce that harm. According to many feminists, by pursuing sex for pleasure in the absence of political reflection, sex radicals ignore the very foundations of feminism.

According to a cultural feminist, man/boy love is simply another example of the patriarchal authoritarianism of male sex: children do not have the social, legal, or financial resources that adults do, making it tempting for mature pedophiles to extract sexual favors from children who may acquiesce to their demands out of fear or insecurity. Some feminists have joined more politically conservative groups in suggesting that cross-generational sex is just a euphemism for child molestation. Therefore, according to feminist critics, issues of consent become moot in man/boy love relationships where the boy's real access to behavioral alternatives is nil. From this perspective, the boys that gay men typically approach are either boys with little knowledge or experience of sex, boys without stable families, or boys whose sexual experience has so convinced them of the necessity of their submission to men as to make their informed consent to sex meaningless. While the men in these relationships do not have the special authority of an incestuous parent to press their demands, many feminists still see in such relationships a kind of emotional and material extortion that makes man/boy love morally reprehensible.[67]

Furthermore, from this view, if early in life young boys experience sex as something an adult male forces on his sexual partner, they will grow up thinking that this is the appropriate sexual role model for them. Thus, such relationships only reinforce men's patriarchal role as the subordinators in sex. Even if a young boy is a teenager who asserts that he likes sex with older men and tends to seek out his own partners, some feminists would respond that the mere fact that he is violating a heterosexual and generational norm makes it impossible for him to have sex without feeling victimized by a guilt and fear imposed on him from without. Thus, he would again reach adulthood with an attitude toward sex that is anathema to a cultural feminist's conception of egalitarian sex.[68]

Marilyn Frye suggests that the relationship between knowledge and power becomes complex when we consider that boys who say they enjoy submitting to the sexual power of a dominant man may have convinced themselves that they want to do what their partners request of them (even if they would not do so in less confining circumstances), because there really is no other alternative that would not create discomfort in the relationship. This conviction in turn endorses the belief on the part of a man that his much younger partner does indeed want to do what he requests, and a man's superior power position assures himself that his beliefs must be true.[69] For all these reasons, a cultural feminist requires that power be shared, if not eliminated, from sex.

Shared attention and reciprocity of affection in sex are also required by cultural feminists, since from this perspective, egalitarian sex is not only a sharing of power but also a sharing of intimacy. According to this view, sex between equals means that no one person is attending to the sexual needs of her partner without also getting her own needs met. Reciprocity of affection means that each partner values emotional intimacy, rather than one partner desiring affection while the other cares for nothing other than physical performance. For a cultural feminist, such sharing of attention and affection means that there will be a loving understanding and promotion of each other's sexual needs. From this perspective, butch/femme sexual roles and lesbian sadomasochism do not allow reciprocal attention and affection since their *modus operandi* is the kind of polarized sex play that makes intimate sharing impossible. According to this view, sadomasochism in particular emphasizes the humiliation and degradation of the masochist and the rejection of intimacy by the sadist. In addition, the power imbalance in man/boy love makes such love suspect, since attentiveness and affection may easily be coerced from a young lover who is emotionally or materially dependent. Furthermore, from this view, boys will be more vulnerable to physical abuse and to the contraction of sexually transmitted diseases when they are in casual or anonymous relationships that are not governed by an equality of intimacy. Thus, for cultural feminists, sex that is equal in power, attention, and affection is essential for a feminist program of reclaiming a woman-identified sexuality. According to this perspective, only through the practice and advocacy of an egalitarian sex that equalizes, not polarizes, sexual roles can there be the kind of care respect that acknowledges, understands, and promotes the real needs and interests of women.

Sex Radical Feminism's Consensual Eroticization of Power   A sex radical feminist who advocates removing the social stigma against cross-generational sex, butch/femme sexual roles, and lesbian sadomasochism responds by claiming that it is she, not a cultural feminist, who practices and promotes a woman-identified sexuality. From a sex radical's perspective, by forcing women to accept what Esther Newton and Shirley Walton call "one look and one role for all,"[70] cultural feminists restrict women to as narrow a range of sexualities and preferences as the status quo. Indeed, from this view a cultural feminist appears to be joining forces with patriarchy in her stigmatization of sexual deviance. According to a sex radical feminist, this much is to be expected, since the moral self-righteousness of cultural feminism engenders a plea for political correctness that is nothing more than a monolith of orthodoxy and totalitarian control. According to a sex radical feminist, the most insidious coercion of women is not in dominant/submissive sex but in the ways that the politically correct sexuality of cultural feminism prevents women from exploring and pursuing sexual difference.[71]

Sex radicals also claim that by rejecting all dominant/submissive sex as degradingly patriarchal, cultural feminists give patriarchy the ability to define the eroticization of power for women. A sex radical feminist would explore dominant/submissive sex to discover what the eroticization of power can mean for women's passion and pleasure. From this view, by absorbing women's sexuality into patriarchal politics, a cultural feminist offers women a so-called egalitarian sex that cannot distinguish between the subordinating sexual power of patriarchy and the liberating sexual power of women. Such confusion only results in oppressing individual women's sexual exploration, pleasure, and agency by misidentifying it as yet another example of women's victimization by men. According to a sex radical feminist, there is every reason to encourage women to defy sexual norms that have so distorted women's needs in the past. Joan Nestle suggests that a cultural feminist's adoption of the status quo's rejection of sexualities that do not match the norm "turns a language of liberated desire into the silence of collaboration."[72] Given the extent to which the feminist movement has endorsed, even embraced, the sexual "deviance" of lesbianism, many sex radical feminists believe that it is nothing less than hypocrisy for cultural feminists to reject other deviations from the sexual norm, especially when they are practiced as a way of reclaiming women's sexuality. Indeed, Gayle Rubin observes that cultural feminism has so politicized lesbianism that nonfeminist and nonpolitical lesbians are regarded with suspicion by many within the women's movement, while lesbianism itself has all but lost its distinction as a sexual orientation as opposed to a political preference.[73]

Furthermore, sex radical feminists point out that if men's sexual victimization of women implies that women's consent to dominant/submissive sex is meaningless, then a cultural feminist's recommendation of consent to more "egalitarian" sex is meaningless as well. This claim suggests that when the sexual victimization of women is made an essential component of the patriarchal landscape, not only is a sex radical unable to define a woman-identified sexuality, but a cultural feminist is denied that power also. In this way a cultural feminist condemns women's sexuality to be defined without opposition in men's terms. According to sex radical feminists, until women are free of being identified as the sexual victims of male lust, individual women will never be able to define their sexuality in their own terms. Accusing sex radical feminists of internalizing patriarchal values—indeed, of imitating the worst form of compulsory heterosexuality by being brainwashed victims of a false consciousness—is, according to sex radicals like Pat Califia, arrogant, hateful psychologism.[74] According to a sex radical feminist, a cultural feminist's position reveals, if anything, the extent of her own indoctrination by a patriarchy with which she unwittingly colludes. Sex radicals charge that women cannot be sexually liberated when they are attributed an inability to make sexual choices independent of patriarchal constraints.[75]

Sex radical feminists also protest cultural feminists' accusations that those who practice man/boy love, butch/femme sexual role-playing, and lesbian sadomasochism are incapable of expressing the kind of care respect that acknowledges, understands, and promotes the sexual needs and interests of their partners. Equality of power, attention, and affection are all a part of a sex radical's program for the sexual liberation of women and men; far from being an "anything goes" program of sexual license, a sex radical feminist advocates the eroticization of power that is equally accessed, defined, and controlled by all partners.

According to sex radical feminists, butch/femme sexual roles and lesbian sadomasochism are vehicles for individual women to reclaim and redefine power in personal relationships in their own terms. As such, they are vehicles in which the power to explore and pursue the sexual needs of each partner is shared equally. According to a sex radical feminist, in butch/femme sexual role-playing and lesbian sadomasochism, the partners create a drama of dominant/submissive sex that is choreographed entirely by them. "Tops" (butches/sadists) and "bottoms" (femmes/masochists) exercise their power in sex through their mutual enjoyment of sexually stimulating each other and being stimulated in accordance with their own versions of the sexual roles of controller and controlled. Indeed, some feminists claim that the relationship between top and bottom is complex enough to make the opposition of the "active" versus the "passive" partner in sex obsolete. By the same token, according to a sex radical, lesbian sadomasochists use bondage, verbal abuse, physical restraint, and physical pain (from leather straps, whips, clamps, hot wax and the like) not in a Sadean coercive or malevolent manner but as a means to explore forbidden erotic territory and reclaim its significance for individual women's sexual pleasure.[76]

Thus, according to a sex radical feminist, the coercive sexual dominance that some cultural feminists complain about is in fact a consensual agreement to a sexual choreography in which the partners *play at* dominance and submission by *acting out* sexual roles. In this way, according to sex radical feminists, patriarchal power *over* women is transformed and transcended to create new avenues of power *with* women, so that women may experience their own sexual agency and sexual pleasure. Indeed, Anne McClintock argues that sadomasochism's successful display of power as performed or invented rather than natural and normal challenges a social order that would disguise power as inherent in some classes and not in others. Thus, butch/femme sexual roles and lesbian sadomasochism can represent a feminist rebellion against male-identified sexuality and political power.[77] Sex radical feminists regard themselves as the vanguard of the women's movement because, according to Joan Nestle, they "have had the strength and courage to express desire and resistance." For a sex radical feminist, it is an insult to such resistance to reconstitute it as a "phony heterosexual replica" instead of embracing it as a complex erotic and social statement.[78] From a sex radical's perspective, if a cultural feminist insists on regarding radical sex as a patriarchal kindred spirit of degrading dominant/submissive sex, then she has undermined individual women's real efforts to engage in sexual practices that express their liberation from oppressive norms.

Furthermore, many sex radical feminists question cultural feminism's rejection of the eroticization of power for its own sake; according to sex radicals, social psychologists and psychoanalysts tell us that if nothing else, sex is all about power.[79] Indeed, if Freudians are right, it is impossible for women to replicate men's dominant/submissive sex, since such sex is, according to classic psychoanalytic theory, the result of deeply embedded, gender-specific infantile fears of alienation and loss. Some sex radicals believe that this essential power dynamic in sex scares cultural feminists because they believe that *all* sexual power dynamics are constituted by patriarchal (sadistic) power. According to sex radical feminists, this belief leads a cultural feminist to the erroneous conclusion that any reclamation of sexual power by women is impossible. Sex radicals recognize that much of psychoanalysis has been used to marginalize women's sexual needs and repress sexual deviance in the service of the status quo; and many sex radical feminists also recognize that sexual liberation alone will not free women from political oppression. Nevertheless, sex remains for many sex radicals a Foucault-inspired, socially constructed practice whose power can be reclaimed by men or women in the service of their sexual agency and authenticity.[80]

Sex radicals also claim that the complaints by cultural feminists that man/boy love is necessarily exploitative is a myth perpetrated by contemporary Western medical, psychoanalytic, and public health institutions, sensationalized by the media, and re-inforced by law. According to a sex radical feminist, such myths about the essential-ism of adult male power are used to reinforce the sexual mores that invigorate the power relations necessary for the maintenance of the status quo.[81] From this view, social prohibitions against children engaging in sex with either each other or adults make it difficult for children to gain any knowledge about, or experience of, their sex-ual needs. A sex radical points out, however, that this very inexperience is then used as the justification for prohibitions against sex with children. From a sex radical per-spective, such prohibitions also make it difficult for children to find safe, secure, and loving outlets for their sexual exploration. The trauma of public exposure, parental disapproval, and police harassment all militate against the success of man/boy love.[82] Indeed, according to a sex radical feminist, it is persons' "consent" to adult hetero-sexual intimacy that should be questioned, since from her perspective, patriarchy makes available to us so little information about, and access to, sexual alternatives.

Moreover, sex radical feminists contend that the North American Man/Boy Love Association (NAMBLA) is not a pimping or procurement service but a formalized network established to help gay men and boys meet one another in much the same way as other associations (of bird-watchers, classical music buffs, and the like) whose members share similar interests. NAMBLA's members report interest primarily in boys aged fourteen to nineteen, who approach them for sexual favors as much as or more than they approach young boys. The British Paedophile Information Exchange (PIE) reports that their major adult interest is in boys aged twelve to fourteen and that social stigma remains more of a problem in man/boy relationships than coer-cion or abuse.[83] Sexual radicals would also point out that if cultural feminists brand cross-generational sex between adults and teens as in any sense inherently exploita-tive, then they have paradoxically condemned any lesbian sex between adults and teens that might otherwise fit cultural feminism's conception of egalitarian sex. A sex radical does not deny that there are abuses in sexual relationships between men and boys. She only suggests that the trouble lies more with the contemporary (and rela-tively recent) Western perception that sex corrupts the young than with some intrin-sic exploitation in man/boy love. The adult fear of children's active, healthy sexual de-sires often appears to sex radical feminists to be the real reason why anyone would reject outright the exploration by children of their own sexuality. Moreover, sexually aware and knowledgeable children may threaten adults by being more confident in getting what they want and refusing what they do not want, including reporting abu-sive situations and resolving them. For a sex radical, it is an adult's responsibility to provide education and guidance to children in the area of human sexuality, not to promote stigmatization and dogma in an effort to control childhood sex.[84]

For a sex radical feminist, equality of attentiveness and equality of affection trans-late, among other things, into a mutual concern for the health and safety of each part-ner. Cynthia Astuto and Pat Califia discuss how important it is to be wary of "top's disease" and "bottom's disease" in butch/femme sexual role-playing and lesbian sado-masochism.[85] As in heterosexual relationships in which one sexual partner is dominant and one is submissive, Astuto and Califia warn against the top's demanding more than a bottom wants to give and against a bottom's feeling so insecure that she believes any top will do no matter how coercive or unsatisfying the sex. For a sex radical feminist, this is hardly an admission that no such sex is caring, attentive, or affectionate. On the contrary, a sex radical would argue that being on the lookout for such abuses belies a sensitivity and consideration for how each partner defines her role in sex as well as what each partner can expect from the other.

Astuto and Califia also point out that some consensual sadomasochistic sex is plainly unsafe, harmful, or unhealthy. Neck clamps can be too tight, time spent in bondage can be too prolonged or unmonitored, penetration can be with sharp or unclean objects. However, before any practice begins, partners can share with each other their sexual concerns, limitations, and needs, from emotional discipline such as humiliation and verbal abuse to the physical discipline of whipping, abrasion, and bondage. Code words that mean "Stop now!" are agreed to beforehand, so that begging to stop or refusing to stop can be incorporated into the erotic play of power; yet each partner maintains control of the encounter by defining the code and the roles played.[86] For a sex radical feminist, stop codes are themselves symbols of an attentiveness that each partner contributes to the sexual play. While a sex radical does not demand the intimate loving relationship that a cultural feminist does, a sex radical feminist nevertheless demands that there be the kind of care respect for each partner that turns the harm in sadomasochism into a mutually directed and mutually pleasurable drama of erotic discipline, quite the contrary from a unilateral perpetration of violence. From a sex radical's point of view, such discipline is intentionally *not* gentle, *not* sweet, and *not* romantic, because as I pointed out in chapter 2, sex radical feminists are skeptical of any version of sexual intimacy that imitates or reinforces patriarchal norms of romantic love. However, the practitioner of s/m protests that her practices should not be equated with rape, torture, and murder simply because her sex is not "vanilla" sex. Nor should her practices be equated with social pathology due to cultural feminists' belief in the essentially intimate and bonding nature of women's sexuality. If the burden is on a sex radical to show that her sex is truly liberating, there is an equal burden on cultural feminists from a sex radical's perspective to show that lesbian or heterosexual "vanilla" sex is not just another instance of an oppressive patriarchal norm.

Thus, a sex radical claims that she cannot be accused of encouraging *violence* against women since, she would argue, she is not being cruel or vicious to women at all. On the contrary, sex radical feminists would assert that cultural feminists encourage violence against women by restricting women to traditionally repressive romantic norms and by refusing to see the radical reclamation of dominant/submissive sex as anything other than the mirroring of women's sexual victimization by men. According to a sex radical, if the public mistakes legitimate attempts to reclaim women's sexuality as encouraging violence against women, that mistake is due to a lack of public sensitivity to sexual practices that deviate from the sexual norm, not to the practices themselves. The solution is public education about the methods and aims of a variety of sexual practices, not social ignorance and public ridicule.

Sex radicals also remind cultural feminists that because the s/m community is scattered and marginalized, it has difficulty in securing proper facilities and equipment for safe individual s/m use and in disseminating its health and safety concerns either to neophyte practitioners or to the public at large. Such difficulties serve the interests of the status quo, since in this way abuses can be publicly isolated and distorted. Yet according to Gayle Rubin, "far more people end up in the hospital as a result of playing sports, driving cars, or being pregnant than from having s/m sex."[87] Furthermore, the community is small enough that practitioners with bad reputations are identified relatively quickly. For a sex radical feminist, it is both predictable and sinister that patriarchal society tolerates wife beating, child abuse, rape, and war more easily than it tolerates lesbian sadomasochism, since lesbian s/m represents a threat to the heterosexual monogamy and repressive intimacy that restrict women's sexual roles to those of subordinates to men.

Furthermore, according to sex radical feminists, butch/femme sexual roles and lesbian sadomasochism can be healing exorcisms of the daily psychological battering women often receive from male coworkers or acquaintances. Such sex provides a cathartic reenactment of a power struggle that they cannot seem to win at work but that they can win at home. For many, dramas of sexual dominance and submission help heal old wounds of childhood neglect, abuse, or incest, even the current wounds of rape. In addition, many sex radicals see in lesbian sadomasochism a revelation of the subtler relationships between sex and power. Master/slave theater and reenactments of political fascism add a dimension to sex that for some women is both provocative and deeply erotic. From this view, to deny women access to such erotica is to deny them exploration into that which is most personal about each woman's sexual needs.[88] Since the pursuit of women's sexual agency and self-definition is a feminist goal, sex radical feminists claim that the pursuit of alternative sexual practices can not only mean safe, healthy, and mutually enjoyable sex but can also be an important part of a feminist sexuality.

Similarly, a sex radical points out that man/boy love relationships can be equally safe and healthy. Indeed, for many gay men and boys, any other sex would be anathema to their sexual desires. Advocates of man/boy love say that their relationships can be as mutually attentive and affectionate as any cultural feminist's ideal of woman-identified sex, since such partners are, like cultural feminists, looking for alternative ways to satisfy a sexual need oppressed under hetero-patriarchy.[89] Though their sex may recreate dominant/submissive patterns that do not fit a cultural feminist's vision of egalitarian sex, sex radicals warn that feminists cannot assume that such sex is dangerous, inattentive, unloving, or bad. Here too, according to sex radicals, if feminists are to break patriarchy's stranglehold on defining the relationship between sex and power, we must refrain from assuming that man/boy, dominant/submissive sex is the degrading patriarchal sex of the status quo. Children must be protected from sexual abuse; but according to this view, it is a mistake to trust such protection to social institutions designed to stigmatize children's sexuality in the service of oppressive norms.[90]

Still Antifeminist and Morally Wrong   A cultural feminist's response to sex radicals' arguments for butch/femme sexual role-playing and lesbian sadomasochism is to point out to radical feminists that by their own admission, their purported reclamation of power in sex is nothing more than *play-acting*. As such, a sex radical's eroticization of power is merely a parody of the real power over women that men wield under patriarchy. Cultural feminists claim that such parodies have no way of releasing women from heterosexual submission, since the fantasy world in which they reside leaves the concrete political world behind. From such a view, dramas of dominance and submission can only delude women into believing they have gained control over their sexual lives when they have not. Cultural feminists contend that such fantasies of power are typical of those for whom power is out of reach, who resign themselves to a kind of childlike magical thinking that would appear to make their real adult oppression disappear with the crack of a whip.[91]

Not only is a sex radical's sexual power illusory according to cultural feminists, but as I mentioned earlier, some feminists argue that this illusion is *not* harmless. According to this view, what may be one person's erotic play at power may be another's real efforts at domination. If feminist dominant/submissive sex is defined in terms of role-playing, there will be no way for play-actors to discern at the outset whether their partners will in fact act out their roles or make real attempts to dominate them. From this perspective, code words and health and safety rules do not protect women from those who would exploit partners expecting everyone to play by those rules. Some feminists suggest that the emphasis on trust in lesbian s/m implies the very danger of its abuse.[92]

Lorena Leigh Saxe and Melinda Vadas argue that the sadomasochistic eroticism derived from simulations of Nazism, slavery, prostitution, and incest exists in virtue of the real oppression such simulations represent. Thus, practitioners of this kind of s/m are not *playing* at dominance and submission at all; rather, they are recreating degrading scenarios constitutive of the very kinds of oppression that as feminists they should ideologically reject. Melinda Vadas writes, "The experience of the simulation is mediated by the meaning of the injustices simulated. To take pleasure in the simulation is to make one's pleasure contingent on the actual occurrence and meanings of rape, racist enslavement, and so on. Pleasures taken in this way are not feminist, and cannot be."[93] Moreover, even if lesbian sadomasochistic sex is a mere performance of violence, grounded in artifice and subversion *for the performer*, it is contended that such play-acting will not undermine the attitudes of those whose entrenched conceptions of sexual deviance allow them to see only perversion, not subversion. Indeed, whether the violence is illusory or real, many cultural feminists argue that a sex radical's eroticization of power merely serves to reinforce the image of woman as Other, inferior, marginalized, dominated, and degraded. Such an image is necessarily public in virtue of the public dress, habits, and community activism of sexual minorities and so reinforces the social stereotype of women as the sexual subordinates of men.[94]

Cultural feminists respond to sex radical arguments for man/boy love by pointing out that boys' approaching men for sex does not make such sex acceptable. Such claims only show cultural feminists once again how pervasive and deeply internalized patriarchal subordination in sex really is. For a cultural feminist, a sex radical's mistake is to invest an inherent rightness in sexual desire that makes sexual pleasure a good in itself.[95] Yet while sexual pleasure may be prima facie good, cultural feminists argue that such pleasure must always be evaluated by the social context in which it arises. Because the social context in which a sex radical practices is defined in terms of adult male dominance, cultural feminists claim that sexual pleasure must be defined in terms that do not imitate and reinforce that dominance. For cultural feminists, the sexual difference advocated by sex radicals remains sexual perversion in its subversion of a truly woman-identified sexuality.

Negotiating the Social Meaning of Sexual Difference

On the one hand, this feminist debate over sexual difference appears to be a debate between diametric opposites. According to cultural feminists, man/boy love or lesbian dominant/submissive sex is necessarily nonconsensual, dangerous (if not abusive), and antifeminist. For sex radical feminists, man/boy love and lesbian dominant/submissive sex can be consensual, safe, healthy, mutually pleasurable, and profoundly feminist. For cultural feminists, gay men's and lesbians' dominant/submissive sexual roles are replications of the oppressive sex of hetero-patriarchy. Sex is a gendered political practice whose traditional heterosexual model victimizes women. For sex radical feminists, gay men's and lesbians' dominant/submissive sexual roles are vehicles for the liberation of men and women from the oppressive sex of hetero-patriarchy. Sex is a socially regulated but potentially liberating practice whose variety can be tapped to subvert the stigma of sexual deviance designed to advance the power and privilege of the status quo. For cultural feminists, women's sexual pleasure, agency, and self-definition are a function of our ability to pursue and develop intimate relations between moral equals in nonpolarized roles. For sex radical feminists, women's sexual pleasure, agency, and self-definition are a function of our ability to pursue and develop a wide range of sexual interests, which include anonymous or casual sex between partners exploring the eroticization of dominance and submission.

However, both cultural and sex radical feminism have a broad range of similar goals. Both cultural and sex radical feminists believe that women's sexual pleasure, agency, and self-definition are values that require the freedom and responsibility of women individually and as a class to define our sexuality in our own terms. Furthermore, both groups would agree that any sex that conforms to, replicates, or reinforces ideological and institutional patterns of male dominance is oppressive to women. Cultural and sex radical feminists both regard their agendas as advocating the kind of care respect for women that acknowledges, understands, and promotes the individual sexual needs of women. Yet ironically, each feminist group accuses the other of undermining women's sexual autonomy, conforming to ideological formulas of male dominance, and misunderstanding the needs of individual women.

The similarity in goals of the two feminist groups is aptly illustrated by the fact that it is often difficult to discern which side is doing the talking. For example, Wendy Stock, a strong opponent of lesbian s/m, writes:

[W]e have the ability to imagine a different sexuality and to struggle to create it. We must continue to question our assumptions and, through feminist analysis, to detoxify ourselves from a culture that hates women. Through these experiences we are formulating new ways of living and being. Deconstructing patriarchal sexuality and abstaining from patriarchal sex may be a stage in the articulation and creation of a feminist sexuality. . . . By turning our backs on our own sexuality, we are admitting defeat to the same degree that we would if we accepted the patriarchy's constructed version of sex. We must sustain a vision of what the erotic can be. By nurturing our sexuality with a critical feminist awareness, we can resist the social structure that would take away this vital part of ourselves.

On the same side of the debate, Judy Butler conceives of women's sexual power as

the power gained through re-claiming my sexuality as an expression of *my* life, shaping my choice to honor my desires, and desiring my own sense of choice more than any other desire. The failure to do this is what Adrienne Rich calls "the worst thing of all . . . the failure to want our freedom passionately enough."[96]

Yet given the aims of sex radical feminism, there is no reason to think that a sex radical feminist would disagree with these conceptions of the meaning and value of the erotic.

Therefore, I propose that we adopt the perspective of the "view from somewhere different" to explore how the feminist tensions I have detailed can be incorporated into an inclusive feminist philosophy of sex. First, adopting this perspective means understanding sexual relations in terms of a dialectic between gender and sexuality. This dialectic situates women's sexuality in terms of women's victimization under patriarchy and women's pursuit of sexual exploration, pleasure, and agency. Thus, both cultural feminism, whose emphasis is on the ways gender oppression informs sexuality, and sex radical feminism, whose emphasis is on the ways that sexual liberation informs gender, can find an audience within the perspective of this broader dialectic.

Second, recall that the "world"-traveling implicit in the "view from somewhere different" recommends that we not only acknowledge the partiality of our own locations but also make an effort to understand the locations of others. Adopting this perspective precludes advocating the kind of politically correct sexuality that would derogate all but those deferring to a favored ideology. Therefore, such a perspective rejects the moral authoritarian approach of any cultural feminist who would restrict women's sexuality to all but a narrow range of ideal preference in deference to a "view from somewhere better." So, too, such a perspective reminds sex radicals not to press the exploration of sexual difference on women whose personal desire for more traditional sex may only reinforce the expectation that all women will want the same. Adopting the "view from somewhere different" shows women how their choices can be both constrained by patriarchy and liberated by their own sense of agency and self-definition, so that their sexual lives can be lived creatively *and* responsibly.

Given the ways in which gender location intersects with other social locations, the women whose sexual agency both cultural and sex radical feminists would maximize will be of diverse races, classes, sexual preferences, ages, nationalities, religions, and physical abilities, among other categories. Therefore, a feminist philosophy of sex from the "view from somewhere different" contextualizes its perspective so that the specific sexual concerns of any given group can be heard. Such a perspective points out, for example, that a cultural feminist's advocacy of egalitarian, nonpolarized sex, particularly as part of an essential female sexuality, will simply not ring true for those women whose strongly identified nationalities or religions cherish different sexual values. Some women's desire for increased sexual experience may make performance-oriented or power-polarizing sex more satisfying, or less of an effort, than monogamous sexual commitment. A woman's age, self-confidence, emotional vulnerability, and physical ability also influence how she views her sexual life. Yet social location is not a predictor of desire, since one woman with a full life of sexual experimentation may long for a relationship of more constancy, while another may wish fewer of her partners wanted "the same old thing." So, too, the"view from somewhere different" will suggest to an advocate of sadomasochistic sex that her choice to "play at power" is as much a function of her race and class as it is her gender. Poor and working-class women often resent middle-class feminists who advocate sexual power plays as a means to liberation, because affluent women already have the power of time, money, and opportunity to explore sexual alternatives. For many more women, however, such sexual experimentation is a luxury that does not address their needs to find food, clothing, and shelter for their families. The reifying effects of interlocking oppressions are also exemplified when sexual difference among the affluent is tolerated as amusing eccentricity, while the same sexual variation in the poor or homeless community is labeled deviant or perverse. Furthermore, women of color may feel insulted by mostly white women's desires to dramatize and eroticize the roles of master/slave. Such dramas only arouse in many women of color profound and painful associations with white imperialist enslavement, making any play at such slavery a disrespectful one.[97] The "view from somewhere different" acknowledges that the disempowered do not have the power of parody and that racism and classism are potent forces in the oppression of women and in the marginalization of sexual difference.

The sexual difference sex radical feminists advocate is itself a social construction located in a milieu in which women are stereotyped as the sexual subordinates of men. Therefore, personal explorations of the relationship between sex and power will have profound political meaning for both sexual minorities and members of the status quo. The erotic play of power that is the sexual rebellion of the sadomasochist has meaning as social rebellion and not mere private fantasy precisely because of the dialectic between the personal and the political.

It is in virtue of this dialectic that a sex radical must recognize the dangers of misinterpretation that her dramas of dominance and submission carry. From the "view from somewhere different," her "world"-traveling commits her to ask of herself, "What is it like to be me in their eyes?" Without the ability to create a woman-identified model of the relation between sex and power, feminists have no way of loosening the patriarchal stranglehold on defining sexual power as the power of victimization. Yet it is in virtue of existing patriarchal constraints that sex radical feminists must, with renewed emphasis, work on ways to educate the larger community regarding crucial differences between patriarchal plays at sexual power and feminist ones.

Some sex radicals complain that this strategy assumes that a sex radical cannot practice a truly liberating form of sexuality until she can convince a disbelieving public that she is not doing something morally wrong. Such dependence on patriarchal approval for their sexual liberation strikes many sex radicals as hypocritical, if not patently absurd. From this perspective, a sex radical's responsibility is not to persuade a patriarchal status quo to accept her but to learn to accept herself. Sex radical feminists would argue that such acceptance is difficult when feminists treat women who enjoy the type of sex that eroticizes dominance and submission as co-opted victims of patriarchal brainwashing.

Yet I would argue that without recognizing and militating against the strength of her opposition, a sex radical feminist undermines her activism by reducing the political to the personal. If a sex radical feminist's aim is to transform the social meaning of sexual power, she cannot expect her practice of sexual difference alone to do the job. As Jeffrey Weeks points out in his argument for a radical sexual pluralism, recognizing what I have been calling the dialectic between gender and sexuality compels us to be "sensitive to the workings of power, [and] alive to the struggles needed to change the existing social relations which constrain sexual autonomy."[98] Indeed, the "view from somewhere different" requires the dismantling of the traditional opposition of the normal versus the perverse, precisely because sex radical plays at power cannot subvert real political power when the status quo retains the option of remarginalizing them as perverse. Unless sex radical feminists actively seek to educate a wary public regarding a radical reconceptualization of sexual perversion, they will have done no more than convince the status quo of their internalization of traditional sexual norms.

Moreover, misinterpretation of a radical feminist sexual practice by women of color may be detrimental to feminism. As I noted earlier, women of color suffer from multiple plays at power that many white women do not. At a time when women of color struggle to find a place for feminism within the context of their struggle against racial oppression, women who claim the power to eroticize sex in their own terms may be regarded by women of color as simply white, *female* imperialists with whom women of color have little in common. By adopting the "view from somewhere different," sex radical feminists can open a dialogue about sexual difference with those whose social location represents oppression on many fronts.

Sex radical feminists can also work to deinstitutionalize aversion to children's sexuality by advocating strongly against the sexual abuse of children at the same time that sex radicals advocate in favor of children's sexual education and sexual play. The "view from somewhere different" encourages attempts to understand the individual sexual needs of children and to acknowledge that adults ascribe symbolic and sexual meaning to acts that children do not. This means recognizing that children's emotional vulnerability and eagerness to please make them easy targets for adult sexual exploitation. Moreover, because children lack economic or social independence from adults, children's ability to make informed sexual choices will be influenced by adults still in control of children's lives. The "view from somewhere different" also acknowledges the patriarchal context of adult heterosexuality in which children's social introduction to sex typically occurs. Therefore, judgments about adult/child sexual relations must be sensitive to the particular personal context of power dynamics within those relations as well as those cultural dynamics external to it. Indeed, there will be those for whom adult/child sex taps into deeply repressed horrors and fears. Because human sexual practice exists in a social milieu that influences and is influenced by sexual norms, sex radicals face the daunting task of restructuring the social and economic relationship between adults and children, if safety, dignity, and care is to be afforded to sexual relationships between them. The larger issue remains as to whether children under any social circumstances are psychosexually mature enough to make free and informed decisions about their sexual lives and exactly who is to decide when such maturity occurs.[99]

From the "view from somewhere different," sexual preference is problematic when advocated by either a cultural or sex radical feminist alone, since both cultural feminism's egalitarian sex and sex radical feminism's eroticization of power are rebellions to patriarchal norms that fail to acknowledge the full range of individual women's erotic needs. Cultural feminism's epistemological presuppositions about female nature and sex radical feminism's essentializing marriage of sex, power, and pleasure must be questioned if we are to avoid a "view from nowhere" that would profess to know the truth about women's sexuality.[100]

Both cultural and sex radical feminisms can be expanded and transformed by the incorporation of their visions for women's liberation into the dialectic between gender and sexuality. Feminist sexuality from the "view from somewhere different" captures a cultural feminist's contention that women's sexuality must be contextualized by the patriarchal climate in which women live. The "view from somewhere different" also captures a sex radical's warning that we should not restrict women's self-conceptions to male-identified definitions but should offer individual women the opportunity to experience sexual autonomy by exploring their sexual lives in their own terms. This perspective has the advantage of advocating a sexual agency and self-definition for women that recognizes and promotes sexual diversity over a broad spectrum of gender, race, and class, since from the "view from somewhere different" no single sexual difference is the only sex worth knowing.[101]

The "view from somewhere different" acknowledges that there are divisions among feminists within cultural and sex radical factions and that simply defining the issue as a debate between two discrete brands of feminism may be practical for the exposition of argument but is misleading in its apparently rigid categorization of types. As I noted earlier, for example, some feminists do not object to sadomasochism restricted to the bedroom. They simply reject the notion that such sex advances the feminist agenda of women's sexual agency and self-definition. Some sex radical feminists are much more interested than others in community activism in support of sexual difference. I also mentioned previously that many feminists who do not consider themselves cultural feminists have many of the same complaints against sex radicals that cultural feminists do. Similarly, many feminists who are not sex radicals also have trouble with aspects of cultural feminism. The "view from somewhere different" maintains a healthy skepticism toward the idea of a *resolution* to the variety of problems feminists raise concerning women's sexual difference, as the dialectic between gender and sexuality is a fluid and flexible one defined by historical and political context. As Muriel Dimen writes:

> Where does this leave us? In an ambiguous, uncertain spot. The idea of political correctness masquerades as eternal truth which we would all like to believe is possible, because it makes us feel much more secure. But everything changes—except the existence of contradictions. With social transformation come new ones. I do not believe that an eternally true consciousness of what is politically correct in sexuality, or in anything, is possible. Or, to say the same thing in other words, the road to false consciousness, no matter how you wish to define it, is paved with politically correct intentions.[102]

Given the added importance, mentioned in chapter 1, of recognizing bias in the philosophical investigator's social location, any attempt on my part to offer a final conceptual or moral solution to the question of sexual difference would be hypocritical. Indeed, the "view from somewhere different" is itself partial to sexual diversity in ways that cultural feminism is not. As I argued in the previous section, the "view from somewhere different" recommends an appreciation of sexual diversity in order to open, not close, the question of the normative status of a variety of sexual practices and preferences. Pat Califia has argued that sexual difference should be a matter of taste ("vanilla" versus "rocky road"), not morality. Other feminists have argued that sex should engage our moral attention precisely because the personal obligations and social benefits that make up our sexual lives are so important to us.[103] The "view from somewhere different" recognizes that there will be contexts in which oppressive sexual relations command our political attention as well as those contexts in which the most sexually intimate affairs recommend pleasure over politics. However, all such contexts are superseded by a feminist ethic of care respect from the "view from somewhere different," which acknowledges, understands, and promotes the individual sexual needs of one's partner from a historicized and socially located perspective. Such a perspective is also partial to difference in order to capture the sexual variety that would be lost if we were to deconstruct the notion of difference by adopting the "view from everywhere." By stressing the importance of the dialectical relationship between gender and sexuality, the "view from somewhere different" paves the way for a dialectical approach to understanding the relationships between the political and the personal, the dominant and the submissive, the moral and the aesthetic. My contention is that such a perspective provides both a theoretical and a practical basis for understanding the presuppositions of contemporary feminist debates over sexual preference as well as a basis for believing that to try to resolve such debates is to foreclose the pursuit of women's sexual liberation.

This perspective also makes questions about women's "real" sexual preferences moot, since from the "view from somewhere different," social location makes all "real" choice partial and historicized. Therefore, it seems misleading to ask Ellen Willis's question, "What would we choose if we had a real choice?"[104] From the vantage point of the "view from somewhere different," claims about women's sexuality make sense only when women's "real" choices are understood as contextually and politically situated ones, not socially isolatable choices free of cultural constraints. Whether or not women consent to their sexual relations cannot resolve the dispute between cultural and sex radical feminism, since there is no clear sense in which our socially constructed desires can truly be said to be "free" of political and ideological forms. Sarah Lucia Hoagland admits that we have all been "infected erotically . . . by the patriarchal ideology of authority, of dominance and submission." Moreover, Sandra Lee Bartky makes the important observation that feminists should not underestimate what she calls the "obsessional dimension of sexual desire," which would militate against feminists easily or satisfactorily changing our sexual preferences to match our politics.[105] However, I believe Bartky would agree that any difficulty we may have in adjusting our sexuality to suit our feminism does not mean that women cannot break free of sexual restraints imposed on us by an oppressive patriarchy; nor does it deny that consent and coercion have real meaning within specific contexts of exploitation, intimidation, and violence against women. The notion of choice is a vital one for feminism of any form, since it is only within the realm of real and accessible alternatives to women's sexual subordination that the feminist project of women's liberation can be achieved. A feminist sexual ethic from the "view from somewhere different" abjures the personal practices and social forces that attempt to stifle women's sexual agency and self-definition. This ethic is one of care respect, detailed in the concluding section of this chapter.

Sexual Ethics from the "View from Somewhere Different"

In chapter 2 I described a woman's sensitivity to the particular sexual desires of her partner and an active willingness to promote those desires as constitutive of a care respect for her sexual partner. I have also noted that while most cultural and sex radical feminists would agree on the inclusion of care respect in a comprehensive feminist sexual ethic, they disagree as to the nature, purpose, and extent of that respect. In this chapter, for example, a cultural feminist is understood as advocating the kind of care respect that recognizes the desire in many women for affectionate personal bonding with their sexual partners. From a cultural feminist's point of view, such affection precludes the adoption of power-polarizing sexual roles. On the other hand, a sex radical feminist advocates care respect by recognizing the desire in many women for the freedom to explore their sexuality, which can foster experimentation with consensual, power-polarizing sexual roles. In the previous section I suggested that the "view from somewhere different" can negotiate the tensions between these two feminist perspectives by circumscribing them within a feminist philosophy of sex that appreciates the dialectic between gender and sexuality.

In this remaining section I will expand on the sexual ethic of care respect introduced in chapter 2. I will show how a feminist program for promoting women's sexual agency and self-definition is a fundamental feature of this sexual ethic, in part by showing how care respect in sex encourages "world"-traveling and in part by showing how care respect informs and is informed by Marjorie Weinzweig's "autonomous relating to others." This autonomy further recommends what Joyce Trebilcot refers to as women "taking responsibility for [our] sexuality," a responsibility that encourages individual women to take an active role in determining their own sexual needs and to understand the social context in which those needs arise.[106] Like the "view from somewhere different" from which it derives, a sexual ethic of care respect can negotiate the tensions between cultural and sex radical feminists by recognizing in both perspectives the goal of sexual agency and self-definition for women whose lives are circumscribed, but not determined, by individual and institutionalized male dominance. Such a goal can then be incorporated into a feminist philosophy of sex that encourages resistance to, and transformation of, women's sexual subordination. Thus, a sexual ethic of care respect may serve as a normative guide to the examination of other issues in feminist philosophy of sex in subsequent chapters.

Robin Dillon describes care respect as "valuing an individual in her specificity, seeking to understand her in her own terms, and caring about and seeking to promote her well-being."[107] For Dillon, valuing an individual merely for some capacity she shares with all other persons may make all persons equally valuable but ignores the ways in which each individual is special. Ignoring these, we tend to forget that not everyone has the same specific needs and interests that we do, encouraging what I have referred to as a "view from nowhere" that can be coercive or intrusive of the needs of others. Moreover, we typically regard our lovers, friends, and family as valuable in ways we do not regard all other people. Thus, there will be some people in the world about whom we feel it is appropriate to care more than others or to whom we feel we ought to be partial. Since all persons are unique, valuing a person in her specificity has the advantage of valuing her not only for the ways her uniqueness makes her equally valuable among persons but also for the particular ways in which she is unique. Thus, care respect promotes a fundamental equality among persons by particularizing individuals instead of generalizing about them. This fundamental equality is important for establishing a moral baseline of respectful treatment of persons from whom we may otherwise be very different, a baseline below which no moral agent may fall without censure. In so doing, care respect balances an ethic of justice that prescribes universal respect for persons with an ethic of care that recommends considerations of context and particularity in personal relations. In Dillon's words, "[C]are respect has the resources to maintain a constructive tension between regarding each person as *just as valuable* as every other person and regarding this individual as *special*."[108]

The "view from somewhere different" specifies the nature of this dialectical tension. A sexual ethic of care respect asks us to value the particularity of each person's sexual desires, pleasures, and preferences as well as the shared particularity of all of us. From the "view from somewhere different," this shared particularity translates into a shared partiality of social location that individually biases the interests of every person. As I argued in chapter 1, unless we acknowledge this shared partiality, we are liable to adopt the "view from nowhere," which mistakes the bias of social location for the assurance of absolute truth. On the other hand, from the "view from somewhere different," I, like everyone, am always "somewhere," different in my particular situation, yet the same in my being situated contextually, politically, historically in ways that will inevitably bias my worldview.

However, one of a sex radical's complaints against cultural feminism is its apparent advocacy of a politically correct sexuality that refuses to acknowledge the legitimacy of alternative sexual preferences. If an equality of moral worth among very different individuals were not established, a sexual ethic of care respect that consisted solely of recognizing the particularity in all of us as well as the particularity of each of our sexual needs would still be consistent with the claim from the "view from somewhere better" that some persons' needs are more worthy of pursuit than others. Therefore, Dillon's care respect not only includes valuing what is the same and different in all of us but also includes trying to understand the worldview of others. A sexual ethic of care respect recommends that I treat my sexual partners as moral equals by recognizing that their particular and perhaps very different sexual desires, pleasures, or preferences are no less worthy of satisfaction than my own. The feminist philosophy of sex advocated thus far neither advocates a single sexual preference as the "right" one nor treats any one person's social location as superior in sexual privilege or access. Care respect assures that we will acknowledge the particularity of worldviews without assuming that our own worldviews are the only ones worth know-ing. The "world"-traveling of the "view from somewhere different" recommends that we ask ourselves what it is like to be someone else and what it would be like to be ourselves in someone else's eyes. Dillon quotes Elizabeth Spelman, who writes, "We treat others as the persons they are just insofar as we try to respond to the way they choose to be seen, and not through our favored ways of seeing them."[109] By trying to see the world from the social location of my sexual partner, I can then begin to un-derstand what my partner's sexual desires are *as my partner sees them* and seek to pro-mote their satisfaction in ways that do not disregard the care respect of others.

A sexual ethic that encourages "world"-traveling in this way is one that encour-ages women's sexual agency and self-definition. A woman's care respect for her sex-ual partner involves actively attempting to discover what her partner's individual sex-ual desires, pleasures, or preferences may be and realizing the value of listening and responding to those desires. "World"-traveling in her sexual relations means that a woman will learn more about others' sexual preferences and so expand her own awareness of the sexual differences open to her. By asking "What is it like to be my-self in my partner's eyes?," she may also expand her sexual awareness of herself and so be better able to match what she values in sex with her actual sexual experience. A sexual ethic of care respect also encourages respecting the limits of others' sexual privacy and experimenting with ways a woman can understand her partner from her partner's perspective without invading anyone's "personal space." This kind of un-derstanding could facilitate dialogue regarding such issues as using contraceptives, asking partners to use protection against sexually transmitted diseases, and asking partners to be tested for the AIDS virus.

From the "view from somewhere different," gender, race, class, and sexual pref-erence, among other social locations, intertwine to create distinctive sexual per-spectives among each of us. The objections that many women of color lodge against sex radical feminism suggest that persons adopt a sexual ethic of care respect that rec-ommends both acknowledging the interlocking of women's social oppressions and understanding the complex ways in which a woman's sexuality is affected by her so-cial location. The resulting diversity of voices suggests that it is not enough to treat our sexual *partners* with care respect. A sexual ethic of care respect acknowledges the feminist goal from the "view from somewhere different" that women and men re-spect each other's sexual agency and self-definition within a larger social framework of a caring and cooperative community. Within such a community, women and men can begin to define our own particular sexual needs and help each other do the same.

This means that *listening* to the diversity of women's voices is not sufficient for a feminist sexual ethic. I may understand what your particular needs are but do noth-ing to help you pursue them. A feminist sexual ethic of care respect is an *activist* one, because it advocates that I not only attempt to understand the sexual needs of others but also do my best to help fulfill those needs. Thus, a feminist sexual ethic of care respect reinforces the larger feminist project of promoting the sexual agency and self-definition of women in all their multiplicity. Dillon suggests that care respect rec-ommends that we do more than simply not interfere with a particular individual's pursuit of her well-being. We are responsible for making a positive contribution to it. According to Dillon, in doing so we acknowledge the need in each of us for the help and support of others. Dillon writes, "[C]are respect can be seen as connecting individuals together in a community of mutual concern and mutual aid, through an appreciation of individuality and interdependence."[110]

Thus, a sexual ethic of care respect is not limited to personal sexual relations alone but is an ethic that extends outward to individuals and institutions that are a part of one's larger community. Dillon is the first to remark that we will extend care respect to persons in different ways and to varying degrees. We have neither the time, energy, nor resources to understand and promote the well-being of *everyone*; indeed, family and close friends cannot always be cared for in the ways they or we would like. Perhaps more to the point, we cannot promote everyone's well-being even if we restrict our energies solely to promoting everyone's *sexual* well-being; and not everyone will want *us* to help *them* discover their own sexual interests, much less promote or pursue them. What an ethic of care respect does suggest is that we approach all human relationships with the kind of sensitivity to individual context and individual needs that can help guide us in our judgments of whether and how to care for the persons in those relationships. This ethic does not provide a set of abstract principles for making such judgments, nor does it provide the terms and conditions of "world"-traveling that would be applicable to every case. Such abstractions would be antithetical to the appreciation of context and particularity that is definitive of care respect. What this ethic does provide is a framework for treating our sexual partners and understanding others' sexualities in ways that allow them to be the agents and defining subjects of their sexual experience. My claim is that with such an approach, we can better determine whose needs should be met and how than if we assume a moral superiority in deference to the "view from somewhere better," invoke a set of abstract moral principles applicable to all in deference to the "view from nowhere," or assume that all perspectives are of equal value in deference to the "view from everywhere."

For example, I may listen to what your sexual needs are, only to find out that pursuing those needs violates the care respect of other persons that the "view from somewhere different" advocates. An ethic of care respect would be self-defeating if we did not insist that the feminist promotion of the sexual agency and self-definition of others be consistent with an ethic of care respect. Rape, sexual harassment, sexual battery, or other forms of sexual violence against, and intimidation of, women are neither tolerated nor promoted from this point of view, since the encouragement of sexual oppression as well as the oppression itself constitute a violation of the care respect of the one oppressed. On the other hand, a sexual ethic of care respect recommends that we not automatically disdain the sexual pleasures or preferences of others simply because we do not like or agree with them. A sexual ethic of care respect from the "view from somewhere different" expands our worldviews precisely because this perspective does not commit us to a single interpretation of a satisfying sexual life. As a result, such an ethic will be extremely unsatisfying for anyone determined to find a set of moral principles that will prescribe what persons ought and ought not do in every case of sex. Some anonymous sexual partners may share intimate sex; other partners' sexual intimacy will require time and familiarity. For still others, intimacy will not be a prerequisite for safe and satisfying sex at all, while the most exciting sex for some will be *unsafe* sex to which applying standards of care respect would reduce the eroticism. It may also be that the kind of lesbian sado-masochism in which each partner attempts to satisfy the other's particular sexual preferences is *both* power-polarizing sex *and* egalitarian sex. I have been arguing that trying to determine what kind of sex is the "right" sex, by excising the concept of care respect from its application in a caring and cooperative community of difference, forecloses sexual debate and arbitrarily stifles the sexual needs of some in favor of others. As I suggested at the end of chapter 1, adopting the "view from somewhere different" means destabilizing our notions of moral rightness or political correctness toward a more uncertain future that nevertheless has the distinct feminist advantage of freeing oppressed voices to pursue their identity in diversity. In this way my sexual ethic of care respect reflects Raymond Belliotti's "engaged fallibilistic pluralism" and Laurie Shrage's moral pluralism, both of which are neither absolutist nor relativist; rather, these moral perspectives appreciate the ways in which culture and context define the parameters of ethical behavior in ways that make moral judgments meaningful even if they are not universally binding.[111]

It could be argued that this ethic of care respect reinforces the nurturing role that has restricted women to domestic and sexual servitude. Women take care of *others*, but no one takes care of *them*. My suggestion is that we adopt Marjorie Weinzweig's model of "autonomous relating to others," which I introduced in chapter 2. This model requires knowing what we want and enjoy for ourselves, a knowledge gained from the state of personal moral development that Weinzweig calls "autonomous being oneself" in which we choose to act for ourselves alone, not because "we hope that somebody else will take care of us if we act as they wish."[112] This kind of autonomy is meant to limit the advantage often taken of the woman whose identity is so bound up in the needs of others that everyone's needs are met except hers. Yet Weinzweig, like Dillon, recognizes the importance of an active care and concern for others in a world that is composed of interdependent members of *communities*, not of isolated individuals. Thus, Weinzweig advocates the further development of an "autonomous relating to others" in which a woman attempts to understand how her own needs and the needs of others may be met within a community of both shared and competing interests. A woman who develops this way of living recognizes that she is part of a larger community in which the satisfaction of her individual needs will influence, and be influenced by, the pursuit of the needs of others. In this way she can be sympathetic, available, and understanding of others in ways that do not undermine her agency or self-definition. Sexual relationships in which this kind of care respect is mutual can enhance each partners' ability to express her or his individual preferences without forcing those preferences on others or ignoring the preferences of others.[113]

Moreover, from the "view from somewhere different," women's autonomy in an actively caring community includes what Joyce Trebilcot calls "taking responsibility for one's sexuality." Taking responsibility for one's sexuality encourages women's sexual agency and self-definition by asking each woman to reflect on the meaning and value of sexual difference in her life. Trebilcot's responsibility for one's sexuality echoes the "view from somewhere different" when she recommends that women begin to get in touch with the "dissonant, unacceptable, threatening, puzzling aspects of ourselves."[114] In this way women can begin to discover our own sexual needs and appreciate the differences of sexual preference and desire within and among women. Such responsibility implies being sensitive to the ways in which an individual woman's race, class, age, nationality, cultural and family history, and physical ability or appearance shape her sexual life. This responsibility also encourages women to consider in what ways our sexual desires and preferences may be a function of patriarchal rules and standards that have been defined without listening to women's voices. In taking responsibility for their sexuality, women help each other recognize the extent to which women may contribute to, as well as overcome, the oppressive sexual stereotypes outlined in chapter 2. Thus, a sexual ethic of care respect in which each person takes responsibility for her or his sexuality is one that recommends that we acknowledge, understand, and promote the agency and self-definition of a community of persons with a wide variety of sexual experiences, preferences, and desires. In this way individual sexual needs can be reflectively identified in the social context in which they arise and can be met with the active care and concern of a community of persons responsive to those needs.

In summary, a feminist sexual ethic of care respect is an ethic reflective of, and derivable from, the "view from somewhere different." A feminist sexual ethic of care respect recommends that all persons express an active and sensitive concern for sexual difference by advocating care respect not only in our personal sexual relations but also in our attitudes toward the sexual lives of others. Thus, it is an ethic that eschews any notion of a politically correct sexuality that would stifle sexual diversity in deference to the "view from somewhere better" or the "view from nowhere." Nevertheless, it is an ethic that can condemn the sexual exploitation or abuse of women by recognizing sexual oppression as both the failure to respect persons of diverse social locations as equally valuable and the failure to "world"-travel in order to promote the sexual agency and self-definition of others. Instead of deconstructing difference from a "view from everywhere" in which "good" versus "bad" sex no long has any meaning, the "view from somewhere different" constructs a sexual ethic to accommodate difference within the moral parameters of care respect. Within such parameters, individual women can decide for themselves how the erotic figures in their lives, so that their sexuality will have meaning and value for them. Weinzweig's autonomous relating to others insures that women's lives combine caring for themselves and caring for others. Trebilcot's concept of taking responsibility for one's sexuality requires that women understand the context of the eroticization of power from which many of our notions of what counts as good sex springs.

Adopting a feminist ethic of care respect implies not assigning normative status to sexual difference without considering the particular historical and social location in which that difference is practiced. Paula Webster has suggested that many feminists have been afraid to embrace sexual difference simply because difference has traditionally meant deviance and division within the movement; tolerating, much less encouraging, the dominant/submissive sex of lesbian sadomasochism or butch/femme role-playing was believed to splinter feminism by alienating those women for whom a woman-identified sexuality means eschewing power-polarizing sexual roles. Yet Webster strongly contends that "[t]he more we know about the dimensions of our hungers, their finite limits and requirements, the more entitled we may feel to speak of our own wishes and listen with compassion to our friends."[115] By adopting the "view from somewhere different," we recast sexual deviance as one of many different sexual practices, none of which is the object of feminist condemnation without the contextual analysis that the dialectic between gender and sexuality and the sexual ethic of care respect recommend. From this perspective, the bonding, nonpolarized sex of the cultural feminist becomes only one of many sexual practices for which women may take responsibility; such responsibility involves reflecting on the ways in which encouraging bonding and intimacy in women's sexual relationships may reinforce women's subordination to, or debilitating dependence on, our partners. So, too, from the "view from somewhere different," the more polarized sex advocated by some sex radical feminists is understood as one of many avenues of sexual exploration open to women; at the same time, recognizing the dialectical relationship between gender and sexuality means recognizing that radical sexual practices exist within a sexually politicized milieu in which the eroticization of power is notorious for the sexual oppression of women as well as children. Recognizing such possibilities is not "giving in" to the power of the patriarchs. Such recognition is essential if we are to minimize misinterpretations of women's reclamations of erotic power and use them to transcend an oppressive sexual politics and head toward a new vision of feminist sexual liberation.

Conclusion

The "view from somewhere different" is a perspective that recognizes the complexity of normative judgments by refusing to close discussion that would reduce tensions among alternative points of view. This perspective recommends that we attempt to negotiate such tensions so that a diversity of normative voices can be heard. Such negotiation reflects the fact that the "view from somewhere different" approaches issues in feminist philosophy of sex with an appreciation for the dialectic between gender and sexuality, which is itself a relation of tension and instability. Thus, earlier in this chapter I argued that sexuality should be reconstituted as a differentiated category of nonstigmatized sexual variation. From such a perspective, both normal and perverse sex become forms of sexual difference. Within this framework, no sexual preference is advantaged by being "normal," yet quite different normative evaluations of sexual practices remain morally meaningful within a broader context of care respect. Indeed, understanding both the normal and the perverse as two types of sexual difference from the "view from somewhere different" has the added benefit of revealing the ways in which normative judgments about sex may involve pragmatics *and* aesthetics *and* ethics. The "view from somewhere different" recognizes social locations in which our normative judgments about sex will include a variety of value concepts that cannot be easily separated.

I argued that the "view from somewhere different" can reveal the strengths and weaknesses in both cultural and sex radical perspectives on sexual difference. The "view from somewhere different" incorporates the tensions between them into an inclusive feminist philosophy of sex whose ethic is defined in terms of care respect. Cultural feminism's emphasis on the way gender informs sexuality is important for recognizing the patriarchal context in which women's sexual desires and preferences develop. A sex radical's emphasis on the way sexuality informs gender is important for recognizing women's desire to transcend sexual oppression toward a broad-ranging conception of sexual exploration, pleasure, and agency. The "view from somewhere different" recommends that we explore the often tempestuous tensions between these two views in an effort to reflect the complexity and contradiction in much of our thinking about the relationship between gender role–playing and erotic role–playing, between the sexes and sex.

A paradox of liberation is that complete freedom in a world of scarcity and competing self-interests results in conflict; but partial freedom means making decisions favoring some values over others, which also produces conflict. Adopting the "view from somewhere different" means questioning the presupposition that there is some politically correct set of sexual values that one individual or group can define for the rest. By neither ignoring, rejecting, nor transcending difference, the "view from somewhere different" positions us to begin learning how to talk to each other in ways that help mediate conflict but do not ignore the internal tensions of debates over sexual practice.[116]

As feminists, we must be mindful of the ways in which women's attitudes toward sexual difference, from conservative to subversive, are affected by the patriarchal milieu in which they develop. The "view from somewhere different" is itself socially constructed from within this milieu, which will inevitably tend to bias its conceptual and normative frameworks. Feminists should be both sympathetic toward, and suspicious of, that which is made other, different, or outside the status quo, since otherness has been the historically oppressive place of women. Yet as sex radical feminists contend, it would be a mistake to continue to allow male-identified sexual values to command all the attention of women in pursuit of a woman-identified life. By questioning the presupposition that difference is bad, feminists pave the way for a reassessment of sexual difference that can promote the sexual agency and self-definition of all women. From this perspective, we can continue to explore the dialectic between gender and sexuality in the debates over sex work discussed in the next chapter.

4

I Only Do It for the Money

Pornography, Prostitution, and the Business of Sex

Overview

Feminists from a variety of theoretical backgrounds target the sex industry as a paradigm of the institutionalized sexual subordination of women. Many radical feminists contend that dancing in strip bars, working as prostitutes, or posing for pornography reduces women to marketable sexual commodities in a patriarchal environment that legitimizes men's unconditional sexual access to women. Socialist feminists expand on the radical critique of androcentric sexual politics with their own critique of patriarchy's class hierarchies and economic exploitation of women. Many socialist feminists contend that commercial sex workers are primarily driven to the trade by a combination of poverty and inexperience in a discriminatory economic climate and that they tolerate their work in virtue of cultural stereotypes of women as the sexual objects of men. Under such circumstances, many sex workers are exploited by male porn producers and club managers or bullied and abused by photographers and pimps. Similarly, it is charged that young girls are coerced by their parents to have oral or anal sex with each other and adults for pornographic videos or films; and teenage runaways suspicious of social agencies that would return them to abusive parents are easy targets for sweet-talking but dominating pimps.[1] Kidnapping and confinement for the purpose of prostitution are not uncommon, particularly in less industrialized countries with large populations of homeless and destitute women and children. Liberal feminists, who believe women's sexual liberation can be won with women's equal protection under the law, would add that even where prostitution or pornography is legal, it typically remains extremely difficult for sex workers to demand better pay or working conditions or to expose their mistreatment by clients and employers. Poor women of all ethnicities seeking employment comprise a traffic in women who are procured under false pretenses for the purpose of prostitution. In Southeast Asia and the Philippines, "sex tourism" is a thriving industry in which tour operators contract with club owners to provide "hospitality girls" to foreign male visitors and businessmen. Asian mail-order and military brides who are deserted by their husbands often have no other recourse but prostitution.[2]

Feminist critics of the sex industry also point out that rape, bondage, and sexual abuse provide the content for some of the more popular pornographic books, magazines, films, and videos. The most popular visual pornography is that which shows real sex rather than simulated sex; thus, penetration by foreign objects, sexual violence, mutilation, even murder become pornography's cinema verité. As one porn model reported, "I knew the pose was right when it hurt."[3] Some feminists emphasize that wives and daughters are shown pornography by husbands and fathers to teach them the sex men want. Racial stereotypes are exploited in pornography through depictions of black women as untamed sexual animals whipped and chained by white masters or of Asian women as exotic seductresses who are passive in their bondage. Pornography's multi-billion dollar industry, much of which is black-market, combined with prostitution's underground economy make the sex industry attractive to drug dealers and organized criminals who cater to illegal but lucrative market demands. Corrupt police both threaten prostitutes with arrest unless they receive regular "servicing" and accept bribes from customers and pimps.[4]

Thus, many feminists argue that a sex worker determined to support herself and her family but compelled to engage in socially stigmatized and often dangerous work becomes the victim of a patriarchal system that entices her into sex work paying more than she could otherwise make with the same skills; and her fear of legal incrimination combined with the threat of exposure make it difficult for her to get out. Such conditions have prompted ex-prostitutes like Evelina Giobbe to organize WHISPER (Women Hurt in Systems of Prostitution Engaged in Revolt) in order to document "the violence and manipulation used to recruit and trap women in the sex industry."[5]

Moreover, given the pervasiveness and accessibility of strip bars, live sex shows, escort agencies, and adult book shops, including X-rated home video, cable, computer, and telephone service,[6] the sex industry appears well positioned to perpetuate an ideology that all women are the proper sexual subordinates of men, craving whatever humiliation, abuse, or physical violence men are willing to dish out. In the absence of a feminist consciousness that recognizes a patriarchy's often coercive sexual politics, some feminists contend that women depicted in pornography as blissful in their bondage and begging to be brutalized convey the message that any sex can be recreational, pleasurable, and fun *because it is sex*. As Catharine MacKinnon has claimed, "[P]ornography eroticizes and thereby legitimizes forced sex."[7] Women who "choose" to be strippers and prostitutes under economic and psychological duress are mistakenly understood as freely and willingly performing sex work, despite the fact that such work may be the only way they can survive or the only work they see themselves capable of performing. From many feminists' perspectives, such an industry not only degrades individual sex workers from autonomous sexual subjects to exploited sex objects but also degrades all women, reinforcing a prevailing sexist ideology that encourages the toleration and promotion of sexual violence against women.

Women (and children) report that pornography has been used to break down their self-esteem, train them to sexual submission, season them to forced sex, and intimidate them out of a job. Sex offenders have been reported to imitate the violence they read about in porn. Some feminists have suggested that the sex industry is central to a larger system of the intimidation of women through sex that includes sexual harassment, child abuse, wife battering, and rape. Such an image has prompted Susan Brownmiller to comment that "[p]ornography is the undiluted essence of anti-female propaganda" and Robin Morgan to write, "Pornography is the theory, rape is the practice."[8] From this point of view, the high-class call girl is at best the brainwashed victim of internalized, male-identified sexual values; at worst, she is a neurotic and self-serving collaborator in a system of women's sexual subordination, who lives well from the coercion and abuse that her own sex work reinforces but mistakes a career choice to live the good life for the ubiquity of her oppression.

Feminists who are critical of the sex industry and who are otherwise at odds with moral conservatives over political issues such as AIDS, sex education, and reproductive, gay, and lesbian rights have formed an uneasy alliance with the political right against civil libertarians and sex radicals. Various factions of the political left regard attempts to ban pornography or close nude bars as yet another wave of Victorian sexual repression and renewed attacks on the First Amendment. New Right conservatives condemn sexually explicit material as appealing to "the prurient interest," regarding the moral indecency of sex work as threatening the institution of the family and the fragile moral fabric of the country. Yet many feminists are both dubious of the propriety of the traditional patriarch who defines the conservative's "family values" and suspicious of who is chosen to weave the fabric of the conservative's moral community.[9] Therefore, feminists who oppose male-identified sex work as degrading to women are vociferous in their assertion that a condemnation of women's sexual subordination is neither a condemnation of sex itself nor a political platform in favor of sexual decency over obscenity. In this vein, some feminists have taken great pains to draw a conceptual and moral distinction between "erotica" and "pornography" to permit, if not applaud, the creation of a sex industry that would produce egalitarian, nonsexist, sexually explicit material.[10] Other feminists have rejected this distinction as failing to recognize the essential male dominance that comprises all sexually explicit material produced under conditions of patriarchy. Andrea Dworkin claims that "in the male sexual lexicon, which is the vocabulary of power, erotica is simply high-class pornography: better produced, better conceived, better executed, better packaged, designed for a better class of consumer . . . but both are produced by the same system of sexual values and both perform the same sexual service."[11] From this perspective, any distinction between erotica and porn collapses, since the patriarchal sex depicted in either case constitutes the degradation and violation of women. As Catharine MacKinnon writes, "In pornography, the violence *is* the sex. The inequality is the sex" (MacKinnon's italics).[12]

Despite such differences, feminists critical of the sex industry are united in their suspicion of a multi-billion-dollar commercial enterprise that profits from women's sexual objectification but defends the private use and public expression of women's sexuality in the name of a less repressed erotic life. Especially for radical feminists, who regard the male appropriation of women's sexual and reproductive life as pivotal to women's oppression, what is proffered as sexual liberation is all too often equivalent to men's sexual freedom to control women, thereby repressing, if not silencing, women's voices as girlfriends, wives, mothers, and wage earners. Indeed, some feminists have suggested that both conservative and liberal male hierarchies conspire to keep women oppressed by simultaneously telling every woman that she should be sexually subordinate to one man in marriage and that she should be sexually available to any man who wants her: the classic double message to the "good" girl who is "best" when being "bad."[13]

All of the above suggests that there is substantial evidence to support the claim that the sex industry is a paradigm of the institutionalized sexual subordination of women. However, from both within and without the sex industry, women have been organizing to change the image and conditions of the sex worker and her work. Some feminists note that violent pornography comprises a relatively small percentage of the total amount of sexually explicit materials on the market and that pornography is increasingly bought by heterosexual women who have the financial and political bargaining power in their relationships with men to demand a type of pornography that suits their own sexual tastes. From this perspective, feminists claim that women ought to be able to enjoy pornography without at the same time conveying the message that women like being abused. Lesbians have become much more visible producers and consumers of woman-identified pornography in an effort to provide the lesbian community with its own alternative for erotic arousal. From this point of view, given the variety of sexual styles portrayed in pornography and available through prostitution, sex work can liberate women who are not in the trade to explore their own sexual styles and to learn new ones. Indeed, some women in the sex trade contend that if a woman is given the money and the permission to use prostitutes, she will.[14]

Many strippers and prostitutes report that they enjoy the money, the flexibility, and the independence that their work offers. Many of them are neither pimped, poor, nor wildly promiscuous, but working women with their own preferred clients, hours, and bosses. Such sex workers report that they are not coerced, abused, or mistreated, although they acknowledge that these are some of the hazards of the profession. They contend that allowing prostitutes to file criminal and civil charges against their clients, along with stricter enforcement of fair wages and working conditions for strippers and porn actresses, would greatly reduce the risks typically associated with their work.

What these sex workers demand are their rights as workers to legal protection and the negotiation of the terms and conditions of their work. As women who advocate financial independence, sexual self-determination, and protection against sexual abuse for all women, they consider themselves feminists as well as sex workers who acknowledge the intimidation and abuse of sex workers worldwide but who reject feminists' and moral conservatives' identification of all sex workers as victims. From this perspective, if prostitution gives a woman the financial independence to choose what to do with her life, feminists who value women's sexual agency and self-definition must not condemn women for pursuing sex work. Therefore, sex workers are skeptical of feminists whose apparent moral and practical insensitivity to the diverse daily needs of individual sex workers makes them look like the same reactionary sexual puritans that feminists disavow, especially if romance novels, music videos, and fashion magazines may be equal if not greater culprits in the perpetuation of women's sexual oppression. From this viewpoint, attacking the sex industry in order to save its victims is precisely the kind of patronizing moralism that feeds a patriarchy's obsession with defining women's sexuality in men's terms.[15]

Sex radical feminists join ranks with sex workers when radicals accuse feminists critical of the sex industry of reinforcing the traditional heterosexual values of monogamy, intimacy, and romance that stripping, pornography, and prostitution flatly reject. From a sex radical perspective, feminists who are unable or unwilling to confront their own sexuality and who see little if anything that is not degrading about sex work under patriarchy are the natural allies of a sexual conservatism that condemns the anonymous, recreational, pleasure-seeking sex in sex work. Moreover, many feminists from a variety of theoretical perspectives believe that such an alliance results in the association of feminism with an antisex moralism that makes feminism unappealing to women who consider themselves both politically liberated *and* sexually adventurous.[16]

For a feminist philosopher of sex interested in approaching the topic of sex work from the "view from somewhere different" introduced in chapter 1, speculating about whether or how the sex industry may contribute to women's sexual liberation is no simple matter. Feminists appear to side with what would otherwise be their political opponents and disagree vehemently among themselves. Some liberal feminists want to abolish current discriminatory prostitution law and protect the legal rights of sex workers; others would abolish prostitution altogether and reform those laws that limit women's economic and political access. Some socialist feminists consider pornography an ugly by-product of capitalism that is best gotten rid of by a socialist economy of moral egalitarianism and community responsibility, while others see a new vision of pornographic eroticism brought about by men's and women's renewed acquaintance with nonalienating labor.[17] Radical feminists differ on the distinction between pornography and erotica. Antiporn radical feminists differ over whether pornography is primarily about violence or about sex and whether sex education, censorship, or the filing of civil sex discrimination suits are the best solutions.[18] While most feminists find at least some form of sexually explicit material unobjectionable, this stance typically disallows s/m porn and depictions of consensual pedophilia. Such a stance consequently draws the ire of sex radicals, who grow tired of defending their sexual difference against the charge of false consciousness.

The variety of opinion within the sex industry is equally wide-ranging. Male and female porn producers (and feminists) have remarked that pornography often parodies itself and pokes fun at antiporn feminists. How else, they ask, could one interpret the 1978 *Hustler* cover photo depicting a woman's torso and legs being run through a meat grinder with the caption, "We will no longer hang women up like pieces of meat"?[19] Women who are managers, lawyers, and publicists of porn producers often find feminist antipornography rhetoric irrelevant to what *they* experience: women and men signing contracts to work long hours, doing strenuous work that not everyone has either the stamina or the ability to do, and being well paid for it. These industry professionals ask what the feminist charge of degradation could possibly mean in such contexts other than that sex for pure pleasure and public enjoyment is indecent. The searing description by Linda Marchiano, a.k.a. Linda Lovelace, of her coercion and abuse throughout the making of the film *Deep Throat* is in stark contrast to the reports of porn models and actresses who attest to agreeable directors, steady incomes, and the chance to feel glamorous in front of a camera. Some activist prostitutes reject feminist support that requires them to leave prostitution, regarding prostitution as one of many legitimate occupations that women should have the opportunity to pursue.[20] Other prostitutes and ex-prostitutes regard poverty and women's refusal of poverty as the cause and attraction of prostitution. From this perspective, prostitution is a last resort in the absence of dignified and economically sustaining work. Until such work is available, such women advocate the recognition of prostitutes as legal workers. As Nina Lopez-Jones remarks, "We are not interested in legitimizing prostitution, but in legitimizing all prostitute women."[21] Still other ex-prostitutes are much more adamant in their condemnation of prostitution. They perceive all prostitutes as victims and reject decriminalization of prostitution as its solution, since such a measure would, in their opinion, perpetuate "the lie that turning tricks is sexual pleasure or agency for women."[22] In addition, nonpolitical, mostly silent sex workers who simply want to be left alone to support themselves and their families often find feminists' and prostitutes' rights organizations inevitably serving white, middle-class interests and needs. From this perspective, using sex work to subvert the sexual status quo presumes a political platform and power base that women of color in the industry and poorer sex workers, particularly those from less industrialized nations, simply do not have.[23]

Legal responses to sex work as well as research attempts to locate a causal connection between pornography and violence against women are similarly inconsistent. While the 1970 U.S. Commission on Obscenity and Pornography concluded that there was no significant correlation between the use of pornography and crimes against women, the 1986 final report by the Attorney General's Commission on Pornography cited evidence of increased sexual violence against women due to men's exposure to violent sexually explicit material. The commission further claimed that such exposure encourages belief in the myth that women want to be raped. However, questions have since arisen concerning the research methods used for such reports, indicating that the 1970 commission tended to rely on surveys whose data was derived from exposure to nonviolent pornography, while the 1986 commission used surveys by researchers most of whom exposed their subjects only to violent pornography. Still other data suggest that harmful effects can result from pornography that is either violent or nonviolent in its depictions. To further complicate matters, published accounts by researchers and other academics suggest that surveys on how people react to pornographic material may be skewed by the artificiality of the surveys' surroundings, the undetectable duplicity of the respondents, and the fact that what respondents may *say* they will do may not reflect how they would in fact *behave*.[24]

In 1983, Minneapolis passed an antipornography civil rights ordinance drafted by Catharine MacKinnon and Andrea Dworkin that would allow women to sue pornographers for damages that women claimed were the result of using pornography.

While the ordinance was drafted at the request of the Minneapolis city council, it was ultimately declared unconstitutional, as it was perceived to have the effect of illegally censoring freedom of expression.[25] Gail Pheterson reports that in some countries, like Norway, pornography is censored but prostitution is decriminalized, while in the United States pornography flourishes and prostitution is illegal.[26] Nevada law allows prostitution in townships of 250,000 or less, yet regulations prohibit prostitutes from socializing in many public places after business hours. In most states it is not a crime to *be* a prostitute or to have sex *with* a prostitute, but it is a crime to do any business *as* a prostitute or *for the purposes of* prostitution, such as solicit, pimp, or pander. Since pimping is defined as "living off the earnings of a prostitute," a sex worker's elderly aunt, boyfriend, or baby-sitter can be arrested for pimping. Ironically, the state may collect fines from arrests and not be so charged. Feminists argue that such laws are designed to protect customers, who can be accused of no crime simply by being found with a hooker.[27]

Instead of trying to locate a single politically correct voice from within the sex industry, social research, feminism, or the law, I suggest that we adopt the "view from somewhere different" to understand some of the complexity of a commerce in sex whose culture both rewards and punishes women for being the sexual objects of male desire. In this way we can move the dialogue away from the polarization that arises from attempts to reduce and not embrace the tensions that exist among sex workers and feminists alike. My claim in this chapter is that stalemate in feminist dialogue about the nature and value of sex work is inevitable if we require that sex work taken up for profit or pleasure be degrading to women. I will argue that one way to make progress toward understanding whether and how sex work is constructed in the lives of individual women is to reconceptualize a sex worker's life in terms of a dialectical relation between commodified object and active subject, which allows us to view sex work both in terms of women's sexual subordination and in terms of women's sexual liberation from oppressive sexual norms.

For those sex workers who view themselves or would like to view themselves as the sexual subjects of a self-determined life, feminists' accusations of victimization or patriarchal brainwashing appear misplaced. Because the only alternative explanation for the accusation of degradation appears to sex workers to be one of sexual indecency, and because feminists have aligned themselves with moral conservatives on the issue of sex work (albeit for different reasons), feminists who lodge such charges are inevitably stamped with the moniker of sexual puritan. Furthermore, because they fail to appreciate the subject/object dialectic of sex work, feminists critical of the sex industry appear to condemn sex workers who are the true victims of coercion and abuse to a life in which they cannot transcend their subordination by men.

On the other hand, too strong an emphasis on a sex worker's subjectivity ignores the ideological, economic, and legal constraints of patriarchy within which the sex worker plies her trade. My aim is to show the interplay of the subject/object dialectic within sex work and to argue that such an interplay helps explain the apparently contradictory claims that women and men inside and outside the industry make about sex work. I contend that not to acknowledge this interplay forestalls discussion and polarizes debate on the meaning and morality of sex work; and I argue that to acknowledge this interplay is to reaffirm an appreciation for the dialectic between gender and sexuality that recognizes the contradiction, complexity, and diversity in the sexual lives of women and men.

In the following pages I describe some of the variety of sex workers and their work. I use this analysis to examine what some feminists mean when they say that sex work is degrading to women. I argue that this ascription of degradation risks investing an undesirable sexual puritanism and moral condescension in many of the legitimate objections feminists raise against sex work. I also contend that viewing sex work as degrading tends to universalize questions of degradation that are context-sensitive and precludes ascriptions of agency or autonomy to sex workers with which many may resist or transcend their subordinate status as dehumanized sexual commodities. I then examine the claim of some sex workers and sex radical feminists that sex work can be pleasurable, profitable, and liberating for women. I argue that unless sex work is situated within a larger cultural framework circumscribed by patriarchal constraints on women's sexuality, the freedom of sex workers to define the terms and conditions of their work is a more restricted one than many sex workers or sex radicals might think. I suggest that understanding sex work as a dialectical relation between commodified object and active subject can better represent women's participation in the sex industry than either anti-industry or sex radical perspectives alone; and I argue that this dialectic reflects the "view from somewhere different" by describing women's sexuality in terms that are neither exclusively oppressive nor unilaterally liberating. In the closing section I show how a feminist sexual ethic of care respect that appreciates the dialectic between gender and sexuality can help feminists and sex workers understand the strengths of each others' positions and find common ground in our efforts to secure the sexual agency and self-definition of all women.

Sex Work, Degradation, and the Sale of Women's Bodies

> I may be missing something, but I don't see a lot of women lawyers, feminist or otherwise, selling their asses on the street or looking for a pornographer with a camera in order to fulfill their sexual agency and I don't think it is because they are sexually repressed.
>
> —Catharine A. MacKinnon, *Feminism Unmodified:*
> *Discourses on Life and Law*

Any normative evaluation of the sex industry is a complex one, made so by the variety of work that is performed and by the diversity of people who perform it. In the following section I describe some of that variety in an effort to avoid definitions of sex work and sex workers that marginalize or silence some of the voices within the industry. I also examine some of the ways in which the sex industry may mirror sexual relations purported to be of a noncommercial sort, in order to question the severe dichotomy between sex work and nondegrading sex that some might claim. I will then discuss some of the difficulties with arguing that sex work is degrading to women, as a way of previewing the subject/object dialectic that I believe better represents the variety of sex workers and their work.

Conceptual Issues

Stripping, erotic dancing, prostitution, and pornographic film acting or photo modeling are the most common and best-known forms of work within the sex industry; they also comprise the sex work most often discussed by feminists. The picture becomes immediately complicated, however, by the variety and hierarchy within the professions themselves. Is the removal of a stripper's costume total or partial? Is it done at a private party or a public club? Does it include table dancing where customers are in close proximity? Does it include stage dancing in which the dancer performs with more theatrical autonomy? Does the strip show include a live sex show? Is the sex heterosexual or homosexual, group or in pairs, s/m or vanilla? Who owns the club, and how are dancers hired?[28] Is the prostitute a streetwalker or a call girl? Teenager or adult? Beaten or befriended? Part-time or full-time? Man or woman?[29] Is the prostitute's work in a private home, motel room, massage parlor, car? Does the work include bondage or discipline? Does the work involve intercourse, fellatio, or only masturbation, the "hand finish" of some massage parlors?[30] Does the work require genital contact with a sex partner, some contact, or none? Is the pornographic work for film, video, magazine layout, computer digitalization? Is the actress also a writer or director? Is the film sex simulated or real? Do we see her bound? Do we see her face? Do we see her unclothed? Is she Anglo or a woman of color? Young or old? There is also a debatable class hierarchy within the industry, in which porn modeling or private club dancing is at the top and prostitution is at the bottom. Within prostitution itself, expensive diplomatic escorts rank high and streetwalkers rank low. In Western industrialized nations, women of color tend to be concentrated at the lower end of the hierarchy, often comprising the majority of streetwalkers in any given city but the minority of prostitutes over all. Streetwalkers in less industrialized nations will rank lower than women of color in countries with greater capital incomes.[31]

My point is that even when we limit a moral analysis of sex work to just one profession within the industry, this limitation does not guarantee that we will capture all of the variety within that profession. The social location of any one sex worker will affect how she sees herself; how club managers, customers, or porn producers treat her; how feminists understand her circumstances; and how society stigmatizes her, and all of these factors will affect any assessment of the "degradation" of her work. One of my aims in this chapter is to fill out the general charge that sex work is degrading to women, by supplying a variety of examples from the sex industry to illustrate both the charge and any responses to it.[32]

This is not to suggest that there is no overlap across genres. Strippers service private customers in hotel rooms after club performances, porn models do table dancing, call girls get hired for magazine layouts. On the other hand, the hierarchy in the sex industry that I mentioned earlier can make it an insult to call a stripper a whore, whereas prostitutes often refer to themselves and each other as whores as a positive declaration of their work.[33] Indeed, some erotic dancers who refuse to dance "totally nude" regard their dancing as much in aesthetic terms as sexual ones.[34] Some sex workers regard pornographic work as safer and more familiar than the street, while others report abuses by photographers and producers that rival the exploitation and coercion of pimps, customers, and cops. Some feminists condemn pornography as more oppressive to women than prostitution, since porn models and actresses typically have no control over the distribution of their work.[35]

The term "pornography" comes from the Greek *pornographos*, meaning the writing or depiction (*graphos*) of the life and manner of prostitutes (*porneia*) and their patrons.[36] Andrea Dworkin has contended that these sexually explicit depictions were part of an entrenched institution of female sexual slavery in ancient Greece. Gayle Rubin, on the other hand, finds no evidence for the claim that such depictions are in any way historically or teleologically linked to modern pornography.[37] The sexually explicit depictions likely served as aphrodisiacs for patrons in the houses of prostitution of ancient times and could be used by prostitutes to advertise their particular services. This sales technique is given an ironic twist when contemporary pornography, often depicting violence or abuse, is used to show prostitutes what customers want. Evelina Giobbe argues that since much of the contemporary pornography shown to prostitutes by customers is of various sexual perversions, many of them dangerous or painful when attempted, prostitutes who may be averse to such sex are simply raped.[38] Rubin would argue nevertheless that this is a far cry from suggesting that pornography is part of the history of ancient Greek sexual experience designed to exploit, debase, and violate women in forced sex.

Despite oppositional hierarchies within the sex industry, when California defines prostitution as "a lewd act in exchange for money or other consideration" and strippers who perform live sex shows are the equivalent of live pornography, the lines between pornography, prostitution, and stripping become extremely thin. Sarah Wynter flatly rejects all conceptual and moral distinctions between prostitution, pornography, and stripping, since she believes that all sex work reduces women to commodities for the pleasure and profit of men. The only descriptive difference she does acknowledge is that "in pornography there is a permanent record of the woman's abuse."[39] Diana Russell rejects the expressions "porn actress" or "porn model" because in her opinion, pornography is just prostitution in front of a camera.[40] On the other hand, Robert Stoller reports that most performers he has interviewed disagree with Russell's assessment. They point out that their sex is with other performers, not customers, so that their partners are not hiring them to do their performing. All performers are hired by some third party, and all parties know that the performers are acting, *especially* when the sex is not simulated. They also appreciate the circumstances and special skills involved, such as men ejaculating in artificial settings, long hours of frontal or anal penetration, and complex dramas of bondage and discipline and/or oral sex under hot lights and in uncomfortable positions.[41]

While there is considerable conceptual disagreement over the various categories of sex work, there are a number of striking similarities between sexual relations outside the industry and commercial sex work. As Alan Soble has pointed out, sex in exchange for money (or some other consideration) could describe dates, marriage, even sex therapy.[42] Indeed, radical feminists have regarded prostitution as the paradigm of the sexual subordination of women to men in any context: women "sell" their sexuality daily, in exchange for dinner and a movie, for a promotion, for financial security and social status. From this perspective, if prostitutes accept paintings, flashy cars, and apartments for sex, how different are they from man-hunting social climbers? At least, so sex workers say, prostitutes are *honest* about the exchange and can say no or send men away in the absence of coercive pimps, who eerily imitate the role of demanding husbands. Thus, it is claimed that what makes prostitution especially threatening to "respectable" women is that it reveals the fundamentally commercial nature of sex.[43]

For example, Frederich Engels was convinced that a bourgeois wife differs from a prostitute only "in that she does not let out her body on piecework as a wageworker, but sells it once and for all into slavery."[44] Sex workers, like wives or girlfriends, can be exploited, abused, and threatened by men, especially if women want to end their relationships with them. A sex worker, like a wife or a girlfriend, can appear to "choose" her life yet still be coerced into sex because she has no other alternative for men's acceptance or support. A prostitute may not be dependent on a single man for making a living, but she is dependent on men, whose fortunes turn with the vagaries of the economy. As one prostitute reports, "If the stock market falls, it's just like any other business."[45] Some prostitutes' rights organizations contend that sex workers are stigmatized, even criminalized, because their efforts at true financial independence from men, unlike the social climber's financial parasitism, are a threat to men's oppression of women.[46] Therefore, if feminists wish to condemn sex work as degrading to women, we must also look critically at our more traditional economic and social institutions whose sexual exchange for goods and services may be degrading to women as well.

Without a raised consciousness regarding the oppressive nature of heterosexuality under patriarchy, prostitutes remain the "bad girls" who perform the dirty, indecent, promiscuous sex that "good" girlfriends/wives cannot or will not do in order to retain their "good girl" status in the eyes of men. As Gail Pheterson points out, the "bad girl" stigma is a stigma of *blame* for her abuse, *shame* for her sexuality, and *punishment* for her independence.[47] Thus, the good girl/bad girl standard for women's sexuality only exacerbates the alienation of prostitutes from wives or girlfriends by teaching good girls what will happen to them if they do not toe the line. Yet some prostitutes contend that what men really want is for their wives to be whores, the virgin nymphomaniacs of some pornography, who represent the impossibly simultaneous good girl/bad girl discussed in chapter 2. According to one sex worker, if a prostitute could perform the sex her male clients asked for, while successfully pretending to be in love with them, she would be rich.[48] Prostitutes often see themselves as therapists for their customers' problems with their wives, while wives condemn prostitutes for pursuing a line of work that they believe encourages errant husbands and panders to, even promotes, men's worst sexual fantasies. Such condemnation is only reinforced by men who bring their wives with them when they visit prostitutes, to coerce their wives into doing what they must pay prostitutes to do.[49]

Given the diversity and overlap within the sex industry and the complex relationship between the sex industry and other social relations, I propose using the expression "sex worker" to refer to those persons whose sexuality is a commodity for the commercial exchange often referred to by workers themselves as the sex *trade*.[50] The extent to which women (and men) make a *business* out of trading sex for personal gain is the extent to which we can call their sexual relations "sex work." Sex workers are conceptually distinguishable from others who work in the sex industry, such as accountants, lawyers, producers, directors, writers, managers, or pimps, whose sexuality is not for sale but who engage in the production and distribution of sex. Sex workers can also be producers or pimps, but they are not to be conceptually confused with them. Thus, "sex work" can be understood as the commercial exchange within the sex trade of the sexuality of the worker for some other commodity of value. This expression alone does not decide whether the work is that of entrepreneur, employee, or unwilling victim nor whether the work is done for $100 an hour or simply to stave off starvation. Nor does the expression "sex work" presume the gender, race, sexual preference, or other social location of the sex worker. In other words, sex work does not presume freedom or force, pleasure or pain, respect or humiliation. Work, as Karl Marx has reminded us, can be impoverishing, alienating, or exploitative for some, humanizing or liberating for others.

Politicized sex workers have often advocated using the expression "sex work" to advance the view that prostitution, stripping, and pornographic posing are simply occupations deserving of employment protection under the law, equal to that of other occupations. Many sex workers report that while making an independent living as a woman is difficult enough, taking money *for sex* stigmatizes sex workers most. Emphasizing the *work* in sex work is thought to reduce this stigma, by eliminating the negative connotations many people associate with words like "whore" or "stripper." From this perspective, if sex workers have more trouble than other working women in determining the terms and conditions of their work, it is the *sex* in sex work that is the reason.

Yet sex work is attractive to many women who are sex workers precisely because sex is a powerful tool for women's economic independence. As one prostitute has said, "The erotic image is our bread and butter."[51] Some politicized sex workers refer to themselves proudly as "bad girls" and "whores" as a way of subverting the negative connotations typically attached to them and announcing their pride in exchanging sex for money. Indeed, as I mentioned earlier, the fact that a woman's sexuality can be a source of freedom from dependence on any one man may be one reason for the stigma of sex work.

Consequently, feminists who want to convince sex workers that feminists are not sexual puritans must convince sex workers that we are worried about women's potential *subordination* through sex, not the (purported) indecency of tainting sex with anonymity and money. Feminists who are skeptical of sex work fear that it makes the degradation of women *sexy* and hence natural, desirable, pleasurable, and defensible. Yet in claiming this, even feminists who presume that only some kinds of sex work are degrading appear to complain about *sex* and so alienate many sex workers from the start. Because I wish to explore the tensions between sex worker and feminist concerns, my conceptual emphasis will remain balanced between the two terms "work" and "sex." This approach is in keeping with my thesis that the work itself comprises a dialectic between sexual subject and object that both affords and explains the variety of interpretations of it.

Normative Criticisms

The feminist complaint that sex work is degrading to women is typically both a complaint about work that degrades women who participate in the industry and a complaint about the degradation of all women. The degradation is typically described in terms of the commerce in sex in which the sex worker engages: sex work is degrading because the sex worker treats herself, and allows others to treat her, as a commodity to be bought and sold on the open market. Evelina Giobbe characterizes the sex industry as one in which "women's or children's bodies are bought, sold, or traded for sexual use and abuse." Diana Russell and Laura Lederer remark that "even the most banal pornography objectifies women's bodies."[52] According to this view, the sex worker does not treat herself, nor is she treated by others, as a person whose feelings, interests, and needs are worthy of respect, equal to that of any other person. She is treated as a mere body, toy, tool, prop, or pet to be used and abused by the men who purchase her. Not only does her work define her as the proper sexual subordinate of men, but her work, insofar as she appears to choose it, encourages and reinforces the view that her only pleasure is to service men and that what she wants and needs from men is their use and abuse. From this perspective, because sex work is situated within a patriarchal milieu whose sexual ideology is already one that defines women in terms of our sexual availability to men, sex work only reinforces the view that all women, even those who would not choose it, wish to devote our lives to the sexual service of men. Feminists argue that such false beliefs about women not only are degrading in themselves but also inevitably result in the sexual exploitation and violation of women, regarded as the unconditional sexual objects of men. Thus, the complaint that sex work degrades women is both a deontological and a teleological complaint: sex work is wrong per se, because it is degrading to (all) women; and sex work is wrong because it has harmful consequences that are the result of degradation, in that sex work encourages the exploitation of women and promotes the tolerance and exercise of violence against women.

However, one of the ways that feminists may forestall open debate on the morality of sex work is by *requiring* that sex work be degrading to women. Helen Longino defines pornography as "the degrading and demeaning portrayal of the role and status of the human female." According to this view, by portraying herself in demeaning ways, a pornographic model or actress performs work that is degrading to all women. Andrea Dworkin and Catharine MacKinnon define pornography in their Minneapolis ordinance as "the graphic, sexually explicit subordination of women in pictures and/or words." Sarah Wynter defines prostitution as "a type of commercial sexual exploitation and abuse which reduces women to commodities for the pleasure and profit of men."[53]

The negative normative content of sex work need not be a function of defining sex work as degrading; some feminists argue that the degradation is implicit in the patriarchal context in which the sex work is practiced. For example, Laurie Shrage posits that cultural settings specify the meaning and value of our activities. Thus, depending on the culture in which commercial sex work is practiced, such work may or may not be degrading to women. However, according to Shrage, in contemporary Western industrialized nations like the United States, prostitution is necessarily degrading to women in virtue of the patriarchal culture in which it is practiced. She states that "if [contemporary Western] prostitution were sufficiently transformed to make it completely nonoppressive to women, though commercial transactions involving sex might still exist, prostitution as we now know it would not."[54] Thus, Shrage notes that in a contemporary Western society imbued with patriarchal values, prostitution differs from marriage in that marriage does not necessarily involve relations of dominance and subordination.

One difficulty with these approaches is that they invest prostitution and pornography with negative normative content that closes the question as to whether sex work under current patriarchal constraints is degrading to women. Sex workers whose lived experience is that of freedom, mobility, and pride in their work are denied any philosophical foundation from which to contest such a view. While Shrage admits to an important cultural and historical incommensurability when it comes to sex work across cultures, she does not apply a similar incommensurability to the multicultural, diversely experienced community of women living in the United States. Indeed, she states that "the meaning of sex work in American society *is determined by* sexist, classist, and racist ideologies" (my italics) in a way that the meaning of sex work in social contexts absent those ideologies may not be. Shrage is certainly correct about much of contemporary American sex work; but to claim that sex work is necessarily oppressive to the women who practice it not only assumes that her interpretive categories for analyzing American prostitution cover every possible case but also denies prostitutes the ability to conceive of their sex work as in any way liberating to them.[55]

Moreover, when sex work is *defined* as degrading to women, feminists cannot ask the questions "Is there anything wrong with prostitution?" or "Is pornography degrading?" without being redundant. Such definitions also preclude discussions of gay male pornography and are "conveniently expandable," to use Gayle Rubin's phrase, to fit the most violent or the least sexually suggestive material, making "pornography" a buzz-word for any sexual depictions that feminists find objectionable.[56]

Many feminists have defended their definitions of sex work on the grounds that they are only referring to *one type* of sex work. The sex work performed to produce "erotica," for example, would not be degrading to women because, in Gloria Steinem's words, such work is produced to depict "a mutually pleasurable, sexual expression between people who have enough power to be there by positive choice."[57] Individual models and actresses can be degraded in their sex work by producers heaping abuse on actresses' performances of "erotica" as well as "pornography," so Steinem is referring here to the degradation of women as a class through degrading depictions of sex. However, much of the sexually explicit material to which many feminists object simply depicts women happily serving men's sexual needs, most of which appear totally self-serving but none of which are expressly coercive, violent, or abusive. Such scenes are thought to be objectionable in that they depict women as mere sex objects of male lust, not as the sexual subjects of a self-determined life. For example, Diana Russell and Laura Lederer contend that even nonviolent pornography can encourage rape by depicting women "not . . . as human beings but as things."[58] Nevertheless, such pornography can just as readily evoke the "sensuous and voluptuous" sexual interest that would satisfy Eva Kittay's condition on erotica as the "lewd or prurient" interests she identifies with porn. Moreover, this latter description of pornography does not meet Steinem's condition that pornography be material whose message is "violence, dominance, and conquest."[59] Indeed, if sexual subservience is part of a woman's self-determined plan of seduction, she might wonder where to locate the objection of degradation.

Suppose, as some philosophers have suggested, that we add to mutual consent and mutual pleasure an *equality* of partnership that requires that the materials depict people satisfying each other.[60] Then, however, the requirement is too strong for still photographs, which necessarily describe only one instant or aspect in the life of their subjects (Do respectful lovers always and simultaneously respond to the needs of each other? How would a still photograph show this?); and the requirement is too weak to preclude s/m porn, which antiporn feminists reject but which, according to sex radical feminists, can depict consent, mutuality, *and* moral equality, just not equality of sexual roles. Kittay argues that since many viewers of s/m porn cannot see the moral equality that the practitioners promise, the sex depicted is illegitimate.[61] However, as I suggested earlier, moral equality is difficult to show even in more vanilla contexts; and Kittay's view confines s/m sex work to an interpretation solely in terms of a patriarchal ideology that eroticizes power in oppressive, not parodying or liberating, terms. Dominatrixes who do s/m work primarily because it pays well report that they are not aroused by it, much less oppressed by it, while others say that they can happily combine business with pleasure.[62] Alan Soble suggests that a specifiable set of internal and external cues can help us distinguish depictions of lovemaking from those of pure sex, or consensual from coercive s/m sex. However, one difficulty with Soble's suggestion is that if the same cues are not shared by all viewers, or if we cannot be sure that the intended cues are received, then we are as much at a loss for one single, appropriate interpretation as before. I agree that if feminists do not want to condemn all sex work, we need ways to distinguish the degrading from the nondegrading sort; but sexual and social bias, institutional setting, and personal taste and moral judgment will all have an effect on what is to count, for individual men and women, as legitimate sex and legitimate sex work. In short, the context in which the sex work occurs is just as important as, if not more important than, the content of the work itself.[63]

Helen Longino recognizes the importance of context when she points out that sexually explicit depictions of women being degraded can be used as educational tools to help us understand the harm that pornography does (Longino's "moral realism"). Therefore, Longino adds, for sexually explicit material to degrade women, there must be "no suggestion that this sort of [degrading] treatment of others is inappropriate." Longino proposes that women are degraded in pornography when they are depicted as women whose sole purpose *ought* to be their sexual subordination to men, and women whose sole pleasure *ought to* consist in serving men's every sexual whim no matter how destructive or abusive. That is, the degradation must not just be depicted in pornography for it to be objectionable; it must also be *endorsed*.[64]

The strength of Longino's argument rests on pornography's ability to both depict and endorse degradation. Exactly what does it mean to depict degradation and endorse it? Judith M. Hill makes the important point that being degraded requires more than being subordinated, exploited, or abused: degradation implies that the victim *deserves* the treatment received—that she is perceived, by either her tormentors, herself, or the public at large, as *unworthy* of anything better.[65] This analysis is consistent with Longino's claim that the subordination of women in pornography is degrading, because it is endorsed as well as depicted. Given this analysis of degradation, however, it is unclear how a photographer might unambiguously depict such an endorsement on the part of either the subordinators or the subordinated, or instill such a perception in the viewer. A woman photographed as appearing pleased to be sexually accessible to any man who wants her does not alone constitute her own or anyone else's perception that she is subordinating her sexuality to dominating men or that she is worthy only of degradation. Indeed, such a photograph is consistent with a woman's initiating such encounters after an honest and self-reflective assessment of what sexually excites her most. Moreover, this image is also consistent with the subject's belief that if she does not appear to enjoy herself and mollify those who would gratify themselves at her expense, only worse (and equally undeserved) treatment will follow. Those whom she services may simply have targeted her as an easy mark, to vent their frustration at work or to fulfill a gang initiation requirement; but this is not equivalent to their contemptuous abuse of her because she (or any woman) deserves it. Thus, the degradation must be inferred by the viewer, not from any pleasure taken in her accessibility, subordination, or abuse but from the depiction of a woman whose sole purpose is to serve men sexually. Since it is not inherently degrading to depict a woman acting with a single purpose (imagine Mother Teresa serving the poor), the degradation must be inferred from the depiction of a woman whose sole purpose is (hetero)sexual service. Consequently, some feminists have argued that depicting unconditional female sexual service is degrading to women, even if depicted as initiated by women, because *such depictions are situated in a patriarchal culture that endorses the sexual subordination of women*, reinforcing the sexual abuse and exploitation of, and violence against, women in that culture.

However, such arguments must be advanced without assuming that sex work subordinates women and without requiring that all women who work in the porn industry contribute to the degradation of women; otherwise, we beg the question of the moral status of sex work in *any* context. Moreover, such arguments need not claim that all heterosexual sex is degrading to women, since feminists can specify more liberating contexts within patriarchy in which nondegrading sex occurs. While some antiporn feminists appear to adopt the view that heterosexual sex and violence are synonyms in a misogynist society, not all feminists critical of the sex industry agree. One result of such a condemnation of heterosexual sex has been the alienation from feminism of sex workers and of women outside the industry who regard such an attitude as repressively antimale and antipleasure.

Nevertheless, even if the sexual subordination of women is depicted in a patriarchal society that endorses it, it is still unclear whether or how pornography and, by implication, pornographic modeling or acting recommends or endorses women's degradation. In the same theater in a single cultural setting, some people may see a recommendation of women's subordination and a "come hither" look in a pornography model's smile, especially if she is only doing what a viewer expects; others may see only sex that outrages, disgusts, or disturbs them. Still others may simply enjoy an unanticipated arousal, oblivious to any social messages about women that the depictions might send. Depicting me happily indulging in large quantities of raw liver without any suggestion that this is inappropriate does not itself count as an endorsement of the indulgence. The saturating repetition of this message in a culture already predisposed to encourage the eating of raw meat probably *would* count as an endorsement, even propaganda, but then any objection to the depiction would be an objection to the cultural ideology and its gastronomic attitudes, not the depiction itself. Using this analogy, attacking pornography is only attacking the symptom—in fact, one among many symptoms that include romance novels, soap operas, fashion advertising, and music videos—and not the disease.[66] One reason that some feminists have made efforts to show a causal connection between pornography and violence against women is to argue that eliminating pornography is itself an attack on the "disease" of a misogynistic and androcentric culture.

What this discussion suggests is that even if we were to argue that pornography were successful at *being* an endorsement of degradation, the further question remains as to whether the endorsement is *successful at persuading* its audience to act on its endorsement. As Alan Soble has pointed out, celebrities endorse all sorts of products that we are not automatically persuaded to buy. Not all men (or women) react and feel the same way about pornography or about sex work generally, nor will such reactions necessarily remain consistent over time. In the same society, some men enjoy pornography and strip bars but eschew prostitutes; others never pay for commercial sexual excitement.[67] F. M. Christensen has argued that women exert enough power in sex by their approval and disapproval of men that pornography simply does not maintain the unilateral control over women that feminists think. He contends that sex is so shame-laden in Western culture that feminists find humiliation and degradation in porn where there is only sex. What is degrading to Christensen is telling men that their sexual desires are always exploitative and degrading, or that men are so depraved as to be driven to violence by pornography.[68] Alan Soble suggests that it is men's powerlessness in the wake of feminist advances at home and at work that is expressed in pornography, not men's power. Laura Kipnis echoes this view when she calls pornography a failed attempt at power over women, expressive of "compensatory mechanisms and empty signifiers" that reveal the impotence of men's sexual fantasies.[69]

My sense is that such claims tend to underestimate the extent to which a patriarchal culture reinforces the sexual subordination of women by using many sources, of which pornography is one. The fact that not all readers of violent porn are motivated to rape does not mean that hard-core pornography has no effect on a male readership bombarded with images of the sexual accessibility of women, nor does it mean that pornography cannot encourage many men to express dominance and control through sex. Companies pay celebrities enormous amounts of money for their endorsements, so at least some people think endorsements do make a difference. Indeed, without *my* acting on an endorsement of a product, I may still persuade *others* to buy it. Similarly, the simple fact that many men are not made violent by pornography is no reason to think that pornography does not succeed in endorsing violence against women in people's minds. This endorsement can then be communicated to others in ways that are successful at persuading them to act on the endorsement or to adopt attitudes degrading to women.

Moreover, sadomasochistic pornography featuring dominatrixes and their whips might express men's sexual submission or symbolize their fear at the power of women, but some pornographic movies and videos also depict women submitting to all manner of sexual abuse in a culture whose sexual ideology characterizes women as men's sexual objects who want and deserve to be sexually dominated by men. Until relatively recently, wives and girlfriends could not expect to press successful charges of rape against their partners, in part because of such ideological beliefs. It would be more than a little ironic to find that men feel so threatened by, much less powerless in the face of, women's sexual rejection of them that their only recourse is to murder, rape, batter, harass, and humiliate women worldwide.[70] Furthermore, it is clear from sex workers' personal descriptions that not all pornography depicts only *simulated* rape and abuse; among other things, some viewers' arousal (and pornographer's profits) will be a function of whether viewers can be convinced that what they see depicts an actual event. Harry Brod believes that pornography is both an expression of men's public power as members of the institutionally dominant gendered class and an expression of their lack of personal power; however, radical feminists have contended that such distinctions between public and private politics only serve the interests of men by characterizing women as capable of greater freedom of choice in the domestic privacy of their "personal" lives than institutionalized discrimination, patriarchal family values, and husbands' sexual intimidation actually allow.[71] I believe that feminists can effectively argue that at least some products and practices of the sex industry are degrading to women; but we must be prepared to show, without begging any normative questions, that such practices somehow fail to treat women living under patriarchal constraints as moral equals who deserve what I have called care respect. Engaging in sex work in which the primary purpose is to satisfy men's sexual desires, to be depicted as doing so, or to endorse doing so will not be considered degrading unless we can show that the social location of either the sex work or the sex work's depictions endorses the degradation of women. Because many feminists believe that patriarchy defines just such a location for modern prostitution and pornography, sex work in these industries is thought to be degrading as it is currently practiced.

However, I have suggested that considerations of individual social location *within patriarchy* are vital to determining the nature and scope of the sexual degradation of sex work. Such contextual considerations appear to be absent in the description of depictions of sexual subordination in the Minneapolis ordinance written by Andrea Dworkin and Catharine MacKinnon. These include: "women presented dehumanized as sexual objects, things, or commodities; or women presented as sexual objects who enjoy pain or humiliation; . . . or women presented in scenarios of degradation, injury, torture, shown as filthy or inferior, bleeding, bruised, or hurt in a context that makes these conditions sexual."[72] Dworkin's and MacKinnon's ordinance would thereby appear to condemn objectifying or violent sexually explicit material that might be used in aversive sex therapy as well as material that simply happened to be sexually stimulating to its audience, even in educative or explanatory contexts. This is particularly odd, given Dworkin's publication of her own novel *Mercy*, which depicts considerable acts of violence against women—ostensibly as a contribution to the feminist debate over pornography—but which could easily be read for the express purpose of sexual arousal.[73] Sarah Wynter's definition of prostitution, alluded to earlier, equally condemns the sexual commodification of women, who are degraded from their status as persons by "exploitation and abuse." However, given the positive testimonials of prostitutes described in this chapter's overview as well as Judith Hill's previously cited claims about the nature of degradation, Wynter cannot assume that all prostitution, much less all sex work, is necessarily exploitative and abusive of its workers or that such exploitation constitutes their degradation.

Furthermore, neither Wynter's definition nor the Dworkin/MacKinnon ordinance answers the question of *why* treating a woman as a sexual object, thing, or commodity is degrading. While many feminists often equate a woman's objectification with her degradation, treating a person as an object is not in and of itself objectionable; people who own treasured mementos and prized pets sometimes treat them better than they treat other people. Paula Webster suggests, in a positive vein, that all porn actors are objectified by being represented as paradigms, fantasies, or cultural icons of a sexuality challenging traditional notions of sexual conservatism. Many sex workers describe their work and themselves in terms of bodily barter without any sense that they are being treated, or are treating themselves, inappropriately. As one prostitute puts it, "I think women and men and feminists have to realize that all work involves selling some part of your body. You might sell your brain, your might sell your back, you might sell your fingers for typewriting. Whatever it is that you do you are selling one part of your body. I choose to sell my body the way I want to and I choose to sell my vagina."[74] Feminist film critics have viewed pornography as the extreme instance of the voyeuristic, fetishizing male gaze that dominates film direction, production, and viewing. Yet this criticism implies that all film actresses are collaborators in men's sexual perversions; and such complaints interpret men's viewing of film, especially pornographic film, as perverse, reinforcing the moral conservative's attacks on sexual deviance.[75] Diana Russell locates the objection to pornography in the fact that women are not portrayed as "multi-faceted human beings deserving equal rights with men." A similar line is taken by John Stoltenberg whose sexual ideal is "when the integrity within everyone's body and the whole personhood of each person is celebrated whenever two people touch."[76] But how would even the most tame of erotic photographs portray me as a lover *as well as* a committed vegetarian and a philosophy professor? Do I fail to treat the cashier at the supermarket as a person when I simply treat her as a cashier? Philosophy may be a deep part of my personhood, but I may not want to discuss Cartesian dualism in bed; I may simply want to *have sex.*

Locating the degradation in the "sexual" of the expression "sexual object" is also problematic. Defining the sexual as degrading defeats any feminist attempts to promote the erotic, instead of the pornographic, in heterosexual sex. Furthermore, it invites the sexual puritan charge that obscenity, not subordination, is the issue. Merely describing some sex acts as degrading invites the contextual criticisms noted earlier: *how* and *for whom* is *which* sex degrading? Ann Garry and Robert Baker suggest that being a *harmed* object is what is degrading about being a *sex* object. Their point is that there is a conceptual connection in the way we think about sex, between being a (female) sex partner and being harmed. According to Garry and Baker, this conceptual connection is reflected in such language as "Screw you!" and "Up yours!"

and captures the complaints women make when they are treated as sex objects. However, conceptually connecting sex with harm that men do to women appears to condemn all heterosexual sex, not just the degrading sort, reinforcing the view of sex workers that antipornography feminists are anti–heterosexual sex.[77] Moreover, as I noted earlier, a woman can be harmed without being regarded as an inferior or subordinate and without being regarded as a commodity and not a person. Therefore, if we address only the "sex" in "sex object," without addressing her complex "object" status, those contexts that turn a woman's objectification into her degradation remain indeterminate.

Along similar lines, in their Minneapolis pornography ordinance Dworkin and MacKinnon describe sexual objects as "women presented in scenarios of degradation," indicating subordination of some type. However, this begs the question as to what makes being an object degrading. Being depicted as filthy, bleeding, bruised, or hurt may be disgusting to view but may not show that the person being hurt is being degraded. Many feminists do not see that expressions like "I choose to sell my body" indicate precisely the dialectical subjectivity in the commodification of women's bodies under conditions of male supremacy which prompts pro-industry sex workers to assume that the charge of degradation must be a charge of sexual conservatism.

I have suggested that if feminists wish to argue that at least certain forms of sex work constitute degradation or the endorsement of degradation, then we must locate sex work within an institutionalized ideology of men's sex objectification of women without begging the question of whether sex work endorses women's subordination or abuse within such constraints. Prostitution, pornography, and stripping will reinforce the erroneous message that women are the natural, proper, and willing sexual subordinates of men only when that message is already an integral part of the gender stereotypes and social role expectations of the culture in which the sex work exists. Furthermore, such expectations combine with economic discrimination against women to narrow many women's choice of work to sex work. This is precisely the criticism that Carole Pateman lodges against Lars Ericsson's claim that prostitution is the free and informed contractual selling of a service, not an instance of sex inequality.[78] Saturation of explicit sexuality in a culture whose sexual ideology is oppressive to women has the effect of desensitizing the consumer: women and men become more accepting and imitative of what Naomi Wolf refers to as "beauty pornography" in fashion magazines and advertising, which increases our tolerance of hard-core pornography, thus our tolerance of real violence against women.[79] Nevertheless, to say that sex work is degrading to women is misleading, since this implies that the degradation somehow originates from the work itself and not from within the social milieu in which sex work is practiced. By recognizing that the endorsement of women's degradation is a function of our society's social construction of sexuality and not a function of commercial sex work, women can legitimately use sex work to subvert and transform the construction of sexuality that is oppressive to them.

The adoption of the "view from somewhere different" that I have described in the preceding chapters recommends that a feminist philosophy of sex locate women's sexuality, among other things, within a male-identified social framework whose sexual double standard *circumscribes* women's sexuality in terms of the subordination of women. But when feminists *require* sex work to be degrading under such constraints, feminists may be guilty of reinforcing a view of sex work that oversimplifies and overdetermines particular cases. Laurie Shrage makes the important point that in a society whose role expectations for women are that they deserve no more than sexual subordination by men, commercial sex will ring a false note. However, while not condemning all commercial sex work in all cultural settings, Shrage then concludes that prostitution will be oppressive for all women living under the patriarchal constructs that support the subordination of women. My quarrel with this line of argument is that if prostitution is oppressive under patriarchy, such that *without being oppressive it would not be prostitution,* prostitutes' arguments that their work is sexually or economically liberating under patriarchy must be dismissed out of hand. Feminists like Longino, Dworkin, and MacKinnon who condemn pornography appear to make the case that pornography is degrading to women only after they have assumed that pornography unequivocally depicts and endorses degradation. Feminists will reinforce the very victimization we wish to transcend if we describe sex work solely in terms of those role expectations that are oppressive to women. What I will argue in the next section is that sex work admits of a general characterization in both subject *and* object terms that can accommodate the variety of interpretations of it from women both within and outside the sex industry.

The Subject/Object Dialectic of Sex Work

As much as feminists have described sex workers as commodities and not persons, there is much about sex work that suggests an agency, personhood, or subjectivity that is in dialectical opposition to sex workers' treatment as sex objects. This is especially clear under conditions that are not outrightly coercive or abusive; but even when conditions are less than ideal, a dialectic between a sex worker's subjectivity and her objectification remains. Sex workers sign contracts, accept payment for services rendered, and act out scenes, not always or even often, of necrophilia or fetishism, but of *people having sex.* Customers who visit prostitutes and not boutiques specializing in sexual paraphernalia do so because they want sex with a *woman,* not an anatomically correct rubber doll. Strippers are enticing precisely because they are scantily clad, seductive women, not windup toys or automatons. Alan Soble points out, "To be aware of the woman [depicted in pornography] as one who is licking her lips in anticipation of sex or as an invitation to engage in sex, is to affirm rather than deny her humanity. . . . [T]he ordinary viewer of pornography responds somewhat to the woman's *showing* him her body or its parts; he responds to an action performed by a person expressing intentions."[80]

Particularly in prostitution, part of the arousal can come from feeling power over a woman who willingly accepts payment to be objectified. Agency "cattle calls" in which photographers choose women for their bodies, breasts, or buttocks reduce such women to their body parts in the way portrait artists reduce women to their faces: it is this *woman* with this body that is required. Sexualizing her body parts or politicizing her objectification to further distinguish the two cases is crucial. Nevertheless, such distinctions do not obliterate the fact that stripping, pornography, and prostitution are successful because they proffer real women for sale. Andrea Dworkin notes with some irony that sexual arousal by a fetishized object is usually considered abnormal, but arousal from the objectification of a woman is not.[81] There is no irony here, however, if we locate the source of the arousal in the fact that this is a *woman* being reduced to the status of object, a woman in dialectical relation to her objectification. Dworkin says as much when she states that "[t]he object is allowed to desire if she desires to be an object; to be formed; especially to be used." Dworkin also tells the story of game hunters who rape and abuse a Girl Scout resembling the women depicted in their pornography. On seeing her, they shout, "There's a live one!"[82] Men who become aroused by having sex with especially sick or filthy prostitutes may become excited, at least in part, because they are associating themselves with a *person* whom they regard as defiled, abject, degenerate, someone who has fallen from grace and who can thus represent the ultimate corruption of the subject. For this reason I disagree with those who would describe sex objectification in terms of "regarding women's bodies, functions or sexual parts as sexual stimuli independently of their connection to a human person."[83] Indeed, if the objectification of a woman is erotic, it is because she is *reducible from* the status of woman to that of object.

Part of a standard pornographic fantasy is the overcoming of a woman's will to resist. She is ultimately subdued, but only after we see her as someone who has a will to be overcome. As Nancy Hartsock points out, "Without the boundary to violate, the thrill of transgression would disappear." She argues that by distancing themselves from an embodiedness of sensuality and feeling that can only remind them of their own mortality, men distance themselves from the embodiedness of woman by attempting to control her will. Robert Stoller has suggested that men need aggression for their sexual excitement, which expresses revenge for an infantile powerlessness in the face of an all-powerful mother. She is recognized as a fearsome subject defining others in terms of her subjectivity. Lynne Segal sees porn as a means for men to revenge themselves on a castrating mother; yet since the revenge remains in the realm of fantasy, men succeed without fear of reprisal, disapproval, or humiliation from a "real" woman. Eva Kittay describes the dialectic between subject and object in pornography when she remarks that women are depicted simultaneously as menacing and inferior, needing to be conquered and having been conquered. Since woman is perceived as menacing, power must be exerted over her; since she is regarded as inferior, power can be exerted with impunity.[84]

An interesting irony of this type of objectification is that men who become dependent on pornography or the use of prostitutes/dominatrixes for their arousal have themselves become objects of a sort, controlled by the sex worker's subjective will to arouse. Anne McClintock describes dominatrixes who take out their aggressions on male clients, feel good about being in control, know just how far to push their "punishment," and keep male "slaves" as real domestics; yet by feeling indispensable to men whose special needs are both acknowledged and fulfilled, the dominatrix's subjectivity restrains and reconstitutes the objectification of her clients. At the same time, McClintock does not believe that a dominatrix's complex psychology of sexual power easily translates into women's political liberation or social power.[85] Harry Brod contends that in depriving women of their sexual subjectivity, a dehumanizing heterosexual partner deprives himself of any meaningful human interaction, turning himself into a performance-oriented, genitally fixated sexual object. "The necessary corollary to pornography's myth of female perpetual availability is its myth of male perpetual readiness."[86]

On the other hand, such a dehumanizing partner may so consume his object that he annihilates her, thereby destroying the very object that defines him as subject. Thus, says Jessica Benjamin, the man who commodifies women "must be careful never to wholly consume her as will-less object, but rather to command and consume her *will*" (Benjamin's italics). This analysis suggests that pornographic "snuff" films, depicting the purportedly real torture and murder of women, are arousing precisely because of the slow and steady annihilation of a woman's will. When the woman is dead, she has become literally nothing more than body, and the film, necrophilia excluded, is over.[87] Even drugged pornographer's models, raped and filmed while only semiconscious, are sex objects whose ability to arouse lies in a subjectivity that is being ravished or subdued. Since some of the most popular porn, unlike R-rated mainstream love scenes, enacts the sex that is depicted, Catharine MacKinnon has commented, "the speech of pornographers was once someone else's *life*."[88]

The dialectic between subject and object characteristic of sex work is also recreated in the dialectic of reality and fantasy that is the sex worker's modus operandi. A stripper provides her customers with fantasies of real sex because she is a sexually enticing woman often no more than an arm's length away. Prostitutes are paid to give reality to their customer's sexual imaginings: one of the reported hazards of the job is the extent to which a customer will force his fantasies on a woman he has paid to service him. Live sex shows, purported "snuff" films, even ceiling mirrors in hotel rooms attest to the arousal of an audience by real subjects; yet much of pornography is arousing in part because of its fictional portrayal of a patriarchal "pornotopia" in which every social aspect is sexualized and in which women are depicted as unconditionally available to men.[89] Diana Russell suggests that pornography is backlash, men's fantasy solution to the reality of "uppity females"; but she also wants to make the case that such fantasy solutions inspire nonfantasy acts of abuse, humiliation, and violence against women. Catharine MacKinnon makes an even stronger claim by stating that pornography constitutes violence against women, such that "[i]t is not that life and art imitate each other; in sexuality, they *are* each other."[90] Few feminists take such an extreme view of the realism in pornography; indeed, Gayle Rubin challenges this claim by noting that (1) it conflates the *image* of violence with the *institution* of violence, and (2) 90 percent of pornographic images are not of violence but of frontal nudity, frontal or anal intercourse, or oral sex.[91] However, in either case, a fascinating dialectic between reality and fantasy in sex work emerges: if the sex work includes too much fantasy, the sex object can become a distant, inaccessible, unreal thing; too real and she will become either too mundane (the accessible, accepting wife), too judgmental (the complaining girlfriend), or too much trouble (the promiscuous and oversexed "ball breaker"). Thus, the female stripper, prostitute, and porn actress symbolize the ambivalence of sexual desire in heterosexual men, reflected in the dialectic of reality/fantasy and subject/object at the heart of sex work. When pornography is claimed to be therapeutic or cathartic, it is because the fantasies depicted in porn are regarded as allowing the viewer to work through dangerous or repressed sexual feelings that the viewer does not wish to make real.[92]

One of the strongest claims to a sex worker's subjectivity ironically comes from the very complaints of objectification that feminists often lodge against her: she is perceived as not only the proper sexual subordinate of men but also someone who wants, needs, even begs for whatever humiliation or abuse to which men are willing to submit her. Part of the arousal of pornography, stripping, and prostitution for many men consists in their belief that this is a woman who is enjoying herself, conveying the message (that feminists object to) that any sex goes. If women's perceived willingness and desire to be men's sexual subordinates is what legitimizes women's subordination in men's eyes, then the heterosexual male image of women as *willing* and *desiring subjects* endorses women's sex *objectification*. Thus, a dialectical relation between subject and object that recognizes the varied, complex, even contradictory range of interpretation of sexually explicit material and sex work may better represent women working in the sex industry than simply reducing sex work to the commodification and degradation of women.

Male sex workers who cater to a gay clientele can combine the dominating subjectivity of the male heterosexual stereotype and the objectification of playing a feminine sexual role that is also assumed by many gays. In gay pornographic depictions of men being sodomized, men who sodomize in return are depicted as objects of male supremacy without being its victims. However, some gay writers contend that gay porn does not always recreate the performance orientation and correlative sex objectification of heterosexual porn but is often more reciprocal, goal-less, and mutual.[93] Gay and heterosexual sex workers of color often complain that their white customers doubly dehumanize them as objects of racial and sexual subordination, especially when whites regard men of color as sexually threatening competitors. White, heterosexual, male sex workers would seem to benefit most from a culture that associates their sexual desirability with a superior masculine agency. Relatively few heterosexual men are professional "gigolos" compared to their gay or female counterparts in prostitution. The catcalls of women in clubs with male strip dancers and the voyeuristic gaze of the female viewer of pornography are no match for the objectifying gaze of a man, whose cultural ideology assumes that his sexuality, not hers, does the subordinating. Some feminists argue that it will not serve feminism to offer heterosexual women our own porn and prostitutes, since such de facto equality under current patriarchal constraints would simply legitimize men's continued subordination of women, encourage women to dehumanize men, and fool women into thinking we are successful.[94] From this perspective, male sex work does not convey or reinforce the belief that men are deserving of humiliation or abuse. On the contrary, toleration of gratuitous violence as well as the infliction of violence are a large part of the cult of macho. When such violence is depicted in gay porn, it is designed, according to some, to assure gays that they are really *men* after all. John Stoltenberg believes that all gays should be antiporn, since heterosexual pornography is an instance of sex discrimination against women, and sex discrimination encourages homophobia: gay men are regarded as participating in the degraded status of the female. In 1972, the readers of a female-oriented soft porn magazine, *Viva*, reported to Bob Guccione, publisher of *Viva* and *Penthouse*, that all of the nude male models looked gay: does this observation reflect women's difficulty in objectifying heterosexual men? Are these women underscoring the ways that sexual objectification imposes a sexual submission associated with gay men but not heterosexual men? Are gay men simply more willing, or more qualified, to pose nude in front of a camera? Porn actors who want to go mainstream often cannot get nonpornographic work, because their value remains fixed on penile erection and ejaculation. (One male porn star has come to be known by porn producers as "The Hose.") This suggests that a restrictive commodification of sexuality in the sex industry is not an exclusively female domain.[95]

Social context, normative perspective, and the psychoanalytic dynamics of power and powerlessness all play key roles in the interpretation of sexually explicit material and sex work. Highly controversial Robert Mapplethorpe photographs of nude women and men have been denounced as reducing African American men to nothing more than penises and praised as explorations into the historical invisibility of the black male nude in European aesthetics.[96] Is s/m sex work an objectifying endorsement of degradation or a self-defining parody of the battle between the sexes? Is a woman stripping a humiliation of the female body or a celebration of it? Is a depiction of a grimace from anal intercourse a depiction of pleasure or pain? Is a prostitute's posh apartment after years of poverty a symbol of the corruption of capitalism or a triumph over adversity? Instead of silencing alternative voices whose interpretations give meaning and value to the diversity of sex work, I have proposed that we regard sex work as a dialectic between subject and object, one that appreciates the sex industry's variety, complexity, contradiction, and ambiguity. In doing so we adopt the "view from somewhere different," which encourages the recognition and promotion of alternative points of view.

Feminists' objections to the coerciveness and abuse that exist in much of the sex industry are well justified. Many prostitutes endure rapes and beatings from pimps and customers without legal or economic recourse. Margo St. James reports that at least 20 percent of the violence against prostitutes is inflicted by the police. Pornographer's models and actresses report being drugged and raped by photographers and coerced into sex on film that they do not wish to perform. Feminists point out that the business of pornography alone is a multi-billion-dollar industry that feeds into, as well as profits from, an institutionalized ideology that devalues women's sexual subjectivity and self-determination in deference to the sexual needs of men. Herein lies the dehumanization and the degradation in treating a woman as a sex object.[97]

My point, however, is that sex work is not merely about treating a woman as an object nor merely about dehumanizing her. Sex work is a complex dialectic between subject and object in which a woman's dehumanization is successful precisely because she is perceived as a person whose will, seductiveness, and power is properly subordinate to men. From a feminist perspective that condemns sex work, since women are defined largely in sexual terms, a woman who sells her sexuality makes herself into a commodity; but from a sex radical feminist perspective, women provide a commercial service when they sell sex, thus opening the door for sex workers as sexual subjects to determine the terms and conditions of their work.

When a woman becomes a sex worker because her society affords her little in the way of alternatives for supporting herself, her sexuality becomes both the means to her survival and her power, often the only resource that gives her some sense of control over her life, even though that very sexuality is a feminist symbol of her oppression. When feminists appear to take that power away from a sex worker by treating her as a victim, a sex worker's understandable response is to accuse feminists of self-righteous moralizing and middle-class interference. Many would argue that Catharine MacKinnon's sardonic comment quoted earlier about lawyers not choosing sex work betrays a social classism that blinds her to the struggle to make a living that sex work often mitigates. Yet when women already experienced in the job market or otherwise capable of other work choose stripping, pornography, or prostitution, they typically see themselves as taking advantage of the profits in a capitalist economy that otherwise discriminates against women. From such a perspective, if sexual self-determination and economic independence are feminist goals, sex workers are the quintessential feminists, taking advantage of the power of a woman-identified sexuality. In these women's eyes, they are combating the very dehumanization to which feminists seem determined to resign them—feminists who blame sex workers, not men, for promoting violence against women.[98] Combine this sense of her own personal agency with the subjectivity of the intentionally seductive stroke, glance, or gyration, and the self-appointed sex worker cannot comprehend where the submission is located about which feminists complain. For a sex worker, submission lies in giving anyone the power to keep her away from using recreational sex as a way to make money. Thus, the only sensible way such sex workers can translate accounts of their degradation is as complaints about the sexual indecency of their work, and this translation is reinforced by feminists' apparent confederacy with the political right.

Catharine MacKinnon's cynicism about the sexual agency in sex work is typical of feminists who see such unequivocal dehumanization in sex work that they cannot imagine or condone any woman's consent to it. By conceptualizing sex work solely in terms of women's object status, however, feminists forfeit the possibility for transcendence to greater subjectivity afforded women when sex work is regarded as work that contains the reality and possibility of both objectification and agency. My contention is that unless feminists are willing to acknowledge the dialectical subjectivity in sex work, we will continue to be regarded as sexual puritans and only contribute to the dehumanization of the sex worker. We can now turn to some of the more specific arguments offered in favor of sex work.

Sex Workers and Sex Radical Feminists Join Ranks

[F]or some women to get paid for what all women are expected to do for free is a source of power for all women to refuse *any* free sex.

—Nina Lopez-Jones, "Workers: Introducing the English
Collective of Prostitutes"

I didn't join the feminist movement to live inside a Hallmark greeting card.

—Pat Califia, "Feminism and
Sadomasochism"

Sex workers skeptical of feminists' anti-industry stance have found a more permissive approach in sex radical feminism. This approach eschews analyses of women's oppression solely or even primarily in terms of patriarchal victimization, in favor of analyses in terms of the repression of sexual deviance and the promotion of alternative sexualities for women. Both sex workers and sex radical feminists point out that sex workers struggle against stereotypes perpetuated by both feminists and the media—that they are either greedy glamour girls who cannot get enough sex or sexually abused and exploited women who turn to drugs to assuage the disgust of work foisted on them by a discriminatory patriarchy. From this perspective, all sex workers are either physically coerced into their work, compelled by their circumstances to live a life otherwise abhorrent to them, or victims of an internalized patriarchy that has convinced them that theirs is a freely chosen life, not without risks, but with the promise of greater financial reward and independence than other jobs demanding the same hours, level of training, or education. What politicized sex workers demand is that feminists stop making such blanket assumptions about an industry as diverse as women are themselves and recognize that for at least some sex workers, their livelihood can be pleasurable, profitable, and liberating.

Such sex workers desire to be recognized as plying a legitimate trade so that they can better determine for themselves the terms and conditions of their work. This means jettisoning the stigma attached to associating female sexuality with earning power. Many prostitutes argue for the abolition of laws against soliciting so that they can file legal grievances against abusive or exploitative conditions that cannot be addressed under current restrictions without landing them in jail. Politicized sex workers typically want to educate the public about the spread of AIDS and other sexually transmitted diseases and to dispel the myth that just because someone works in the sex industry, she is incautious about infection. Heterosexual customers have been known to offer prostitutes as much as four times their going rate if they will dispense with using condoms. On the other hand, prostitutes would *prefer* that their customers use condoms, belying the claim that prostitutes' indiscriminate sex is largely responsible for the spread of AIDS in the heterosexual community. Sex workers complain that they are doubly stigmatized: as morally incorrect by conservatives for their sexual license and permissiveness, and as politically incorrect by feminists for making sexual transactions with sexists and for taking advantage of a capitalist enterprise that profits from exploiting women's sexuality. From a sex worker's point of view, her stigmatization gives feminists a way to remain good girls who join the moral and political right in righteously condemning sex workers for being bad. Moreover, while political liberals or civil libertarians may be more inclined than conservatives to accept the sex industry in the name of freedom of expression, according to some sex workers and sex radical feminists, liberals do not give the needs of women in the sex industry the priority that many feel they deserve.[99]

Sex radical feminists claim that the sex industry affirms sexual pleasure, promotes diverse sexual styles, and gives a voice to oppressed sexualities. They claim that prostitution affirms the validity of sex divorced from intimacy or romance. Lesbian and gay pornographic literature, s/m videos, and magazines featuring cross-generational sex are regarded as important erotic outlets for those interested in exploring sexual alternatives. Many sex radicals point out that the vast majority of pornography depicts women liking sex in all its variety and initiating sexual encounters, confirming, not denying, women's sexual agency and subjectivity in a world that benefits from women's sexual submissiveness. From this perspective, the very public depiction of women's sexual agency combined with the revelation that sex for money is not fundamentally different from sex in exchange for social status, marriage, or children is what moral conservatives of both genders find truly "obscene." Sex radicals contend that the sex industry is poised to redefine women's sexuality in women's terms and to end the stigma associated with combining female sexual pleasure and recreational sex. Instead of feminists telling other women what kind of sex they can have, sex radicals and sex workers advocate organizing more groups like Pink Thread, a liaison group of women from both inside and outside the industry advocating financial independence, sexual self-determination, and protection against sexual abuse for all women.[100] Strengthened and emboldened by such reforms, women will then be in a position to decide for themselves what kind of sex or sex work is best for them.

Instead of asking "What kind of woman would choose sex work?," sex radicals suggest that feminists should ask, "What kind of woman *wouldn't* choose sex work?" Indeed, both sex workers and sex radicals censure the society that would stigmatize and marginalize an economically productive worker, demanding her existence and her invisibility all at once. Sex workers and sex radicals contend that since many feminists would ignore the social and economic needs of sex workers, feminists' complaints about sex work are really concerns about bonding versus recreational sex and about confronting the power of our own sexuality.[101] From this perspective, until feminists are willing to expand our notion of appropriate sexuality, the chasm between sex workers and feminists will remain.

My contention is that just as some feminists overemphasize the objectification of the sex worker, some sex workers and radicals see only the potential for subjectivity and female agency in the sex industry. In the discussion that follows, the claim that sex work can be pleasurable, profitable, and liberating will be expanded in some detail. My aim is to show that without taking a close enough look at the ideological milieu in which their sex work is performed, sex workers can too easily rationalize their occupations as nonoppressive, indeed, liberating for women. What I do believe is that sex work contains both liberating and oppressive elements, circumscribed by the dialectic between subject and object described in the previous section. This dialectic reflects the broader dialectic between gender and sexuality that acknowledges the victimization and the agency in women's sexuality under patriarchy. From such a perspective, we can then describe in the closing section of this chapter a care respect for sex workers from the "view from somewhere different" that can embrace some of the tensions and highlight some of the complexity in our attitudes toward sexuality and the sex industry.

It has been argued by sex workers that sex work can be pleasurable, just like any other occupation. The money, independence, and flexibility afforded many single women and working mothers means more time for leisure, more time with children and family. Many porn actresses and strippers report feeling sexy and glamorous on the screen or stage; some prostitutes enjoy the company of their customers.[102] Porn actresses get satisfaction out of the fact that their photographs, films, and videos will offer viewers new sex techniques or sex therapy, or simply provide their audience with sexual pleasure. Some prostitutes say they are only too happy to provide (for a fee) the sex that men are often too ashamed, unable, or unwilling to ask their wives or girlfriends to provide. According to this view, if women and men were willing to confront their sexual fears and frustrations and share them with their partners, they would contribute to the breakdown of the good girl/bad girl sexual standard that separates sex workers from feminists. Sex workers like to point out that as long as sex work can be stigmatized, *any* woman can be made into a bad girl. Thus, feminists aligned with sex workers argue that women's freedom from male sexual intimidation and control of sexual pleasure will always be limited as long as sex workers are stigmatized and criminalized. As Deirdre English has noted, the whole point of a feminist politics of sexuality is not to have to choose between being a good girl or a bad one.[103]

Moreover, many sex workers and sex radical feminists argue that pornography is consumed for arousal and produced to make money. From their perspective, the claim that it represents or promotes violence against women is simply unwarranted, given the conflicting claims of researchers, and especially given the fact that such a small portion of the industry is devoted to depictions of violence. As Ellen Willis remarks, "It is men's hostility toward women—combined with their power to express that hostility and for the most part get away with it—that causes sexual violence. . . . [I]f *Hustler* were to vanish from the shelves tomorrow, I doubt if rape or wife-beating statistics would decline." Gayle Rubin adds, "It is important to recall that rape, violence against women, oppression and exploitation of women, and the attitudes that encouraged and justified these activities, have been present throughout most of human history and predate the emergence of commercial erotica by several millennia."[104] Accordingly, if feminists are concerned about media expressions of violence against women, we would do just as well to boycott selected mainstream television, movies, music videos, and "bodice-ripper" romances (all the more insidious because they are mainstream), or to promote more woman-identified, heterosexual and lesbian pornography. Sex radical feminists contend that women can be aroused by visual depictions of sex; women just need to be looking at sex that appeals to us. This contention is in response to authors like Beatrice Faust, who suggests that women are not aroused by visual erotic stimuli in ways that would make pornography appealing to them the way it is to men.[105] Such feminists argue that they only wish to delegitimize the primary significance of the penis for women's eroticism, not reject heterosexual porn, especially since many women report liking and buying it. Furthermore, they would argue that prohibiting pornography is just another way to repress sexual minorities whose "deviant" sexualities are made explicit in porn. According to this line of reasoning, anti-industry feminists and former sex workers deceptively portray themselves as representative of the feminist movement and all sex workers, when there are plenty of women who would like to experiment safely with using pornography or engage in sex work. Furthermore, feminists have argued that saving the sex worker from her purported victimization has a history of being subverted to serve moral and legal conservatism.[106]

Sex workers admit that abusive porn producers, club managers, pimps, and customers are hazards of the profession. They also admit that the personal pride as well as survival of many sex workers often precludes their dwelling on how and why women get hurt.[107] But many prostitutes claim that eliminating discriminatory laws against prostitution would reduce violence against them, by making it more difficult for the men they work with, or for, to get away with it. Strippers and porn actresses suggest that if their work were not so marginalized by a sexually conservative politics, they would be better able to take cases to court without being humiliated by the exposure. Because sexual harassment is such a common feature of working women's lives and sexual abuse so pervasive among wives and girlfriends, sex workers see no special reason for targeting them other than the purported sexual indecency in their work.

Indeed, because prostitutes as a group are identified as promiscuous (averaging a reported 1,500 clients a year), female prostitutes have been targeted as a primary cause of the spread of AIDS among heterosexuals. However, the U.S. Department of Public Health reports that while up to 35 percent of sexually transmitted diseases in the United States are related to teenage sex, only 5 percent are related to prostitution. Margo St. James reports that in every age group, the venereal disease rate among prostitutes is lower than the rate among the general public. As I mentioned earlier, sex workers insist that prostitutes have always been careful about sexually transmitted diseases, because disease-free sex is their bread and butter. When they do not use condoms, it is often because they are too financially desperate to insist on them when customers are willing to pay several times the going rate to go without. Police officials are not much more helpful when they confiscate condoms as evidence of solicitation.[108]

Moreover, surveys on the transmission of AIDS through prostitution are often biased, targeting IV drug users in the sex industry or prostitutes already visiting HIV clinics. Customers are seldom officially tested, and where prostitution is regulated and legal, prostitutes can be subjected to compulsory isolation and public censure for testing positive for HIV. Thus, sex workers argue that the real AIDS threat is in forcing sex work underground, resulting in a lack of customer education about, and responsibility for, HIV transmission. Sex workers also point to the dearth of education of heterosexual couples on the importance of the use of condoms and the fight by a conservative public to keep condom distribution out of public schools. In a culture in which women's sexuality has been associated with dirt and defilement, women in the industry complain that they are assumed to be the diseased ones, blatantly displaying a sexuality that does not defile the men for whom they work.[109]

Women of color in the sex industry feel the bite of racism and classism in the maintenance of the good girl/bad girl standard, since cleanliness and purity are associated in many Anglo minds with upper-class whites: for many white men, "black woman" means "whore." Black women who simply stroll in or near red-light districts are often arrested as prostitutes, and antiloitering laws make it easy to press charges. Consistent with the white stereotype of black males, pimps are often assumed to be black, since black men are regarded by many whites as violent, irresponsible, and sexually powerful. Indeed, such a description fits some pimps, but not all of them.[110]

Some sex workers simply say that they are tired of rationalizing their work. If sex work is not always pleasant, at least *it's a job.* They remind feminists that most of us compromise when it comes to work, since the jobs we have are often not our ideal. Moreover, most of us do not work "by choice" but do so in order to support ourselves and our families. Nevertheless, sex workers are talked down to and considered sick, neurotic, or abused just because they honestly and openly exchange sex for money. Sex workers complain that feminists can only see the reinforcement of male power in commercial sex work and not the power a woman has in making a successful sale. Women of color have argued that activism against the sex industry has been largely a white, middle-class issue, since abolishing prostitution or censoring pornography would only mean more unemployed women of color who do not have the luxury of choosing their line of work and who find white social service agencies alienating, isolating, and ineffective. According to this view, if middle-class feminists were to argue for better working conditions for sex workers, such feminists would have to admit that their own middle class, perhaps some of their own husbands, are sexually exploiting working women. From such a perspective, feminists who tell sex workers what kind of work they should or should not do sound exactly like racist and sexist men who say women ought to make coffee and not laws; and feminists who tell sex workers what kind of sex they should or should not have sound exactly like moralizing prudes. Sex workers say that picketing through their districts and humiliating them on organized tours through strip clubs and porn shops only shows them that feminists do not believe that sex workers' voices count. Such workers demand that feminists either contribute to their cause for better working conditions or simply let them get on with their work.[111]

As in other occupations, when sex work is profitable, the mundane or even unpleasant aspects of the work are often more tolerable. When a stripper in a fancy New York club or a call girl for a studio executive makes more money in an evening than she can make in a month of typing, the money itself can be exciting. Sex workers say that because there is big money to be made in the sex industry, feminists should want women to get a piece of what is still a preserve whose economic base is determined primarily by male producers, directors, photographers, club managers, and pimps. When madams like Heidi Fleiss in Los Angeles are arrested for pandering, they are made into media spectacles and moral examples of good girls gone bad. The facts that Heidi Fleiss grew up in an upper-middle-class vegetarian household and that her parents are a pediatrician and a schoolteacher have often been cited to imply that she was not always "that kind of girl."[112] Such denigration is the price, some prostitutes contend, for making good money in an industry that stigmatizes women but not men for commercializing sex.

If pornography is used to coerce women into sex they do not want, the problem is not with the sex industry but with the fact that women are not in positions of economic or social power to refuse. According to this view, legalized sex work empowers women to say yes or no to sex, thereby challenging the belief that women are the proper sexual subordinates of men; censoring or prohibiting the industry does not. Some sex workers contend that if feminists want women to be economically independent, there is no better way to earn a living *and* have power over men than working in the sex industry, whether as producer, manager, or sex worker. Indeed, sex workers point out that legitimizing sex work might even prompt women to be more honest about the negotiations they make in exchange for sex or give women permission to see dating and marriage as the sex work that it is.[113]

The English Collective of Prostitutes asserts in its policy statements that laws against prostitution punish women for refusing poverty and deny them the right to make money.[114] Arrests only reinforce dependence on pimps who can arrange bail, attorneys, and child care; constant surveillance of known offenders often drives women to other cities, where pimps are enticing in the absence of a known support network. Constant fines and bail fees encourage a revolving door whereby prostitutes are forced back out on the street in order to pay their fines, prompting some sex workers to accuse the state of being the biggest pimp of all. Runaways from parental abuse tend to stay in underground sex work largely because public agencies and police charged with their protection are legally required to notify their families of their whereabouts. According to sex workers, the money spent on arrests alone could be used for support services for women, including alternative job training, child care, continued education, and counseling. The fact that such broad-ranging support is not forthcoming is evidence, according to this view, of both a cultural dependence on and abhorrence of prostitution. Indeed, many feminists are convinced that antipornography and antiprostitution campaigns drain energy away from more productive feminist efforts to secure adequate employment, education, housing, and health care for women who would then be better able to resist men's exploitation and abuse. As Betty Friedan admonishes her more radical antiporn sisters, "Get off the pornography kick and face the real obscenity of poverty." Sex workers believe that feminists can "save" women from sex work only if they help women secure enough education and job skills to make their own decisions about how to live.[115]

On the other hand, many sex workers admit that minimum-wage job training or its equivalent will fail to draw women away from the real profits, independence, and flexibility in much of sex work. From this perspective, the view that pornography is a propaganda tool to degrade women is a trap feminists fall into that blinds us to the real profits to be made in the industry. Moreover, simply to ban all sex work underestimates the real humiliation and desperation of women who cannot feed their children or pay their rent without sex work. The prohibition of sex work simply drives it underground, making it a feeding ground for drugs and crime. Sex work advocates want the world to admit that the sex industry is here to stay: as retired stripper Amber Cooke has said, "People will actually pay for sex, and that makes it a valuable commodity to a woman. That's her right. As long as people are willing to buy sex, there will be people who choose to make their living in the sex trade."[116] Thus, say sex workers, they should be accorded proper social status, unionization, and protection under the law.

This is not to advocate legal *regulation* of sex work, however. Sex workers and feminists alike point out that state regulation of prostitution has been historically oppressive to women. In regions like Nevada, where prostitution is legal in communities under 250,000, prostitutes are licensed with the state and confined to brothels for their work. Any criminal offense constitutes the automatic withdrawal of the license, yet the social stigma of being a prostitute remains public record for any future employers, loan officers, or landlords to check. Her regulation not only limits her hours of work but also limits where she can socialize after hours, making brothels places of confinement, not employment. Police are notorious for using such regulations to make regular sweeps of brothels for minor infractions in order to bring a fresh supply of prostitutes into town for regular customers. Such sweeps are often racist: in Las Vegas, where prostitution is illegal, black prostitutes are often not allowed into the casinos or hotels where white prostitutes mingle; instead, they return illegally to the street, where they are picked up, do more jail time, and pay more fines than whites. Street life is the lowest paying work for prostitutes, comprising a reported 10–20 percent of all prostitution, yet 85–95 percent of prostitution arrests are off the street. The percentage of women of color among all women arrested for street soliciting is much greater than the percentage of women of color working the street. Women of color picked up for soliciting constitute 85 percent of all prostitutes who serve jail time.[117]

Licensed prostitutes are the subject of frequent mandatory venereal disease checks to which their customers are seldom subjected. A positive test for HIV can mean loss of a job and an identifying photograph in the local newspaper. Priscilla Alexander notes that California's confidentiality laws preclude such exposure, but AIDS fears projected onto prostitutes may challenge them. There are typically no regulations on condom use and no requirements that brothels provide disability benefits, health insurance, or pensions. Strippers and porn actresses complain of exploitative "consultant" contracts that provide no benefits but restrict their dress, hours, and activities in ways that make them more employees than independent contractors. Licensing strippers has the same discriminatory effect on alternative employment that licensing prostitutes does. While nude dancing is illegal in many cities, club owners may require it to compete with underground clubs who offer it; but when police raid the clubs, it is the dancers who are busted. Sex workers note with some irony that while feminists would restrict sex work in the name of preventing violence against women, the least restrictive prostitution laws are those that have been correlated with the least violence or theft against prostitutes and the least juvenile prostitution. Feminists aligned with sex workers point out that while sex work regulations are purportedly designed to protect prostitutes and facilitate their work, the laws nevertheless exist within a cultural ideology whose sexual double standard and sexist attitudes subvert the law to reinforce women's unconditional sexual access to men.[118]

Despite the admitted risks and real dangers of the job, however, many women who are sex workers claim that their work is personally and politically liberating. They contend that their work gives them an economic independence, freedom, and flexibility that they could not obtain otherwise. Sex work is regarded as financially empowering when a woman controls a valuable commodity for which a man is willing to pay. By the same token, sex work can be sexually liberating in that it is work that severs the bonds between sex and love and hence affords female sex workers the opportunity to explore a sexuality of pleasure and entertainment not confined to intimacy or monogamy. Some sex workers argue that feminists are hiding behind issues of degradation and violence against women because we are unwilling to confront the potential for liberation in our own sexuality. From this view, the fact that a sexually repressive society has rejected anonymous or casual sex is no reason for women to reject it too. In this respect, sex work can also be politically liberating in that it conveys a message to women and men that women are the sexual subjects of a woman-identified life. Thus, roller hockey team owner Jeanie Buss is reported to have posed for *Playboy* as a way of celebrating her divorce, advertising roller hockey, and (ironically) compensating for her father's constant company of Playboy "bunnies" when she was growing up. In this way, sex work is believed to be subversive of the sexual status quo and radical in its goal of freeing women from the subordination, humiliation, and abuse that accompanies women's economic and social dependence on men.[119]

However, many sex workers admit to creating an intentional barrier between themselves and the dominant culture for their own protection. Prostitutes risk their livelihoods by coming out politically in favor of workers' rights and the abolition of laws against prostitution. Women in the sex industry who are found to be organizing, striking, or agitating are quickly blackballed: jobs become scarce, and fellow workers become frightened and stay away. Exposed sex workers risk loss of alternative employment, housing, custody of children, scholarships, and loans and alienation from friends and family. The sex industry remains a netherworld where many women seek shelter from abusive spouses and families. Thus, it is even more important from the sex worker's point of view that feminists take the time to uncover, in a conscientious and caring way, their individual stories of survival.[120]

From this perspective, feminists who regard sex workers as either victims of an overpowering patriarchy or collaborators in collective brainwashing are themselves collaborators in refusing individual women the freedom to define their sexuality and their economic lives in their own terms. If all heterosexual prostitution, stripping, and pornography is based on male power backed by force, then autonomous choice for women within the industry collapses. When Pat Califia points out that dominatrixes and others on the s/m game do not mock the oppressed but, rather, *are* the oppressed, her aim is to give such women tools to fight their sexual oppression, not to condemn them to it. Compare Califia's comments to those of Catharine MacKinnon, who accuses the editors of *Powers of Desire* of false consciousness for thinking that they can define and express a distinctively women's sexuality under patriarchy: "Women often find ways to resist male supremacy and to expand their spheres of action. But they are never free of it. . . . From pornography one learns that forcible violation of women is the essence of sex."[121]

Most adult sex workers have very strong views about the abuse of children in pornography and prostitution and do not deny that the kind of work women and men do in the sex industry has its exploitative and violent side. Sex workers argue, however, that such dangers are present in order to silence women who would dare to use their own sexuality as a source for economic and erotic power. Degrading sex work inevitably results in degrading the commodity that sex workers offer; thus, women whose real poverty makes sex work their only option or whose sex work has liberated them from incest or abuse at home have been effectively stigmatized by feminists simply for trying to make a living. From this perspective, therefore, feminists who would deny sex workers their work are doing precisely what a patriarchy interested in keeping women economically dependent on men, and dividing women against themselves, would want. Sex workers only hear contempt in patronizing comments to the effect that to save an otherwise wounded pride, sex workers simply do not want to confront the reality of their victimization. For example, Catharine MacKinnon observes: "Women who are compromised, cajoled, pressured, tricked, black-mailed, or outright forced into sex (or pornography) often respond to the unspeakable humiliation, coupled with the sense of having lost some irreplaceable integrity, by claiming that sexuality as their own. Faced with no alternatives, the strategy to acquire self-respect and pride is: I chose it." Compare such comments to those of former porn actress Candida Royalle: "I was never forced or coerced to do *anything*. . . . [Antiporn feminists] don't want to hear that *I made the choice to do this*" (Royalle's italics).[122]

Sex workers and sex radical feminists also warn that sex-related materials vital to public education about AIDS and family planning, agendas for the promotion of gay and lesbian rights, and sexually explicit materials that could enhance the exploration and enjoyment of women's sexuality are all endangered by a feminist diatribe against sex work. Feminists like Alisa Carse worry that censoring pornography will only serve to restrict a feminist liberation of sexuality by supporting "a strenuous politics of silence and repression."[123] Moreover, sex radicals argue that if feminists encourage women to breach the boundaries of traditional erotic and social territory by being lesbians, then feminists must support sex workers, many of whom are lesbians, in their own challenge of the sexual landscape. Indeed, women-only escort services, strip clubs, erotic videos, and lesbian pornographic novels represent a small but growing segment of the sex industry, and safer sex initiatives using sexually explicit depictions have begun to take off in gay male and lesbian communities. Heterosexual and lesbian women who use pornography report that it allows them to detect their own repressed sexuality and confirm existing desires and empowers them to define their own sexual agendas. They increasingly demand erotic videos with real plots, showing women living full lives of which pleasurable, mutually satisfying sex is a part. Lesbian porn and prostitution mirror radical lesbianism outside the industry in aiming directly at subverting the sexual ideology that says only men get to have pleasurable, recreational sex. There has also emerged a category of bisexual pornography aimed at subverting prescribed sexualities without identifying exclusively with men or women. From a sex radical view, women of all classes, ethnicities, and sexual preferences must work together in a sex-positive, not sex-negative, approach to free women's pursuit of the sexual subjectivity and economic self-definition that is at the heart of sex work.[124]

Objectification without Victimization

My contention is that the extent to which sex workers are the defining subjects of their sexual lives is the extent to which they can begin to transcend patriarchal limitations of their choice of work and male-identified definitions of women's sexuality. A woman's socially constructed sexuality under conditions of male dominance is so closely identified with *who she is as a person* that when she sells her sexuality, she appears to sell her *self*—namely, her subjectivity, her agency. Moreover, if sex in such a culture turns good women into bad, then the degradation of a woman, through the identification of her with her sexuality, is a fundamental one, affecting her identity as a self-determining moral agent.[125] When feminists complain that sex work is degrading to women, many of us do so in the belief not that sex work cannot be pleasurable for women but that such pleasure resides in the identification of women with a subordinating, male-identified sexuality that does not allow women to explore our sexuality in our own terms.

Sex work is pleasurable, profitable, and liberating for women in an environment where women's options for both work and social status compared to those of men are

circumscribed by a feminine stereotype that relegates women to the private, domestic, sexual, and reproductive sphere and men to the public, professional, intellectual,
and political one. Men's power in such a culture is the power to define the public
world as more valuable than the private and to convince women that our real value
lies in the sexual and reproductive roles that fulfill men's interests and men's needs.
Professional career women can still be expected to take responsibility for child care
and housework, hiring other women to perform the necessary day labor; sexual harassment, violence, and abuse, no matter what a woman's social or economic status,
are reminders of her primary gender identification as the sexual subordinate of men.
In a culture that fully approves of women only when we are heterosexually attractive,
women will appear "naturally" to gravitate to those social and economic roles that
portray us as the proper sexual objects of men as a way of gaining prestige, social acceptance, and financial support. Such prestige is tenuous, however, as I pointed out
in chapter 2, since a woman's socially constructed sexuality, reconceptualized as the
"nature" of woman, is as much an excuse for her degradation and abuse as for her
approval by men. Thus, when women choose sex work, they do so within a political
hierarchy that circumscribes their legitimate social and economic choices in terms
of women's natural and proper sexual subordination to men.

Women who choose sex work under such ideological conditions must be regarded
as both the subjects and *objects* of their sexual experience. They remain subjects in
that even sex workers victimized by poverty or blackmailed into sex work are women
whose eroticism derives in part from their being perceived as women whose wills can
be subordinated and controlled. Moreover, many self-identified sex workers enjoy
what they do, agree to basic terms and conditions of work that earns them a supporting and sometimes superior income, and take pleasure in the personal satisfaction of a job well done. Nevertheless, all such women are also the male-identified
objects of a subordinating sexuality that is reinforced by the prevailing culture and
made real by rape, sexual harassment, battery, and abuse that are justified by appeals
to female inferiority. A woman's willingness to model sexual bondage or abuse, to
portray rape for sport, or simply to parade naked in high heels before high-paying,
fully clothed men is a sign to many feminists of just how successful her indoctrination into her own subordination has become. From such a view, the sex industry
functions as a medium of social control for insuring women's sexual compliance and
reinforcing our political silence. As Catharine MacKinnon points out, "[W]ho listens to a woman with a penis in her mouth?"[126] Such control is particularly defam-
ing, according to some feminists, because while Jews and blacks have been treated
like laboratory rats or plow horses, no one ever assumed that those persecuted *wanted*
to be treated that way. Therefore, even the work of the most self-identified female sex
worker will be circumscribed by a subject/*object* dialectic that commits her to examining how her actions encourage and reinforce the prevailing sexual ideology.

For example, when sex worker Valerie Scott says that most of her married clients
still love their wives but that sometimes men just need a sexual change of pace,[127]
she fails to situate her prostitution within a sexist ideology in which women have no
similar outlet for our adulterous peccadillos nor a way to maintain our status of
"good girl" if we had. Thus, even if Scott is right that "lust will never replace love,"
so that truly loved wives need not be threatened by prostitution, she does not take re-

sponsibility for the fact that her prostitution reinforces a sexual double standard that deprives women's sexuality of an eroticism fully defined in our terms. As Anne McClintock points out:

> Sure, men don't get enough sex; but then neither do women. Men have privileged access to the global emporium of porn and prostitution — not to mention that hardy perennial the double standard. Women's desire, by contrast, has been crimped and confined to history's sad museum of corsets, chastity belts, the virginity cult and genital mutilation. Alongside women's erotic malnourishment, men's sexual scarcity looks like a Roman banquet.[128]

Given this double standard, the power the prostitute says she has over her customer is temporary and socially invisible relative to his; thus, Scott may fail to see how easily her power can be subverted to empower her customer's sex objectification of his whore *and* his wife (*and* his secretary *and* his girlfriend . . .). The fact that sex workers tend not to share their real horror stories in public and consider violence to be one of the risks of the job suggests that even their occasional abuse and humiliation by men has to some degree undermined their ability to be liberated from it.[129] It also suggests that while no one likes to be a victim, sex workers must recognize that they do not act in social isolation from a patriarchal culture of sexual violence and submission given tacit approval by women who appear to choose their own objectification.

When feminist women of color object to stereotypical depictions of them in pornography, especially s/m porn, they see women who pose for such depictions as women who accept their identification by both black and white males as sexual slaves and bestial whores. Alice Walker suggests that pornography bonds black men to white men *as men*, so that black women are no longer sisters in a common struggle with black men against racial oppression but sexual objects to be consumed. Alice Mayall and Diana Russell complain that racism in pornography is largely ignored because it is made sexy, thus desirable and pleasurable. When black women complain about their portrayal in pornography, they are attacked by black men as aligning themselves with a feminist movement of white, overprivileged "hags."[130] From within such a cultural milieu, the facts that the proportion of black prostitutes in countries like the United States and Canada is much higher than their percentage in the general population, and that they typically comprise the majority of street prostitutes where the life is most dangerous and least lucrative, bespeak a racism in education, housing, and employment that forces black women into the streets. Nina Lopez-Jones claims that many madams, escort services, massage parlors, and clubs refuse to hire black women; services that do hire them tend to keep minimum quotas that restrict black women to streetwalking.[131] Since street work is highly visible, women of color not only are more frequently arrested but, ironically, also serve to reinforce the black stereotype entertained by many whites of the insatiable sexual animal. When women of color are hired by escort services, they are advertised as especially hot or submissive, and men who call such services ask for them specifically if they want "kinky" sex. Perhaps this image is reinforced by the fact that while white women make up the majority of women depicted in pornography, women of color tend to fall into the "special interest" categories of s/m, bondage, lesbian sex, and sex with children.[132]

Feminists are predictably split over sex work's political priorities. While conference pro-industry feminists talk about reform, education, and self-esteem, conference women of color talk about racism, feeding their children, and economic powerlessness.[133] The contention of women of color is that commending sex work as pleasurable, profitable, or subversive in its exploration of alternative sexual styles will be commendations of both racism and sexism if care is not taken to understand the cultural framework of interlocking oppressions within which such sex work takes place.

Ironically, in their demand that sex work be treated like any other occupation in light of the bread and butter of its eroticism, sex workers underestimate the extent to which the *sex* in their work represents a primary tool for the subordination of women under patriarchy. The husband watching a pornographic video who says, "Honey, I want to do this," is not watching a cooking video to encourage his wife to try out new recipes. The woman whistling at a male stripper is not applauding a male violinist. The customer visiting a prostitute has come to exchange money for *sex*, not encyclopedias. Sex is what makes pornography, stripping, and prostitution so attractive to so many people, and sex is what makes women's and men's personal relations such a complex potential of the unpredictable, the dangerous, the frustrating, the pleasurable, and the political. Without recognizing that sex workers cannot choose to ply their trade outside an institutionalized ideology of sexism and sexual subordination in which their industry plays a part, they adopt the "view from nowhere," which distorts their choices by suggesting that they can be made from within a social vacuum. When sex workers compare their work to nursing or typing, they not only ignore the training and social skills that make such professions those to which a poor and inexperienced woman cannot turn as a last resort; they also fail to acknowledge that sex work is a highly stigmatized and often criminalized occupation to which poor and inexperienced women are forced to turn. Society does not teach women that if all else fails, women can always get attention and money *by typing*; society teaches women that if all else fails, women can always offer *sex*. In offering such comparisons, sex workers downplay the dangers of coercion and abuse that accompany a job with such a high degree of illegitimacy and inferiority attached to it; and they also tend to underestimate the extent to which the economic restriction and sex objectification of women may subvert their efforts at control of their lives. Feminists are doing fundamental consciousness-raising when we urge sex workers who could pursue other lines of work to understand that they choose a profession whose socially illicit nature reinforces the institutionalized marginalization and silencing of women, despite the profits involved. Yet because one of the ways women are politically oppressed is through the linking of moral defilement and inferiority to women's sexuality, what sex workers usually hear in feminists' laments about the oppressive nature of sex work is that sex is morally wrong. While sex workers are justified in objecting to their characterization as symbols of women's oppression, their work symbolizes a powerful means whereby men reaffirm their claim to the unconditional sexual availability of women. Unless sex workers see their work in such terms, they will inevitably alienate feminists whose fight to extricate women from the grip of patriarchy begins with an acknowledgment of its power.

Sex workers are correct in asserting that they cannot control any man's particular penchant for regarding women solely as a means to his own sexual gratification. In fact, they will say that being such a means is exactly what their job requires. What sex workers deny is that their being treated as sex objects is always, or even often, treatment that enhances their customers' sense of erotic and economic power at the expense of their own. Nevertheless, as a sex worker in an industry still dominated and profit-driven by the cult of macho and the subordination of the female, she must recognize that the power of her market value or her ability to capitalize on the sexual desire of men may be exploited to serve male financial and sexual interests at her expense.

In view of such contradictions, I have argued that we should regard sex workers as both the subjects and the objects of their experience. They create their own burlesque theater; they contract for and write pornographic scripts; they act as therapist, social worker, and confidante to the men they service. Under such conditions it is difficult to describe their work as reducing them to nothing more than "tits and ass." Indeed, the subject/object dialectic that I contend is at the heart of sex work suggests that the reduction of a woman to a sexy body is as much a function of her erotic power as her powerlessness. Therefore, I suggest that a sex worker's choice can be objectifying without always being *victimizing*. Sex workers can be treated as commodities by their customers without being the victims of abusive pimps or exploitative club managers. Sex workers can make a profit from selling their bodies without needing sex work to keep them from starvation. Nevertheless, the words of one former pornography model put the issue of women's sexual exploitation at the heart of the sex work debate: "The thing is, with enough stress or enough need any woman will do things she never thought she would do before."[134]

My claim is that all sex work must be described and evaluated from within the social construction of oppressive sexual institutions that circumscribe women's lives. Such evaluations, however, must not so determine women's sexuality that women cannot, even in principle, define for ourselves what is to count as satisfying sex and sex work. To do so would effectively condemn the feminist enterprise of constructive change in heterosexual relations from within the patriarchal institutions in which feminists live. By characterizing sex work in terms of a dialectic between subject and object, sex workers are in a position to use their work as a source for their liberation from the economic and sexual subordination of men. The desire for liberation, however, must be characterized and evaluated in terms of the objectifying gaze that defines the subordinate position from which she would liberate herself. Thus, the subject/object dialectic that characterizes sex work reflects the broader dialectic between gender and sexuality that I believe gives voice to the diversity of women's sexuality. Treating sex workers with a care respect circumscribed by the "view from somewhere different" and convincing sex workers to take the same view toward both their own work and the concerns of feminists is the subject of the following section.

Treating Sex Workers with Care Respect

Is the prostitute the quintessential oppressed woman or the quintessential liberated woman? Or is the prostitute simply a woman who, like all women in this society, is struggling to understand and live her own sexuality?

—Rosemarie Tong, *Women, Sex, and the Law*

In other words, there is no real stereotype of who a prostitute woman is—
she could be any of us.

—Rachel West, "U.S. PROStitutes Collective"

The debate over the meaning and morality of sex work is a debate easily polarized by sex workers and feminists alike. Some feminists accuse sex workers of overestimating the agency and autonomy of sex work in a social milieu whose institutionalized ideology defines women as the sexual subordinates of men. Some sex workers accuse feminists of overemphasizing the status of woman as victim in a patriarchal society, such that women have no possibility of subverting the sexual status quo to meet the needs and goals of women. Some feminists argue that sex work symbolizes male dominance backed by force; sex workers argue that such a description makes all consent to sex work and all nonviolent sex work meaningless. Feminists accuse sex workers of mistaking an internalized patriarchy for sexual freedom; sex workers accuse feminists of recreating an oppressive patriarchy by not affording sex workers the means to their own sexual liberation. Indeed, from a sex worker's perspective, if women's brainwashing by men is so complete, then the feminist agenda itself must be suspect. In short, feminists accuse sex workers of not gendering their sexuality; sex workers accuse feminists of not sexually liberating our politics of gender. My claim has been that recognizing sex work as a dialectical relation between subject and object means recognizing the dialectic between gender and sexuality that negotiates the tensions between those who regard sex work as oppressive to women and those who regard sex work as liberating to women. Such a dialectic affirms that sex work can be objectifying at the same time that it can provide workers with a subjectivity and potentially liberating sexual agency. The dialectic between gender and sexuality affirms that sex work within patriarchy can be self-determining at the same time that sex work can be degrading in a culture in which women's sexuality has historically been circumscribed by men's subordination of women.

Such an analysis is consistent with the view of Irene Diamond, who warns that overemphasizing the violence in pornography makes porn evil without challenging traditional attitudes about sex but that conceiving of pornography solely as sexually explicit material cannot account for the ways in which pornography functions to maintain and encourage the domination of women.[135] It is also consistent with the suggestion by Rosemarie Tong quoted at the beginning of this section that a sex worker need not be construed exclusively as either oppressed or liberated but can be regarded as a woman struggling amid the objectification and subjectivity of her work in order to find some meaning and value in it.

In this section I introduce what it would mean to treat sex workers with the care respect outlined at the end of chapter 3, in order to capture the dialectical elements of women's sexuality and sex work described thus far. I will suggest that feminists' "world"-traveling to a sex worker's social location can help feminists acknowledge, understand, and promote the agendas of sex workers who wish to use their profession as a source for personal growth, entrepreneurial profit, or economic survival. In addition, I will show how Marjorie Weinzweig's notion of autonomous relating to others and Joyce Trebilcot's notion of taking responsibility for one's sexuality can help a sex worker situate her work within the larger social context of men's sexual subordination of women. Thus, by listening to each other with the particularized sensitivity and social responsibility implied by a sexual ethic of care respect, both feminists and sex workers can better promote our common goal of sexual self-determination for all women.

Recall from chapter 3 that treating a person with care respect means not only valuing her as one among many unique individuals worthy of respect but also valuing the particular ways in which she is unique. This perspective allows us to acknowledge the shared partiality of social location in all of us as well the contextual specificity of each person. An ethic of care respect also requires that we try to understand an individual in her own terms and not through our favored ways of seeing her and that we try to promote, where possible and desirable, the interests of individuals consistent with that ethic. Thus, a sexual ethic of care respect is not confined merely to personal sexual relations but extends outward to individuals and institutions that are a part of one's larger community.

This perspective reiterates the recommendation from the "view from somewhere different," introduced in chapter 1, that each one of us "world"-travel in order to understand and more effectively promote the particular worldview of others. Such traveling reminds us to ask the questions "What is it like to be them?" and "What is it like to be myself in their eyes?" It is a point of view that requires me to recognize that my "world" is not the only one worth knowing, and that my perspective will always be partial to *my* needs and *my* interests in a way that will often make it difficult to understand the partiality of others.

Therefore, treating sex workers with care respect will mean trying to see the world from their point of view and, even more important, to respect each worker as a unique individual whose social location specifies her needs and interests in ways that may be quite different from other sex workers' or my own. Such a relationship requires establishing open lines of communication and trust between feminists and sex workers through which we can exchange points of view. Former stripper Amber Cooke cautions, however, that politics is a luxury that most sex workers cannot practically or legally afford.[136] Thus, care respect for sex workers means realizing that only those sex workers (and feminists) who know about seminars, attend conferences, or will risk speaking in a public forum will be heard. Such women show that they already have the freedom of choice that many sex workers do not. This means that sex workers who do politicize their profession must recognize that they are not representative of sex workers as a whole and must work, in deference to the "view from somewhere different," to find ways to include otherwise silenced agendas on the table.

As I mentioned earlier in the chapter, sex workers who politicize their work must also face an often humiliating and skeptical public eye when they voice their concerns about the terms and conditions of their work. They also risk losing their means of financial support and custody of their children for coming out as illegal workers. For this reason it is all the more important that feminists wishing to align ourselves with sex workers in pursuit of women's economic and sexual self-determination be willing to listen to, and speak on behalf of, sex workers with the time and money to be political as well as sex workers with no such opportunities. Feminists must also remember that many sex workers will mistrust our political agenda, since concerns about the degradation of women in sex can sound exactly like moral prudery. By asking "What is it like to be myself in this sex worker's eyes?," feminists can sensitize ourselves to such misunderstandings in order to better establish lines of connectedness with sex workers. Inviting nonintrusive and safe conversations with sex workers in bars, clubs, and on the street; visiting them during a studio session; buying them dinner; helping them pay the bills; finding them affordable housing; meeting their child-care needs for a day—in other words, meeting sex workers on their turf without intruding on their turf: these are the practical strategies that Amber Cooke believes will show sex workers that feminists are committed to addressing their specific, daily needs as well as the longer-term needs of women within the industry as a whole.[137]

Just as feminists are required to "world"-travel epistemologically and practically to an individual sex worker's social location in order to find common ground, so, too, a sex worker must adopt an ethic of care respect from the "view from somewhere different" if she is to understand a feminist's emphasis on the historical and social context in which she works. In this respect, developing the autonomy characterized in chapter 3 as autonomous relating to others and taking responsibility for her sexuality under conditions of patriarchy will be vital for any sex worker, both to "world"-travel successfully to a feminist's critical perspective and to make better sense of her own. For example, when a sex worker stigmatized by some for her association with the sex industry chooses to make an economically better life for herself in sex work rather than in social work, she exercises an autonomous *being oneself* in which she chooses to act for herself alone and not in virtue of how others might want her to act; but a woman who exercises an autonomous *relating to others* recognizes both her own individual needs *and* the needs of others. Such an autonomy requires that she see her actions within the context of a larger community of women whose own needs and interests may conflict with her own. In this way a sex worker may locate her work within a feminist community that will ask her to question some of her presuppositions about the benefits of sex work.

Therefore, a sex worker who adopts a sexual ethic of care respect will be required to take responsibility for her sexuality. She does so by reflecting on the extent to which her sexuality originates with her, and also the extent to which her sexuality is a function of male-identified, institutionalized sexual values that she has adopted for the sake of survival, approval, or profit. This is not to suggest that such reflections are easily parsed out or that her awareness of her gendered context will necessarily alter her pursuit of sex work. Her responsibility for her sexuality will recommend locating the common feminist complaint that sex work is degrading to women in a political context, not a context of moral and sexual conservatism. ("What is it like to be them?") Also, by asking herself "What is it like to be myself in their eyes?," a sex worker can better understand why some feminists might regard sex work as collaborating with the enemy or as work so infused by patriarchal approval that sex workers assume the pleasure from their work to be self-determining. Such "world"-traveling can be motivated by the conviction, based on the "view from somewhere different," that sex workers' happiness and well-being will be improved when they see their lives as part of a larger community of women whose combined efforts at securing women's liberation are stronger than any single effort alone. Such a perspective will also allow a sex worker to see the variety within feminism, so that she need not think that feminists are unilaterally against sex work or against one form of sex work. Furthermore, taking responsibility for her sexuality will allow her to see the diversity among sex workers, especially those whose work may be much less lucrative or satisfying than her own. In this way her considered judgments about her own work and sex work generally will be better informed and more sensitive to feminist politics than before.

From this perspective, the relevant question for both sex workers and feminists is not "What kind of sex do women like?" but "What kind of sex (if any) does *this woman* like?" If both women's and men's contemporary sexuality is a complex social construction under conditions in which patriarchal institutions define the norms of the sexual, then it makes no sense to ask, paraphrasing Freud, "What do women *really* want?" Enmeshed as we are within the social framework that circumscribes our sexuality, we cannot know which aspects of our sexual lives are defined by conditions of women's sexual subordination by men and which are the "natural" conditions of women. Alan Soble critiques a Reichian sexual philosophy on the basis that we cannot know what kind of sexuality will emerge from repressive capitalist conditions, when all we know about that sexuality is circumscribed by those conditions. On this basis, however, I do not think that Soble can argue for his thesis that there will be pornography under communism with any more epistemological certainty than Reich has at his disposal.[138] The question of whether or not there will be sex work in the ideal society assumes that there is one ideal to which individual women and men universally subscribe and to which we all have the same epistemological access, a perspective firmly ensconced in the "view from nowhere," which I have argued greatly misrepresents the variety and complexity of women's sexuality. What we can say is that our individual attitudes toward our own and others' sexualities is quixotic and complex enough to warrant skepticism about making generalizations concerning what women (and men) may derive politically or personally from sex work. As with Andrea Dworkins's *Mercy*, the subject/object dialectic in sex work makes distinctions between pornography, erotica, and feminist moral realism tenuous even when their contexts are carefully noted. Robert Stoller has pointed out, "In both art and erotics, *each episode feels different and is done differently from every other episode,* even in the same person" (Stoller's italics).[139] Feelings of power and powerlessness, fear and rage, tenderness and intimacy often paradoxically combine to form a single human sexual relationship. Sex work, like sex, is simply too complexly motivated to lend itself to easy analysis or simple categories.

To affirm this ambiguous, contradictory, and uncertain space is typically unpopular with philosophers and feminists who require analytically and morally determinable foundations from which to argue their positions. My thesis throughout this book has been that while both feminism and philosophy are essential to clarify the issues that divide people over sex, it is a mistake to treat sex itself as capable of conceptual and moral clarity. What we do need is more women talking *and listening* to each other, so that we will feel united, not divided, by our diversity; and we need more women talking to men who perform sex work, more women listening to men who are embarrassed, confused, or themselves enraged by sex work, and more women willing to "world"-travel to the social location of men who simply cannot get enough of what the sex industry has to offer.[140] Exploring the tensions in women's and men's attitudes toward sex work without the superiority of the "view from somewhere better" or the univocal perspective of the "view from nowhere" means negotiating the tensions—accommodating, even embracing them, not disregarding or ignoring them after attempts at resolution have failed. Indeed, I contend that such attempts at resolution arbitrarily and artificially close important conceptual, moral, and political questions, thus dividing women against each other when openness to such questions would unite sex workers and feminists.

Efforts at eradicating specific sex work practices commonly ignore those women whose only sense of identity and autonomy derives from sex work. On the other hand, celebrating the subversiveness of the self-identified "bad girl" can minimize the ways in which sex work is used to justify and reinforce men's sexual subordination of women. Both run the risks of polarizing the dialogue and alienating women from our common goal of sexual subjectivity and self-definition for all women. Both sex workers and feminists must recognize that a debilitating sexual double standard that turns "good" girls into "bad" ones, combined with economic discrimination that drives many women to a profession stigmatized by that standard, are the real enemies, not sex workers or feminists. Without such recognition, women may unwittingly fall prey to the socially ubiquitous "blame the woman" syndrome that both sex workers and feminists contest. The extent to which sex work will be liberating for women will be the extent to which individual women of diverse perspectives can define their sexuality in their own terms and, as members of a caring community of women, live differently together in ways that help secure for all women the educational and economic opportunities necessary for informed vocational choice.

Conclusion

Driving the sex industry underground with accusations of political incorrectness will not constructively address those aspects of the trade that promote or reinforce the degradation and abuse of women; nor will successfully eliminating abuses within the sex industry change the content of billboards and soap operas that also capitalize on the equation of a woman's identity with her sexual availability to men. The sex industry is a conducive environment for the exploitation of women, since the industry exists within a culture in which heterosexual sex has been, and continues to be, a primary means of intimidation of women through rape, sexual harassment, wife battering, incest, and the forced traffic in women.[141] However, this is not equivalent to saying that every female sex worker is a victim nor that sex workers must work for feminist producers, procurers, or club managers in order not to be collaborators in patriarchy. Moreover, pinning harm to women on the sex industry, its workers, or its images absolves rapists and batterers of their responsibility for their violence against women.[142] Indeed, sex workers are often assigned the impossible role of being both the brainwashed victims of an oppressive patriarchy and the willful causal agents of men's violence against women.

The goal of feminists working to separate pornography from erotica is to give women sex work and sexually explicit material that is nonsexist and nondegrading to women. Yet many such feminists err in assuming that we can easily distinguish the pornographic from the erotic or that women who perceive themselves as feminists would not want to be turned on by bondage, discipline, anonymous sex, group sex, telephone sex, computer sex, and other alternative sexual styles depicted or otherwise offered for sale by the sex industry. This is not to suggest that sexual pleasure is its own justification. It is simply to remind feminists that women must be given the freedom to explore sexual difference if we are to transcend the restrictive standards of women's sexuality under patriarchy. It is also to remind sex workers that such standards are easily reinforced by behavior that can be reframed by the status quo and mistaken by feminists as women desiring our sexual subordination by men. Characterizing sex work as a dialectic between subject and object allows feminists and sex workers to talk to each other about the meaning and morality of sex work without devolving into the polarization and alienation that has characterized so much of the dialogue in recent years. By adopting a sexual ethic of care respect derived from the "view from somewhere different," feminists and sex workers can better understand how a woman's sale of her sexuality can be both a vehicle for her subordination and her liberation.[143] How this perspective can help us understand the pervasiveness of women's sexual intimidation at home and at work is the subject of the final chapter.

5

Appropriating Women's Bodies

The Form and Function of Men's Sexual Intimidation of Women

Overview

The woman who says, "He talked me into it" after having consensual sex is still seen as a good girl. The young woman who says, "I invited him up to my place; we got naked and had a blast" is often still deemed a slut.

—Rene Denfeld, *The New Victorians: A Young Woman's Challenge to the Old Feminist Order*

As the previous chapters suggest, one of the ways that individual women are punished for defying patriarchal models of feminine sexuality is by being denigrated to the status of "loose woman." When a woman chooses to be promiscuous, or when she questions the desirability of a compulsory and traditional heterosexuality, or when she turns a profit from selling sex, she becomes tantalizing proof of a potential for sexual agency and self-definition that must be discouraged if she is to continue in the sexual service of male desire. Moreover, as Rene Denfeld implies, so-called good girls acquire and maintain their good-girl status by acquiescing to the sexual intimidation of men—if not by appearing to submit to men's sexual persistence, then by actually relenting to ultimately coercive sexual advances. Still other women acquiesce to sexual intimidation by remaining silent in the face of sexual violence or psychological abuse. From this perspective, men's sexual harassment, rape, battery, and abuse of women and girls are the visible exemplars of men's attempts to insure that women stay well within the boundaries of male-identified conceptions of women's "proper place."

Indeed, many feminists point out that sexual violence against women in the United States is considered staggering enough in scope and intensity that many mental health professionals, social scientists, and legal theorists refer to it as a national epidemic.[1] However, these same feminists contend that characterizing sexual violence as *epidemic* may leave many with the impression that the violator is a mentally ill, deviant, or otherwise deranged individual whose personal responsibility for his actions is mitigated by serious psychopathology. Feminist researchers of sexual violence against women point out that such acts are perpetrated by men of every class, nationality, race, age, sexual preference, or religion, men whose personality profiles most often put them well within the range of "normal" and whose victims are themselves equally diverse.[2] The 1990s have seen a dramatic increase in various highly publicized sexual harassment, rape, or battery allegations, including Anita Hill's 1991 charges of sexual harassment against then Supreme Court Justice nominee Clarence Thomas; allegations against former U.S. Senator Bob Packwood for sexual harassment over the past two decades of several female secretaries and aides; Paula Jones's allegations of sexual harassment by President Bill Clinton when he was governor of Arkansas; charges of sexual assault at the 1991 Tailhook Association Convention in Las Vegas, at which over 100 female officers were allegedly accosted by Navy and Marine Corps men; allegations of rape against Mike Tyson (1991, convicted) and William Kennedy Smith (1992, acquitted); charges of sexual harassment and intimidation against the 1993 Lakewood, California, high school men's Spur Posse, whose members would compete for the best female "score"; and O. J. Simpson's alleged harassment and assault of his former wife Nicole Brown Simpson, whose murder he was charged with (1994) and acquitted of (1995). Such cases paint a very public picture of workplace, domestic, and campus life that, together with researchers' survey data, would appear to reflect women's widespread sexual intimidation by men.

Feminism is often identified with the claim that the pervasive and often violent sexual intimidation of women by men is by no means a coincidental series of isolated, spontaneous, or unrelated events; rather, it is evidence of the systematic and institutionalized sexual subordination of women whose intimidation serves a patriarchal status quo. Indeed, many feminists contend that while women are less likely to be the victims of violent crime than men, men prey on other men (and women defend themselves against men) in ways that do not maintain and reinforce a cultural ideology that encourages the devaluation and sexual subordination of the male sex.[3] It is argued that in a patriarchal society in which social and economic power and prestige lie in the hands of men, the sexual intimidation of women is an especially successful means of maintaining dominance over and control of women, when that intimidation is built into the very fabric of our laws, education, economics, media, culture, and family life. From this perspective, tacit institutional approval of women's sexual harassment and abuse creates a climate of paranoia and fear in which women gain no social recognition for the violence they experience nor any economic independence or legal protection from it. Coerced into unconditional sexual accessibility by men in positions of social and economic power who define the terms and conditions of women's lives, women become the sexual victims of men. Marilyn French refers to the insidiousness of such socially sanctioned appropriation of women's bodies by men as the "slime under the rug of patriarchy."[4] The sexual victimization of women is successfully reinforced by patriarchal sex role socialization that teaches men to be sexually dominant and women to be sexually submissive, and the resulting model of woman's fundamental inferiority and passivity justifies and legitimizes the violence done to her. This is the thrust of many feminists' claim that men abuse women because they can.[5] From this view, sexual harassment, rape, woman battering, and the sexual abuse of girls become the tools of sexual intimidation whereby men establish and maintain their dominance and supremacy over women. Men's sexual violation, terrorization, coercion, and dehumanization of women insure this dominance by turning women into sexual victims. The ultimate elimination of such victimization, according to such a view, would require the wholesale dismantling of the hierarchical structures of our current patriarchal politics and sex role socialization within the family that reinforce, and are enforced by, the sexual intimidation of women. Feminists who subscribe to the general tenets of this theory claim that unless men's sexual intimidation of women is exposed and vilified for its systematic and pervasive violence against women, women will never be free to control our own bodies and so our own sexual and reproductive lives.[6]

However, socially constructing the problem of individual women's sexual intimidation by defining women *as a class* as sexually subordinate to men has appeared to at least some feminists only to reinvigorate the debilitating feminine stereotype of the sexually passive and vulnerable woman. Such feminists argue that much of feminist theory in effect *defines* or *determines* women as victims in ways that ironically succeed in performing patriarchy's own task of inhibiting women's sexual agency and self-definition. Critics claim that the victim mentality apparently promoted by many feminists absolves women of their responsibility for taking undue risks in sexually dangerous environments that common sense would dictate avoiding altogether; and sexual harassment policies only succeed in communicating that women need special protection in an overwhelmingly hostile male environment. Critics contend that date rape brochures advise an unrealistically sterile approach to sex that denies the inevitability and legitimacy of flirtation and temptation in sex, depicting women as helpless victims of coercive male sexual power. Many of these same critics would agree that individual men count on the passive and silent suffering of women to perpetuate men's crimes against women and to reinforce a legal and social services system that discriminates against women. These feminists would acknowledge that when that silence is broken, as it is in the consciousness-raising forums of public speak-outs, marches, educational seminars, and community-sponsored public meetings, the community becomes accountable for the ways in which it has blamed, ignored, or trivialized the violence that many men inflict on women. It is contended, however, that more than a few members of that community feel bombarded by feminists' antimale and antisex propaganda that says all men are potential rapists and no heterosexual bedroom is safe for women. Feminists critical of antirape marches and incest victims' speak-outs believe that these activities produce a "groupthink" hysteria about male violence against women that results in false accusations of men's sexual abuse of women and effectively closes women's minds to the possibility of satisfying sexual exploration and pleasure with passionate and pleasure-seeking men. From this perspective, presuming that an institutionally entrenched, ubiquitous, and all-powerful patriarchy sexually oppresses women at every opportunity alienates many women who would like to call themselves feminists but are hesitant to align themselves with a political platform that does not match their own experience of either men or sex. Indeed, it is argued that the evidence for a so-called epidemic of sexual violence against women is based on ambiguously worded surveys and misleading statistics that overestimate the actual battering and rape women suffer at the hands of men and underestimate individual women's causal role in their own abuse.[7]

The dilemma is a deeply troubling one for feminists: if we ascribe to women too much sexual victimization and not enough sexual agency, we are at risk of reasserting patriarchy's message that women are to be identified as the proper sexual subordinates of men. If we ascribe to women too much sexual agency, however, and fail to see the ways in which women's condition is a socially constructed and institutionally subordinated one under conditions of male dominance, women's sexual harassment and abuse become personal failures that, had *women* only acted differently, would never have happened. In ascribing to women a sexual agency that places the responsibility for their abuse on women, men are able to shirk their own responsibility and reap the social benefits many of them share for intimidating women into men's sexual service. Feminists seem to be left with one of two equally unpalatable choices: a victimization model of woman's condition that appears to essentialize her sexually subordinate situation, despite the political necessity of exposing it; or an agency model of woman's condition that disguises the structural nature of her oppression but affords her the practical and moral basis for her liberation. How can feminists establish and promote women's sexual agency and sexual self-definition from a position of sexual subordination without either overwhelming individual women with a personal responsibility for their sexual abuse that they do not deserve or overdetermining women as sexual victims in ways that alienate women and men from feminism and reinforce debilitating patriarchal values? How do we recognize and politicize the pervasiveness and severity of men's sexual intimidation of women through sexual harassment, rape, woman battering, and the sexual abuse of girls yet at the same time empower women to transcend the status of victim to one of self-determining sexual subject?

I propose that the answer can be found in analyzing women's sexual intimidation under patriarchy from the "view from somewhere different," the perspective I introduced in chapter 1 to provide a viable context and legitimacy for the diversity of voices within feminist debates over women's sexuality. This perspective requires that we recognize not only the ways in which gender politicizes sexuality under conditions of male dominance but also the ways in which sexuality informs gender with liberating strategies for women's (and men's) sexual pleasure, agency, and self-definition. In this chapter I will suggest ways in which we can facilitate a continuing dialogue among feminists of diverse viewpoints concerning the politics of women's sexual intimidation in the face of the apparently irreconcilable views already expressed.

The discussion that follows poses these questions: How should we understand the feminist claim that a woman is the "victim" of a man's sexual intimidation? What do feminists mean when we say that women as a class are sexually "victimized" by male-dominated social institutions? To answer these questions, I offer a detailed summary of several feminists' denunciations of men's sexual harassment, rape, battering, and sexual abuse of women and girls to reveal the normative forms that such victimization takes: (1) the violation of and violence against women; (2) the terrorization of women; (3) the coercion, deception, and manipulation of women; (4) the dehumanization of women. I then look more closely at the feminist counterclaims that by describing women's sexuality as institutionally and pervasively male-dominated, feminists condemn women to the very condition of sexual passivity, feminine fragility, and physical vulnerability from which feminists would extricate women, and that this perspective leaves many women with the impression that feminists are antimale and antisex, if not outrightly misogynistic, when it comes to women who refuse to accept their "victim" role.

After framing the debate, I invoke the "view from somewhere different" to argue that men's sexual intimidation of women can be better represented by socially locating women in dialectical contexts that are both institutionally oppressive and personally liberating. As in the previous chapter on sex work, I contend that women's sexuality in contemporary Western culture can be described in terms of a complex and dynamic subject/object relation; I then use this relation to think and talk about women as both the objects of men's sexual victimization and the defining subjects of our sexual experience as women, capable of transcending the victimization we may suffer. Specifically, using the notion of woman as *survivor*, I argue that a woman's experience of being sexually victimized by men can generate within her a renewed sense of sexual agency and political activism. I contend that women can be reinvigorated by feminist consciousness-raising efforts at identifying men's sexual intimidation of women, not revictimized by them. However, women's sexual subjectivity will be impossible if men and women do not make an effort to dismantle the hierarchical structures and values that reinforce the male dominance of women. Therefore, in the closing section I sketch what is required for men to treat women with care respect in their sexual relations with them, and what women need to understand about men's socially complex power position under patriarchy in order to make that respect a shared one.

Sexual Victimization and Male Dominance

[M]en initiate, women consent—that's mutual?

—Catharine A. MacKinnon, *Feminism Unmodified:*
Discourses on Life and Law

[B]eing a woman [is] a life time occupational hazard in itself.

—Robin Morgan, *The Demon Lover:*
On the Sexuality of Terrorism

Funny, every man I meet wants to protect me. I can't figure out what from.

—Mae West, quoted in Susan Brownmiller,
Against Our Will: Men, Women, and Rape

In this chapter's overview, as well as in previous chapters, I have outlined feminists' arguments for the claim that women's sex role socialization and economic discrimination maintain and reinforce men's power over and control of women. Thus, when a feminist argues that women are sexually victimized by men, she has in mind a victimization circumscribed by an oppressive framework that I refer to as *institutionalized* intimidation. Marilyn Frye describes such a framework as "a network of forces and barriers which are systematically related and which conspire to the immobilization, reduction and molding of women and the lives we live."[8] From this view, any woman is oppressed in that she belongs to an oppressed group whose members are other women, all of whom live in a patriarchal society in which women are devalued, marginalized, or silenced by oppressive social institutions. Because these institutions—law, government, education, religion, medicine, media, culture and the arts, the family—are regulated and controlled at the highest administrative levels by men, it is contended that men effectively dominate women's daily lives, specifically women's sexual and reproductive lives. According to this view, the sexual intimidation of women is central to consolidating male advantage under patriarchy. Thus, when some feminists argue that social and economic institutions support a "rape culture" or that woman battering has been "normalized" under patriarchy, they refer to the power of these institutions to determine the terms and conditions of women's sexuality. While not all feminists contend that every man is a potential rapist, many do believe that sexual harassment, battery, and rape lie on a continuum of violence against women and that all men benefit from the sexual intimidation engendered by some men's rape.[9] From this perspective, sexual harassment, rape, woman battering, and the sexual abuse of girls are designed so effectively to intimidate women that women become dependent *on men* for protection *from men*. Mae West's comment about men's urge to protect her captures the irony and the frustrating paradox of this situation: men maintain their institutional superiority over women by sexually intimidating women, only to reinforce male dominance by convincing women that we need a man's protection from *other* men's abuse but not his own.[10]

In the following pages I will review much of the evidence and many of the arguments that feminists offer in support of the claim that men's sexual intimidation of women maintains and reinforces cultural, political, and economic institutions that are oppressive to all women. My aim is to show how and why many feminists have come to believe that sexual harassment, rape, woman battering, and the sexual abuse of girls have common normative features that bind them together in a pervasive system of sexual intimidation that facilitates men's control over women's sexuality and rationalizes men's unconditional access to women's bodies. This is not to deny that male children are common objects of adult neglect or emotional or physical abuse, although studies suggest that sexually abused girls far outnumber sexually abused boys. My primary concern in this chapter is to examine how *women's* sexual intimidation under patriarchy manifests itself.[11] I begin this discussion with some indication of the conceptual overlap between sexual harassment, rape, woman battering, and the sexual abuse of girls and suggest that this overlap is consistent with the feminist argument offered earlier that such treatment of women is part of a larger, overarching effort aimed at men's sexual domination and control of women. I then discuss in considerable detail the normative features that feminists most often cite as common to men's sexual intimidation of women: (1) sexual violation and violence; (2) sexual terrorization; (3) sexual coercion, deception, and manipulation; and (4) sexual dehumanization. Such normative categories are not conceptually discrete or independent, since they circumscribe common features of interrelated types of sexual intimidation. Nevertheless, these categories are helpful in illuminating the variety of complaints individual women make when they are sexually victimized by men; and they are helpful in situating women's sexual intimidation within the socially constructed context of male dominance and control on which many feminists base their condemnation of the sexual oppression of women. Furthermore, while such categories point out the ways in which the variety of forms of sexual intimidation may be linked, they also reveal some of the finer distinctions between sexual harassment, rape, woman battering, and child sexual abuse. Thus, my analysis both draws from and contributes to contemporary feminist theorizing on the sexual victimization of women. My goal in this section is to provide a normative framework for thinking and talking about women's sexual intimidation that is consistent with the feminist claim that such intimidation maintains, and is facilitated by, men's institutionalized dominance and control of women. I can then proceed to explicate and evaluate the critical responses to such a claim, which counter that conceiving of women's lives as pervaded by male heterosexual dominance only serves to reinforce and legitimize men's sexual victimization of women.

Conceptual Confusion

There is wide disagreement among political theorists, moral philosophers, mental health professionals, and legal authorities as to what counts as a clear case of either sexual harassment, rape, woman battering, or the sexual abuse of girls. Because each form of sexual intimidation involves some type of sexual violation, questions typically arise as to how to identify its occurrence. For example, Ellen Frankel Paul feels that we should define sexual harassment sufficiently to exclude the "merely trivial" sexual innuendo yet not equate all sexual harassment with a serious injury like rape. While sexual harassment is a serious violation, Paul, like Rosemarie Tong, believes that merely offensive or annoying sexual behavior must be differentiated from the extreme violation of bodily integrity that is at the heart of rape.[12] On the other hand, to say simply that sexual harassment is *unwanted* sexual behavior condemns all accidental or unintentional slights and includes offenses taken by the sexually paranoid or vindictive person.[13] Both sexual harassment and rape share the feature of being unwelcome sexual overtures that are not asked for and not returned, but this means that the two forms of sexual intimidation also share the ambiguity of the word "unwelcome." Quid pro quo sexual harassment in which sex is made a condition for employment or promotion may be a relatively straightforward case of coercion, but what about a request for a date by a supervisor? In her discussion of harassment within the academy, Nancy Tuana believes that actions count as sexually harassing if a professor or thesis adviser *should have known* that those actions would be construed as an implied threat;[14] yet what may be construed as threatening to one graduate student may seem ludicrous to another or a harmless flirtation to a third. On the other hand, if the harasser's *intent* is the sole criterion of harassment, then sexual harassment claims will deflate in the face of unverifiable excuses like "I didn't *mean* to upset her. I was just . . . [horsing around, trying to flatter her, impress the boys, etc.]," when discernible harm has been done in contradiction to company or educational policy guidelines. This is why the conduct of the harasser and the effects on the harassed, not the intent of the harasser, are the criteria for determining sexual harassment specified by the Equal Employment Opportunity Commission guidelines.[15]

An intruder's violation of a woman in her own bedroom may be a more obvious case of an unwelcome advance than the successful pressure placed on a date to "put out" after an expensive dinner; but a woman who feels manipulated into having sex when it is late and her date is her only ride home feels the sexual violation nevertheless. Feminists are also deeply divided over how a woman's responsibility for her own conduct and choice of male companionship should figure in any moral assessment of his sexual violation of her. John Bogart suggests that raping a woman who is intoxicated makes sense because rape can be both voluntary and nonconsensual, an observation typically overlooked in favor of the more common assumption that a woman's rape always constitutes a sexual assault against her will.[16] These are the very kinds of "hard" cases that have made sexual harassment and rape so difficult to prosecute successfully, a fact made especially painful given the statistics showing that the vast majority of sexual harassers and rapists are men that the victim knows and often knows well. Despite the fact that sexual harassment is a form of gender discrimination that is illegal under Title VII of the Civil Rights Act of 1964 and Title IX of the Education Amendments of 1972, local and federal judges in sexual harassment cases are notorious for their inconsistent interpretation of what constitutes a "hostile environment" for women in the workplace; what an employer "could or should have known" about the harassment; what is "severe or pervasive" treatment of an offensive sort; or what a "reasonable person" would be offended by.[17] For the purposes of my own discussion, *sexual* harassment will be distinguished from *gender* harassment in which the sexuality of the harassed is absent from a description of the gender discrimination against her.

Woman battering can be a form of *sexual* intimidation among teen and adult intimates, because physical abuse or psychological abuse (attacks on self-esteem, scare tactics, or threats) can be used to enforce sexual compliance, and because a woman's breasts, pregnant abdomen, and genitals are often the focus for her abuser's physical attacks. While Rosemarie Tong notes that such sexual battering ideologically links sexual harassment and rape to woman battering, other feminists warn that since it is still legal in some states for a man to rape his wife, a wife's rape and her battering should be kept conceptually separate for the purpose of successfully filing assault charges that can distinguish rape from the beating that may or may not accompany it.[18] On the other hand, if Catharine MacKinnon and others are right that sex is the weapon of choice for men because of its effectiveness in violating women, how do we determine which batterings are "sexual" and which are not? Sex and aggression are not easily parsed out; the slap that is, for some, a sexual turn-on is not easily differentiated from a "merely violent" punch. When some social scientists declare that they do not include sexual aggression in their assessment of violent behavior, they only succeed in biasing their own data with presumptions about the nature and legitimacy of the distinction.[19]

Diana Russell also notes the lack of agreement among researchers as to which sex acts constitute the sexual abuse of children, as well as the researchers' confusion over how to define the term "child." Some researchers distinguish the vaginal or anal rape of children from their "mere" sexual abuse; others refer only to the abuse of a child by an adult but do not consider abuse by peers or younger children to be in the same category. Physical or emotional assault or neglect accompanying the sexual assault of children presents the same problems of identification and differentiation as those concerning woman battering. Legal statutes vary: what is "forcible rape" in one jurisdiction is "impairing the morals of a minor" in another. While focusing on father-daughter incest acknowledges the special power dynamics involved in such an assault, many assume the incestuous father to be the biological father, although there is good reason to think that stepfathers and legal guardians are much more common perpetrators of the sexual abuse of children than biological fathers. The question then arises as to whether or not the sexual abuse of a child by an adoptive parent constitutes incest, and what social inhibitions are minimized if it does not.[20]

The sexual abuse of a four-year-old girl and the physical battering of a teenage girlfriend can both constitute rape; a stepfather's threatening demands for the sexual compliance of his young stepdaughter or the psychological battering of his wife constitute the unwelcome sexual overtures definitive of sexual harassment; a foster father's verbal and sexual abuse of a mature teenager is as much a case of woman battering as child abuse; a rubber penis thrown into a woman's lap at the office is as much psychological battery as sexual harassment. In light of such conceptual overlap, any attempt to draw hard and fast distinctions between cases would be misleading. Indeed, this conceptual overlap in the forms of sexual intimidation mirrors the ways in which the correlative normative concepts of violation, terrorization, coercion, and dehumanization are related: for example, a woman who is battered by her husband is sexually *terrorized* by his threats to her well-being, which are *coercive* and in *violation* of her sexual autonomy and integrity, which in turn *dehumanizes* her to the status of mere object for her husband's sexual consumption.

What I suggest is that the conceptual and normative overlap between various forms of sexual intimidation has instructive, if paradoxical, political implications for feminists. On the one hand, if the systematic sexual intimidation of women is most successful when it is not exposed for public scrutiny and, when exposed, only confuses many women and men by its complexity and variety, then it will behoove feminists not only to call for fairer legislation of men's sexual intimidation of women but also to make fine distinctions between cases. Such distinctions would also help insure that feminist surveys conducted to gather data on various forms of sexual intimidation would not be open to charges of vagueness, self-serving interpretations of the data, or the making of mountains out of molehills. On the other hand, when some feminists make a point of noting the overlap between cases—that sexual harassment looks like woman battering, that rape is a form of sexual battery, that sexual abuse is often rape, and so on—they can more persuasively argue that there exists a continuum of sexual intimidation that pervades women's lives at home, at the workplace, in campus dormitories, in parking lots, in public bars: in a word, *everywhere*. As Sandra Lee Bartky points out, "To apprehend myself as victim in a sexist society is to know that there are few places where I can hide, that I can be attacked almost anywhere, at any time, by virtually anyone."[21] The variety of any one form of sexual intimidation only appears to offer further evidence of its pervasiveness: rape can be perpetrated by a stranger, acquaintance, or lover, and stranger rape itself can be gang rape; anal, oral, or vaginal rape; rape with objects; a planned rape; or a crime of opportunity. Sexual harassment can be quid pro quo or hostile environment harassment; but a hostile environment can itself consist of comments, gestures, leers, cartoons, or photographs.[22]

What this paradox implies is that even the most conceptually clear, woman-centered legislation will be ineffective if sexual intimidation case law continues to be interpreted under the aegis of a pervasive and institutionalized sexism. Feminists who believe that such structural sexism exists require instead a normative feminist framework for sorting through the variety of complaints that women make when they are sexually intimidated by men—a framework that condemns the patriarchal institutions themselves. Such a framework will be intentionally redundant in order (1) to reflect the conceptual and normative overlaps in men's sexual intimidation of women; (2) to capture the pervasiveness and reiteration of men's sexual intimidation of women; and (3) to galvanize women victimized in this way into individual and collective political resistance. To this framework we can now turn.

Sexual Violation and Sexual Violence

One of the strongest arguments feminists can make against the sexual intimidation of women is that it constitutes a violation of a woman's sexual integrity and autonomy. Women who are sexually harassed, raped, battered, or sexually abused as children or teenagers all express a sense of being both emotionally and physically violated by their victimizers. Victims feel injured, invaded, and defiled in ways that linger long after any physical scars have healed. Sexual harassment is a complex and often misunderstood case of sexual violation, since unwelcome sexual jokes, comments, gestures, ogling, touching, or pinching are invasive to women yet not physically violent. Even quid pro quo harassment does not typically involve consistent verbal abuse or physical beating, although the sexually coercive nature of sexual harassment has led feminists like Marilyn French to describe it as *threatening* physical violence: "male co-workers' derogatory comments on women's sexuality, appearance, and competence express hatred: the men tacitly threaten rape or battery and appropriate the woman's sexuality to themselves."[23]

Edmund Wall suggests that sexual harassment primarily involves wrongful communication that is marked not so much by the content of the harassment as by the invasiveness of the approach. In Wall's opinion, sexual harassment is simply a failure to show respect for the victim's right to privacy. Many feminists argue that such an analysis of sexual harassment is misleading because it fails to situate sexual harassment in a patriarchal context in which discrimination against women as a class is a means of establishing and maintaining institutionalized male dominance. Catharine MacKinnon argues, for example, that when they are "[u]nsituated in a recognition of the [structural] context that keeps women secondary and powerless, sexual injuries appear as incidental or deviant aberrations which arise in one-to-one relationships gone wrong."[24] The harassed woman may feel especially exposed if she reports her harassment, fearing that questions about her sexual life may arise despite grievance procedure guidelines to the contrary. Such fears cause her embarrassment and shame in a culture ambivalent about the value of sexual privacy and, along with fear of reprisal, make rates of reporting sexual harassment low relative to its incidence. The sexually harassed woman may be required to fend off advances sustained over long periods of time, causing her not only tension, anxiety, and frustration but also physical ailments such as headaches, nausea, and insomnia.[25] Feminists have argued that these very illnesses can severely hamper her job performance—indeed, in some cases force her resignation—justifying the prejudice that women are too fragile for the stresses of the workplace. One of the difficulties in proving that a hostile working or educational environment exists for a woman is precisely the difficulty of showing that unsolicited, deliberate, or repeated sexual comments, leers, or gestures violate a woman's sexual integrity in a way comparable to the coercion of quid pro quo harassment. The subtlety, variety, and ubiquity of hostile environment harassment diffuse and normalize it, so that many women simply accept it as a fact of life. If both women and men accept the view that women trade sex for money, status, and security through commercial sex work, dating, and marriage, then sexual harassment will be understood as the intrusive but necessary price women pay for social goods.

The grievances of women of color often include complaints of sexism, racism, and classism, since their harassment by white males will appear to many such women to be vestiges of colonial imperialism or slavery, threatening the livelihoods of female heads of single-parent households or poor households in ways that a more wealthy white women's harassment might not. Women of color whose sexuality is stereotypically associated in some white men's minds with promiscuity and sexual accessibility may be especially vulnerable to harassment. Furthermore, even if the courts decide to base their assessment of hostile environment harassment on what a reasonable *woman* might find offensive, as opposed to what a reasonable *man* might, such a judgment may still be biased in favor of white, middle-class women.[26] Yet many African American women may be more resistant to sexual harassment than white women because they have both everything (their livelihood) and nothing (their economic advantage) to lose by reporting it and, given their history of sexual exploitation by whites, are particularly sensitive to the structural oppression that their harassment represents. On the other hand, a white woman may be accused of being racist if she officially complains of her harassment by a man of color, appearing to castrate him for attempting to accost a white woman.[27] Lesbians harassed by heterosexual men may feel the special intrusion of a man, whose very sexual preference is invasive and presumptuous. Indeed, lesbians often suffer harassment as punishment precisely because they refuse to make men their choice of sexual partner. However, lesbians cannot sue under Title VII or IX for loss of a job or an education due to discrimination against them as homosexuals unless their claims of discriminatory harassment are also claims of gender discrimination.[28]

Understanding women's sexual harassment in terms of gender discrimination means recognizing that if the harassed were not a woman, she would not be treated this way. Catharine MacKinnon has argued that the harassment is *sexual* precisely because women as a class are identified by men as their sexual subordinates; thus women's *sexual* harassment (as opposed to harassment based on women's managerial or culinary skills, such as "This memo stinks!" or "I wouldn't feed this to my dog!") constitutes the discrimination against women and becomes the source for women's exploitation and humiliation. For feminists like MacKinnon, sexual harassment is an abuse of sex as well as an abuse of educational status or economic power; otherwise we could not explain the effectiveness of coworker and peer harassment of women by men. From such a perspective, the invasiveness of sexual harassment, like all sexual intimidation, stems from the attempt to use sex to dominate and control the harassed.[29] Women as a class do not control men's employment destinies or wield economic power to the extent that men do, and women are not socialized to be the sexual initiators in the way that men are. As women move up the corporate ladder, more women are harassing men; but the man who perceives his harassment as a compliment or who feels fully justified in retaliating with a harassment report is in a better social and psychological position to resist than a woman. Such asymmetries are used by many feminists to point out the power of a Western gender role socialization that defines men as aggressive and self-confident and women as submissive and indecisive to maintain and reinforce the sexual intimidation of women.

A woman's sexual harassment has been called her "little rape" because, among other things, harassment involves an invasive sense of sexual violation. Rape, on the other hand, is invasive in its *violence* to women's sexual integrity and autonomy. In rape, a woman's body is physically appropriated and sexually used in ways only hinted at in hostile environment sexual harassment. Even quid pro quo harassment coerces with incentive: sex is offered *in exchange for* a promotion or sex *in exchange for* a good grade, and the price of refusal is rarely the threat of imminent death. In rape, a woman's sexuality is overwhelmed by an attacker uninterested in cutting deals and unfazed by women who "just say no." Whether in stranger, acquaintance, date, or marital rape, the rapist shows his victim in unequivocal terms who is in control of her sexuality. In Judith Lewis Herman's words, "In rape . . . the purpose of the attack is precisely to demonstrate contempt for the victim's autonomy and dignity. The traumatic event thus destroys the belief that one can *be oneself* in relation to others." Carolyn Shafer and Marilyn Frye suggest something similar when they argue that rape is the transgression of one's personal domain, in which one's body is central. John Bogart describes rape as a violation of bodily integrity. Jacquelyn Dowd Hall contends that rape and the fear of rape enforce a "bodily muting" and a "self-censorship" that make it impossible for women to express our sexuality on free and equal terms with men.[30]

For some rape victims, every sexual contact has been tainted, a constant reminder of the personal invasion that the victim would sooner forget. Catharine MacKinnon states that rape is no less than the violation of a woman's sexuality, whose control is lost to her by an attack that is "intrusive or expropriative of a woman's sexual wholeness."[31] Specifically, the violation constitutes a personal invasion or intrusion on a part of the self that is *sexual*, a paradoxically privatized and intimate part of the self given massive public exposure in Western culture, largely through depictions of women's bodies. According to Pamela Foa, since a woman's sexuality in such a culture is characteristically used to identify her, rape makes evident the essential sexual nature of woman; in rape, a woman is *sexually* assaulted, not merely robbed or beaten. Furthermore, because her sexuality has traditionally been used to brand and degrade her (as whore, adulterer, temptress, bitch), rape may be cause for her humiliation in ways that a robbery or mugging is not. The rape victim becomes the transgressor of sexual mores, not simply an unfortunate victim of brutal assault.[32] This analysis matches the fate of the raped Muslim wife I described in chapter 2, who was socially ostracized as punishment for her "promiscuity."

Ironically, rape was originally conceived as a violation of a *man's* right to his daughter's or wife's body. According to this tradition, a rapist has either robbed the father of his daughter's marketable virginity or robbed the husband of his certainty of paternity and stigmatized a prized possession. So conceived, a rapist is always a stranger or an enemy to the family, never a friend or acquaintance and *never* a husband or father. Thus, from this view, the proverbial unknown rapist lurking in the bushes for an unsuspecting victim relieves men of the burden of responsibility for the rapes of women by their friends, lovers, and spouses that some surveys suggest comprise 85 percent or more of all rape incidents.[33] The tradition of a marital exception rule to rape stems from the belief that a man cannot violate that to which he already has total and legitimate access. If an extramarital rapist is found innocent in court, the victim herself is often condemned as an adulterer. While feminism has made legal headway in dispelling the notion that women are men's property, and women can now file *assault* charges against their husbands, marital rape exemption rules still exist in some states in the fear that vindictive wives will falsely cry rape for better divorce settlements or in order to justify not having sex with their husbands.[34]

The violation of rape is not confined to penile entry or vaginal penetration: objects, fingers, and tongues can penetrate, and rape can be oral or anal. The rapist can be motivated by rage, a strong need to control, and/or by an obsessive and sadistic aggressiveness that has perpetuated the myth of the rapist as the rare but dangerous madman. The psychological violation of rape, the humiliation, embarrassment, and sense of personal invasion, are often not confined to the incident itself but continue for many rape victims through the process of reporting and prosecuting their rape. One reason why many rape victims do not press formal charges is to avoid the ordeal of the courtroom. Feminists have succeeded to a large extent in sensitizing police, prosecutors, judges, and juries to the psychological injury often done to the rape victim by the criminal justice system—for example, by insisting on rape shield laws that make the victim's prior sexual history inadmissible as evidence in court in most states. Nevertheless, such a history can still come out in the course of questioning the victim for evidence of her credibility or in private hearings to determine whether such history is crucial evidence in the case.[35]

Such an intrusion is especially galling when victims of robbery or mugging are not routinely asked such questions as "Have you ever been robbed before?," "Why didn't you take precautions?," "What did you do to resist?," or "Were there any witnesses?" Julie Allison and Lawrence Wrightsman observe that "[r]ape is the only crime in which the credibility of the victim is considered relevant to the issue of whether the defendant's behavior constitutes rape." The authors also point out that according to prosecutors, the rapist's use of a weapon makes rape more credible, since a weapon is independent corroboration of the victim's inability or unwillingness to resist. Yet a majority of states still require that the victim put forth "reasonable" resistance in order for the event to be considered rape. Under feminist pressure, judges in California have stopped routinely advising jurors that the accusation of rape is easy to make but difficult to prove. A victim's habit of drinking or drug use has also been known to lead jurors to doubt whether rape has occurred, despite the absence of such use immediately prior to rape. Her moral weakness and sexual attractiveness can often lead directly to perceptions that the victim was somehow responsible for what occurred, often prompting the rape victim herself to wonder what she could have done differently, despite the assertions of stranger rapists that "it could have been anyone." Women on the witness stand often fare little better with their church or families, who may find it easier to blame the victim than face the reality of an acquaintance rape by one of their own. Indeed, the victim herself may remain emotionally dependent on the man who raped her or be convinced that she could not survive with her children alone, making either his arrest or his prosecution that much more unlikely. The emotional dependency of a marital rape victim will be especially acute if the rape has been preceded by months of physical and verbal abuse that effectively destroy her self-confidence and self-esteem.[36]

A single, ninety-year-old woman who is raped by an intruder in her own home is not provocative, in the wrong place at the wrong time, drunk, "asking for it," "loose," or putting herself at risk, outside of living alone and independently. Yet such beliefs about the stereotypical rape "victim" are precisely those that have encouraged prosecutors, judges, and juries to look for special evidence that would reveal the victim's "true" predicament. Many feminists point out that it has been largely through feminist efforts that changes have been made in recent years in the legal requirements for corroboration and proof of resistance for successfully suing against rape, which more closely resemble such requirements in assault cases. On the other hand, some feminists argue that comparing rape to assault underestimates the psychological trauma the rape victim suffers and fails to critique the violence done to women *through sex*; others charge that overemphasizing such trauma restigmatizes women as hysterical and would reduce the penalties for the "lucky" rapist whose emotionally stable victim was not seriously traumatized.[37]

The prostitute and the promiscuous woman are especially vulnerable to the charge that their livelihood or lifestyle makes it impossible for anyone to have raped them. From this perspective, women as sexual subjects demanding payment or initiating sexual advances are already "used goods" whom forcible sex cannot further defile, who like being "forced" into sexual acts that they really want and thus are responsible for whatever sexual abuse they receive.[38] Such beliefs are consistent with a Western cultural ideology, epitomized in female representation from pulp novels to pornography, that encourages female sexual accessibility with the curious rationale that since women really want to be raped (taken, used, ravished), there is no use asking them: "no" will always mean "yes." Men's gender role socialization in such a milieu is that male *violence* toward women is a legitimate expression of what men want or need from women. It is for this reason that Diana Russell describes rape not as a deviant behavior but as an *overconforming* one, an extreme acting out of qualities regarded by the rapist's culture as masculine: aggression, force, power, strength, toughness, dominance, competitiveness, independence. Russell refers to a belief in the appropriateness of such qualities in men as a belief in the "masculinity mystique" or the "virility mystique." Julie Allison and Lawrence Wrightsman contend that such overconforming behavior derives from an identification with "hypermasculinity," which encourages a man to believe that danger is exciting and that violence is desirable and a sign of masculinity. As a result, hypermasculine men's sexual attitudes toward women are exploitative and callous. Allison and Wrightsman also found that such attitudes are exhibited more strongly in men who engage in coercive sex than those who do not. Catharine MacKinnon and others would argue that rape is a conforming behavior *simpliciter*, since heterosexuality and violence are culturally congruent. Whether conforming or overconforming, such socialization brings down reporting rates and causes many young girls and women to expect (and tolerate) at least some abuse from their husbands or boyfriends.[39] Heterosexual men have been known to try to "cure" lesbians by raping them, while rape between lesbians, when it occurs, may recreate or reflect masculine/feminine sexual power dynamics more than it exposes an underlying violence in the lesbian community. Lesbians are understandably reticent to politicize sexual violence among lesbians, since the tendency in the heterosexual community is to use such exposure as a way of condemning women's homosexuality.[40]

Women of color are especially wary of making rape a political priority. Given the white world's stereotype of the violent black male or the sexually volatile Latino, these women believe that the men of color in their communities will inordinately bear the responsibility for rape. Furthermore, given the stereotype of the prostituted, sexually voracious black woman, African American women who are victims of sexual violence are even more skeptical than their Anglo counterparts that they will be believed by police, judges, and juries. In addition, poor women who do not own a car or who live in high-crime districts are particularly vulnerable to rape. Even though most rapes are intraracial and black women are raped four times as often as white women, black feminists note that African American men have been disproportionately executed for rape, and they argue that rape reform laws need to be enforced fairly against white and black men alike and enforced with equal diligence when whites perpetrate such crimes in the black community. Vindictive, southern slave-owning white women were known to accuse slaves and black freemen of rape, and black men were lynched for purported assaults on white women that never in fact occurred. As a result, black feminists are wary of dismissing out of hand the claim that women lie about being raped and suggest that many white women have little conception of surviving in a culture that encourages intraracial violence as a way of maintaining dominance over women and men of color.[41]

Racism is a factor in the violence and violation of woman battering as well. A young black woman may refrain from seeking help if she thinks that a white establishment will not take her seriously or if she sees only a limited educational or career future for herself, staying in an abusive relationship where she believes she can "make things better." Because they combine a gender identity that keeps young women dependent economically and socially with a youth that inhibits access to resources for power and independence, young women of color are especially vulnerable to sexual abuse by their husbands or boyfriends. Teen pregnancy only adds to this powerlessness. Social pressure to be a "couple" and a desire to become more independent of her family are further inducements to stay in a relationship that nevertheless may be unremittingly invasive. Men of color are arrested more often than white middle-class men for similar battering, despite the pervasiveness of abuse within white, bourgeois communities. Feminist women of color argue that such com-

munities can simply hide women's violation better from legal authorities, whose profile is higher in poorer and more racially or ethnically mixed neighborhoods, where
private therapy is less accessible. Also, women of color may feel the pressure alluded
to in my discussion of rape to protect their partners in order to avoid the disintegra-
tion of a family and community already suffering from racism; in doing so, men of
color may feel the power of patriarchy at home even if they do not feel it in the public domain. Believing that the only system designed to protect women of color has
historically subjugated and exploited them, many women of color will be suspicious
of the social services and legal resources designed to aid the battered woman. Poor
women may simply perceive violence in the home as part of their overall struggle to
feed, clothe, and shelter their families.[42]

Invasion and intrusion of the battered woman's sense of self are the hallmark of
abusive relationships, identified by hypercritical or demeaning verbal barrages, with
or without physical or sexual violence, alternating with the batterer's displays of affection, remorse, or passionate sex. In this way the batterer effectively physically and
emotionally ties the battered woman to him. Rosemarie Tong describes the general
character of woman battering as assaultive behavior between adults in an intimate,
sexual, theoretically peer, usually cohabitating relationship; the relationship can involve physical, sexual, and/or psychological abuse, or the destruction of property or
pets. Cigarette burns, sleep deprivation, enforced social isolation, deprivation of
medical care, beating, and threats of increased violence are not uncommon. Ola
Barnett and Alyce LaViolette add that battering is not an isolated, incidental instance
of hitting or verbal abuse but a systematic means of dominance and control of the
battered. Some men are thought to batter to reestablish the traditional sexual division of labor lost with feminist advances at home and in the workplace.[43]

The sexual intimacy of the partners distinguishes woman battering from at least
some sexual harassment and rape and makes the criminal justice system especially
reticent about interfering. Feminists debate over how much the state should regulate
family, sexual, and reproductive life. However, we typically agree that many women's
emotional and economic dependence on abusive partners makes it almost impossible for them to escape their sexual violation without readily available social services
and legal resources. Given that almost 25 percent of all police homicides result from
handling family disturbance cases, and that a woman's credibility is still a thorny issue with some policemen who may themselves be batterers, police may be slow to
respond to domestic violence calls. Indeed, police arrest more women who batter in
self-defense than men who offensively batter, despite the fact that a woman uses extreme violence against her partner less often than men and that women's violence
against men is more often retaliatory than offensive. When a battered woman refuses
to press charges out of fear of reprisal, community recrimination, or isolation, she
only reinforces in the minds of the police that their call was unnecessary. Yet restraining orders are difficult to enforce even when police adopt a "pro-arrest" policy
in battery investigations to inform a battered woman of her legal options, and shelters are often already full of women and children without the financial or family resources to move elsewhere. Issuing restraining orders that successfully ban the batterer from the house may only further enrage him, with no guarantee that he will not
continue to threaten and harass his partner when she leaves. Thus, she effectively be-

comes a prisoner in her own home with or without his presence. Prosecutors and judges are often insensitive to the emotional or economic predicaments of the battered. If the batterer is charged and convicted, his prison term may mean real financial hardship on his family. Therapy as a condition of probation is often met with indifference, if not outright hostility, and is often without the radical feminist slant that many women feel is necessary for ultimate prevention. Many women may simply feel too overwhelmed by a legal bureaucracy that cannot appreciate the fact that they do not have the time or energy to appear at court hearings and that they still care for their partners; they just want the battering to stop.[44]

The same tradition of woman as sexual property that is used to rationalize rape is used to justify the battering of women. Some sociologists have called a contemporary marriage license a "hitting license," reminiscent of traditional "wife chastisement" laws that permitted a certain level of physical abuse for purposes of patriarchal stability and control within the family. Rosemarie Tong reports that as late as 1977, the courts treated a husband's assault on his wife as "acceptable practice." Barrie Levy notes that as of 1991, only three states included dating relationships within the definition of relationships under the protection of domestic violence laws and allowed women under age eighteen to seek redress under those laws.[45] If violence is (hetero)sexualized by a cultural ideology of male dominance and control, then a battered woman's violation will often be sexual in that she will be battered into sex, battered on the breasts or genitals, or battered by a man whose sexual satisfaction derives from being dominant and abusive. Conversely, if heterosexual pleasure translates into male sexual conquest and his conquest into brute force, there will be little of her heterosexuality that will not involve battering. Together, these claims are the driving force behind Catharine MacKinnon's assertion that men's erotic arousal from depictions of violence against women means that the violence just *is* the sex.[46] Denise Ganache reports that compared to other battered women, women sexually abused in their battery are significantly more severely injured, frequently beaten, ashamed of their bodies, likely to have stress-related physical symptoms, more likely to blame themselves for the abuse, and more in danger of either murder or committing murder.[47] The irony is that in the absence of social services or legal resources, or lacking any community awareness and support of such resources in isolated or rural communities, women do not report their abuse for fear of reprisal, social isolation, or homelessness; thus, such resources are not developed in response to the need. Lesbian couples are especially vulnerable if they live in areas where they fear that homophobia will punish them for attempting to seek help. Experiences of sexism and internalized homophobia can create the kind of low self-esteem that inhibits some lesbians from taking any action against their abusive partners.[48]

The same woman who complains that a man's abuse of her is a violation of her emotional and physical integrity may also say that she regards her battering as his plea for her support or for more affection and tolerance on her part. A boyfriend's jealousy or abrupt and uncontrollable anger is often cited by a teenage girl as a prelude to his battering, reinforcing her belief that her batterer really does love her but that *she* is responsible for the unhappiness in the relationship. Battered women's shelters and judge's restraining orders are not always available to juveniles suffering from battering by their boyfriends. High school administrations often have no public policy of preventing and responding to this kind of intimate violence, despite a batterer's constant presence on campus.[49]

Gender role socialization that prompts many women to take full responsibility for the success of their relationships convinces them that if only they were better lovers, housekeepers, mothers, or support systems for their families or their partners, the abuse would stop. These beliefs persist despite the clinical documentation of battered woman syndrome, a psychological condition much like the post-traumatic stress disorder suffered by war veterans and concentration camp and hostage survivors. Those who suffer from such conditions reexperience the traumatic events in dreams and externally stimulated memory, have difficulty concentrating, feel detached and alienated from loved ones, and suffer insomnia and nightmares. As with victims of sexual harassment and rape, a battered woman's psychic life features fear, shock, shame, anger, distrust, sadness, guilt, and helplessness. Suicide rates among battered women are high, as if they were carrying their abusers' destructiveness with them.[50]

The sexual violation of a young girl is perhaps the most difficult to countenance. Florence Rush notes that the youngest victims of sexual abuse may suffer from internal hemorrhaging and ruptures from penises and objects too large for their fragile bodies; they can also enter clinics ravaged by disease and infection.[51] Not all of the sexual abuse of girls is this physically violent, at least not in the beginning: Sandra Butler reports that in the majority of father-daughter incest cases, the abuse begins with fondling, then escalates to intercourse at puberty, after a history of sexual play justifies to the father the move to the next step.[52] Even in the absence of violent abuse, the sexual molestation of girls is invasive in its violation of the trust that a young girl has been taught to place in those adults who are responsible for her protection and well-being. Like the rape of teen and adult women, the sexual violation and abuse of a prepubescent girl is perpetrated largely by men she knows and often loves or trusts: a father, stepfather, mother's boyfriend, brother's schoolmate, uncle, grandfather, foster father. Such men are typically not regarded by their community as self-serving pedophiles, mental misfits, or criminals on the loose but as law-abiding, church-going "family" men.[53]

If a man's emotional security, sexual virility, and social status define his masculine identity yet are constantly being threatened by other men equally driven to establish their power positions in a male hierarchy, powerless children can be exploited to reassert a man's masculinity, particularly in the privacy of his home. Women's entry into the workforce in ever-increasing numbers and feminists' challenges to men's presumption of institutional dominance have often been blamed for men turning to their domestic lives to reestablish their perceived loss of control. Diana Russell argues that men far outnumber women as perpetrators of child sexual abuse because of men's gender role socialization to initiate and control the sex they want, to divorce sexuality from affection or intimacy, and to sexualize emotions that women regard as maternal and caring. As with rape, Russell attributes the sexual abuse of girls to the social and economic power disparity between women and men and to a culture of violence that dominates the effectiveness of social institutions to control the abuse.[54] Like adult women, children have traditionally been viewed as the property of the family patriarch. Many feminists argue that such a tradition lives on in the lack of credibility and legal rights we afford the contemporary child. The belief in a male right to the unconditional sexual accessibility of children certainly appears to live on in the booming global business in child pornography and prostitution. Some feminists critical of pederasty and pedophilia suggest that this same sense of entitlement comes into play in the male sexual "deviant."[55]

Sexual activity between children and adults is a crime in every state in the United States: statutory rape and sexual molestation laws prohibit vaginal, oral, or anal sex with a legal minor as well as the fondling of her genitals or private parts. Physicians, psychologists, teachers, social workers, and other professionals who closely supervise children are required by law to report all suspected cases of such activity to law enforcement agencies; police are required to investigate reports made; prosecutors are required to prosecute. Yet the horror at the offense by some professionals, their need to find serious physical injury before they report abuse, the predisposition of police and prosecutors to disbelieve children in the face of denials by adults, and children who are manipulated or forced into retractions all contribute to a system that often fails to protect children from adults who wish to abuse them sexually. Often the child is the one who feels punished by being removed from the only home she knows. Indeed, the irony in this is that sexual abuse commonly exists in juvenile halls and foster care as well.[56]

When the perpetrator of child abuse is white but the victim is not, women of color find convictions more difficult to get than when the perpetrator is a man of color. The most common convictions still involve a black perpetrator and a white victim. As I mentioned earlier, researchers report that offenders are overwhelmingly male. Female perpetrators of child sexual abuse are not only much rarer than males but use less violence and verbal threats to get what they want, are less likely to molest children much younger than themselves, and almost never molest girls. Nevertheless, a young girl's fear of reprisal, of being disbelieved, of breaking up her family, or of hurting or leaving her parents, combined with her confusion over what is actually happening to her and her ignorance of where to turn when she believes something is wrong, make the probability that authorities will discover her abuse from an adult of either sex extremely low.[57]

Survivors of incest who have endured many years of oral, anal, and/or vaginal intercourse by their fathers often struggle to develop self-esteem and self-confidence. Adult sex can be difficult, reminding them of their vulnerability and failure of control as children. One woman writes of her feelings of violation and intrusion, "How do I feel? Empty—lost—disgusted—angry—guilty—suicidal inside. I am exploding with emotions, but outside I am empty—I feel like my eyes are black holes to my soul."[58] Some women develop split personalities from incestuous abuse as a way to metaphysically and psychically dissociate themselves from their trauma. Ironically, this personality profile is often judged *normal* for women, since the feminine stereotype is that of a "charmingly unsure, ambivalent and slightly confused" person.[59] Judith Lewis Herman has documented how the emotional upheaval of many incest victims matches the post-traumatic stress disorder of the rape trauma victim and the traumatized battered woman, including not only the dissociation of the split personality but also insomnia, nausea, overreaction, nightmares, and the intrusion of constantly reliving the trauma in memory. Herman wryly points out that only after successful efforts by combat veterans to legitimize post-traumatic stress disorder did the trauma suffered by victims of sexual violence become recognized as not just another form of female hysteria. Young women's antisocial behavior; problems with drugs, diet, or alcohol; or difficulty with adult authority can often be traced to earlier sexual abuse.[60] Mothers of incest victims are often blamed by authorities and by their own children for not protecting them from men's abuse, for being already too burdened to handle the strain of the exposure, or for not staying home and being a "real" mother. Many mothers' frustration with their own powerlessness within the family, their loyalty to their husbands, and their competition with their children make intervening in the abuse a difficult task. In their preoccupation with social recrimination and personal guilt in a society that has acculturated them to take full responsibility for the emotional well-being of their families, many mothers simply choose to ignore what is going on.[61]

While some sex radicals and mental health professionals have claimed that children have a right to sex, I suggested in chapter 3 that children have little experience in saying no to adults who tempt them either with attention and affection or with physical and emotional security in exchange for sex. Often they do not understand their own or others' sexuality, ignorance of which is used to the advantage of the abuser. Even some politically active gay pedophiles assert that heterosexual pedophilia under conditions of gender inequality is a "reprehensible form of power tripping."[62] Yet even if it is insured that children in nonhierarchical settings have the sexual knowledge and economic freedom to make informed and unfettered sexual choices, sexual activity between adult and child, especially adult male and female child, will always carry with it the burden of proof that such activity is not exploitative of a child's emotional immaturity. To stress this point, Sandra Butler has characterized incest in terms of incestuous assault, in which an adult family member imposes sexual contact on a child "who is unable to alter or understand the adult's behavior because of his or her powerlessness in the family and early stage of psychological development." Florence Rush asserts that children are entitled to be free of their violation by exploitative and violent adults and to legislation that insures against abuses of power.[63]

Sexual Terrorization

Several feminists have argued that the sexual intimidation of women is victimizing not only for its violent and violating intrusiveness but also for its success in instilling *terror* in women. According to this view, a woman who is intimidated by the possibility of sexual harassment, rape, woman battering, and child sexual abuse feels a wariness, paranoia, and fear that come from not being able to predict if or when her actual violation will occur, who the perpetrators will be, or whether she will be able to protect herself adequately from the abuse. This is the thrust of Sandra Lee Bartky's comment quoted earlier that a woman living under conditions of male dominance can experience her sexual violation by almost anyone, anytime, anywhere she goes. In this way, a climate is created in which a woman's fear becomes a part of her everyday life. Robin Morgan has called the daily insistence of this fear "the normalization of terror," which functions, among other things, to keep individual women from properly assessing the extent of their sexual danger. Morgan compares a woman's daily condition to a population terrorized by subnational groups or clandestine state agents whose political, premeditated motivation "is not to kill or to destroy property but to break the spirit of the opposition."[64] Bat-Ami Bar On suggests that terrorism is a formative process that produces people who are psychologically and morally diminished by a constant, threatening surveillance. A terrorized woman no longer has control over what happens to her. From this point of view, a woman who is not individually terrorized by a boyfriend or husband must still live with institutional terrorism in the fear that at anytime, any one man might victimize her. Thus, every woman is terrorized because she is a member of a class all of whose members are potential targets. Susan Brownmiller comments, "That *some* men rape provides a sufficient threat to keep all women in a constant state of intimidation."[65]

From this perspective, a woman's terror is exacerbated by the fact that her sexual intimidation is enforced by a secrecy and silence for which she perceives a real threat of punishment if broken. A woman who is sexually harassed at work or at school often does not report her abuse for fear that the harasser will "get her later" either by impugning her own character or by actually raping her. Her lack of confidence in the grievance procedures available to her, her lack of self-confidence due to the humiliating attacks, and her embarrassment at having to describe such attacks reinforce this fear.[66] Men who create a hostile environment for women with off-color jokes, comments, cartoons, sex toys, or pornography often do so with just enough irregularity and variety that a woman cannot know how to prevent what is happening or defend herself against it. Sandra Lee Bartky writes:

> Feminist consciousness is a little like paranoia, especially when the feminist first begins to apprehend the full extent of sex discrimination and the subtlety and variety of the ways in which it is enforced. Its agents are everywhere, even inside her own mind, since she can fall prey to self-doubt or to a temptation to compliance. In response to this, the feminist becomes vigilant and suspicious.[67]

If her harasser is her supervisor or professor, a woman may fear for her job or academic standing if she does not comply. She may wonder whether it is her work quality or her sexuality that got her the position in the first place. Despite legislation designed to allay such fears, the process of reporting and prosecuting a harasser is still a harrowing and uncertain experience for many women.[68]

Unlike sexual harassment, stranger rape is an act of violence that, according to Susan Griffin, "always carries with it the threat of death." Among many women, only murder is feared more than rape. Susan Brownmiller calls stranger rapists "anonymous agents of terror" whose rape is "designed to intimidate and inspire fear."[69] Griffin refers generally to rape as a form of what she calls "mass terrorism," where women are victimized indiscriminately then blamed for behaving as though they were free. I would qualify Griffin's remark by noting that date rapists can be quite particular about whom they rape; their purpose is not just to dominate and control some woman or other but to dominate *this* woman sexually. Ironically, the threat of stranger rape can terrorize women into seeking intimate relationships with men as a means of protection, even though women are more likely to be raped by an intimate than by a stranger. Indeed, some black feminists contend that the historical lynching of black men for uncommitted crimes against white women had the intended effect of terrorizing white women into dependency on white men. Lynching thus served to convince white women that they were "ever threatened by black men's lust, ever in need of white men's protection."[70]

Some feminists have pointed out that just knowing that she can be raped in a public place can make a woman constantly wary, sometimes incapable of venturing out alone or in groups of women. A rape in her own home may terrorize her into moving to another city or retaining an unlisted phone number or post office box. As Kathleen Barry notes, "In the face of terrorism people reorganize their lives."[71] Men who are raped in prison may feel some of this kind of terrorization, since they live in the kinds of controlled environments where men are the sole available instruments to express sexual conquest and to validate masculinity. However, many heterosexual and gay men may also display a well-socialized machismo in prison that motivates outrage and offense rather than resignation and submission. Indeed, without the adoption of a masculine stereotype on both sides of the attack, we could not make sense of the heterosexual male prisoner's claim that "[a] male who fucks a male is a double male."[72]

As with sexual harassment, a woman often does not report her rape out of fear of reprisal. In many cases, the man whom she may be living with or going to classes with or who is the father of her children is the perpetrator, and his capacity for reprisal terrorizes his victim into silence. The trauma of reliving the event in the police station and the courtroom makes this fear even more real. Publicity about rape or attempted rape can have deleterious effects on women's reporting, when women read about or see the agony, humiliation, sexual publicity, and alienation of women who prosecute the men who raped them. In one study it was found that almost one in five victims of rape attempted suicide, indicating for many feminists that the power of the rapist to terrorize his victim extends far beyond the rape itself.[73]

Ann Jones calls rapists and woman batterers within the family "domestic terrorists" whose tactics of physical and verbal abuse are designed to enable the terrorist to dominate and control the terrorized, to destroy any sense of autonomy or authority, "to erase identity" through careful manipulation of her practical and emotional life. Ola Barnett and Alyce LaViolette regard battering as the creation of an atmosphere of fear informed by a variety of abuse increasing in frequency and intensity over time. That fear is intensified by the unpredictable nature of the violence, which forces a woman to worry about the time, place, or reason for the next attack. From the batterer's perspective, the more frightened and humiliated a battered woman is, the easier it is to control her. The batterer may threaten his partner with murder or his own suicide if she tries to leave him, and his prior physical abuse may convince her that he means what he says. Ironically, a woman threatened in this way must also fear state retribution in the form of extended prison sentences if she kills her threatening partner in self-defense.[74]

A battering husband may threaten to stop payment on his wife's checks, take the children, or lock her out. An abusive boyfriend may obsessively follow his girlfriend to school or work, harass her friends, monitor her phone calls. A battered girlfriend is often too embarrassed and confused to ask her parents for help, afraid that they will forbid her to see a boy she still cares about or fears too much to leave. A battered wife knows that her batterer will come looking for her at the homes of family or friends. Living in motels and moving her family from place to place may severely deplete her already limited financial resources. She has been told by police that they can arrest him on assault charges but cannot physically restrain him prior to sentencing with anything more that a court order. Her fear of reprisal may keep her from reporting her abuse at all. Simply not knowing when he will appear or what he will do next may undermine her will to resist his presence in her life. Judith Lewis Herman remarks that what mental health professionals have called a battered woman's "learned helplessness" should be understood not as passive submission in the face of danger but as an active decision to comply with her batterer, a decision marked by a profound wariness based on the legitimate belief that every action is watched and transgressions paid for dearly.[75]

Her terrorizer may so dominate a woman's life that she perceives escape as impossible. If he shows any signs of affection or reprieve, she may come to believe that she can secure her safety only by becoming hypervigilant and attentive to her batterer so that he will refrain from abusing her. In her efforts to survive, she may then begin to identify his wants and needs as her own. In this way she imitates the psychological profile of terrorized hostages and concentration camp victims, who adopt the behavior patterns or values of their aggressors as a means of staying alive.[76] This identification, combined with a socialization that may compel her to stay to try to "make things better" and a fear of being alone in a world unfriendly to single women, conspire to undermine any determination she may have to make a better life for herself or her children outside the confines of her battering.

Even if a battered woman escapes her abuse, she may be terrorized by old fears. A playful hand on the neck or face, a sudden outburst by an otherwise sensitive lover, can recreate painful and paralyzing images. She may struggle with the nightmares and overreaction of battered woman syndrome in a way that reinvigorates the feeling of being out of control of her life. Feminists remind us, however, that such feelings are not misplaced. As Ola Barnett and Alyce LaViolette point out, the terrorism in woman battering is that "[a] woman cannot know with complete certainty that the man she loves and plans to marry will not eventually abuse her. A battered woman could be any woman or *every woman*" (Barnett's and LaViolette's italics).[77] If a woman can be convinced that aggression against women is an acceptable expression of masculinity and proof of it, she will live in a state of constant fear of what men will do and resign herself that women must accept what is done to them. Therefore, even men who do not abuse their partners may benefit from the dominance or authority conferred by their gender but bear the burden of being regarded with either suspicion or fear by their female partners.

Young girls who are the victims of sexual abuse may be terrorized most of all, since as children they are even more vulnerable than battered women to the sexual dominance and control of adult men. A sexually abused girl often does not understand what is happening to her. If she does, she may fear that her own reluctant complicity or lack of resistance will destroy her credibility. She may also fear what will happen to herself or her family if she tells anyone. The trauma of having her life or bodily integrity threatened at such a young age is sufficient to inspire in her feelings of terror and helplessness. Incest survivors recall the fear of knowing that their abusers were *always there* when they came home from school, when their mothers were working or away. A young incest victim's terror of her abuse becomes the overriding preoccupation of her life. She wonders not only when the abuse will end but why it is happening at all. When her abuse does not stop, she often blames herself, since she cannot believe that someone she has loved and trusted would choose to treat her this way.[78] Even if her image of her abuser is too fragmentary to be one of love or trust, she may simply be unable to sort out why someone with so much power over her would subject her to such violation.

A young girl abused by a stranger may remain fearful of adult men for many years afterward, indoctrinated into sex by way of insecurity, confusion, and terror. Some survivors fear their own sexual arousal, as its heightened state may be associated with real physical pain and emotional chaos. A survivor's capacity for intimacy may be irreparably damaged by oscillating feelings of need and fear. Judith Lewis Herman documents the terrorizing symptoms of post-traumatic stress disorder that many survivors of sexual abuse feel: a state of hyperarousal in which the survivor believes that danger could return at any moment; intrusion, in which survivors continue to relive the event, never sure when some reminder of the trauma will reactivate painful memories; and constriction, a state of surrender or dissociation in which the survivor tries desperately to block the traumatic event off from conscious memory.[79]

Mothers of incest victims fear for their children's safety when abusive fathers continue legal visitation. If mothers flee with their children from such visits, they are often hounded by their husbands and by the police, held in contempt of court, or jailed. Mothers contemplating intervention often fear family division, community stigma, or what may appear to be an overwhelming legal bureaucracy. When mothers do interfere in their children's abuse, they are often beaten or abused themselves. Thus, they may harbor deep feelings of guilt for allowing the abuse to happen or for having ignored it for so long. Young girls who attempt to run away from their abusers at home often end up being reterrorized by pimps whose livelihood is threatened by young prostitutes who think or act too independently. Indeed, Kathleen Barry compares the pimp's abduction, seasoning, and criminalization of young girls to the sexual intimidation of battered women.[80] Such intimidation communicates to many of these young women that sexual danger is inescapable and sexual victimization inevitable.

Sexual Coercion, Deception, and Manipulation

Several feminists have noted that the violation and terrorization of women would be unsuccessful if women were not physically forced or psychologically threatened to have sex we would not otherwise choose. Such sexual coercion captures the sense that women often feel betrayed and trapped by men into sexual compliance, misunderstood by deceptive myths about women's sexual needs and desires, and manipulated by economic and legal institutions that appear to facilitate the sexual violation of women by men. Feminists who argue that sexual intimidation is an institutionalized part of women's lives under patriarchy claim that sexual harassment, rape, woman battering, and the sexual abuse of girls are each special cases of a pattern of systematic and pervasive sexual coercion, deception, and manipulation.

Ellen Frankel Paul refers to quid pro quo sexual harassment as a form of extortion of property in which a woman's body is appropriated using the leverage of fear for her job.[81] Many feminists have argued that women are vulnerable to sexual harassment precisely because women's job opportunities are limited and our work devalued, suggesting structural or institutional inequities that individual women have little power to overcome.[82] Indeed, before the success of Title VII lawsuits, women were often fired for not acquiescing to quid pro quo harassment. Some feminists suggest that female graduate students are well advised not to become sexually involved with their professors, noting young women's vulnerability to male abuses of academic power and to accusations of "asking for it." Many institutions officially condemn such liaisons to protect both students and faculty from defamation and false accusation. According to Rosemarie Tong, sexual offers ("Sleep with me and I will promote/hire you") that are not overt threats ("If you don't sleep with me I'll flunk/fire you") are equivalent not to seduction but to coercion, given the charged hierarchical contexts of the workplace or the academic office. Tong suggests that while the seducer's goal is ultimately to win over a willing (and equal) partner, the sexual coercer's goal is ultimately to satisfy his own sexual needs whether or not the object of his coercion really wants to sleep with him. If a woman refuses her senior's sexual offer, she must face the possible repercussions of her refusal. If she accepts, she must face the possibility that her supervisor will not follow through with the promised employment or promotion or that her professor will not give her the promised grade or academic rank. She may wonder whether she will in fact please him or if others of his professional status will get a similar idea. Edmund Wall contends that sexual threats are too often confused with sexual offers. He contends that not all offers of promotion in exchange for sex *in fact* promise harm to the employee if she does not accept nor are they seen by all women as placing their situations in jeopardy. I would argue that an employee or student's standing *is* compromised by her superior's sexual offers, because she cannot confidently predict their outcome, nor can she participate equally in defining the terms and conditions of the relationship, given her less dominant position in the company or academic hierarchy. The coerciveness of such offers, whatever the outcome, lies not in their likelihood of being injurious to women nor in women understanding such offers as implicit threats; their coerciveness lies in their success at turning requests, which in more egalitarian relationships can be freely refused, into issues of dominance and control.[83]

A sexually harassed woman may feel coerced into not reporting her abuse out of a perceived loss of privacy or fear of retribution. It may cause her extreme hardship to look for another job or change classes or advisers, much less leave school. If she reports her harassment, she often feels manipulated by a harasser who charges that she either provoked his advances or asked for them and whose social status and assumption of superiority may protect his credibility and insure his safety from reprisal. A harassed woman may be made out to be a spurned and vindictive lover, an employee dissatisfied with her salary, or a student whining for a better grade. Some students reluctantly but successfully short-circuit their professors' harassment by dropping classes, switching majors, or leaving school rather than risk matching their credibility against their professors. Such avoidance, however, has the unintended consequence of leaving other students vulnerable to the same fate. Women who try to diffuse their harassment by joking about it or appearing to be flattered have been regarded by some judges as making the kinds of suggestive remarks that purportedly show that they were not in fact harassed. Some harassers threaten countersuits for defamation of character, which often also succeed in reducing the harassed to silence or in rehumiliating her.[84]

Catharine MacKinnon has referred to sexual harassment as "economic coercion, in which material survival is held hostage to sexual submission," and as "economically enforced sexual exploitation."[85] While such coercion may be true in cases of quid pro quo harassment, some philosophers and feminists have wanted to make a distinction between quid pro quo and hostile environment harassment on the basis that the former, but not the latter, is actually coercive.[86] Others have contended, however, that sexually harassed working women are often less able to work as productively and efficiently as they might if they were not working in a sexually hostile environment. Their inefficiency may then be used as an excuse to lay them off, pay them less, or fail to promote them. The environment may become so untenable that rather than risk further alienating her coworkers with a harassment report, a harassed woman may quit her job or request a transfer. Such transfers can result in virtual job segregation by gender, which can perpetuate lower wages and middle-management glass ceilings for women. While hostile environment harassment does not imply forcing a woman to perform sexually, some feminists charge that this kind of harassment is coercive because it forces women to perform their work under conditions unfairly adverse to their success on the job.[87]

Hostile environment harassment at colleges and universities is also perceived as coercive. Campus peer harassment can be manipulative of a female student's attention and performance in the classroom. Unsolicited sexual advances from students do not carry the weight of professorial power behind them, but they can nevertheless undermine a young woman's efforts to concentrate on her studies or simply to live a campus life free of unwelcome sexual intrusion. Nancy Tuana argues that a professor's sexist remarks or sexual ogling in class can carry the implicit, even if unintended, threat that unless his female students allow him to continue to speak and act this way, their grades will suffer. A hostile environment created by such a professor becomes coercive in virtue of his power position. If sexual harassment is part of a system of sexual intimidation reinforced by economic and social discrimination against women, then both quid pro quo and hostile environment harassment can be said to coerce women oppressed by such a system into sexual compliance.[88]

The traditional English common law definition of rape is coercive sex: "illicit carnal knowledge of a female by force against her will." Just as rape is considered to be more physically violent than sexual harassment, so the rapist may display more physical force as well. However, there is notoriously wide disagreement among legal theorists, sociologists, feminist activists, philosophers, and lay people alike over what is to count as "against her will." For example, John Bogart notes that coercive sex may not capture every case of rape, since a woman may be raped not by being forced to have sex but by being too intoxicated to be able to give her consent. On the other hand, if "forcible sex" and "sex without one's consent" are regarded as synonymous expressions for rape, all rape is sex against one's will to resist.[89] Until fairly recently, one of the difficulties rape victims have had in pressing legal suits against rapists has been to prove lack of consent. Unnecessary in other criminal assault cases, such evidence at one time required proving the kind of resistance that caused serious bruises, internal injuries, or lacerations, sometimes in addition to showing that the rapist had a gun or knife. A majority of states still require victims to show "reasonable" resistance in order for the event to be considered rape, lest vindictive women falsely accuse tiresome or unacceptable partners, or willing women later blame their partners for their lost virtue. However, as Robin Abcarian has pointed out, many women are taught to say no to a rapist, then not resist further for fear of being killed. She notes that women who are raped by their friends, acquaintances, or dates often do not physically resist because women think that such men will listen to them. Moreover, it is argued that what may appear to be reasonable resistance for a man may not be so for a woman, and rape prosecutions are so emotionally harrowing that few women would submit to them for the sake of simple revenge. In fact, the percentage of false charges of rape is reported to be no higher than the percentage of false charges for other crimes.[90]

The traditional legal requirements for proving sexual coercion appear to be based on the beliefs that men are naturally sexually aggressive and women naturally resistant and in the stereotype of the woman as liar and temptress, so that only an inordinate amount of verifiable resistance would constitute nonconsensual sex. Moreover, the feeling persists among many people that a truly virtuous woman would fight to the death to retain her chastity or would never have gotten herself in such a situation in the first place. This feeling is consistent with the common rationalization that prostitutes and black women cannot be raped, since their purported promiscuity "proves" that they really want all the sex they can get. If men and women continue to believe that even stranger rape is brought on by the woman herself, then the more intimate the rapist and the more voluntary the setting, the less the sex will look like rape. Yet as Rosemarie Tong points out, boyfriends can be just as forceful or violent as strangers, and husbands can use even more clever methods of deception or manipulation *because* the victim is well-known to them. Indeed, acquaintance rape can be more psychologically devastating than stranger rape, since a divorced spouse or spurned lover may rape out of hatred or vindictiveness directed at *this* victim.[91]

The myth that women want to be raped is matched by the belief that rapists are suddenly overcome with uncontrollable lust in the presence of a seductive and tantalizing woman. From this view, such lust is thought naturally to reside in men, all of whom are potential predators against whom women must take appropriate precautions or be ready to accept the consequences. The fact that most rapes are planned and that fifteen-month-old babies are raped do not seem to make much headway in dispelling such myths. Many feminists argue that women are blamed for rape so that men, particularly educated or affluent white men, can be absolved of responsibility for their own violence; and men justify rape by claiming that women "want it."[92] Feminists encourage women to prosecute their rapists because women's silence or unwillingness to file charges is regarded as unwitting collaboration in the elaborate deception notoriously referred to under the general heading "blame the woman." Women's silence also encourages men to continue to rape in the belief that women who value their femininity will quietly submit to it and encourages in women a stereotypic passivity that itself encourages rape.

According to Catharine MacKinnon, myths about rape also undermine women's ability to see or admit how much "normal" sex is coercive or unwanted, obscuring the extent to which rape has been defined in terms of what *men* perceive as forced sex. From this view, separating rapists from "normal" men encourages women to believe (falsely) that we can protect ourselves by associating only with the "right" men.[93] Py Bateman notes that many young women as well as men consider a certain amount of forced sex to be an acceptable part of a date: when he initiates the date, pays for it, and takes her back to his apartment for coffee and she *still* says no, he may feel justified in taking the sex he thinks he deserves. Thus, his control over the context of the date encourages his belief that he has control over *the person* who is his date as well. Diana Russell speculates that men will continue to extort the sex they want if they resent the price they have to pay for it: money, status, and security for women.[94]

What Susan Rae Peterson calls the "social coercion" of rape refers not only to rape's restriction of the freedom of individual women's bodily movement by individual men; the expression also refers to the structural coercion of all women that presents ubiquitous barriers to women in our pursuit of equal participation in both public and private life. From this view, a woman's social coercion through rape exists whether or not she is conscious of it, because she is unable to express herself or go almost anywhere without moderating her behavior in response to unknown sexual danger.[95] Accordingly, rape is punishment for transgression of the sexual double standard that rewards chaste girls with moral virtue while denying them social mobility and rewards promiscuous men with sexual virility and social independence. As Marilyn Frye points out, "[T]o coerce someone into doing something, one has to manipulate the situation so that the world as perceived by the victim presents the victim with a range of options the least unattractive of which (or the most attractive of which) in the judgment of the victim is the act one wants the victim to do."[96]

Indeed, according to some feminists, raping a woman is part of the masculine ideal for at least some men. Diana Russell quotes Norman Mailer, who has written, "A little bit of rape is good for a man's soul," and Ogden Nash, who writes, "Seduction is for sissies; a he-man wants his rape."[97] Yet according to this view, since no woman is exempt from unconditional sexual accessibility to men, heterosexually inactive women must be raped too—indeed, must *want* to be raped—since they are deeply repressed from having been taught to say no when they really mean yes.[98] The traditional psychoanalytic description of women's unconscious masochism has only contributed to such beliefs, as have romance novels and soap operas that depict the heroine falling in love with her ravisher. Thus, it is no surprise that estimating the incidence of rape is troubling for some feminists, since not all women characterize forcible sex by someone they know as rape. Julie Allison and Lawrence Wrightsman observe that many women believe that women enjoy men's use of force in sex, that relationships between men and women are normally manipulative and adversarial, and that many women say no initially so as not to appear too eager, when they have every intention of having sex. If (1) men continue to be socialized to believe that men know what women really want out of sex, (2) women continue to be socialized simultaneously to guard our "reputations" yet encourage, indeed *want*, a sexually aggressive response, and (3) women submit to men's sexual advances only when we have been sufficiently "paid" with money, status, security, or a good time, then the possibility for misinterpretation, miscommunication, and forced sex among sexual partners will remain high.[99]

The battering of women is regarded as an especially complex case of coercion, as it often involves a combination of isolation, mental manipulation, and physical violence that succeeds in narrowing the victim's choices of action to those defined by the batterer. As in the pimp's seasoning of his prostitutes, the strategy of the woman batterer is to capture and attach his partner to him.[100] A battered woman is often made to think she cannot survive without her batterer's protection, yet his verbal and physical abuse tell her that she may be killed or abandoned if she displeases him. Her total enslavement requires that her own interests actually become the batterer's interests. Her enslavement is only partial when she regards doing whatever her batterer wants as the best means to her own survival. Her belief in her own responsibility for the abuse, her conviction that things will not get better, and the unpredictable nature of her violation often induce in her what I referred to earlier as a learned helplessness that paralyzes her into inaction.[101] As in rape, many women, particularly young women, often do not regard battering as coercive, since the violence against them signifies attention, affection, even love. Such beliefs are consistent with the claim of some feminists that violence against women is so normalized and institutionalized that women themselves often fail to recognize its coercive and manipulative quality.

Several feminists point out that myths surrounding the battered woman parallel those of the rape victim: a battered woman wants, needs, or deserves her abuse, and if she will not take responsibility for her battering, then it simply did not happen. Such myths reinforce accusations that battered women always choose violent men, have a history of repeated sexual abuse as children, and are never seriously harmed (otherwise they would always have their partners arrested). Some feminists have contended that the very language of woman battering contributes to such myths by failing to identify the perpetrator: "woman battering" *by whom*? "spousal abuse" *by whom*? "The wife was beaten with a hose until unconscious" *by whom*? This linguistic analysis also suggests that the expression "domestic violence" succeeds in obfuscating the identity of the victim as well as the abuser, while "domestic situation" obscures that any violence occurred at all. Just "*slapping* a woman around a little" might be condoned by some (unfortunately), until it is revealed that such *hits* can be so hard that some women's jaws have to be wired shut.[102] As in rape, such myths make it difficult for women to establish credibility during police investigations and in the courtroom. If the battered woman is a woman of color, she may confront white police officers or judges who believe such violence to be normal and inevitable among a people many of whose members reside in a racial or ethnic ghetto. Yet because of the general lack of privacy and heightened police presence in such communities, people of color tend to become statistics more readily than whites.

Battered women can become susceptible to myths about themselves, since beliefs in their inferiority and blameworthiness for abuse are often reinforced by the very men from whom they have received love and support in the past. A battered woman may feel total responsibility for the emotional health of her family because of her gender role socialization, which is then manipulated by the batterer into absolving him of any blame for a violent household. She may still want to believe that her home is a safe haven, a loving, happy place protected from the ravages of the outside world, instead of the beleaguered place descriptive of so many homes divided by traditional gender hierarchies. She may be made to believe that good women stay no matter what and that she can love him if she tries hard enough. Thus, if she stays, she is blamed for her own abuse. If she leaves she is accused of having no commitment or concern for the welfare of her family. This may be especially true in African American communities, where black women have often felt obligated to protect black men from whites' stereotypes of intraracial violence.

If a battered woman does not complain the first time she is beaten, she may find it increasingly difficult not to blame herself for continued abuse. In addition, any financial or emotional dependence on her batterer is exploited to attach her to him at the same time that he abuses her. ("I'll always take care of you, darling," "You know I would never hurt you," or "That was all in the past.") Women are more apt to consult clergymen than any outside source other than the police. Yet many women are told simply to forgive, be patient, and remain committed, even in the face of visible evidence of serious abuse. Psychiatrists are much less apt to label battered women paranoid or hysterical today than in the mid-1970s, yet many physicians still prefer prescribing painkillers, tranquilizers, and sleeping pills to helping a battered woman prevent her abuse from continuing, especially if she shows any ambivalence about separating from her partner. Many feminists have argued that unless we provide battered women with access to food, clothing, shelter, job training, child care, and feminist psychological counseling, legal resources, and health services, all of which also recognize the special needs of battered women of color, women will not be in a free and informed position to take action against their abusers.[103]

In many cases, the frequency and severity of a woman's abuse increase over time. Some women succeed in adjusting to the escalating violence by making the former into the new baseline, so that a punch or slap is "just nothing really." Other women who see themselves trapped in a pattern of repeated violence by men physically stronger than they are may resort to violence themselves. Yet because quite often their retaliatory violence has been in anticipatory self-defense—killing their battering husbands in the certainty that they would be killed themselves in the foreseeable future if they did not do so—judges and juries have been wary of acquitting such cases. The law has also traditionally been hesitant to acquit battered women who kill battering husbands who brandish no weapon other than their own fists. As with rape, however, more courts are becoming sensitized to what a reasonable woman would consider imminent danger or justifiable force in defense of her life. Such sensitivity is largely the result of feminists determined to write domestic assault case law from a woman's point of view.[104]

Some feminists remark that young girls can be coerced into sex even more easily than adult women, since young girls tend to be less sexually experienced, less strong, and more trusting and dependent on adults for their emotional and material well-being than mature women. Young girls may have been successfully taught not to take candy from strangers but not taught to be wary of the sexual advances of adults they know and love. These girls may be more impressed by threats of bodily harm or sexual exposure than mature women, more vulnerable to incentives offered by adult men, and more easily forced into retractions or denials of sexual abuse they do report. A typical scenario is that the abused girl is taken from her home to the local youth authority or juvenile hall, while the perpetrator is out on bail. One or both of her parents then say that if she wants to come home, she must recant her story.[105] Some professionals believe that issues of consent to sex are meaningless with regard to very young children, since they are unable to alter or understand what is happening to them. Children often have even less credibility than adult women: young girls must confront both sexism and the bias of age when they report their abuse by adult men who may be otherwise respected members of their community. If sexually abused girls sustain no discernible physical injuries, their reports may be dismissed out of hand. The pressure on girls to keep silent is even greater when their abuse is within their own families, often perpetrated by the very men to whom they would turn if they were abused by strangers. Disbelieving mothers may unwittingly contribute to their daughters' sexual coercion by failing to comprehend what their husbands or boyfriends are doing. Others who are themselves battered or economically dependent on their husbands may believe they have no choice but to allow the abuse to continue. Some may fear social stigma strongly enough to look the other way or remain passive in their perceived role as subordinate to their husbands. Still others simply never hear of the abuse, when fear of reprisal or of witnessing her mother's emotional breakdown may maintain a young girl's silence.[106]

The causal claim that victimized children become victimizing adults must be seriously questioned, when it is acknowledged that the vast majority of perpetrators are men but the vast majority of victims are women.[107] Many feminists contend that insisting on accusing mothers of incest victims of being primarily responsible for their daughters' abuse, by being failed wives and spiteful, competitive, "unfit" mothers, is yet another example of blaming women for men's violence. The claim by some feminists that rape is normal sex for many men is consistent with men's claims that they did no harm to the girls they molested. ("She needed to be taught the facts of life," or "She needed to be protected from other men.") If injury is obvious, then little girls are turned into temptresses and tarts who brought their abuse upon themselves. Such rationalizations are invoked to justify young girls' use in pornography as something they enjoy and to encourage men who view such pornography to assume the same. Young girls running away from abusive households are sometimes accused of wanting a faster life, when they may be at the mercy of coercive pimps and indifferent law enforcement officials who appear interested only in returning them to their original incestuous abusers.[108]

If young girls and adult women alike are made to believe that men's unbridled lust makes violence against women inevitable, justified by both biology and gender hierarchy within the family, then they will fail to see any legitimate line of defense against their abuse. "Family" therapy too often manipulates both mother and daughter into feeling compelled to admit some complicity in the crime. According to some feminists, Dr. Benjamin Spock has misleadingly overemphasized the relatively rare occurrence of the lonely, confused, and socially inadequate pedophile confronted

by a sexually precocious and seductive child. It is argued that Spock, a highly regarded child psychologist, has also overplayed the image of the benevolent and unsuspecting baby-sitter who is approached for sex by his charge. The myth of the seductive child persists when children respond to adults' approval of their charm,
popularity, or physical attractiveness or when they imitate what they see their parents
do. Yet children become frustrated and confused when they are inconsistently punished for a seductiveness that they are told is never to be used "that way." Parents often teach their children that child molesters are not responsible for their behavior,
because molesters are emotionally deprived or "friend-sick." However, this lesson
only encourages children to think that *they* are responsible for their abuse. Upwardly
mobile parents are also notorious for painting a picture of incest as something that
happens in *other* families, when such abuse does not confine itself to one class, race,
nationality, or religion. The Freudian legacy that teaches analysts to regard reports
of women's sexual abuse as girls as mere fantasy, revealing a search for resolution of
their own Oedipal conflicts, has been difficult to dispel among psychiatrists unfamiliar with feminist criticism of traditional psychoanalysis. Florence Rush notes that
such a legacy has led contemporary professionals to believe not only that many
women's reports are false but also that their fantasies encourage the abuse that does
occur. Thus, Rush calls a young girl's sexual abuse "a system of foolproof emotional
blackmail," the exposure of which would incriminate herself as well as her abuser.
In this way incest remains "the best kept secret in the world."[109] Moreover, the fact
that middle-class incest often remains in the privacy of a physician's or therapist's office means that its occurrence may fail to be recorded as a significant social statistic
in the way that sexual abuse documented in public hospitals and police stations
among the poorer classes is recorded. Coerced into sex they do not want, betrayed
by adults they have been taught to trust, if not love, deceived by myths about girls'
and women's sexuality that confuse and frustrate them, and manipulated by men into
sexual activity that can have severe consequences for their emotional and sexual life
for years after the abuse has ended, women who are survivors of child sexual abuse
are confirming evidence to many feminists of an entrenched and pervasive sexual
ideology that encourages the sexual intimidation of women by men.

Sexual Dehumanization

A woman who has experienced a man's sexual insensitivity and sense of propriety will
often assert that she feels as if she were nothing more than a *sex object* to serve his
own sexual needs. Her complaint is one of being treated as if her sexuality made her
something less than a man's equal in power, authority, or dignity and that her own
needs and interests were insignificant compared to his own. This sexual *dehumanization* of woman from active subject to expendable object captures the feeling many
women have of being degraded, humiliated, and exploited in their sexual relationships with men. From this perspective, sexual harassment, rape, woman battering,
and the sexual abuse of girls reduce women to sexual toys, tools, props, and pets that
men can appropriate and control. Some feminists claim that one of the primary ways
men can assert their superiority and dominance is through their pervasive and institutionally sanctioned sexual dehumanization of women.[110]

Quid pro quo sexual harassment is degrading to many women in the workplace and academia, because it sends them the message that they are primarily valued not for their professional or practical skills but for their sexuality. Women who are subjected to this form of harassment often begin to question their own job or intellectual performance and wonder whether they were ever hired, promoted, or evaluated on any basis besides their sexuality. Hostile environment sexual harassment lets a woman know that she is not respected as a fellow worker or student but used as the brunt of sexual jokes, comments, cartoons, or photographs that reveal how men prefer women: as ready and willing sexual objects of male desire. An especially interesting case of sexual harassment as sex objectification appeared in a 1991 sexual harassment suit filed by five women against Stroh's Brewing Company. The women alleged that Stroh's sexually provocative beer commercials—showing bikini-clad Swedish girls bearing six-packs and parachuting into a male campsite—encouraged Stroh's male workforce to treat the women who worked at Stroh's as sexually available and exploitable objects.[111] Thus, quid pro quo and hostile environment sexual harassment both express the attitude that women are to be identified in terms of their sexual attractiveness (or unattractiveness) to men.

The question immediately arises: what is *wrong* with being valued primarily, if not solely, for one's sexuality? First, some feminists argue that when sexually harassed women complain about being treated as sex objects at work or in academia, they are typically complaining not about being found sexually attractive by the men in the office but about being *dominated and controlled* through sex, or about being *humiliated and degraded* through sex, as though their own feelings or desires were of no consequence. When sexually harassed women are accused of lacking a sense of humor or misinterpreting the intent of sexual jokes or sexual touching, they are accused of politicizing sexuality by the very men whose gender dominance defines what counts as a sexual joke and what does not. Sexually harassed women are not just being reduced to their sexuality; their sexuality is being exploited by men whose expression of appropriate masculinity begins with the presumption of sexual propriety.[112] Women's complaints about feeling victimized by sexual harassment are considered by some feminists to bolster the view that as a form of institutionalized sexual intimidation, sexual harassment is about power and control over women, about imposing an inferior status on a person otherwise deserving of respect as an equal, and about reinforcing that status with the message that a natural inferior should expect no better. Furthermore, from this view, men will resent and resist being exposed as perpetrators of sexual harassment at the same time that they take advantage of the opportunity.

Second, because of the often public nature of hostile environment harassment, a woman bears the added humiliation of being sexualized in a culture that teaches her that "good" girls put a premium on sexual privacy and discretion. Sexual harassment often makes a woman feel embarrassed or ashamed, because her sexuality is made part of a public domain that she would prefer to keep private, or that she knows that *others* would prefer to keep private. And third, because women as a class are socialized to identify ourselves primarily in terms of our heterosexual attractiveness, often to the exclusion of other aspects of our character or abilities, when a man attempts to exploit a woman's sexuality, that exploitation may strike at the very core of how she sees herself as a woman. Many women who consider themselves sexually attractive to men are often upset by sexual harassment precisely because they feel they are being punished for appearing and behaving exactly the way men would insult them for were they *not* sexually attractive. In fact, many women, lesbian and heterosexual alike, report sexual harassment based on sexual slurs and epithets that let them know that they are not measuring up to their male coworkers' definitions of sexual desirability. Older women have complained that they have been harassed out of their jobs to make way for younger women whose youth *and* gender make them more accessible and desirable sexual objects. If heterosexuality is socially constructed on the foundations of male dominance and female submission, as radical feminists claim, then *sexual* harassment is an ideal venue for women's exploitation and abuse. As Catharine MacKinnon asserts, "[G]ender distributes power as it divides labor, enforcing that division by sexual means." Indeed, the sexual harassment of women who work in the sex industry has been dismissed by some courts, who regard it as "a rational consequence of such employment."[113]

Feminists like Susan Brownmiller have argued that rape should be understood as a violent attempt to humiliate, degrade, or defile women, not to alleviate men's oversexed nature or quell their sexual fears or anxieties. Such a thesis is consistent with the tradition that rape is the seizing of another man's property as his own, such that a woman's value to her original possessor is severely diminished. If a woman is identified either by herself or by her culture in terms of her sexuality, then a rapist's violation of a woman's sexuality is a violation of her*self*, a diminution of her*self* to that of exploitable and expendable object. Kathryn Larsen remarks, "Rape is a death of sorts. It slowly chokes the spirit and drains one's sense of self."[114] Furthermore, in a culture whose sexual double standard can demean women merely for being sexual, rape stands out as just one more way to sexualize women and thus demean them. For this reason, some feminists remark that rape degrades women in a way that mugging does not, even though both are attacks on the body. On the other hand, women are given the implicit message that we deserve no better than rape by men who normalize rape as heterosexual sex and by legal institutions who question women's accounts of sex by force. As in the case of sexual harassment, the dialectical message of rape is that a woman is an innately inferior creature whose sexuality is deserving of violation and abuse, as well as an active subject whose sexuality is a means of devaluing her.

Women of color are multiply dehumanized by race and by gender, and often by class: white men often regard women of color as already inferior in virtue of their race or poverty so that their gender makes them even more vulnerable to the myth that women want, need, and deserve to be raped. Black feminists point out that the exploitation of female black slaves by white masters involved sexual appropriation as much as economic exploitation. Indeed, when women are perceived as having no claim to our own bodies, the myth that a promiscuous woman never has sex against her will gains force and legitimacy.

Some feminists claim that a feminine socialization that encourages kindness, compassion, patience, and acceptance and emphasizes connectedness in human relations may make women more susceptible to rape, particularly acquaintance rape. Many women do not want to hurt their dates' feelings or appear rude or unfeminine and believe they will bear the blame if the relationship sours. A young woman who is raped is blamed for dressing too seductively, but when she refuses to beautify herself on men's terms, she is marked frigid, lesbian, or just plain ugly. In this way the social expectations placed on women to be sexually seductive while at the same time sexually discriminating are themselves dehumanizing, insofar as they encourage a woman to submit her feelings about her own sexual needs and preferences to the service of male sexual desire. Some feminists have argued that many college fraternities that brutalize and degrade their initiates with epithets of "wimp" and "pansy" reinforce the masculine mystique of toughness and domination that is then acted out on campus women in the form of battering and rape. While boys are taught how *not* to be weak and submissive, "like a girl," many girls are taught that this is exactly what they are.[115] Many feminists bemoan the reemergence of "the waif look" among models, in the fear that associating female beauty with physical fragility and vulnerability can only encourage rape and the submission to rape.

One of the manipulative techniques of the woman batterer is to degrade the object of his abuse with verbal assaults on her self-esteem. "You can't do anything right," "You're a worthless bitch," and "I'll show you who's boss" are typical examples of the verbal abuse that undermines the self-confidence and self-worth of the battered woman. If he batters her by destroying her property or pets, she is being told that she too is breakable and expendable. The batterer's physical abuse is often accompanied by verbal abuse precisely because in this way he can most effectively communicate to her that she is deserving of nothing better. She can be so terrorized that her sense of her own personhood, of herself as an autonomous being in control of her own life, is effectively shattered. Bat-Ami Bar On remarks that such terrorization results in "a self [that] is intentionally eroded and a will [that] is intentionally broken." Larry Tifft contends that battering "deconstructs the self," causing the battered to lose the ability to observe, express, and identify herself as someone whose consciousness and being in the world are independent of the will of the batterer.[116] If the batterer is successful at attaching the battered woman to him at the same time that he abuses her, he has at least partially succeeded in disintegrating her own independent interests and reintegrating them into his own. If he is too successful, however, she becomes so completely will-*less*, abject, and emotionally flat that his abuse no longer expresses power *over* any agent at all. His despair at her total inattentiveness may drive him to kill her as a final attempt at control. Jessica Benjamin observes, "Violence is a way of expressing or asserting control over an other, of establishing one's own autonomy and negating the other person's. It is a way of repudiating dependency while attempting to avoid the consequent feeling of aloneness. It makes the other an object but retains possession of her or him." Of the sadists and their object in *The Story of O*, Benjamin writes: "When her [O's] objectification is complete, when she has no more will, they cannot engage with her without becoming filled with her thing-like nature. They must perform their violation rationally and ritually both in order to maintain their boundaries and to make her will the object of their will." Many feminists believe that O. J. Simpson's alleged history of battering and verbally abusing Nicole Brown Simpson was directly relevant to his murder trial, precisely because Nicole's express rejection of his attentions could have been overwhelming enough for her batterer to turn to murder.[117]

Failing to see herself as someone capable of living on her own, a battered woman becomes convinced that she does not deserve a better life than she is living and so fails to seek help or confide her abuse to anyone. If she has been successfully socialized to be submissive or at least acquiescent in the face of the demands of men, or if she has learned to question her own behavior before she accuses others, she may accept her degradation as normal and expected. Even women who are the primary breadwinners in their families will stay in abusive households, because such socialization often means that they are unable to imagine themselves outside of their relationships with men, that they are confined to thinking of themselves primarily as men's wives and as the mothers of their children. If a woman believes love equals her denial and self-sacrifice, then the more she tries to do what he wants, despite his beatings, the more she will feel she loves him and the more this belief in reform can be used by her partner to keep her from leaving.[118]

Men of color who have themselves experienced a demeaning sense of powerlessness in a racist world may seek to reestablish that power at home by subjecting their partners to the kind of physical or verbal abuse that makes women feel worthless. A perceived breakdown of patriarchy in the public domain in the wake of feminism has led many to believe that men of all races and classes are reverting to the privacy of the home to reestablish their dominance and authority. Feminists remind us that white women were legally beaten under English common laws that suspended a woman's legal existence during marriage: whipping a woman was likened in many men's minds to breaking a horse, since both women and horses were considered property acquired or exchanged at the will of the family patriarchs.[119]

Daughters have also traditionally been regarded as the property of their patriarchs, a tradition that many feminists contend lives on in men who feel entitled to sexual access to their daughters, as if they were objects or possessions to be taken when wives are unwilling, unavailable, or unsatisfying. A little girl's sexual dehumanization by a male family member is a function not only of an inequality of gender but also of unequal generational power and unequal custodial power. Researchers such as David Finkelhor suggest that adult male abuse of female children is the most common form of child sexual abuse, because such abuse tends to gravitate to the relationship with the greatest power differential.[120] Mothers who cannot protect themselves or their children from abuse further devalue and berate themselves for being unable to act. When a young girl's mother feels powerless to stop her daughter's abuse, the young girl's dehumanization can become even more devastating: she has no role model for equality and respect in a heterosexual relationship; she learns very early that women are to serve at a man's sexual whim and that without either protection from the abuse or the resources to convince another adult of her violation, she concludes that she *must* be inferior after all. She sometimes sees herself as evil, as a witch, dog, rat, or snake, in order to stigmatize herself and save her attachment to her parents. Incest survivors commonly resort to self-injury in order to reestablish some semblance of control over their own lives and to experience themselves as something more than a mere object. As one survivor remarked, "I do it to prove I exist."[121]

Women who are survivors of child sexual abuse also struggle to develop self-esteem and self-confidence, feeling used by someone who had no feelings at all for their emotional or sexual needs. A survivor may denigrate herself while idealizing others in an attempt to seek the love and affection she feels was denied her as a child, or she may become permanently dependent, passive, and unable to make her own needs known to her adult partner. If her abuse is severe enough, she may dissociate herself completely from a world she no longer sees as safe or just. She may completely lose any sense of positive value in herself or any meaning or purpose to her life. Mental health professionals can also dehumanize survivors of child sexual abuse by reducing them to personality profiles, implying that the survivor is equivalent to some stereotypical set of characteristics that determine her abuse.[122]

The aim of this extended discussion has been to show why feminists believe that men's sexual intimidation of women must be exposed as an entrenched and ubiquitous feature of the patriarchal social institutions under which women live. From this view, the sexual harassment, rape, battering, and abuse of individual women and girls constitute the systematic victimization of women as a class, whose pervasive sexual violation and violence, terrorization, coercion, manipulation, deception, and dehumanization come to be regarded as a normal and inevitable part of women's social psychology and sexual agency. Many feminists believe that a necessary element in the liberation of women from men's sexual harassment and abuse is to actively and publicly continue to make both women and men aware of the form and function of men's individual and institutionalized sexual intimidation of women, and the excruciating pain, fear, anger, and anxiety such intimidation produces in women. According to this perspective, such consciousness-raising is vital if we are to effectively move women from our sexually subordinate position under patriarchy to a position of informed and autonomous choice concerning the nature and value of women's individual sexual lives. The following section fleshes out the general counterclaim that far from liberating women from men's sexual intimidation, such a perspective only succeeds in revictimizing the very women feminists wish to empower.

Feminist Paranoia, Male-Bashing, and the Avoidance of Personal Responsibility

A girl who lets herself get dead drunk at a fraternity party is a fool. A girl who goes upstairs alone with a brother at a fraternity party is an idiot. Feminists call this "blaming the victim." I call it common sense.

—Camille Paglia, *Sex, Art, and American Culture*

We'd rather see a woman spend her money on a .357 magnum than contribute to her therapist's BMW payments for the next 30 years.

—Nikki Craft, quoted in Amber Coverdale Sumrall and Dena Taylor, eds., *Sexual Harassment: Women Speak Out*

While some feminists have been organizing Take Back the Night marches decrying sexual violence against women, distributing leaflets about sexual harassment and date rape on college campuses, and staffing shelters for battered women and their abused daughters, other feminists professing equal commitment to the cause of women's sexual agency and self-definition have been calling for a fundamental reevaluation of how women can best procure our sexual liberation. These feminists are concerned that activists' consciousness-raising practices are too full of "victim" talk, of how sexually oppressed women are and how violated and misunderstood women feel. Such critics charge that this kind of feminist thinking is both patronizing and alienating to many women: women who do not feel harassed at work, endangered on the street, or paranoid and worthless at home are regarded as either pitiable, dull-witted, or co-opted women who need their consciousnesses "raised" with all manner of marches, speak-outs, seminars, brochures, and "woman-identified" therapy to discover how truly oppressed they are. Feminists who object to this approach to understanding women's sexuality do not deny that *some* women *some of the time* are subjected to sexual intimidation by insensitive and overbearing men. Indeed, they do not deny that *some* women are brutalized by inexcusably violent men. What such feminists object to is a picture of women's lives in a world in which men are pervasively victimizing, hostile, and oppressive. Critics charge that such a picture reinvigorates an image of woman as a fragile flower whose vulnerability must be protected. This picture also paints an image of a savage male whom women would surely want to avoid at all costs, especially when considering sexual partners or families.

Critics further contend that the so-called evidence many feminists have adduced to make their case for the pervasive sexual violence against women is overblown in virtue of sloppy research methods and biased interpretations of the data. It is charged that such interpretations overestimate the severity of violence against women and disguise how women are complicit in much of their own abuse. Indeed, critics argue that the female victimization alleged to be fundamental to an institutionalized sexism effectively eliminates any personal responsibility that women have for being harassed, raped, or abused. Taking such responsibility, according to these critics, would encourage the kind of liberating mentality that not only results in better resistance to abuse but would conceivably keep a woman from getting into her abusive situation in the first place. Some sex radicals are unusually aligned with more conservative liberal feminists on this issue, as both camps tend to agree that treating women's sexual intimidation as, first and foremost, a gender issue is patronizing, presumptuous, and hostile to women (and men), and plays directly into the hands of those who would benefit socially and politically from women thinking of ourselves as sexual victims.[123]

In the discussion that follows, I will further delineate how the feminist contention that women's sexual intimidation is an institutionalized and integral part of an oppressive patriarchy has been criticized by other feminists for disempowering and alienating women. From such an analysis we can then determine to what extent the "view from somewhere different" can offer a working model for thinking and talking about women's sexual intimidation that mediates the tensions of the debate without silencing the voices within it.

Developing a Thick Skin

Some feminists who wish to differentiate bona fide cases of sexual harassment from the sexual innuendo and trivial double entendre common to office banter are concerned that sexual harassment has become a catchall for any and all offensive remarks men make about women. Ellen Frankel Paul believes that all women become the unavoidable victims of an oppressive male sexuality when feminists regard sexual harassment as *any* unwelcome or offensive sexual behavior, since she contends that "[n]o one, female or male, can expect to enjoy a working environment that is perfectly stress-free, or to be treated always and by everyone with kindness and respect."[124] According to Paul, if we define sexual harassment in terms of sexually offensive behavior that fails to respect the rights of others or that creates a hostile environment for women, we have no way to distinguish between patting a woman's fanny and raping her, a position she suggests women should find unacceptably extreme. In fact, researchers who have documented the different ways women and men assess the seriousness of sexual comments and behavior in the workplace have noted that those who think of themselves as victims tend to regard specific behavior as more harassing than those who take up the perspective of the actor.[125] Paul's suggestion is that women "develop a thick skin" in order to survive and prosper in the workforce, even to "dispense a few risqué barbs" toward annoying men now and then, to diffuse their obvious satisfaction at watching women squirm.

Paul is not atypical of those concerned with the victim status they see foisted on women by feminists who would politicize and institutionalize the sexual harassment of women. Camille Paglia also worries that the hostile environment category under the Equal Employment Opportunity Commission guidelines for sexual harassment confuses coarse or ribald language with real sexual intimidation. Paglia is convinced that this confusion makes women appear to be sexual puritans and moral elitists who cry wolf at the slightest off-color remark; and policies against hostile environment harassment return women to the traditional status of "delicate flowers who must be protected from assault by male lechers" by demanding a procedural advantage outside men's workplace rules.[126] Both she and Paul would rather women be given the message to be more resilient and self-reliant when it comes to sexual provocation by male coworkers, instead of encouraging women to file gender discrimination suits that only give men the message that women are *not* equal in the workplace. Paul comments, "Equality has its price and that price may include unwelcome sexual advances, irritating and even intimidating sexual jests, and lewd and obnoxious colleagues." Paglia simply asserts, "It is anti-feminist to ask for special treatment for women."[127]

Such "special treatment" can indeed backfire: male supervisors may hesitate to include women in business dinners or in informal gatherings where "shop talk" is looser, or men may fail to include women on teams that travel out of town for fear that they will take offense at coarse jokes made in airport or hotel bars. Kate Walsh argues that "the gender issue" has made men impossibly paternalistic in their dealings with women in order *not* to be sexist or in any way offensive. Now, instead of "What is a pretty girl like you going to do with a Ph.D.?," it is "What a bright girl you are!," as if, according to Walsh, it is a surprise that a woman can be smart. From this perspective, claiming to be victimized by an oppressive patriarchy has resulted in women being handled with a kid-glove approach that militates against frank discussion and direct criticism. Camille Paglia notes that climbing up the corporate ladder has always been cutthroat, requiring oppositional stratagems and rank competition. If individual women want to make their way in this environment, according to Paglia, then they had better get over their Victorian moralism, learn how to play hardball, and "talk trash with the rest of the human race."[128]

Moreover, Paglia regards hostile environment harassment as absurdly reactionary and totalitarian in its demand for the curtailment of freedom of speech; she believes such restrictions only confirm the view that feminists who would develop sexual harassment policy guidelines are no more than punitive moral prudes. However, she and other critics agree that a woman should be encouraged to seek redress if she is persistently and injuriously harassed. Researchers have found that ignoring or going along with the harassment is the least effective strategy for reducing its occurrence, while confrontation or reporting the harassment was found to be the most effective.[129] On the other hand, feminists in favor of regarding sexual harassment as a case of gender discrimination have warned women to be wary of making only informal complaints to their harassers or third-party mediators. Compliance by the harasser must be voluntary under such conditions, and the confidentiality of the complaint makes it difficult to identify repeat offenders or gain an accurate picture of sexual harassment within the company or department as a whole. Even formal reporting that follows company or university guidelines on sexual harassment may be biased against the harassed, if those appointed to review the case personally favor the accused or resent a woman's airing the company's or department's dirty laundry. Yet according to some critics, seeking legal redress through the courts in order to obtain a fairer hearing, expose the harassment to public scrutiny, or gain a monetary settlement underestimates the effectiveness of using in-house sexual harassment policies and procedures to settle disputes. Furthermore, such legal action often results in a humiliating revictimization of women on the witness stand, which feminists interested in publicizing the pervasively structural nature of the harassment have themselves deplored.[130] Critics charge that such a public impression can only leave those who take in the proceedings with the sense not only that a woman is unable to manage the stress of the workplace or academic life without whining or blaming men but also that she is unwilling, or unable, to take any personal responsibility for her situation. According to this line of reasoning, since such responsibility is indicative of moral agency and autonomy, women appear to be no more than passive objects to be manipulated and controlled at the whim of men.

Rejecting the Purported Right to Be Comfortable

Katie Roiphe suggests that campus women's concerns about sexual harassment and rape are actually fears and anxieties about heterosexual sex, displaced onto male students and professors. Such displacement, she implies, ignores the real responsibility female students must take for steering the course of their sexual lives. Roiphe also sees hostile environment sexual harassment as making the workplace and academia so sexually sterile and humorless that all semblance of what is valuable in human contact is lost. Like Camille Paglia, Roiphe contends that male sexual aggression is a part of nature, which is not to say that all men are power mongers or real threats to women. Roiphe argues that there is no such right as a woman's right to be comfortable around men; yet according to Roiphe, this is just the sort of impossibly subjective entitlement that feminists are demanding when they demand to be free of unwanted sexual attention. Moreover, Roiphe contends that if young women learn to expect leering coworkers around every corner and a rapist in every date, we will train an entire generation of women to see themselves as sexual victims whom feminists themselves have helped to create. Roiphe's concern is that unless we begin to deal realistically with the problems men and women face in our sexual relationships with one another, we will continue to miscommunicate our intentions and ignore chances for real intimacy.[131]

Furthermore, Roiphe sees white student and faculty feminists' concerns about date rape as revealing a deeper anxiety over multiculturalism, one that characterizes poor but sexually voracious men of color as lusting after rich, white girls who have a reputation to protect. Instead of facing the problems of multiculturalism head-on, such feminists, in Roiphe's view, hide behind the specter of date rape to express their own gender angst about the apparent irreconcilability between races and classes. She also believes that date rape films, seminars, and brochures put women on the sexual defensive at the expense of sexual passion and pleasure. Women who are paranoid about rape, she implies, will not be willing to take the emotional and physical risks that are an integral part of satisfying sex.[132]

Exercising Sexual Power and Handling Lecherous Men

Camille Paglia, on the other hand, describes men in such a way that suggests women *should* be on the sexual defensive, but only in order to assert women's sexual responsibility and exercise women's sexual power. Paglia asserts that men's "natural" state is one of sexual aggression; thus, she insists it is high time feminists embrace male lust and take responsibility for handling it. Paglia writes, "So my motto for men is going to be this, 'Get it up!' That's my thing. 'Get it up!' And now my motto for women: 'Deal with it.'"[133] With college men "at their hormonal peak" and with a "tendency toward anarchy and brutishness" that only socialization can inhibit, a college woman must be alert and ready to fend off those who would sexually assault her. Paglia contends that women do not understand how provocative and inflammatory their sexual signals are to men whose pride and ego combine with their testosterone to demand women's sexual compliance. Yet because of men's pressure on women to "put out," women do not understand the full nature of their sexual power over men. For Paglia, rape is expressive of men's desperation, envy, and revenge for an infantile dependence on an all-powerful mother, a revenge which young women should be taught to predict, confront, and survive. Paglia is convinced that acknowledging that women are the objects of male lust in this way does just the opposite of victimizing them: such a recognition encourages a woman to take up her best line of defense herself. "The only solution to date rape is female self-awareness and self-control," Paglia states. She eschews campus judicial bodies set up to handle accusations of rape precisely because they do not empower women to counterattack publicly and legally.[134] As for stranger rape, former antigun activist Paxton Quigley has made a career out of teaching women how to feel comfortable handling and using firearms, asserting that her courses help women stop seeing themselves as victims and start seeing themselves as confident human beings. As one martial arts teacher who specializes in women's self-defense puts it, "Fear of men turns women into victims."[135]

One of Paglia's main complaints against a feminism grounding women's oppression in structural and pervasive sexual intimidation is that many affluent, sexually curious, but naive young women, armed with a renewed awareness of their own victimization, become convinced that they *can* take back the night, go anywhere, wear anything, and not be accosted. In Paglia's opinion, this attitude effectively places young women in positions of vulnerability for which they are totally unprepared. According to Paglia, when women are taught about their sexual victimization and not about their sexual power and the free-ranging lust it engenders, men get blamed for women ending up in the wrong bed, when it is up to *women* to make men keep their pants on. Such a view is echoed by Nigella Lawson, a London columnist reporting on the acquittal of a twenty-one-year-old male London University student who was accused of raping a female student: "To wake up and find yourself in bed with someone whom sober you wouldn't touch with a barge pole is not such a big deal. We've all been there, honey. It's called student life."[136] According to Paglia, when a woman accepts a date with a man, she accepts the risk that sex may be demanded of her even though she may not want it. It is her responsibility to set the tone for how she is to be treated and what lines should not be crossed; but she should not and cannot expect her date not to take advantage of any sexual opportunity that comes his way. If she is raped, her awareness of such a possibility, combined with the knowledge that she was as prepared to defend herself as she could be, will aid her recuperation much faster than what Paglia believes is revictimizing rape therapy. Such is the state of two sexes "at war."[137]

Some feminists who are sympathetic to the legal difficulties in prosecuting rape described earlier also wonder whether according the rape victim special legal status over and above that of assault victim is most conducive to the cause of equal rights for women. Making too much of the trauma might only reinforce the assumption that women crack easily under stress or are not capable of dealing effectively with physical danger or violence, and that all rape is traumatizing to all rape victims. From this perspective, feminists who claim that women fear only murder more than rape are buying into the sexist assumption that women are physically vulnerable creatures in need of (male) protection. Some feminists also point out that to treat rape as a gendered category glosses over male and female homosexual rape, cases where women actually rape men, and heterosexual rapes by men in which women assist. Defining rape as a patriarchally structured problem of dominant men attacking passive women not only appears to define women as passive but also obscures the very real power struggle and emotional anguish that is also a part of less common, but no less painful, rapes. Furthermore, if patriarchal institutions effectively determine women's sexual choices, as opposed merely to impeding or constraining them, and are so ubiquitous that all heterosexual sex becomes rape, battery, or harassment, then any ability of women to liberate themselves from such conditions is effectively eliminated.[138]

Realistically Assessing a Crisis of Sexual Violence

Critics also contend that "rape awareness" programs, "rape crisis" centers, psychiatric literature that describes "rape trauma syndrome," and even self-defense programs specifically designed to defend against rape are just a few of the many examples of a feminist mindset that makes individual women sexually paranoid about men, often despite the fact that they have yet to experience being victimized. From this point of view, concentrating on helping the victim of injustice allows the perpetrator himself to go unchallenged and, self-defense classes notwithstanding, continues to typecast women as sexually vulnerable objects. Katie Roiphe argues that Take Back the Night marches on college campuses are high on canned rhetoric and group therapy and low on real analysis of what the exact nature of the local problem may be. Rape begins to lose its horror when date rape brochures suggest to campus women that they invest in rape everything they find negative about sex. According to Roiphe, false accusations of rape are the inevitable result of such messages; such brochures can also backfire on women by implying that women cannot take care of themselves, do not have a clear head when it comes to sex, and cannot withstand the verbal and emotional pressure of a heavy come-on.[139]

Indeed, the Violence against Women Act recently introduced in Congress to make rape an act of gender discrimination has been described by its critics as victimizing women by not only making it harder to convict rapists but also making women appear to need special, not equal, protection under the law.[140] Furthermore, from this view, if the sexual intimidation of women is embedded in our legal institutions, then a feminist is wasting her time trying to make any changes from within. Critics like Christina Sommers agree that women who have been brutally raped should have the proper resources to overcome the real trauma they may suffer; but Sommers argues that the very communities who need social resources for combating rape are the ones least likely to receive funds. Monies are directed instead to support rape hotlines on affluent college campuses, where rapes are relatively rare but academic feminist advocacy is strongest. Sommers and Roiphe also contest the feminist claim that rape is ubiquitous and that rapists are "normal" men, since women filling out surveys do not always recognize as rape the sex that feminist researchers say they should. According to this view, when surveys designed to reveal the actual incidence of rape or battering are vague in their questions and manipulable in their responses, it is too easy for feminists to find in such surveys the data that will confirm their original beliefs. Sommers and Roiphe believe that if feminists do not want to assist a so-called oppressive patriarchy in its carefully crafted sexual intimidation of women, then we should restrict our sexual indictments to those men who commit real crimes against real victims.[141]

Critics also charge that high school support groups and workshops for teens who are profiled as high-risk victims of battering or abuse tend to reinforce the view that fragile young women need protection from hostile boyfriends and fathers that overwhelm women's ability to resist. Along similar lines, the claim is made that laws specifically designed to deal with woman battering by taking into account a woman's fear of reprisal and her emotional and economic dependence on her batterer only serve to reinstantiate the view that women lack self-confidence and initiative and cannot fend for ourselves. Recognizing battered woman syndrome or what a reasonable woman finds life-threatening may have created new avenues for a woman's self-defense plea against the charge of willfully murdering her batterer. Nevertheless, some researchers are concerned that without expert testimony in the courtroom to explain a battered woman's feelings of both dependency and fear, juries will simply see her as a mentally unstable woman who should have walked out on her husband long before she chose to retaliate.[142] Similarly, to many ears, a battered woman's learned helplessness is not a reasoned and active response to a life-threatening situation perceived to be out of her control but a pathological retreat to a defenseless feminine passivity that only makes a bad situation worse. Camille Paglia would prefer that feminists both admit the psychological truth that some women stay in abusive relationships because they like them, and quit denying women's free will with epithets that refuse to recognize her power to goad her partner into violence and to be complicit in her own abuse.[143]

From this perspective, expressions like "domestic violence" or "spousal abuse" do less harm to women than expressions like "wife beating" or "woman battering" simply because the less gendered expression does not leave the impression that all and only women are beaten by our partners. Indeed, Christina Sommers contends that men are far more victimized by violence than women and that women do as much minor battery to men as men do to women. Like her complaints about the gathering of rape statistics, Sommers argues that surveys to reveal the incidence of woman battering enlarge on the number of cases by making minor domestic skirmishes equivalent to full-blown physical attacks. She suggests that less biased studies reveal that the great majority of batterers are not "normal" men but criminals with prior records and that battery among noncriminals is a pathology of intimacy, not patriarchy. Sommers decries the violence that men do to women by arguing that without credible and trustworthy information on the incidence and severity of woman battering, feminists will fail to procure the legislation, public funding, and community support necessary to address the problem.[144]

Indeed, Sommers is convinced that "gender feminists," the name she gives to feminists who claim that all women are oppressed by institutionalized male dominance, put the most degrading or humiliating face on women's relations with men. She finds it patronizing and parochial to think that because not all women have the hostility toward men that she believes may be at the foundation of gender feminism, such women must somehow be reeducated *not* to want what men have told them to want, which cannot be what women *really* want anyway. Not only, she says, do gender feminists betray a profound and unmitigated hatred of men, but such feminists also reveal a deep disdain for women who enjoy the feminine traditions that such feminists assert are so oppressive. What results, according to Sommers, is a feminism that is apparently so antimale and antiheterosexual sex that it is no surprise to Sommers that many women are turned off by it.[145]

Rene Denfeld echoes this view when she complains that an entire generation of twenty-something women are rejecting feminism in the wake of its apparent condemnation of men as oppressive brutes from whom helpless women have no hope of escaping. According to Denfeld, this so-called antiphallic campaign is so anti–heterosexual sex as to appear to advocate a return to the Victorian values of moral refinement, chastity, sexlessness, and spiritual purity that have historically been so oppressive to women. Indeed, the current feminist campaign appears to Denfeld to allow individual women no means to redefine their socialized submissiveness, dooming them to a life of unmitigated victimhood. Both Sommers and Denfeld would like to see feminism return to its liberal democratic roots, with a platform demanding such basic goods for women as pay equity, political parity, and reproductive rights. According to both women, feminists' self-preoccupation with spiritual transformation and sexual alienation has taken all of the truly political dialogue out of feminist activism and left it with an overly personalized agenda maimed by feelings of resentment and hurt.[146]

Developing Pro-Active Strategies of Resistance

Critics have also charged that men and women of color will continue to suffer from racism, classism, and sexism if they persist in seeing themselves as nothing more than members of a race on the defensive from the horrors of white, bourgeois oppression. Many African American women already endure sexual and emotional abuse from men they feel must be nurtured when a white world turns its back on them. Evelyn White suggests that black women and men together must stop the cycle of domestic violence that reverberates from, and continues into, the streets by creating their own programs for resistance and prevention targeted to their individual families and communities.[147]

Indeed, critics do not contest the need for pro-active as well as defensive strategies to combat the real problems of woman battering. They would applaud the tactic in some Peruvian shanty towns, for example, of women blowing whistles when they are beaten or abused, drawing a cadre of volunteer women who march to the battered woman's defense. They would not contest Indian women banging pots and pans outside the houses of the most abusive men in their communities, literally humbling their abusers into desisting. Rather, critics' concern is that community programs and services with their seminars and brochures on the ubiquity of woman battering may so undermine a woman's confidence that she comes to expect or resign herself to her abuse, despite such programs' efforts at promoting legal and practical resistance.[148]

Critics further contend that a young girl who is fed a steady diet of scathing indictments about power-driven adult men who sexually exploit young girls will grow up as unsure of herself sexually and as paranoid of men as if she had actually been abused. From this perspective, children need to be protected from adult abuse by being given the tools to resist temptation and the credibility to report their abuse, not more horror stories about "boogie men" who are hiding behind the mask of the friendly next-door neighbor or family friend. Some might charge that the stability of the family unit itself is unnecessarily threatened by inculcating in young girls the suspicion, based on a belief in the ubiquity of an oppressive patriarchy, that her own beloved patriarch is in fact an incestuous monster. Furthermore, from this view, referring to women who were sexually abused as children as "survivors" stamps them with a moniker of the walking wounded that will make the trauma that much more difficult to overcome.

Sonia Johnson contends that part of what it means to be a victim of an enslaving patriarchy is to believe that for women to be liberated, we must get men to change their minds about women. According to Johnson, if women can be convinced that men can and must be "fixed," we will wait forever expecting men to respond to our demands when they never will. Therefore, if advocating freedom from oppressive male dominance means trying to get men to change first, then feminism is truly victimizing after all. According to Johnson, *women* are the ones who must do the changing, so that we do not miss opportunities for making new lives for ourselves outside the system of oppression, not from within it.[149]

Sonia Johnson is committed to the view that women's oppression is ubiquitous and institutionalized. Nevertheless, she questions the road to liberation founded on trying to change men's behavior, believing this tactic gives men more power to dictate the form and function of that liberation. As I have described thus far, other critics are much more skeptical of the theoretical foundations of a feminism that appears to reduce women to sexual victims: how, such critics ask, can we provide women with equality of opportunity at home and in the workplace when many feminists want literally to institutionalize men's sexual harassment and abuse of women? In the discussion that follows, I offer some analysis of the competing views described in the preceding sections and outline a framework for discussing women's sexual intimidation that can circumscribe the concerns of a variety of political perspectives

Sexual Intimidation Revisited

The [feminist] consciousness of victimization is a divided consciousness. To see myself as victim is to know that I have already sustained injury, that I live exposed to injury, that I have been at worst mutilated, at best diminished in my being. But at the same time, feminist consciousness is a joyous consciousness of one's own power, of the possibility of unprecedented personal growth and the release of energy long suppressed. Thus, feminist consciousness is both consciousness of weakness and consciousness of strength. But this division in the way we apprehend ourselves has a positive effect, for it leads to the search both for ways of overcoming those weaknesses in ourselves which support the system and for direct forms of struggle against the system itself.

— Sandra Lee Bartky, *Femininity and Domination:*
Studies in the Phenomenology of Oppression

Feminists who are convinced that an understanding of women's systematic sexual intimidation by men is necessary to freeing women to define the terms and conditions of our sexual lives argue, as does Sandra Lee Bartky, that such an understanding is empowering to women. Such feminists argue that with this understanding, women can recognize that our intimidation is not trivial, inevitable, or deserved, even if it appears "normal"; and when we do come to see our intimidation as imposed by patriarchal social institutions, we are able to map out the specific programs and strategies most effective in resisting what is sexually oppressive to us. An understanding of the structural and pervasive nature of women's sexual intimidation tells abused women that they are not alone in their pain and that there are resources at their disposal designed to help them overcome their abuse. Furthermore, from this perspective, women can understand that the male bias and gender asymmetry within the political and cultural institutions under which we live make it highly questionable whether the economic, legal, academic, or family values of the status quo will work to our advantage.

Thus, I believe feminists critical of views like Bartky's are mistaken when they contend that such a perspective reduces women to no more than victims of an oppressive patriarchy. These critics apparently disregard the strong emphasis that feminists like Bartky place on women's resistance and transcendence of women's subordinate position. Sexual harassment policies, campus rape brochures, battered women's shelters, and abused women's support groups are all designed to encourage individual women to resist their exploitation, defend against possible violence, and change their abusive conditions. For feminists who regard the sexual intimidation of women as pervasive and institutionalized, the raised consciousness of sexual intimidation in a woman's life means that she is aware of her responsibility for assessing the risks of where she walks and with whom, which dorm rooms she visits, and how to avoid unnecessary contact with an employee known for his advances. These same feminists also encourage individual women to take the offensive, by participating in Take Back the Night marches, filing sexual assault and battery charges, and apprising themselves of harassment grievance procedures and how to use them. Many feminists make a point of arguing that a woman who is terrorized and dehumanized is *not* thereby *made* helpless even though she may *feel* helpless. I believe that what many feminists do not want to imply by making women responsible moral agents is that women should always be *blamed* when things go wrong.

However, I would argue that this is precisely what happens when critics like Camille Paglia contend that given men's aggressive nature, women who do not want sex are "fools" for letting men get too close. It is difficult to deny that a young college woman is at least partially responsible for her dating behavior, unless we want to make her into a truly passive victim. Women should be wary of the ways in which their sexual messages may be misconveyed or misunderstood. Yet by removing all behavioral responsibility from men in the name of raging hormones, Paglia places all of the responsibility on women for what men do to them, effectively blaming women for whatever happens in our dealings with men. I think that we can assign individual sexual responsibility to both women and men, in keeping with the "view from somewhere different," in ways that allow us to adjudicate cases contextually according to an ethic of care respect and under current cultural constraints that typecast women, and not men, as heterosexual subordinates. Under such constraints, some female students may get their boyfriends drunk and press them for sex; some women may take sexual advantage of their senior positions in academia to intimidate male graduate students. However, these gender role reversals should not disguise important asymmetries in the general patterns of socially constructed sexual relations between women and men; and a woman cannot be expected to bear full responsibility for the acting out of any one man's lust in addition to her own. My point is that we cannot treat any cases of sexual intimidation in isolation from the particular social locations and dialectical interplay of sexual subordination and liberation that circumscribe each case.

My main criticism of the contention that women's sexual intimidation is a pervasive and institutionalized feature of all women's lives is in its widely mistaken interpretation, not in its intent, since this claim often leaves many with the easily refutable but false impression that all women spend their lives stricken with an immobilizing terror that sexual violence could be their fate at any moment. Few would deny that men's sexual violence against women is a serious problem or that the numbers of women who are abused daily are far too high. Therefore, I believe that feminists would do ourselves a great service by consistently pointing out that the institutionalized sexual intimidation of women does not require women to spend most or even many of our waking hours experiencing the kind of daily wariness, paranoia, or fear that a woman living under the threat of a Salvadoran or Serbian terrorist attack feels when she steps outside her front door. I agree with the feminist claim that battered women and incest victims are terrorized in an analogous way, but that same sense of constant and unmitigated fear cannot be attributed to all women. What I believe feminists do say with accuracy is that women's sexual intimidation is part of the fabric of patriarchal institutions and that it is used regularly and effectively as a means for the subordination of women in contemporary Western society—so effectively, in fact, that women's views of ourselves and our negotiation of our world is profoundly influenced by a pervasive awareness of our vulnerability to male sexual assault. This is what Bartky refers to when she says that women live daily with a consciousness of our own victimization. Indeed, it is a consciousness of sexual vulnerability and access that I believe men as a class do not experience, no matter how victimized by male violence they may be. While self-defense courses and gun classes can better prepare a woman to avoid or combat rape, their growing popularity is testimony to general feelings of sexual distrust and anxiety that are a common feature of women's lives. When a working woman locking up late in the evening is joined alone in an elevator by a man she does not know, she will typically experience a heightened awareness of her own vulnerability that symbolizes, at some level, that her sexual intimidation by men is always with her. Walking alone to my parked car at night in an unattended lot is enough to instill this awareness in me, no matter how much self-defense I know or how assertive I am. Indeed, it is this very awareness that gives women who have never been raped, battered, or abused some understanding and empathy for women whose lives are those of daily trauma or abuse. Men's sexual intimidation of women can be overt or subtle, unmitigated or intermittent, overwhelming or overcome. From the "view from somewhere different," the partiality and particularity of each woman's social location will define the nature and extent of that intimidation.

Therefore, when a woman is advised by feminists wary of an overly victimizing view of women's sexuality to "take the heat" of men's sexual harassment or to dispense a few "risqué barbs" herself, I would respond that women are not always or even often in the social or economic position to fight back with equal power or authority. Nor should women give men the idea that such harassment is acceptable by shrugging it off or, whenever possible, by returning the harassment in kind. The goal of making women's sexual harassment a form of gender discrimination, among other things, is to point out that the harassment is underwritten by a stereotypical view of women qua women as the unconditionally accessible sexual objects of men. Without laws specifically designed to prohibit taking advantage of women's sexuality, employment and academic environments are not level playing fields for women and men. Furthermore, it is because there is a *gender* hierarchy at work, not just an economic one, that sexual harassment of women by men, particularly by coworkers, is such a routine occurrence: in a system defined by patriarchal values whose rule for heterosexual relations is one of male dominance and female submission, sexual harassment indeed becomes the norm. This is why many women are often suspicious of in-house resolutions to their harassment. This is why feminists have taken such pains in the last twenty years to expose women's humiliation and exploitation in school and at work. Thus, I would argue, in response to Katie Roiphe and Rene Denfeld, that younger feminists tired of the apparent sexual conservatism and humorlessness of an older feminist generation would do well to acknowledge the extent to which such women's consciousness-raising efforts on behalf of all women have afforded many younger, more affluent women the sexual freedom that Roiphe and Denfeld value.

I also believe that arming women in self-defense communicates to many men that violence is a legitimate way of settling disputes. A .357 magnum or a black belt in karate may help keep rapists at bay but may also be used as excuses for men to do whatever they think they can get away with. Furthermore, bearing lethal weapons can not only escalate violence between the sexes but can also give both women and men the false impression that the sexual playing field is a level one just because both sexes are armed. However, women are victimized sexually in part because our socialization reinforces establishing connections rather than enforcing hierarchies, and many men know this. Being "armed and female" may be completely useless in acquaintance rape. Will a woman want to shoot her date in the face? Will she want to send her lover to the hospital? Will she want to jeopardize her family's primary source of economic support? Moreover, women's success on the firing range or in the karate studio does not always translate into successful defense against rape. Rape can be painful, humiliating—indeed, traumatizing—precisely because all of one's best-laid plans for self-protection simply did not work. Misfires in the heat of the moment can further enrage a rapist who may himself be armed. Karate can be rendered useless by gang rapists or an attacker with a knife. In short, arming ourselves can give women a false sense of security that may encourage women to enter the dangerous settings of which Camille Paglia and others say women should be *more* wary, not less.

Contra Paglia, if men are strongly motivated by the most basic biological urges of sex and aggression, all the more reason for *men* to reassess *their* shortcomings as successfully socialized human beings, not for *women* to take up the slack. Indeed, a woman can be sending all of Paglia's recommended "clear signals" that she wants a man to keep away from her, but this may only increase his excitement, hostility, or abuse. Moreover, a ninety-year-old widow may be incapable of firing a gun properly or executing a karate chop. As Susan Brownmiller attests, "There can be no private solutions to the problem of rape." From this perspective, unless women and men recognize the political underpinnings of why men rape and why women cannot ignore rape, women will continue to suffer from the contradiction of being perceived as both the victims of male sexual aggression and the agents responsible for sexual assaults against us by men bursting with uncontrollable hormones.[150]

Woman battering is another area where, as with sexual harassment and rape, special laws to handle battering do not upset an already equitable distribution of justice but attempt to restore an equity that does not exist within legislative institutions whose male bias is part of their existing structure. From this perspective, gender blindness in such areas is itself a prejudice from the "view from nowhere" discussed in chapter 1, in which ignorance of individual social location can induce the false belief that standards of neutrality and objectivity will eviscerate gender bias. Furthermore, community speak-outs, support groups, educational seminars, and films are essential for empowering women with the knowledge that woman battering is a function of a system of reinforced male dominance that we can and must take responsibility for transcending, not for merely covering over or coping with. In response to both Rene Denfeld and Christina Sommers, I would argue that it is not antisex or paranoid to gain a realistic assessment of being a woman in a world often hostile and degrading to women, nor is it antimale to suggest that our social institutions advantage men in ways that make it easy for men to convince women that women's sexual harassment and abuse is natural or deserved. Feminists do not need overwhelming statistical evidence to make the claim that men's sexual violence against women is too common and too severe to be tolerated; and legal, economic, and marital institutions can be clearly identified as traditionally conforming to *men's* versions of what counts as the sexual harassment and abuse of women. If women do not identify forcible or abusive sex because this is the only sex they know, then surveys designed to reveal the incidence of rape or battering that do not take this into account will themselves be biased against women. Moreover, without identifying behaviors like battered woman syndrome or learned helplessness, many women are regarded as paranoid hysterics whose emotional state remains psychologized out of its gendered context and so uninterpreted as rational mechanisms for helping a woman survive a subordinating sexual ideology supported by patriarchy.

From this perspective, it is no less important for young girls and their mothers to know of whom they should be wary and why. Certainly *not* knowing has kept the sexual abuse of girls an embarrassing and dirty family secret and has often convinced mothers that they are primarily responsible for their husbands' incestuous abuse of their daughters. Many feminists argue that if female children are disempowered by their age as well as their sex, and if many of them are further victimized by race or poverty, making appeal to the legal system especially difficult, then this is all the more reason to provide public resources advertising their special role in protecting children from adult abuse. The overriding concern by many feminists, including myself, is that unless we continue to voice our opposition to the institutional nature, social pervasiveness, and gender discrimination of women's sexual intimidation by men, then sexual harassment, rape, woman battering, and the sexual abuse of girls will continue to keep women from transcending our sexual victimization and moving toward a new vision of individual sexual agency and self-definition for all women.

Sexual Intimidation from the "View from Somewhere Different"

Feminists remain deeply divided over the issue of the nature, extent, and ramifications of women's sexual victimization by men. Some feminists regard hostile environment sexual harassment as an insidious reminder of patriarchal control of the workplace. Others regard it as indicative of overly sensitive and easily offended feminists who are hostile to men in the first place. Some feminists regard speak-outs against rape as vital to women's self-conscious sexual liberation. Others regard such gatherings as tedious and unnecessary rape hype that only widens the increasing gap between the sexes. Some feminists regard battered woman syndrome as essential for legally arguing self-defense cases against the batterer. Others see the syndrome as reinvigorating the stereotype of the hysterical woman who cannot maintain self-control. Some feminists think protecting young girls from adult male sexual abuse requires recognizing the potentially debilitating hierarchy within the traditional nuclear family. Others think that such gender politics divides otherwise close families by suspicion and false accusation.

My claim is that we can use the "view from somewhere different" to negotiate the tensions among such disparate perspectives. By interpreting women's sexuality as a dialectic between gender and sexuality, we can characterize women's sexual intimidation by men as reflective of men's pervasive and institutionalized dominance over women's sexual lives yet as also carrying within it the seeds of women's growth toward a sexuality more fully defined in our own terms. The "view from somewhere different" asks us to recognize patriarchy's claim on women's sexuality yet at the same time to resist women's sexual intimidation by men, so that women may claim our sexuality as our own. In this sense, progress toward women's sexual pleasure and agency can be a *feminist* goal precisely because it is also progress away from women's sexual victimization. In the remainder of this section I will describe how regarding women as *survivors* of sexual intimidation can allow us to think and talk about women as both the active and responsible subjects of our sexual experience and the victimized objects of men's dominance and control. As in my discussion of sex work in the previous chapter, my aim is to use such a dialectic to negotiate the tensions between those feminists who require that we recognize women's victimization under patriarchy and those who fear that such a recognition diffuses women's sense of sexual responsibility and agency. If women's sexuality under patriarchy is dialectical in the way I suggest, then both sexual victimization and sexual agency have a stake in defining women's sexual preferences and sexual desires.

Suppose, for example, that a woman interprets her sexual intimidation under patriarchy not only as an assertion of male dominance at home and at work but also as a reaction to, and fear of, women's sexual power over men. Traditional psychoanalytic literature is rife with imagery of a punitive and powerful mother whose perceived ability to disempower her son causes him to distance himself from her and align himself with his father. Feminist "backlash" theories claim that women are the increasing targets of men's sexual harassment and abuse precisely because feminism is empowering women in ways that severely threaten men's sexual dominance over them. Under such theories, women are both the unconditional sexual objects of men and the defining sexual subjects of men's experience of their own sexuality. Instead of perceiving herself as a mere victim, a woman may thus begin to see herself as *surviving* victimization by being the defining subject of how men perceive themselves in the world. In doing so, she may begin to gain a sense of her own agency as a woman whose sexual power is to be reckoned with, which in turn helps embolden her to stop tolerating her harassment or to report her date rape or battering. Even the behavior of her rapist or batterer can be interpreted from this perspective as an admission of his own weakness, his own pathos, his own dependence on her to satisfy his own complex emotional needs.

On the other hand, actively reporting her abuse may result in reprisals or humiliation that reaffirm in her mind her own victimization. Actively resisting a rapist or batterer carries real risks: he may desist in search of someone more passive, or he may overcome her resistance and be made even more hostile or excited by it.[151] Alternatively, a woman may simply be so overwhelmed by the male sexual hostility she confronts on a daily basis that any sense that *she* is powerful or fearsome in the eyes of any man remains illusive. Therefore, from the "view from somewhere different," being a *survivor* of sexual intimidation in a patriarchal world where women and men are in constant contact means both *living with* and *living through* the sexual risks of being a woman in a society oppressive to women. Under such conditions, women forge sexual lives in terms circumscribed by patriarchy and also in terms not bound exclusively by patriarchy. The feminist consciousness implicit in the "view from somewhere different" is a consciousness of women's sexual oppression under social institutions that reinforce a cultural ideology of male superiority and enforce a politics of male dominance. I claim, however, that the dialectical relation between the politics of gender and the possibilities of sexual experience that defines women's sexuality from the "view from somewhere different" also implies a consciousness of women's potential for sexual exploration and sexual passion. This consciousness can transform a woman's victimization under patriarchy into something she lives *with* and *through*, but not something she is *defined by*. When she reassesses her life from the dialectical perspective implicit in the "view from somewhere different," her sexual victimization can become a source for her liberation, a lens through which she may see in less distorted fashion the possibilities for, and limitations of, her own sexual agency and self-definition.

From such a dialectical perspective, a woman may begin to understand how some men see her as both a sexual object of their harassment and abuse and a sexual subject wanting, needing, or deserving her attack. From this perspective, she may realize that *her* agency is in fact circumscribed by *his* wants and needs, so that she will be blamed for her partner's abuse, charged with "making" him hit her. She may later reflect that her own learned helplessness was an active decision to comply with the abusive demands of her batterer, a decision that ultimately afforded her the opportunity to gather her children and few possessions and leave her abuse for good. From a dialectical point of view, a woman may begin to recognize how her socialization to empathize with the troubles of others ironically militates against the very act of resistance to rape that would reduce the likelihood of long-term emotional trauma, despite the risks of such resistance. A woman may also understand why no matter how successful *her* career track, how careful *her* choice of date, how perfect *her* housekeeping, she can nevertheless feel and be violated, terrorized, coerced, or dehumanized, and sometimes all of these at once. By the same token, she may understand her own harassment as the objectifying abuse of a woman whose mere presence may be powerful enough to inspire hostility, fear, or anger. On the other hand, a woman who says she does not recognize or experience her oppression in any way is not the object of patronizing feminist derision but a woman who has simply not experienced herself as a sexual survivor in a patriarchal world. To say that she *should* so experience herself is to foist upon her a "view from somewhere better" that is antithetical to the task of credibly listening to the diversity of women's voices recommended by the ethic of care respect from the "view from somewhere different."

By viewing herself as a survivor from the "view from somewhere different," however, a woman can tell other women about her own sexual intimidation and share with them what she feels are the risks of not also seeing themselves as self-determining subjects in dialectical relation to their own sexual objectification. From this perspective, she may be motivated to learn self-defense, join therapy groups, or become a rape crisis counselor after her own rape as a way of seeing herself as the defining agent of her own victimization and as helping other women do the same. Even if she must change jobs, addresses, or lifestyles simply to avoid further abuse, as a survivor seeing herself from the "view from somewhere different," she may regard such changes as positive steps toward her sexual dignity and autonomy as well as steps away from her abuser.

On the other hand, as I noted earlier, a woman's sexual agency under patriarchy is an agency at risk. She may find that confronting or chastising her harasser, when she knows that sexual harassment is not about being flattered or being "nice," still leaves her feeling humiliated and used. Sharing her history of child abuse with a therapist may cause her to reexperience the violation at the same time that she begins, perhaps for the first time, to see herself as a self-confident and self-defining subject in the world. Surviving, therefore, from the "view from somewhere different," is not about moving blithely forward as a sexually autonomous agent without a consciousness of one's own and others' victimization; surviving means using that consciousness as a way of forming personal and communal strategies for liberation in a world where the sexual intimidation of women by men is a fact of contemporary life. Robin Morgan captures the subject/object dialectic implicit in this perspective when she describes what happens to a woman who, having acquiesced to her abuse in the past, finds it impossible to continue to live a victimized life: "At last she begins to fear her own silence as much as or more than the violence he visits upon her if she speaks. Her silence is within her own power to break, even if his violence is not. Silence is the first thing within the power of the enslaved to shatter. From that shattering, everything else spills forth."[152] But that shattering is also frightening, for it requires women to rely on ourselves to give meaning and value to our lives and to appreciate the different ways each woman may wish to define her life for herself. Many women in such situations both want and do not want to be the defining subjects of their sexual experiences with men. They want the freedom to define the terms and conditions of their heterosexual relationships, but they know that with such freedom comes the shared responsibility for making those relationships successful. They know that the personal agency requisite for such responsibility has often been used to blame them for their own abuse but that without the recognition of such agency, they remain no more than sexual objects to be exploited by self-serving men. Being a survivor of sexual intimidation from the "view from somewhere different" means acknowledging that a woman's victimization provides the context and the rationale for her sexual liberation and that her resistance to that victimization is a way of beginning to define her sexuality in her own terms. This dialectic is reflected in Marilyn Frye's observation that "[t]he forces which we want to imagine ourselves free of . . . mark the shape they mold us to, but they also suggest by implication the shapes we might have been without that molding."[153]

The dialectical relation between active subject and manipulable object that defines being a survivor of sexual intimidation from the "view from somewhere different" helps explain why a contemporary woman's experience of her sexuality can be such a fascinating and frustrating experience. The more a woman rejects traditional notions of femininity by going out alone, living independently, or initiating dates, the more she may also find herself vulnerable to violence than if she sought the safety and passivity of membership in a group. The more a woman submits herself to her batterer, the more she may see herself as engaged in her active survival, and the more her batterer must allay the total submission that would turn her into a will-less object of no value to him. A battered woman may simultaneously see herself as the active support system for a troubled partner and the whipping post for his anger and frustration. Resisting her rape may reduce a woman's experience of post-traumatic stress syndrome, but it may also increase the risk of further abuse during the rape itself. Reporting her abuse can aid her recovery, reduce further incidents of abuse, and increase public awareness of the nature of the abuse and the identity of the abuser; but as I mentioned earlier, such reporting can also result in the kind of reprisal, humiliation, reduced credibility, or emotional repetition of the original trauma that makes her feel she has been victimized all over again.

Self-defense courses specifically designed to combat rape can build a woman's self-confidence and self-reliance but can also promote a wariness and hostility that encourage her to see a rapist in every man. Carrying a can of mace in her purse may convince a woman that she is not in sexual danger, yet she may find herself defenseless against an aggressive former boyfriend whom she cannot bring herself to hurt. Many feminists argue that sex education for young girls is incomplete without an explanation of the ways in which a woman's sexuality can be used as a vehicle for her harassment and abuse; yet the goal of such education is not to increase girls' sense of victimization but to strengthen their resolve not to tolerate such abuse or see it as normal. Sexually abused little girls often see themselves as powerful keepers of the dark secret that keeps their families intact and as tempting seductresses of their abusers; yet they can also regard themselves as powerless to stop their own sexual violation. While helplessness may constitute the essential insult of the trauma, reliving it in memory later in life may help restore efficacy and power to the survivor.[154] "Reasonable woman" standards of harassment and self-defense, and rape shield laws limiting the exposure of women's sexual history, can have the combined effect of both encouraging some women to prosecute their abusers and encouraging others to regard women as in need of special protection. Ironically, if a woman makes a relatively quick psychic recovery from the dehumanizing trauma of date rape, she may be accused of not being raped at all. Many women who feel successful at putting their abuse behind them report that a feminist activism of sharing their experience with others has been their best source for recovery. Other women who have been rape victims find that they can no longer tolerate the subordinating sex on demand that was a regular feature of their sex lives prior to being raped. Indeed, Judith Lewis Herman remarks that it is tempting to side with the perpetrator of violence, for while he simply asks you to ignore him, his victim "demands action, engagement, and re-membering."[155]

Kathleen Barry states that surviving is the other side of being a victim.[156] I agree that a woman's survival of sexual intimidation involves her developing coping mech-anisms and formulating strategies in response to her abuse, strategies that require a willful subject. I have argued, however, that from the "view from somewhere differ-ent," surviving places a woman's sexual victimization under patriarchy in a dialec-tical relation to her active capacity for sexual agency and self-definition. From the "view from somewhere different," being a survivor just *is* being *both* a victim or po-tential victim of institutionalized male dominance *and* an autonomous agent who has the capacity to transcend that victimization and move toward a sexuality more fully defined in her own terms. From this perspective, women's sexuality under pa-triarchy constitutes a dialectical relation between defining sexual subject and abused sexual object. This relation describes women's sexual desires and preferences as con-strained by social institutions that are oppressive to women at the same time that women's capacity to define the terms and conditions of our sexual lives affords us the determination to resist oppressive individuals and institutions and, ultimately, to tran-scend them. Valerie Heller, a feminist survivor of years of sexual abuse as a child, re-ports, "I think that our sexuality cannot and has not been taken from us. It has with-out a doubt been thwarted. . . . My sexuality—the inner experience of my sexual energy—is, in actuality, something that I am becoming aware of and experiencing for the first time."[157]

The "view from somewhere different" can accommodate the diversity of feminist voices that speak to the issue of women's sexual intimidation, because the subject/ob-ject dialectic on which surviving such intimidation is based invites viewing women as both victims of men's pervasive and institutionalized sexual violation and as will-ful agents taking responsibility for the direction of our sexual lives. Thinking and talk-ing about women's sexual intimidation from the "view from somewhere different" does not reinvigorate the debilitating stereotype of the fragile and vulnerable woman in need of protection from and by men, because this perspective affords women the capacity to develop a self-confidence and self-reliance that can liberate her from her dependence on abusive men; nor does such a perspective absolve women of all per-sonal responsibility for our heterosexual relationships. Indeed, taking responsibility for one's sexuality is a feature of the ethic of care respect implied by this perspective, which asks women and men to look at how and why we choose the sexual partners we do, and how those choices are affected by the particular cultural and political contexts in which we live. Interpreted from this perspective, men's sexual violation, terrorization, coercion, and dehumanization of women under institutionalized male dominance can be experiences that motivate women to seek out better relationships for ourselves and richer lives for our families and friends. Therefore, regarding women as survivors from the "view from somewhere different" is neither antimale nor antisex, since such a perspective encourages viewing women's sexuality not merely as externally defined by an oppressive patriarchy but also as subjectively de-termined by each woman through her own personal exploration of sexual passion and pleasure. From this perspective, it is through the unique dialectical interplay of these two opposing forces in each woman's life that her sexuality is formed and lived. In the next section of this chapter I will outline how encouraging men to treat women with care respect can help undermine men's sexual intimidation of women.

Encouraging Men to Treat Women with Care Respect

> The only way to understand a woman's survival is to put oneself in her place.
>
> — Kathleen Barry, *Female Sexual Slavery*

Feminists who argue that women's sexual harassment and abuse are pervasive features of contemporary social institutions also argue that it will take the wholesale dismantling of such institutions for men's sexual intimidation of women to be eliminated. Taking this position into account, it is naive to expect men to change their sexist attitudes toward women, when such attitudes continue to be reinforced by cultural institutions that reward male sexual dominance and control. Recognizing this, many feminists satisfy themselves with changes in current law, politics, or education, which they believe will result in better treatment of women. Yet despite changes in these areas, feminists have found that if men's and women's *attitudes* toward the relations between the sexes do not change, the practice of theoretically equitable social systems tends to remain inconsistent and unpredictable. Dismantling institutional sexual intimidation will ultimately be successful only if those who have power over, and control of, existing social structures are themselves amenable to change. Therefore, in this section I present ways that women can encourage men to treat women with care respect, which can begin the process of dismantling those social institutions inimical to women's sexual agency and self-definition. I will argue that one of the ways that women can actively undermine the sexist attitudes that reinforce the sexual intimidation of women is to encourage men to do the "world"-traveling required by the ethic of care respect introduced in chapter 3. First, I explain what it would mean for a man to treat a woman with care respect in his sexual relations with her. I then describe how encouraging men to exercise autonomous relating to others and to take responsibility for their sexuality can help them understand what it means to be a woman in a sexist society and what cultural pressures men may feel to conform to sexist standards. I speculate about whether convincing men (and women) to change their sexual attitudes is either practical or possible, especially if men will be asked to give up their power base. I conclude with the claim that only by simultaneously shifting individual women's and men's sexual attitudes toward those of care respect, as well as working toward changing the cultural and economic institutions that are both created by oppressive sexual attitudes and continue to reinforce them, can feminists hope to afford women the sexual agency and self-esteem necessary to define our sexuality in our own terms.

Encouraging Men to "World"-Travel

In chapters 3 and 4 I discussed how an effort to recognize other persons as both equally valuable and special is fundamental to an ethic of care respect. I suggested that a sexual ethic of care respect also encourages an active concern for understanding and promoting others' sexual wants and needs as they see them and for doing so in ways consistent with the care respect of others. If we want to encourage men to treat women with care respect, then we must encourage men not only to regard each woman as the defining subject of her sexual experience but also to recognize each woman's ability to define her sexual experience in ways unique to her. Attempting to understand an individual woman's experience of her sexuality also requires the "world"-traveling often referred to as "putting oneself in another's shoes": treating a woman with care respect requires that a man ask, "What is it like to be her?," and "What is it like to be me in her eyes?" Through such "world"-traveling, men will begin to understand the particular context of each woman's battle with sexual intimidation as well as her gender role socialization as the sexual object of men's institutionalized supremacy and control. He may also begin to understand why women fail to feel much sympathy for men whose failure in the workplace or in education is so often compensated for by their harassment or abuse of women and girls, yet rationalized by citing "trouble at home."

A sexual ethic of care respect further recommends that men not merely tolerate, or refrain from interfering with, a woman's pursuit of the meaning and value of the erotic in her own life. In doing so, a man would be exercising no more than Marjorie Weinzweig's "autonomous being for oneself," introduced in chapter 3. This kind of autonomy is quite similar to one described by traditional ethical theories of justice, in which mutually self-interested persons make claims on each other only when competing individual rights create conflicts between persons or when impartial duties to act in accordance with those rights are not fulfilled. Instead, a sexual ethic of care respect recommends that a man do what he can to promote a woman's sexual agency and self-definition in ways that encourage her ability to exercise an autonomous relating to others and to take responsibility for her sexuality. In this way a man also becomes one who exercises an autonomous relating to others in the world, a member of a community of persons who share a similar commitment to "world"-traveling and the pro-active care of others.[158] Furthermore, in such a community, a man takes responsibility for his own sexuality by seeing his sexual desires and preferences as themselves rooted in patriarchal social institutions that can afford him an unfair advantage over women and that may make it easy for him to treat women unreflectively as accessible sexual objects. By adopting this moral perspective, men will begin to regard men's sexual violation, terrorization, coercion, and dehumanization of women as violating their respect for women as self-determining moral equals and as antithetical to the empathy and sense of community required of those who value an ethic of care.[159]

Specifically, treating women with care respect in the workplace or in academia means, among other things, realizing that overt physical or sexual contact, sexual comments, jokes, or cartoons may offend a woman and not a man, precisely because she is sexualized by a culture whose economic and social climate makes it difficult for her either to transcend her identification of sexual object or to make that identification a positive feature of her life. By understanding sexual harassment from a woman's point of view, a man may realize that the subtlety, variety, and constant exposure to hostile environment harassment that a woman may be subjected to can be just as destructive to her self-esteem or self-confidence as the quid pro quo variety. Because hostile environment harassment represents an abuse of the social and sexual power men have over women without the more obvious economic or political hierarchies of quid pro quo harassment, for men to understand hostile environment harassment requires that they understand the ways in which social institutions are hierarchically constituted simply by the gender of their members. Thus, the "world"-traveling implicit in care respect may motivate judges and juries to listen with new political sensibilities to what individual women consider a hostile work environment, rather than relying on overly generalized and apolitical standards of what a "reasonable man," a "reasonable person," or even a "reasonable woman" would find harassing. Furthermore, a man who treats women with care respect in the workplace or academia will not automatically assume that a woman's friendliness is a sign of sexual attraction to him and so will not respond to her attentions in ways that are in fact harassing to her. Former U.S. senator Bob Packwood actively supported equal rights for women during his congressional tenure yet allegedly sexually harassed his secretaries and political aides over a period of many years. In the language of care respect, Packwood's failure to "world"-travel to individual women's economic and social situation or to take responsibility for his sexuality under conditions of institutionalized male dominance made it possible for him to depoliticize his very personal attentions. Care respect for women who are sexually harassed also means developing policies and procedures that reflect women's preferences for handling disputes and that recognize how a woman's lower position or economic clout within a company hierarchy may make purportedly gender neutral grievance procedures work against her. Men may also realize from this perspective that while *men* might lie about others' sexual harassment of them to rationalize poor job performance or to punish supervisors unwilling to promote them, a woman rarely does so, if only because of the tremendous emotional and economic price she often feels she must pay for her accusations.[160]

Pamela Foa suggests that once women and men begin really listening to each other, coercive sex will no longer reflect the norm of many women's heterosexual experience. If men were to treat women with care respect, men might begin to understand the social pressures many women (especially young women) feel to say yes to sex when they would rather say no; the desire of some women to be partners with men for social comfort, affection, and companionship but not sex; and the pressures men often feel to "score" or to make their partners' sexual needs secondary to their own.[161] Women and men would begin to realize that there are compelling alternatives to the often debilitating and destructive courtship customs that require that when men "shell out" for a date, women must "put out," making rape and battery a common feature of heterosexual sex. Women would begin to see ourselves as worthy of respect in our own right and less in need of acquiescing to a man to maintain our self-esteem or social image. By asking "What is it like to be me in their eyes?," men would recognize how much more threatening, controlling, and violent they often appear to their wives and girlfriends than they seem to themselves. Compassion and kindness in sexual relations would replace selfishness and cruelty if women and men treated each other with care respect, where compassion, according to Lawrence Blum, involves an "imaginative dwelling on the condition of another person, an active regard for his good, a view of him as a fellow human being, and emotional responses of a certain degree of intensity," and where kindness, according to Tom Regan, implies "to act with the intention of forwarding the interests of others, not for reasons of self-gain, but out of love, affection or compassion for the individuals whose interests are forwarded."[162]

Challenging Social Hierarchies
and Gender Role Expectations

Many feminists claim that eradicating men's violence against women over the long term means eradicating the unequal power relations between the sexes. This eradication would demand a total restructuring of the family, with men and women taking equal responsibility for child rearing, domestic maintenance, and financial security.[163] The successful dismantling of the patriarchal family would also require the widespread acceptance of caring and cooperative alternatives to the heterosexual nuclear family, as well as radical changes in the workplace and traditional child care. However, if feminists are to be successful in teaching men care respect for women, then feminists must dislodge many men's (and women's) gender role association of masculinity with power over women, for unless they do so, men will regard feminists' demands for egalitarian relationships as emasculating. Yet if men's public lives continue to demand that they value and pursue hierarchical social power and authority, then men may find it difficult to give up such pursuits in their personal relationships or may resist doing so altogether.[164] This is one reason why socialist feminists claim that women's liberation requires not only a revolution in our sexual and reproductive institutions but also the dismantling of any political economy that requires human relationships to be defined by the dominance of an elite and wealthy few over an impoverished and oppressed majority.

As with sexual harassment law, "reasonable woman" standards in self-defense laws pertaining to battered women reveal that lawmakers are making an attempt to "world"-travel to the situations of battered women. Judges and juries are being asked to try to understand a woman's fear for her life from her perspective rather than from a man's, who may only have bared his fists or may not have been provocative the moment she assaulted him. Men who treat young girls with care respect will begin to realize a girl's pain, humiliation, confusion, and outrage by being abused and not believed, or by being consistently raped yet asked to feel affection and respect for her abuser. Men will begin to see themselves as adults in whom many young girls place an enormous amount of trust but whose betrayal of that trust can have devastating effects that can last a lifetime in young women already socialized to dependency and self-doubt. In short, for a man to treat women with care respect means *not* objectifying, universalizing, or rationalizing women but trying his best to particularize and empathize with women's daily experience of sexual intimidation by men, *including himself.* Men cannot be women, of course; but men can make every effort to acknowledge, understand, and promote women's sexual lives as women would define them, not as men might wish women to define them.

Therefore, the caring and respectful treatment of women should be understood not as treatment encouraged only under the most sexually intimate conditions but as treatment that should exist in the workplace, in education, in the law, and in the family—indeed, *everywhere* that women and men congregate. There are few such places that do not provide ample opportunity for men's sexual intimidation of women, and few relationships between women and men that could not benefit from the combination of esteem and empathy that an ethic of care respect describes. At the same time, a sexual ethic of care respect should not be understood as giving men blanket permission to intrude on women's sexual lives with the excuse that they are "just trying to get to know women better." What a sexual ethic of care respect recommends is that both women and men be sensitive to the social location and the needs of each individual, a sensitivity in which listening to each other's particular voices is a value. In this way women and men can begin to assess how far their imaginative understanding of another's sexuality should reach and how much effort should be spent promoting the interests of others. An ethic of care respect is grounded in a fundamental respect for persons as self-determining moral agents and so can morally circumscribe the parameters of such efforts with minimum standards of moral conduct below which no one must fall. However, this ethic is deliberately flexible in its decision procedures for particular cases in order to appreciate social context and individual eccentricity and to avoid the distortion of a purportedly more exact ethical theory that advocates the application of universal and abstract moral principles to a wide variety of cases. An ethic of care respect can thus appreciate both the ambiguity and the clarity of the woman described by Robin Morgan, who awakens for the first time to her own sense of herself: "She still doesn't know 'what must be done,' but she is on her way to doing it, and she has no time to waste on those who insist they know when they don't."[165]

Furthermore, just as men must take responsibility for accepting a socially constructed male sexuality often dictated by cultural expectations of dominance and control, so women must take responsibility for acquiescing to our own gender expectations of sexual compliance and understand the complex social pressures that encourage many men unreflectively to dominate women sexually. Thus, neither sex is "off the hook" from the "view from somewhere different," since both women and men who adopt this perspective not only seek to resist making presumptions about the other's sexual needs and preferences but also recognize the difficulties of doing so in a world whose social expectations put pressure on both genders to conform to a hierarchical status quo. The creative collaboration and opportunities for real affection that may result from such efforts, however, may encourage men to give up a power base that they may otherwise feel too vulnerable to relinquish. Yet as I write this, I realize that it may be a question not of losing or gaining power but of transforming the meaning and value of power in sexual relations that will make them personally rewarding for all. Intimacy and shared responsibility without the fear of falling down a notch in a gender hierarchy may create opportunities for individual women and men to understand more clearly their own needs and values.[166] Lesbian and gay relationships would certainly benefit from a perspective that advocates care respect as would any sexual practice that deviates from traditional heterosexual norms, since sadomasochistic as well as vanilla sex can be nonoppressive sex using such a model. If power-transforming, nonintimidating, compassionate, and passionate sexual relationships are both possible and desirable, then we must not only redefine for adults as well as our children the moral parameters of sexual desire under the rubric of care respect; we must also continue to demand that our economic, political, and cultural institutions neither instantiate nor reinforce the sexual intimidation of women. The latter task defines the continuing need for a feminist activism that publicly recognizes and resists the victimization of women. The former task asks women and men to share the responsibility for redefining human sexuality in terms that facilitate the sexual exploration, passion, and pleasure of both sexes.

Conclusion

The "view from somewhere different" is a perspective from which I have claimed that men's institutionalized sexual intimidation of women and women's capacity for determining the meaning and value of our sexual passion and pleasure combine to reflect the dialectic between gender and sexuality that is at the heart of women's sexual experience under patriarchy. This perspective encourages women to understand the pervasive and structural ways in which women are sexually victimized by men in a society that reinforces men's domination and control of women. I have argued that this perspective is vital if individual women are to defend themselves against their sexual harassment and abuse and to liberate themselves to define a sexuality suited to their individual needs. The "view from somewhere different" can accommodate those who believe that feminists victimize women by overemphasizing women's institutionalized oppression; according to the "view from somewhere different," women's sexuality is an active and responsible one that women have the capacity to define in our own terms, yet such definitions are viable ones only when women recognize the extent to which our sexuality is also a function of social institutions structurally biased to advantage men.

Thus, for women to eradicate men's sexual intimidation of women requires profound and difficult changes in women's and men's sexual attitudes that must be incorporated into, and reflected by, the social institutions under which women and men live. Such a perspective in turn recommends that a promising method of resistance against men's sexual intimidation of women is to encourage women and men to treat one another with care respect. This perspective advocates treating all persons as moral equals as well as treating each person as uniquely situated in a way that allows women and men to recognize, understand, and promote the particular and self-determined interests of each other. The intentional ambiguity of how to assess those interests is one of the strengths of this perspective, since it requires women and men to explore actively and communally which actions best suit which contexts and needs within the parameters of moral equality.

On the other hand, the "view from somewhere different" is a frustrating perspective for many, because it is paradoxically noncommittal in its insistence that there is no one epistemological or moral voice that can speak about women's sexual experience in all times and places. What this perspective gains by this approach, however, is a way of understanding women's sexuality that accounts for the variety and complexity of individual women's sexual experience, affords women and men a way of evaluating that experience using an ethic of care respect, and gives each woman the double prism of her patriarchal oppression and her capacity for sexual self-definition from which to discern the meaning of the erotic in her own life.

Conclusion

We face the task of learning how to use our own conflicts constructively, affiliatively, and pleasurably—as sources of pleasure precisely because they can be tools for forging new understanding and new forms of affiliation.

—Marianne Hirsch and Evelyn Fox Keller,
"Conclusion: Practicing Conflict in Feminist Theory"

Feminists continue to disagree over the extent to which individual women may be complicit in their own sexual oppression and the oppression of women as a class. We also differ over what kinds of experience can liberate women individually and collectively to define the terms and conditions of our sexual lives. I have suggested in this book that such disagreements often paint a picture of women's sexuality in mutually exclusive terms: women's sexual choices are *either* the product of an oppressive gender politics *or* the site for a self-defined sexual liberation for women. I have argued that a more representative picture of women's sexuality reveals diversity, complexity, ambiguity, and contradiction in individual women's lives. I have argued that such features reflect a dialectic in a woman's sexual experience between the individual and institutional forces of her sexual oppression, on the one hand, and the possibilities for her sexual exploration, passion, and pleasure, on the other. From this perspective, the profoundly feminist assertion that the personal is political is less an equivalence than a fluid and dynamic relationship between a woman's individual pursuit of her own passions and preferences and her social responsibility for making decisions that do not contribute to women's sexual oppression under conditions of institutionalized male dominance.

I have contended that the perspective of the "view from somewhere different" is an epistemological framework that provides a way of thinking and talking about women's sexuality that captures the dynamic between the personal and the political within and among women. Such a framework recognizes the strengths of a feminism that situates women's sexuality within a cultural ideology that devalues and subordinates women to the advantage of men. Yet it is also a framework that advocates raising our consciousness of this ideology as a first step in the pursuit of women's sexual creativity and power, which along with women's freedom from sexual subordination would allow individual women to determine for themselves how sex and sexuality figure in their lives.

This perspective informs a sexual ethic of care respect that recommends treating women and men as the agents and defining subjects of our sexual experience in actively caring communities of both shared and conflicting interests. This ethic recommends a general application of the principles of care respect to our sexual lives at the same time that it encourages persons to regard sexual relationships as uniquely confounded by the politics of gender. My contention is that sex is not merely a matter of taste, because sex is such an effective tool for the harassment, humiliation, and abuse of women. Power and control are moral issues; thus, our moral sensibilities must be engaged to examine those specific and unique ways in which systemic gender hierarchies turn a woman's sexuality into a vehicle for her oppression and the oppression of women as a class. A sexual ethic of care respect from the "view from somewhere different" is designed as a guide, but not a decision procedure, for considering the meaning, value, and practice of the sexual lives of persons who may be very differently situated from one another. Thus, the "view from somewhere different" can provide a context and a legitimacy for a variety of sexual experiences, preferences, and desires in both women and men and can provide feminists of diverse theoretical backgrounds with a common frame of reference from which to advance our dialogue in women's sexuality. This advance is essential if we wish to represent ourselves as offering constructive voices in different women's lives instead of the unacceptable extremisms often disseminated by feminism's detractors.

This means that we will have to become more comfortable with conflict in the absence of clear resolution and accept compromise or consensus only when it is understood that consensus does not require stasis or sameness. It is much easier to fall back on the "view from nowhere" or the "view from somewhere better," because neither requires the energy and effort of "world"-traveling. On the other hand, being all things to all people is an impossible task not lost on critics of the "view from everywhere." However, from the "view from somewhere different," living with partial coalitions or uneasy alliances need not be divisive, when consensus is not the ultimate goal and when conflict resolution can be oppressively elitist and dismissive of difference. As Raymond Belliotti writes:

> Rather than regretting the loss of fixed foundations and authoritative trumps of reason, we should revel in increased opportunities for freedom and collective deliberation.

Further, we should not assume that convergence of opinion is the necessary goal of rational discussion. . . . [O]ur institutions should not strive to eliminate ideological and political conflict; rather, they should rechannel controversy as a way to invigorate social life.[1]

Moreover, by emphasizing the importance of negotiating the tensions among feminists from a wide variety of theoretical and practical perspectives, the "view from somewhere different" is useful for advancing the dialogue across a broad spectrum of feminist concerns. Such concerns reveal themselves in conflicts over the meaning and value of essentialist claims in feminist theorizing; debates over the place of analytic reasoning and objectivity in women's studies curricula and feminist academic discussion; differences of opinion over whether and how psychoanalytic theory should be used to explore women's oppression; exchanges over the benefits and risks of new reproductive technologies such as in vitro fertilization, embryo transfer, and embryo freezing; and tensions among feminists of differing sexual preferences over what counts as an affirming and expansive sexuality for women.[2] The "view from somewhere different" recommends that all such feminists "world"-travel to the perspectives of those from whom we differ and to remember that ours are not the only "worlds" worth knowing. In this way women and men may build a connectedness without striving for commonality or unanimity, where Marianne Hirsch's and Evelyn Fox Keller's "new forms of affiliation" may be formed and lived.

The "view from somewhere different" encourages us to think of any one woman's metaphysical "self" as both enduring and unstable, since it is a self whose identity as an agent of change is an important element in her capacity for liberation. From this perspective, a woman is in constant flux between the ideological forces that shape her sexuality and the self-consciousness of those forces that can ground her sexual subjectivity and agency. Adopting the "view from somewhere different" means recognizing that gender can be a liberating force in women's lives and that sexuality can be an oppressive one, depending on the context and culture in which the dialectic between gender and sexuality is played out. I believe it is beside the point to wonder what "good sex" means for women outside the current patriarchal constraints that circumscribe our sexuality. Rather, it is up to feminist theory and practice from the "view from somewhere different" to give us an epistemology and ethic that can work within current parameters to forge new pathways for women's sexual freedom, creativity, and satisfaction.

A common framework for thinking and talking about women's sexuality may strike some feminists as uncomfortably presumptuous and inevitably universalizing, necessarily silencing some of the very voices within the discourse that such a framework is purportedly designed to recognize. On the contrary, I am convinced of the necessity and the possibility of a single philosophical perspective from which a variety of issues in women's sexuality can be explored. Indeed, the framework is designed to be simultaneously theoretical and practical in its efforts to facilitate conversation and collaboration. Without feminist praxis to ground theory, such a framework too readily dissolves into the rallying cry of an intellectual elite; without feminist theory to inform practice, feminists cannot credibly argue for structural changes in social policy. In the preceding chapters I have contended that feminist tensions within dis-

cussions of women's sexuality invite critical inquiry and allow constructive negotiation without requiring the final resolution that would silence opposing feminist viewpoints. I believe that this perspective both strengthens and endorses the feminist commitment that women's voices be heard and validated despite a status quo advantaged
by our silence. Such a perspective is more pragmatic than relativistic, more recon-
structive than deconstructive, since this perspective denounces both the legitimacy
of men's sexual oppression of women and any ethic of exclusion that ignores the
unique and varied role that sexuality may play in each woman's life. It is a perspective that seeks to transform and transcend current marginalizing definitions of difference. It is not a complement but a radical alternative to more conservative conceptions of the value of diversity in a global community. I believe it is a perspective
that works to bring otherwise disparate factions together in a single and collective effort to eradicate misogyny and male bias from women's sexual lives and to increase
women's sexual agency and self-definition. In this sense, feminist theory fuses with
feminist practice in ways that show how feminism, philosophy, and women's sexuality, taken together, can further our understanding of the relations between the sexes.
The conviction to continue, not forestall, the dialogue in women's sexuality by constructing a framework for conscientiously listening to the diversity of women's voices
in such discussions has encouraged me to forge ahead, wary of hasty generalization
yet convinced of the value of the effort. I encourage readers to use the discussions in
this book to reflect on the role that sex and sexuality play in their own lives and to
find caring and cooperative ways of sharing those reflections with others.

NOTES

Introduction

1. See Gayle Rubin, "Thinking Sex: Notes for a Radical Theory of the Politics of Sexuality," in *Pleasure and Danger: Exploring Female Sexuality*, ed. Carole S. Vance (London: Pandora Press, 1989), 267–319; Alison Assiter and Avedon Carol, eds., *Bad Girls and Dirty Pictures: The Challenge to Reclaim Feminism* (London: Pluto Press, 1993); Samois, ed., *Coming to Power: Writings and Graphics on Lesbian S/M* (Boston: Alyson Publications, 1987); Pat Califia, *Public Sex: The Culture of Radical Sex* (Pittsburgh: Cleis Press, 1994); Joan Nestle, ed., *The Persistent Desire: A Femme-Butch Reader* (Boston: Alyson Publications, 1992); Annie Sprinkle, *Post Porn Modernist* (Amsterdam: Torch Books, 1991). For a discussion of the ways in which challenging stereotypes of male sexuality can liberate men and masculinity as well as women and femininity, see John Stoltenberg, "How Men Have (a) Sex," and Patrick D. Hopkins, "Gender Treachery: Homophobia, Masculinity, and Threatened Identities," in *Free Spirits: Feminist Philosophers on Culture*, ed. Kate Mehuron and Gary Percesepe (Englewood Cliffs, N.J.: Prentice Hall, 1995), 410–32, 518–20.

2. For some of the ways that patriarchal institutions encourage battered women to stay in abusive relationships, see Ola W. Barnett and Alyce D. LaViolette, *It Could Happen to Anyone: Why Battered Women Stay* (Newbury Park, Calif.: Sage Publications, 1993), chap. 2; also see chapter 5 in this book. For a variety of feminist arguments against the more radical forms of sexual expression advocated by the authors in note 1, see Dorchen Leidholdt and Janice G. Raymond, eds., *The Sexual Liberals and the Attack on Feminism* (New York: Teachers College Press, 1990); Robin Ruth Linden, Darlene R. Pagano, Diana E. H. Russell, and Susan Leigh Star, eds., *Against Sadomasochism: A Radical Feminist Analysis* (San Francisco: Frog in the Well, 1982); Catharine A. MacKinnon, *Feminism Unmodified:*

Discourses on Life and Law (Cambridge: Harvard University Press, 1987); Laura Lederer, ed., *Take Back the Night: Women on Pornography* (New York: William Morrow, 1980); Diana E. H. Russell, ed., *Making Violence Sexy: Feminist Views on Pornography* (Buckingham, U.K.: Open University Press, 1993); Andrea Dworkin, *Pornography: Men Possessing Women* (New York: E. P. Dutton, 1989); chapters 2, 3, and 4 in this book.

3. See Camille Paglia, *Sex, Art, and American Culture* (New York: Vintage Books, 1992) and *Vamps and Tramps: New Essays* (New York: Vintage Books, 1994); Christina Hoff Sommers, *Who Stole Feminism?: How Women Have Betrayed Women* (New York: Simon & Schuster, 1994); Katie Roiphe, *The Morning After: Sex, Fear, and Feminism on Campus* (Boston: Little, Brown, 1993); Rene Denfeld, *The New Victorians: A Young Woman's Challenge to the Old Feminist Order* (New York: Warner Books, 1995); also see chapter 5 in this book.

4. See Janet Radcliffe Richards, *The Sceptical Feminist: A Philosophical Enquiry* (Boston: Routledge & Kegan Paul, 1980), chap. 7; Christina Sommers, "Philosophers against the Family," in *Person to Person*, ed. George Graham and Hugh LaFollette (Philadelphia: Temple University Press, 1989), 82–105.

5. Linda LeMoncheck, "Feminist Politics and Feminist Ethics: Treating Women as Sex Objects," *Philosophical Perspectives on Sex and Love*, ed. Robert M. Stewart (New York: Oxford University Press, 1995), 31–32.

Chapter 1

1. See Rosemarie Tong, *Feminist Thought* (Boulder, Colo.: Westview Press, 1989); Alison M. Jaggar, *Feminist Politics and Human Nature* (Totowa, N.J.: Rowman & Allanheld, 1983); Nancy Tuana, *Woman and the History of Philosophy* (New York: Paragon House, 1992); Susan Moller Okin, *Women in Western Political Thought* (Princeton: Princeton University Press, 1979); Diana Coole, *Women in Political Theory: From Ancient Misogyny to Contemporary Feminism* (Boulder, Colo.: Lynne Rienner, 1988); Linda A. Bell, *Visions of Women* (Clifton, N.J.: Humana, 1983); Genevieve Lloyd, *The Man of Reason: "Male" and "Female" in Western Philosophy* (Minneapolis: University of Minnesota Press, 1986); Lorenne M. G. Clark and Lynda Lange, eds., *The Sexism of Social and Political Theory* (Toronto: University of Toronto Press, 1979); Mary Lyndon Shanley and Carole Pateman, eds., *Feminist Interpretations and Political Theory* (University Park: Pennsylvania State University Press, 1991); Ann Garry and Marilyn Pearsall, eds., *Women, Knowledge, and Reality* (Boston: Unwin Hyman, 1989). On the dangers of describing traditional philosophy as "male" or "masculine," see Jean Grimshaw, *Philosophy and Feminist Thinking* (Minneapolis: University of Minnesota Press, 1986).

2. See María C. Lugones and Elizabeth V. Spelman, "Have We Got a Theory for You!: Feminist Theory, Cultural Imperialism and the Demand for 'The Woman's Voice,'" in *Women and Values*, ed. Marilyn Pearsall (Belmont, Calif.: Wadsworth Publishing Co., 1986), 19–31; Charlotte Bunch, "A Global Perspective on Feminist Ethics and Diversity," in *Explorations in Feminist Ethics*, ed. Eve Browning Cole and Susan Coultrap-McQuin (Bloomington: Indiana University Press, 1992), 176–85; María C. Lugones, "On the Logic of Pluralist Feminism," in *Feminist Ethics*, ed. Claudia Card (Lawrence: University Press of Kansas, 1991), 35–44; Elizabeth V. Spelman, *Inessential Woman: Problems of Exclusion in Feminist Thought* (Boston: Beacon Press, 1988), chaps. 5, 6, and 7; Cherríe Moraga and Gloria Anzaldúa, eds., *This Bridge Called My Back: Writings by Radical Women of Color* (Watertown, Mass.: Persephone Press, 1981); bell hooks, *Feminist Theory from Margin to Center* (Boston: South End Press, 1984); Barbara Smith, ed., *Home Girls: A Black Feminist Anthology* (New York: Kitchen Table: Women of Color Press, 1983); Patricia Hill Collins, *Black Feminist Thought* (New York: Unwin Hyman, 1990).

3. See Alan Soble, ed., *The Philosophy of Sex: Contemporary Readings*, 2d ed. (Savage,

Md.: Rowman & Littlefield, 1991); Robert Baker and Frederick Elliston, eds., *Philosophy and Sex*, 2d ed. (Buffalo, N.Y.: Prometheus Books, 1984); Robert C. Solomon and Kathleen M. Higgins, eds., *The Philosophy of (Erotic) Love* (Lawrence: University Press of Kansas, 1991); D. P. Verene, ed., *Sexual Love and Western Morality* (New York: Harper Torchbooks, 1972); Robert M. Stewart, ed., *Philosophical Perspectives on Sex and Love* (New York: Oxford University Press, 1995).

4. "Western culture" is itself a gloss on a diverse set of nations, peoples, and social institutions. I have tried throughout the book to give some sense of when diverse social perspectives or multiple social oppressions within Western culture require special examination. I have endeavored to do the same for gender relations in many Eastern and less industrialized nations. For an excellent discussion of the dimensions of culture and gender in feminist discourse, see Lugones and Spelman, "Have We Got a Theory for You!"

5. For example, see Catharine A. MacKinnon, *Feminism Unmodified: Discourses on Life and Law* (Cambridge: Harvard University Press, 1987); Susan Brownmiller, *Against Our Will: Men, Women, and Rape* (New York: Bantam Books, 1975); Kathleen Barry, *Female Sexual Slavery* (Englewood Cliffs, N.J.: Prentice Hall, 1979); Susan Griffin, *Pornography and Silence* (New York: Harper & Row, 1981); Andrea Dworkin, *Pornography: Men Possessing Women* (New York: E. P. Dutton, 1989); Susan Schecter, *Women and Male Violence: The Visions and Struggles of the Battered Women's Movement* (Boston: South End Press, 1982).

6. Marilyn Frye, *The Politics of Reality* (Trumansburg, N.Y.: Crossing Press, 1983), 96.

7. See Carole S. Vance, "Pleasure and Danger: Toward a Politics of Sexuality," in *Pleasure and Danger: Exploring Female Sexuality*, ed. Carole S. Vance (London: Pandora Press, 1989); Ann Snitow, Christine Stansell, and Sharon Thompson, eds., *Powers of Desire: The Politics of Sexuality* (New York: Monthly Review Press, 1983); Sheryl Ortner and Harriet Whitehead, eds., *Sexual Meanings: The Cultural Construction of Gender and Sexuality* (New York: Cambridge University Press, 1981); Stephen Heath, *The Sexual Fix* (London: Macmillan, 1982); Susan Suleiman, ed., *The Female Body in Western Culture* (Cambridge: Harvard University Press, 1986); Toril Moi, *Sexual/Textual Politics: Feminist Literary Theory* (New York: Methuen, 1985); Dorchen Leidholdt and Janice G. Raymond, eds., *The Sexual Liberals and the Attack on Feminism* (New York: Teachers College Press, 1990); Adrienne Rich, "Compulsory Heterosexuality and Lesbian Existence," *Signs: Journal of Culture and Society* 5 (summer 1980): 631–60.

8. See Ann Ferguson, Ilene Philipson, Irene Diamond and Lee Quinby, and Carole S. Vance and Ann Snitow, "Forum: The Feminist Sexuality Debates," *Signs: Journal of Women in Culture and Society* 10 (autumn 1984): 106–35.

9. For elaboration of the postmodern critique of feminist theory, see Jane Flax, "Postmodernism and Gender Relations in Feminist Theory," in *Feminist Theory in Practice and Process*, ed. Micheline R. Malson, Jean F. O'Barr, Sarah Westphal-Wihl, and Mary Wyer (Chicago: University of Chicago Press, 1989), 60–64; Sandra Harding, "The Instability of the Analytical Categories of Feminist Theory," in Malson et al., *Feminist Theory in Practice and Process*, 15–20; Linda J. Nicholson, "Introduction," in *Feminism/Postmodernism*, ed. Linda J. Nicholson (New York: Routledge, 1990), 5–8.

10. Linda Alcoff, "Cultural Feminism versus Post-Structuralism: The Identity Crisis in Feminist Theory," in Malson et al., *Feminist Theory in Practice and Process*, 321.

11. See Flax, "Postmodernism and Gender Relations in Feminist Theory," and Harding, "The Instability of the Analytical Categories of Feminist Theory"; also see Sandra Harding, *Whose Science? Whose Knowledge?: Thinking from Women's Lives* (Ithaca, N.Y.: Cornell University Press, 1991), 185, and "Feminism, Science, and the Anti-Enlightenment Critiques," in Nicholson, *Feminism/Postmodernism*, 100.

12. Harding, *Whose Science? Whose Knowledge?*, 179. Harding footnotes bell hooks

(*Talking Back: Thinking Feminist, Thinking Black* [Boston: South End Press, 1989]) as a feminist who has described social relations in this manner; also see Spelman, *Inessential Woman,* chap. 5.

13. Feminist women of color have written extensively on this issue. See Audre Lorde, *Sister Outsider: Essays and Speeches by Audre Lorde* (Freedom, Calif.: Crossing Press, 1984); hooks, *Feminist Theory from Margin to Center;* hooks, *Talking Back;* Moraga and Anzaldúa, *This Bridge Called My Back;* Smith, *Home Girls;* Gloria Anzaldúa, *Borderlands/La Frontera: The New Mestiza* (San Francisco: Spinsters/Aunt Lute, 1987); Gloria Anzaldúa, *Making Face, Making Soul–Haciendo Caras: Creative and Critical Perspectives by Women of Color* (San Francisco: Aunt Lute Press, 1990); Gloria T. Hull, Patricia Bell Scott, and Barbara Smith, eds., *All the Women Are White, All the Blacks Are Men, but Some of Us Are Brave: Black Women's Studies* (Old Westbury, N.Y.: Feminist Press, 1982); Gayatri Chakravorty Spivak, *In Other Worlds: Essays in Cultural Politics* (New York: Methuen, 1987); Maxine Baca Zinn, Lynn Weber Cannon, Elizabeth Higginbotham, and Bonnie Thornton Dill, "The Costs of Exclusionary Practices in Women's Studies," *Signs: Journal of Culture and Society* 11, no. 2 (1986): 290–303; Aída Hurtado, *The Color of Privilege: Three Blasphemies on Race and Feminism* (Ann Arbor: University of Michigan Press, 1996); Cherríe Moraga, *Loving in the War Years* (Boston: South End Press, 1986).

14. For a review of this dialectic and alternative methodologies in the social sciences, see Sandra Harding, ed., *Feminism and Methodology: Social Science Issues* (Bloomington: Indiana University Press, 1987); Dorothy Smith, *The Everyday World as Problematic: A Feminist Sociology* (Boston: Northeastern University Press, 1987).

15. See Thomas Aquinas, *On the Truth of the Catholic Faith,* book 3: Providence Parts I and II, trans. Vernon J. Bourke (New York: Doubleday, 1956); Aristotle, "Politica," book I, chaps. 12 and 13, *The Works of Aristotle,* trans. Benjamin Jowett, ed. W. D. Ross (Oxford: Clarendon Press, 1921); Arthur Schopenhauer, "Essay on Women," in *The Works of Schopenhauer,* ed. William Durant (New York: Simon & Schuster, 1928); Friedrich Nietzsche, *Beyond Good and Evil,* section 144, in *The Philosophy of Nietzsche,* trans. H. Zimmern (New York: Random House, 1954). Discussions of the misogyny in the philosophy of sex of both Schopenhauer and Nietzsche can be found in Robert Baker and Frederick Elliston, "Introduction," in Baker and Elliston, *Philosophy and Sex,* 20–22, 32–33.

16. María Lugones, "Playfulness, 'World'-Traveling, and Loving Perception," in Garry and Pearsall, *Women, Knowledge, and Reality,* 289.

17. For explicit references to the privileged voice of women, see Mary Daly, *Pure Lust: Elemental Feminist Philosophy* (Boston: Beacon Press, 1984); Sara Ruddick, *Maternal Thinking: Toward a Politics of Peace* (Boston: Beacon Press, 1989); Nel Noddings, *Caring: A Feminine Approach to Ethics and Moral Education* (Berkeley: University of California Press, 1984). Arguably, tacit assumptions of women's privileged worldview may be found in Nancy Chodorow, *The Reproduction of Mothering: Psychoanalysis and the Sociology of Gender* (Berkeley: University of California Press, 1978); Dorothy Dinnerstein, *The Mermaid and the Minotaur: Sexual Arrangements and Human Malaise* (New York: Harper Colophon Books, 1976); Carol Gilligan, *In a Different Voice: Psychological Theory and Women's Development* (Cambridge: Harvard University Press, 1982); Mary Field Belenky, Blythe McVicker Clinchy, Nancy Rule Goldberger, and Jill Mattuck Tarule, *Women's Ways of Knowing: The Development of Self, Voice, and Mind* (New York: Basic Books, 1986). The fact that interpretations of these authors' views change depending on the nature of the interpreter's political agenda is discussed in Susan Bordo, "Feminism, Postmodernism, and Gender-Scepticism," in Nicholson, *Feminism/Postmodernism,* 145–49.

18. See chapter 1, nn. 2, 13.

19. See Thomas Nagel, *The View from Nowhere* (Oxford: Oxford University Press, 1986). The following discussion is not intended to be a critical analysis of Nagel's epistemological position. The brief commentary I give is meant as a feminist philosophical interpretation and critique of the concept of an ideal and purely objective observer whose worldview, devoid of any personal or cultural perspective, Nagel describes as being "nowhere."

20. See Sandra Harding, *The Science Question in Feminism* (Ithaca, N.Y.: Cornell University Press, 1986) and *Whose Science? Whose Knowledge?*; Donna Haraway, *Primate Vision: Gender, Race, and Nature in the World of Modern Science* (New York: Routledge, 1989); Helen E. Longino, "Can There Be a Feminist Science?," *Hypatia* 2 (fall 1987): 51–64, and *Science as Social Knowledge: Values and Objectivity in Scientific Inquiry* (Princeton: Princeton University Press, 1990); Evelyn Fox Keller, *Reflections on Gender and Science* (New Haven: Yale University Press, 1984); Evelyn Fox Keller, *Refiguring Life: Metaphors of Twentieth-Century Biology* (New York: Columbia University Press, 1995).

21. See Lorraine B. Code, *What Can She Know?: Feminist Theory and the Construction of Knowledge* (Ithaca, N.Y.: Cornell University Press, 1991); Sandra Harding and Merrill Hintikka, eds., *Discovering Reality: Feminist Perspectives on Epistemology, Metaphysics, Methodology, and Philosophy of Science* (Dordrecht, Holland: D. Reidel, 1983); Garry and Pearsall, *Women, Knowledge, and Reality*; Card, *Feminist Ethics*; Cole and Coultrap-McQuin, *Explorations in Feminist Ethics*; Laurie Shrage, *Moral Dilemmas of Feminism: Prostitution, Adultery, and Abortion* (New York: Routledge, 1994); Eva Feder Kittay and Diana T. Meyers, eds., *Women and Moral Theory* (Savage, Md.: Rowman & Littlefield, 1987); Hilde Hein and Carolyn Korsmeyer, eds., *Aesthetics in Feminist Perspective* (Bloomington: Indiana University Press, 1993).

22. See Immanuel Kant, *Lectures on Ethics*, trans. Louis Infield (London: Methuen, 1930), 162–71, reprinted in Verene, *Sexual Love and Western Morality*, 154–64; David Hume, "Of Polygamy and Divorces," in *Essays Moral, Political and Literary*, ed. T. H. Green and T. H. Grose (London: Longmans, Green, 1975), 231–39, reprinted in Verene, *Sexual Love and Western Morality*, 144–53.

23. See Tong, *Feminist Thought*, chap. 1; Jaggar, *Feminist Politics and Human Nature*, chap. 7.

24. Bordo, "Feminism, Postmodernism, and Gender-Scepticism," 152.

25. Susan Bordo likens the postmodern perspective to "a dream of being everywhere," in ibid., 143. For a succinct review of postmodern philosophy, see Flax, "Postmodernism and Gender Relations in Feminist Theory," 54–55.

26. Respect for diversity on an international scale is discussed in Charlotte Bunch, "A Global Perspective on Feminist Ethics and Diversity," in Cole and Coultrap-McQuin, *Explorations in Feminist Ethics*, 176–85; Harding, *Whose Science? Whose Knowledge?*, chap. 9; Amrita Basú, ed., *The Challenge of Local Feminisms: Women's Movements in Global Perspective* (Boulder, Colo.: Westview Press, 1995); Lourdes Torres and Chandra Mohanty, eds., *Third World Women and the Politics of Feminism* (Bloomington: Indiana University Press, 1991); M. Jacqui Alexander and Chandra Talpade Mohanty, eds., *Feminist Genealogies, Colonial Legacies, Democratic Futures* (New York: Routledge, 1996); Chéla Sandoval, "Feminist Forms of Agency and Oppositional Consciousness: U.S. Third World Feminist Criticism," in *Provoking Agents: Gender and Agency in Theory and Practice*, ed. Judith Kegan Gardiner (Urbana: University of Illinois Press, 1995), 208–26.

27. For example, see Joan Nestle, "The Fem Question," Gayle Rubin, "Thinking Sex: Notes for a Radical Theory of the Politics of Sexuality," and Amber Hollibaugh, "Desire for the Future: Radical Hope in Passion and Pleasure," in Vance, *Pleasure and Danger*, 232–41, 267–319, 401–10.

28. See Bordo, "Feminism, Postmodernism, and Gender-Scepticism," 145, 149. I have based much of my critique of postmodernism on Bordo's analysis.

29. Such claims are expanded upon in Luce Irigaray, *Speculum of the Other Woman*, trans. Gillian C. Gill (Ithaca, N.Y.: Cornell University Press, 1985); Luce Irigaray, *This Sex Which Is Not One*, trans. Catherine Porter with Carolyn Burke (Ithaca, N.Y.: Cornell University Press, 1985); Hélène Cixous, "Sorties," in *New French Feminisms*, ed. Elaine Marks and Isabelle de Courtivron (New York: Schocken Books, 1981), 90–98.

30. See Lugones, "Playfulness, 'World'-Traveling, and Loving Perception," 289–90.

31. Here I paraphrase María Lugones's description of "world"-traveling, from ibid., 289.

32. For example, see Camille Paglia, *Sex, Art, and American Culture* (New York: Vintage Books, 1992), 49–74, and *Vamps and Tramps: New Essays* (New York: Vintage Books, 1994), 19–94; Samois, ed., *Coming to Power: Writings and Graphics on Lesbian S/M* (Boston: Alyson Publications, 1987); Susie Bright (of *On Our Backs*), Nan Kinny and Debi Sundahl (of Blush Entertainment Productions), Marie Mason (of Hot Chixx), and the author Katherine Forrest, in Victoria A. Brownworth, "The Porn Boom," *Lesbian News* 18, no. 7 (February 1993): 42–43, 61–63; Susie Bright, *Susie Sexpert's Lesbian Sex World* (Pittsburgh: Cleis Press, 1990).

33. See Hélène Cixous, "The Laugh of the Medusa," in Marks and Courtivron, *New French Feminisms*, 245–64; Julia Kristeva, "The Novel as Polylogue," in *Desire and Language*, trans. Leon Roudiez (New York: Columbia University Press, 1982), 159–209; Luce Irigaray, "When Our Two Lips Speak Together," in *This Sex Which Is Not One*; Daly, *Pure Lust*.

34. Rubin, "Thinking Sex," 280–84.

35. See Teresa de Lauretis, "Feminist Studies/Critical Studies: Issues, Terms, and Contexts," in *Feminist Studies/Critical Studies*, ed. Teresa de Lauretis (Bloomington: Indiana University Press, 1986), 14.

36. See hooks, *Talking Back*.

37. Naomi Wolf, *The Beauty Myth: How Images of Beauty Are Used against Women* (New York: Anchor Books/Doubleday, 1991), 132–68; Linda LeMoncheck, *Dehumanizing Women: Treating Persons as Sex Objects* (Totowa, N.J.: Rowman & Allanheld, 1985), chap. 2.

38. Compare the social and economic clout of the supermodel who is "made" beautiful by her sponsors and photographers, in Robert E. Sullivan Jr., "Cover Girls Are Made, Not Born," *Vogue*, April 1992, 331–48, to the trials and tribulations of newscaster Christine Craft in *Too Old, Too Ugly and Not Deferential to Men* (New York: Dell, 1988).

39. See Alcoff, "Cultural Feminism versus Post-Structuralism," 325; also see Harding, *Whose Science? Whose Knowledge?*, 185. For more on the ways in which defining the socially constructed parameters of a feminist cognitive framework escapes both relativism and objectivism, see Mary Hawkesworth, "Knowers, Knowing, Known: Feminist Theory and Claims of Truth," in Malson et al., *Feminist Theory in Practice and Process*, 327–51.

40. I have based this summary of the context for the development of an adequate feminist philosophy of sex on Carole S. Vance and Ann Barr Snitow, "Toward a Conversation about Sex in Feminism: A Modest Proposal," in Ferguson et al., "Forum," 135.

41. See Harding, "The Instability of the Analytical Categories of Feminist Theory," 19.

Chapter 2

1. See Deirdre English, "The Fear That Feminism Will Free Men First," in *Powers of Desire: The Politics of Sexuality*, ed. Ann Snitow, Christine Stansell, and Sharon Thompson (New York: Monthly Review Press, 1983), 480; Barbara Ehrenreich, Elizabeth Hess, and Gloria Jacobs, *Remaking Love: The Feminization of Sex* (New York: Anchor Books/Doubleday, 1986), 170, quoting a *Cosmopolitan* reader: "In the past a man used to have to offer a relationship in order to get sex. Tat for tit. But now, since so many women give sex so freely, the

men offer nothing—and we women must accept this, even if we don't like it. Throughout the centuries women have gotten the short end of the stick. We're still getting it."

2. See Kathleen Barry, *Female Sexual Slavery* (Englewood Cliffs, N.J.: Prentice Hall, 1979).

3. See Marilyn Murphy, *Are You Girls Traveling Alone?: Adventures in Lesbianic Logic* (Los Angeles: Clothespin Fever Press, 1991); Irena Klepfisz, "they're always curious," in Snitow et al., *Powers of Desire*, 228; Paul Gregory, "Against Couples," *Journal of Applied Philosophy* 1, no. 2 (1984): 263–68.

4. See Naomi Wolf, *The Beauty Myth: How Images of Beauty Are Used against Women* (New York: Anchor Books/ Doubleday, 1991), 284–88; Ehrenreich et al., *Remaking Love*, chap. 5.

5. For the function that sexual exclusivity in monogamous marriage serves under patriarchy, see Shulamith Firestone, *The Dialectic of Sex: The Case for Feminist Revolution* (New York: Bantam Books, 1970); Kate Millett, *Sexual Politics* (Garden City, N.Y.: Doubleday, 1970); Anne Koedt, Ellen Levine, and Anita Rapone, eds., *Radical Feminism* (New York: Quadrangle Books, 1973). For excellent overviews of both the radical and conservative backlash to sexual liberation, often referred to as "the sexual counterrevolution," see Steven Seidman, *Embattled Eros: Sexual Politics and Ethics in Contemporary America* (New York: Routledge, 1992), chaps. 2 and 3, and Ehrenreich et al., *Remaking Love*, chap. 6. For ways in which the AIDS epidemic has fueled this backlash, see Seidman, *Embattled Eros*, chap. 4, and chapter 2 in this book, "Pregnancy and Sexually Transmitted Diseases."

6. Seidman, *Embattled Eros*, chap. 3; also see the selections in Snitow et al., *Powers of Desire*, and in Carol S. Vance, ed., *Pleasure and Danger: Exploring Female Sexuality* (London: Pandora Press, 1989).

7. Frederick Elliston, whose analysis I take to task in the pages that follow, is one of the few philosophers in the last twenty years who has written a detailed conceptual and moral analysis of sexual promiscuity; see his "In Defense of Promiscuity," in *Philosophy and Sex*, ed. Robert Baker and Frederick Elliston (Buffalo, N.Y.: Prometheus Books, 1975), 222–43. This article does not appear in the second edition of Baker and Elliston, *Philosophy and Sex* (1984).

8. Elliston uses the example of a married man widowed two times or more to show the dangers of trying to stipulate a numerical criterion for promiscuity, "In Defense of Promiscuity," 224.

9. Our "craving for generality" that prompts the philosophically dangerous search for such definitions is discussed in Ludwig Wittgenstein, *The Blue and Brown Books: Preliminary Studies for the "Philosophical Investigations"* (New York: Harper Colophon Books, 1965), 17–19. For a discussion of how the resemblances, but not identity, among English language uses of a single term mark out the particular contexts of its use and so the "language game" in which the term appears, see Ludwig Wittgenstein, *Philosophical Investigations*, trans. G. E. M. Anscombe (New York: Macmillan, 1960), 6–7, 11, 19, 31–34, 48.

10. Examples of using the notion of family resemblance to do conceptual analysis in the philosophy of sex can be found in Janice Moulton, "Sexual Behavior: Another Position," in *The Philosophy of Sex: Contemporary Readings*, 2d ed., ed. Alan Soble (Savage, Md.: Rowman & Littlefield, 1991), 63–71; Richard Wasserstrom, "Is Adultery Immoral?," in Baker and Elliston, *Philosophy and Sex* (1984), 102–3.

11. Kathryn Pauly Morgan, "Romantic Love, Altruism, and Self-Respect: An Analysis of Beauvoir," in *The Philosophy of (Erotic) Love*, ed. Robert C. Solomon and Kathleen M. Higgins (Lawrence: University Press of Kansas, 1991), 402.

12. See Nina Lopez-Jones, "Workers: Introducing the English Collective of Prostitutes," in *Sex Work: Writings by Women in the Sex Industry*, ed. Frédérique Delacoste and Priscilla Alexander (Pittsburgh: Cleis Press, 1987), 271–72; Evelina Giobbe, "Confronting the Liberal

Lies about Prostitution," in *The Sexual Liberals and the Attack on Feminism*, ed. Dorchen Leidholdt and Janice G. Raymond (New York: Teachers College Press, 1990), 68–72; also see Barry, *Female Sexual Slavery*, 45–117.

13. Elliston, "In Defense of Promiscuity," 225.

14. Ibid.

15. In fact, a former mistress of then-married U.S. Congress member Newt Gingrich reported to the press that Gingrich preferred oral sex, because then he could say that he hadn't slept with her. See the *San Francisco Chronicle*, 10 August 1995.

16. Elliston, "In Defense of Promiscuity," 226.

17. See, for example, Elliston's claim that "[i]f one partner is a child, then their behavior is pedophilia. If the child is a son or daughter, it is incest. In neither case is it promiscuity." Ibid.

18. Ibid.

19. Ibid.

20. Marriages can be based on social convenience in the absence of sexual desire, while others may involve partners whose capacity for sex has dissipated through age or accident. For a discussion of the variety of scenarios that one might legitimately call marriage, see Wasserstrom, "Is Adultery Immoral?", and Michael J. Wreen, "What's Really Wrong with Adultery?," in Soble, *The Philosophy of Sex*, 182–85.

21. For example, see Barry, *Female Sexual Slavery*; Susan Brownmiller, *Against Our Will: Men, Women and Rape* (New York: Bantam Books, 1975); Andrea Dworkin, *Right-Wing Women* (New York: Perigee Books, 1983); Catharine A. MacKinnon, *Feminism Unmodified: Discourses on Life and Law* (Cambridge: Harvard University Press, 1987).

22. See Wasserstrom on loving several adults at a time, in "Is Adultery Immoral?," 100–104. For reasons against simultaneous romances, see Bonnie Steinbock, "Adultery," in Soble, *The Philosophy of Sex*, 191.

23. For a discussion of the ways in which privacy enables us to establish and maintain intimacy characterized as the sharing of information, see Charles Fried, "Privacy: A Rational Context," in *Today's Moral Problems*, ed. Richard Wasserstrom (New York: Macmillan, 1975). For a critique of this characterization, see Jeffrey H. Reiman, "Privacy, Intimacy, and Personhood," *Philosophy and Public Affairs* 5 (fall 1976): 26–44.

24. Gregory, "Against Couples."

25. See Firestone, *The Dialectic of Sex*, chap. 6; also see Lal Coveney, Margaret Jackson, Sheila Jeffreys, Leslie Kay, and Pat Mahoney, eds., *The Sexuality Papers: Male Sexuality and the Social Control of Women* (London: Hutchins, 1984).

26. For example, see Gayle Rubin, "Thinking Sex: Notes for a Radical Theory of the Politics of Sexuality," and Amber Hollibaugh, "Desire for the Future: Radical Hope in Passion and Pleasure," in Vance, *Pleasure and Danger*, 267–319, 401–10; also see Samois, ed., *Coming to Power: Writings and Graphics on Lesbian S/M* (Boston: Alyson Publications, 1987).

27. Robert J. Stoller, *Sexual Excitement: Dynamics of Erotic Life* (New York: Simon & Schuster, 1980).

28. See Linda LeMoncheck, *Dehumanizing Women: Treating Persons as Sex Objects* (Totowa, N.J.: Rowman & Allanheld, 1985), chap. 1.

29. Elliston, "In Defense of Promiscuity," 223.

30. A. Ellis, "Casual Sex," *International Journal of Moral and Social Studies* 1 (summer 1986): 157.

31. Seidman, *Embattled Eros*, 105. Proponents of this view include Mary Daly, *Gyn/Ecology: The Metaethics of Radical Feminism* (Boston: Beacon Press, 1978); Janice G. Raymond, *The Transsexual Empire* (Boston: Beacon Press, 1979); Barry, *Female Sexual Slavery*; Andrea Dworkin, *Our Blood: Prophesies and Discourses on Sexual Politics* (New York:

G. P. Putnam, 1981); Susan Griffin, *Women and Nature: The Roaring inside Her* (New York: Harper & Row, 1978); Adrienne Rich, *Of Woman Born: Motherhood as Experience and Institution* (New York: Bantam Books, 1977).

32. See such disparate feminists as Simone de Beauvoir, *The Second Sex*, trans. and ed. H. M. Parshley (New York: Vintage Books, 1974); Betty Friedan, *The Feminine Mystique* (New York: Dell, 1974); Ti-Grace Atkinson, *Amazon Odyssey* (New York: Links, 1974).

33. See Alice Echols, "The New Feminism of Yin and Yang," in Snitow et al., *Powers of Desire*, 441–47; Alice Echols, "The Taming of the Id: Feminist Sexual Politics, 1968–1983," in Vance, *Pleasure and Danger*, 50–72; Seidman, *Embattled Eros*, 98–106. While I hesitate to divide feminism into discrete camps, feminists do draw distinct battle lines vis-à-vis one another, which I have claimed has ultimately weakened the movement as a whole. Therefore, my usage of expressions like "cultural feminist" or "sex radical" is meant to identify a particular feminist point of view that I would prefer were less insular; my usage is not meant to reify existing divisions. For criticism of Echols's interpretation of the cultural feminist agenda, see Haunani-Kay Trask, *Eros and Power: The Promise of Feminist Theory* (Philadelphia: University of Pennsylvania Press, 1986). For an alternative understanding of cultural feminism as an inclusive, not exclusive, feminist ideology and practice, see Katie King, "Producing Sex, Theory, and Culture: Gay/Straight Remappings in Contemporary Feminism," in *Conflicts in Feminism*, ed. Marianne Hirsch and Evelyn Fox Keller (New York: Routledge, 1990), 87.

34. Adrienne Rich, "Compulsory Heterosexuality and Lesbian Existence," *Signs: Journal of Women in Culture and Society* 5 (summer 1980): 631–60; Seidman, *Embattled Eros*, 103.

35. See Dorchen Leidholdt, "When Women Defend Pornography," and Sheila Jeffreys, "Eroticizing Women's Subordination," in Leidholdt and Raymond, *The Sexual Liberals*, 125–35.

36. For excellent overviews of the debate between cultural and sex radical feminists, see Ann Ferguson, Ilene Philipson, Irene Diamond and Lee Quinby, and Carole S. Vance and Ann Barr Snitow, "Forum: The Feminist Sexuality Debates," *Signs: Journal of Women in Culture and Society* 10 (autumn 1984): 106–35.

37. See Kathryn Pauly Morgan's analysis of Simone de Beauvoir, in "Romantic Love, Altruism, and Self-Respect," 396–97.

38. Robert Nozick, "Love's Bond," in Solomon and Higgins, *The Philosophy of (Erotic) Love*, 428.

39. See Firestone, *The Dialectic of Sex*, 131, 149; Elizabeth Rapaport, "On the Future of Love: Rousseau and the Radical Feminists," in Solomon and Higgins, *The Philosophy of (Erotic) Love*, 379.

40. Susan Minot, *Lust and Other Stories* (New York: Washington Square Press/Pocket Books, 1990), 16.

41. Robin S. Dillon, "Care and Respect," in *Explorations in Feminist Ethics*, ed. Eve Browning Cole and Susan Coultrap-McQuin (Bloomington: Indiana University Press, 1992), 73–77.

42. See Wreen, "What's Really Wrong with Adultery?," 180.

43. For example, see G. E. M. Anscombe, "Modern Moral Philosophy," *Philosophy* 33 (1958): 1–19; Alasdair MacIntyre, *After Virtue* (Notre Dame: University of Notre Dame Press, 1981); Bernard Williams, "Persons, Character, and Morality," in his *Moral Luck* (Cambridge: Cambridge University Press, 1981.) For some contemporary feminist criticism of a traditional, rights-based ethic, see Lawrence Blum, *Friendship, Altruism and Morality* (London: Routledge & Kegan Paul, 1980), and John Hardwig, "Should Women Think in Terms of Rights?," in *Feminism and Political Theory*, ed. Cass R. Sunstein (Chicago: University of Chicago Press, 1990), 53–67. For a reevaluation of the place of Kantian ethics in discussions of feminist sexual ethics, see Barbara Herman, "Could It Be Worth Thinking about Kant on

Sex and Marriage?," in *A Mind of One's Own: Feminist Essays on Reason and Objectivity* (Boulder, Colo.: Westview Press, 1993), 49–67.

44. Robert C. Solomon, "The Virtue of (Erotic) Love," in Solomon and Higgins, *The Philosophy of (Erotic) Love*, 499.

45. Firestone, *The Dialectic of Sex*, 128–30, 146; Rapaport, "On the Future of Love," 376–80.

46. Firestone, *The Dialectic of Sex*, 131.

47. Steinbock, "Adultery," 191.

48. See Roger Scruton, *Sexual Desire* (New York: Free Press, 1986), 167–69; Søren Kierkegaard, "The Immediate Stages of the Erotic," in *Either/Or*, vol. 1, trans. David F. Swenson and Lillian Marvin Swenson (Princeton: Princeton University Press, 1944, 1959), 86–102.

49. Firestone, *The Dialectic of Sex*, 132–33, 144, 146.

50. Robert C. Solomon, "Love and Feminism," in Baker and Elliston, *Philosophy and Sex* (1984), 56.

51. Ibid., 56, 63; also see Solomon, "The Virtue of (Erotic) Love," 506, 513.

52. Solomon, "Love and Feminism," 56; also see 54–55.

53. Ibid., 66.

54. Ibid., 64.

55. Ibid., 64, 65.

56. Solomon, "The Virtue of (Erotic) Love," 511; Nozick, "Love's Bond," 428.

57. Solomon, "The Virtue of (Erotic) Love," 506, 510; also see Kathryn Pauly Morgan on Beauvoir's paradoxes of romantic love, "Romantic Love, Altruism, and Self-Respect," 398–401.

58. Solomon, "The Virtue of (Erotic) Love," 513.

59. See Seidman, *Embattled Eros*, 122–23.

60. See Elliston, "In Defense of Promiscuity," 229.

61. See J. D. Unwin, *Sex and Culture*, vols. 1 and 2 (London: Oxford University Press, 1934); Margaret Mead, *Sex and Temperament in Three Primitive Societies* (New York: Morrow, 1935); Reay Tannehill, *Sex in History* (New York: Stein & Day, 1980); Helen E. Fisher, *Anatomy of Love: The Natural History of Monogamy, Adultery and Divorce* (New York: W. W. Norton, 1992).

62. Sigmund Freud, "'Civilized' Sexual Morality and Nervous Illness," in Solomon and Higgins, *The Philosophy of (Erotic) Love*, 167–76; John McMurtry, "Monogamy: A Critique," in Baker and Elliston, *Philosophy and Sex* (1984), 112, 114.

63. Rubin, "Thinking Sex," 277.

64. See Sheila Ruth, "Bodies and Souls/Sex, Sin and the Senses in Patriarchy: A Study in Applied Dualism," *Hypatia* 2 (winter 1987): 149–64; Rubin, "Thinking Sex," 281–82.

65. Rubin, "Thinking Sex," 275, 309.

66. Ibid., 306. On the subject of consenting to sex under patriarchy, see ibid., 304–6; also see Joan Nestle, "The Fem Question," in Vance, *Pleasure and Danger*, 232–41. For further discussion of the appropriateness of sex without love or intimacy, see Raymond A. Belliotti, *Good Sex: Perspectives on Sexual Ethics* (Lawrence: University Press of Kansas, 1993), 74–77, and Russell Vannoy, *Sex without Love* (Buffalo, N.Y.: Prometheus Books, 1980).

67. Elliston, "In Defense of Promiscuity," 235, 236.

68. Ibid., 239–40; also see Kierkegaard, *Either/Or*.

69. Elliston, "In Defense of Promiscuity," 240.

70. Solomon, "The Virtue of (Erotic) Love," 515–16.

71. Ibid., 517.

72. See Marjorie Weinzweig, "Should a Feminist Choose a Marriage-Like Relationship?," *Hypatia* 1 (fall 1986): 139–63; also see Ann Ferguson, "On Conceiving Motherhood and

Sexuality: A Feminist Materialist Approach," in *Mothering: Essays in Feminist Theory*, ed. Joyce Trebilcot (Savage, Md.: Rowman & Littlefield, 1983).

73. A variety of sociological surveys have suggested that married men tend to live longer than single men but that married women tend to die sooner than single women. See Bill Moyers (host), "Healing and the Mind," KCET/PBS television documentary, 23 February 1993.

74. See Dalma Heyn, *The Erotic Silence of the American Wife* (New York: Turtle Bay Books, 1992).

75. Sheila Ruth, ed., *Issues in Feminism: An Introduction to Women's Studies* (Mountain View, Calif.: Mayfield Publishing Company, 1990), 87.

76. Patt Morrison, "War of the Words," *Los Angeles Times Magazine*, 6 December 1992.

77. Mary Daly, *Pure Lust: Elemental Feminist Philosophy* (Boston: Beacon Press, 1984); Clarissa Pinkola Estes, *Women Who Run with the Wolves: Myths and Stories of the Wild Woman Archetype* (New York: Ballantine Books, 1992).

78. A common complaint regarding the 1991 Mike Tyson trial has been that if Tyson were white and affluent like William Kennedy Smith, he would not have been convicted of rape. For a variety of contemporary discussions about race relations in America, see John Arthur and Amy Shapiro, eds., *Color, Class, Identity: The New Politics of Race* (Boulder, Colo.: Westview Press, 1996).

79. The sexual attraction of Latinos can change drastically for white women when they (as "gringas") visit Mexico. For ways in which Mexican men reinforce the macho stereotype and attract American women, see Cecilia Rodriguez and Marjorie Miller, "Muy Macho," *Los Angeles Times Magazine*, 6 December 1992.

80. See Karl Taro Greenfeld, "The Broken Dreams of the Blond Geishas," *Los Angeles Times Magazine*, 8 November 1992; also see Maxine Hong Kingston, *China Men* (New York: Random House, 1989), and Sumiko Iwao, *The Japanese Woman's Traditional Image and Changing Reality* (New York: Free Press, 1993).

81. See Patricia Morton, *The Historical Assault on Afro-American Women* (Westport, Conn.: Greenwood Press, 1991); Rennie Simson, "The Afro-American Female: The Historical Context of the Construction of Sexual Identity," and Barbara Omolade, "Hearts of Darkness," in Snitow et al., *Powers of Desire*, 229–35, 350–67; Evelynn Hammonds, "Black (W)holes and the Geometry of Black Female Sexuality," *differences: A Journal of Feminist Cultural Studies* 6 (summer–fall 1994): 126–45.

82. See Oliva M. Espin, "Influences on Sexuality in Hispanic/Latin Women," in Vance, *Pleasure and Danger*, 149–64. For a moving personal account of life as a lesbian and a Chicana, see Gloria Anzaldúa, *Borderlands/La Frontera: The New Mestiza* (San Francisco: Spinsters/Aunt Lute, 1987); also see Cherríe Moraga, *Loving in the War Years* (Boston: South End Press, 1986).

83. For a discussion of sexual expectations and stereotypes of Asian women, see Xiao Zhou, "Virginity and Premarital Sex in Contemporary China," *Feminist Studies* 15 (summer 1989): 279–88; M. Wolfe and R. Witke, *Women in Chinese Society* (Stanford: Stanford University Press, 1978); also see Amy Tan, *The Joy Luck Club* (New York: Putnam, 1989). For further discussion of how sexual stereotypes break down along racial lines, see Laurie Shrage, "Is Sexual Desire Raced?: The Social Meaning of Interracial Prostitution," *Journal of Social Philosophy* 23 (spring 1992): 42–51.

84. For excellent overviews of abortion and birth control in America, see Kristen Luker, *Abortion and the Politics of Motherhood* (Berkeley: University of California Press, 1984); Rosalind Pollack Petchesky, *Abortion and Woman's Choice: The State, Sexuality, and Reproductive Freedom* (New York: Longman, 1984); Gaye D. Ginsburg, *Contested Lives: The Abortion Debate in an American Community* (Berkeley: University of California Press, 1989);

Linda Gordon, *Woman's Body, Woman's Right: Birth Control in America* (New York: Penguin Books, 1990).

85. See Seidman, *Embattled Eros*, 157–63; Catherine Waldby, *AIDS and the Body Politic: Biomedicine and Sexual Difference* (New York: Routledge, 1996).

86. See Steve Connor and Sharon Kingman, *The Search for the Virus* (New York: Penguin, 1988); Elizabeth Fee and Daniel Fox, eds., *AIDS: The Burden of History* (Berkeley: University of California Press, 1988).

87. See Seidman, *Embattled Eros*, 161–63, 165, 167; Michael Bronski, "AIDing Our Guilt and Fear," *Gay Community News*, 7 October 1983; Tim Vollmer, "Another Stonewall," *New York Native*, 28 October–3 November 1985; also see Charles Turner et al., eds., *AIDS: Sexual Behavior and Intravenous Drug Use* (Washington: National Academy Press, 1989).

88. For disturbing trends in HIV transmission in the lesbian community, see Lee Chiaramonte, "Lesbian Safety and AIDS: The Very Last Fairytale," *Visibilities* (January/February 1988); also see Gena Corea, *The Invisible Epidemic* (New York: HarperCollins, 1993); Fleur Sack and Anne Streeter, *Romance to Die For: The Startling Truth about Women, Sex, and AIDS* (Deerfield Beach, Fla.: Health Communications, Inc., 1992); Beth E. Schneider and Nancy E. Stoller, eds., *Women Resisting AIDS: Feminist Strategies of Empowerment* (Philadelphia: Temple University Press, 1995); Pat Califia, "A Note on AIDS, Lesbians and Safe Sex," in *Macho Sluts: Erotic Fiction* (Boston: Alyson Publications, 1988); Women's AIDS Network, *Lesbians and AIDS: What's the Connection?* (San Francisco: S.F. AIDS Foundation and the S.F. Department of Public Health, July 1986; revised October 1987); Jackie Winnow, "Lesbians Working on AIDS: Assessing the Impact on Health Care for Women," *Outlook* 5 (1989): 10–18.

89. See Jad Adams, *AIDS: The HIV Myth* (New York: St. Martin's Press, 1989); Peter Duesberg, "HIV and AIDS, Correlation but Not Causation," *Proceedings of the National Academy of Sciences USA* 86 (February 1989): 755–64; Clifton Jones et al., "Persistence of High-Risk Sexual Activity among Homosexual Men in an Area of Low Incidence of the Acquired Immunodeficiency Syndrome," *Sexually Transmitted Diseases* 14 (April–June 1987): 79–82; Dennis Altman, "AIDS: The Politicization of an Epidemic," *Socialist Review* 14 (November–December 1984): 93–109.

90. Laurie Shrage, *Moral Dilemmas of Feminism: Prostitution, Adultery, and Abortion* (New York: Routledge, 1994), 160–61.

91. See Paula Webster, "The Forbidden: Eroticism and Taboo," in Vance, *Pleasure and Danger*, 385–98.

92. See Waldby, *AIDS and the Body Politic*; Cindy Patton, *Sex and Germs* (Boston: South End Press, 1985); Cindy Patton, *Inventing AIDS* (New York: Routledge, 1991); Dennis Altman, *AIDS and the Mind of America* (New York: Doubleday, 1985); Richard Goldstein, "The Use of AIDS," *Village Voice*, 5 November 1985; Bronski, "AIDing Our Guilt and Fear"; Vollmer, "Another Stonewall."

Chapter 3

1. Nancy Friday, *My Secret Garden* (New York: Pocket Books, 1974); Germaine Greer, *The Female Eunuch* (New York: Bantam Books, 1972); Anne Koedt, "The Myth of the Vaginal Orgasm," in *Radical Feminism*, ed. Anne Koedt, Ellen Levine, and Anita Rapone (New York: Quadrangle Books, 1973), 198–207; and the Boston Women's Health Collective, *Our Bodies, Ourselves* (New York: Simon & Schuster, 1973), represent some of the many and varied ways that women began to talk about exploring our sexuality in the early stages of feminism's second wave. Shannon Bell offers a fascinating account of the invisibility of any discussion of female ejaculation in contemporary feminist discourse in "Feminist Ejaculations," in *The*

Hysterical Male: New Feminist Theory, ed. Arthur and Marilouise Kroker (New York: St. Martin's Press, 1991), 155–69; also see Paula Webster, "The Forbidden: Eroticism and Taboo," in *Pleasure and Danger: Exploring Female Sexuality*, ed. Carole S. Vance (London: Pandora Press, 1989), 385–98; Barbara Ehrenreich, Elizabeth Hess, and Gloria Jacobs, *Remaking Love: The Feminization of Sex* (New York: Anchor Books/Doubleday, 1986), chap. 3.

2. See Ellen Carol DuBois and Linda Gordon, "Seeking Ecstasy on the Battlefield: Danger and Pleasure in Nineteenth-Century Feminist Sexual Thought," in Vance, *Pleasure and Danger*, 31–49; Judith Walkowitz, "The Politics of Prostitution," *Signs: Journal of Women in Culture and Society* 6, no. 1 (autumn 1980): 123–35.

3. See Sidney Abbott and Barbara Love, *Sappho Was a Right-On Woman* (New York: Stein & Day, 1972), 107–34.

4. See Ann Snitow, Christine Stansell, and Sharon Thompson, "Introduction," in *Powers of Desire: The Politics of Sexuality*, ed. Ann Snitow, Christine Stansell, and Sharon Thompson (New York: Monthly Review Press, 1983), 30–34; Toby Marotta, *The Politics of Homosexuality* (Boston: Houghton Mifflin, 1981); Gayle Rubin, "The Leather Menace: Comments on Politics and S/M," in *Coming to Power: Writings and Graphics on Lesbian S/M*, ed. Samois (Boston: Alyson Publications, 1987), 214–15.

5. The complexity of both the eroticism and the oppression of lesbianism is discussed in Dorothy Allison, "Public Silence, Private Terror," in Vance, *Pleasure and Danger*, 112, and in Julia Creet, "Daughter of the Movement: The Psychodynamics of Lesbian S/M Fantasy," *differences: A Journal of Feminist Cultural Studies* 3 (summer 1991): 135–59. For the equation in the public mind of "gay male" with "child molester," see Jeffrey Weeks, *Sexuality and Its Discontents: Meanings, Myths and Modern Sexualities* (New York: Routledge, 1985), 223–31, and Rubin, "The Leather Menace," 197–98, also see Robin Ruth Linden, Darlene R. Pagano, Diana E. H. Russell, and Susan Leigh Star, eds., *Against Sadomasochism: A Radical Feminist Analysis* (San Francisco: Frog in the Well, 1982).

6. See Pat Califia, "A Personal View of the History of the Lesbian S/M Community and Movement in San Francisco," in Samois, *Coming to Power*, 272; also see Rubin, "The Leather Menace," 213. For responses to NOW's and others' accusations of the internalization of patriarchal values by practitioners of sexual deviance, see *Heresies* #12 "Sex Issue" 3, no. 4 (1981).

7. See Carole S. Vance, "Epilogue," in Vance, *Pleasure and Danger*, 431–39, and 437, n. 1, for additional references to articles describing the controversy. The papers presented at the conference are collected in *Pleasure and Danger*; also see B. Ruby Rich, "Feminism and Sexuality in the 1980's," *Feminist Studies* 12, no. 3 (1986): 525–61.

8. See Janice G. Raymond, *The Transsexual Empire* (Boston: Beacon Press, 1979); Marjorie Garber, "Spare Parts: The Surgical Construction of Gender," *differences: A Journal of Feminist Cultural Studies* 1, no. 3 (1989): 137–59; Marjorie Garber, *Vested Interests: Cross-Dressing and Cultural Anxiety* (New York: Routledge, 1992); Richard Ekins and David King, eds., *Blending Genders* (New York: Routledge, 1996). For more on the social construction of gender and sexuality, see chapter 3, n. 52, in this book.

9. See Louise Armstrong, "Making an Issue of Incest," in *The Sexual Liberals and the Attack on Feminism*, ed. Dorchen Leidholdt and Janice G. Raymond (New York: Teachers College Press, 1990), 43–55; Paul Eberle and Shirley Eberle, *The Politics of Child Abuse* (New Jersey: Lyle Stuart, 1986); Toni A. H. MacNaron and Yarrow Morgan, eds., *Voices in the Night: Women Speaking about Incest* (Minneapolis: Cleis Press, 1981); Janis Tyler Johnson, *Mothers of Incest Survivors: Another Side of the Story* (Bloomington: Indiana University Press, 1992).

10. See Daniel Tsang, ed., *The Age Taboo: Gay Male Sexuality, Power and Consent* (Boston: Alyson Publications, 1981); Pat Califia, *Sapphistry: The Book of Lesbian Sexuality*, 2d ed. (Tallahassee, Fla.: Naiad Press, 1983).

11. For this summary, I have relied on the detailed exposition and critique of opposing fem-

inist views on women's sexuality given by Ann Ferguson, "Sex War: The Debate between Radical and Libertarian Feminists," in Ann Ferguson, Ilene Philipson, Irene Diamond and Lee Quinby, and Carole S. Vance and Ann Barr Snitow, "Forum: The Feminist Sexuality Debates," *Signs: Journal of Women in Culture and Society* 10 (autumn 1984): 106–12. (Ferguson refers to "radical feminists" where I refer to cultural feminists and describes sex radical feminists as "libertarian feminists.")

12. See Chris Straayer, "The Seduction of Boundaries: Feminist Fluidity in Annie Sprinkle's Art/Education/Sex," in *Dirty Looks: Women, Pornography, Power*, ed. Pamela Church Gibson and Roma Gibson (London: BFI Publishing, 1994), 170–71.

13. See Roger Scruton, *Sexual Desire* (New York: Free Press, 1986), 284–321; Thomas Nagel, "Sexual Perversion," in *The Philosophy of Sex*, 2d ed., ed. Alan Soble (Savage, Md.: Rowman & Littlefield, 1991), 39–51; Robert Solomon, "Sex and Perversion," in *Philosophy and Sex*, ed. Robert Baker and Frederick Elliston (Buffalo, N.Y.: Prometheus Books, 1975), 268–87, and Robert Solomon, "Sexual Paradigms," in Soble, *The Philosophy of Sex* (1991), 53–62; Pope Paul VI, "Humanae Vitae," in Baker and Elliston, *Philosophy and Sex* (1975), 131–49.

14. Mortimer R. Kadish, "The Possibility of Perversion," in Soble, *The Philosophy of Sex* (1991), 109.

15. For a more detailed account of Foucault's thesis that power produces and reinforces sexuality, see Michel Foucault, *The History of Sexuality: Volume I, an Introduction*, trans. Robert Huxley (New York: Vintage Books, 1980) and *Power/Knowledge*, ed. Colin Gordon (New York: Pantheon, 1980). For discussions concerning whether Foucault's analysis of the relations between institutional power and sexuality can be recuperated for feminist theorizing, see Jana Sawicki, *Disciplining Foucault* (New York: Routledge, 1991); Irene Diamond and Lee Quinby, eds., *Feminism and Foucault* (Boston: Northeastern University Press, 1988).

16. Michael Slote, "Inapplicable Concepts and Sexual Perversion," in Baker and Elliston, *Philosophy and Sex* (1975), 263.

17. Kadish, "The Possibility of Perversion," 102.

18. For example, see Nagel, "Sexual Perversion," 39; Solomon, "Sex and Perversion," 270; Sara Ruddick, "Better Sex," in *Philosophy and Sex*, 2d ed., ed. Robert Baker and Frederick Elliston (Buffalo, N.Y.: Prometheus Books, 1984), 287–89; Robert Gray, "Sex and Sexual Perversion," in *The Philosophy of Sex*, ed. Alan Soble (Totowa, N.J.: Littlefield, Adams, 1980), 167; Michael Ruse, "The Morality of Homosexuality," in Baker and Elliston, *Philosophy and Sex* (1984), 383; Slote, "Inapplicable Concepts," 263.

19. See Solomon, "Sex and Perversion," 285; Nagel, "Sexual Perversion," 290; Alan Soble, "Masturbation and Sexual Philosophy," in Soble, *The Philosophy of Sex* (1991), 145.

20. See Sara Ann Ketchum, "The Good, the Bad and the Perverted: Sexual Paradigms Revisited," in Soble, *The Philosophy of Sex* (1980), 152.

21. See Gayle Rubin, "Thinking Sex: Notes for a Radical Theory of the Politics of Sexuality," in Vance, *Pleasure and Danger*, 282.

22. Jerome Neu, "What Is Wrong with Incest?," in *Today's Moral Problems*, 3d ed., ed. Richard Wasserstrom (New York: Macmillan, 1985), 224.

23. Slote, "Inapplicable Concepts," 266.

24. Ruse, "The Morality of Homosexuality," 384.

25. For rape as the essence of heterosexual sex, see Susan Griffin, *Rape: The Power of Consciousness* (San Francisco: Harper & Row, 1979); for rape as a sadistic sexual perversion, see Ketchum, "The Good, the Bad and the Perverted"; for rape as a crime of violence, see Susan Brownmiller, *Against Our Will: Men, Women and Rape* (New York: Bantam Books, 1975).

26. See Deirdre English, Amber Hollibaugh, and Gayle Rubin, "Talking Sex: A Conversation on Sexuality and Feminism," *Socialist Review* 11, no. 4 (1981): 43–62.

27. Mary Daly offers just this kind of transformative feminist semantics in *Webster's First New Intergalactic Wickedary of the English Language*, ed. Jane Caputi (Boston: Beacon Press, 1987); also see Mary Daly, *Pure Lust: Elemental Feminist Philosophy* (Boston: Beacon Press, 1984).

28. For a wide range of historical and contemporary essays on lesbian and gay sexualities as forms of cultural resistance, see Donald Morton, ed., *The Material Queer: A LesBiGay Cultural Studies Reader* (Boulder, Colo.: Westview Press, 1996); also see Arlene Stein, ed., *Sisters, Sexperts, Queers: Beyond the Lesbian Nation* (New York: Plume Books, 1993); "Queer Theory: Lesbian and Gay Sexualities," special issue, *differences: A Journal of Feminist Cultural Studies* 3 (winter 1991).

29. Donald Levy, "Perversion and the Unnatural as Moral Categories," in Soble, *The Philosophy of Sex* (1980), 178–81.

30. Scruton, *Sexual Desire*, 289, 346–47.

31. Ibid., 176–77, 295, 298.

32. For further criticisms of Scruton's claim that morally appropriate sexual desire aims at mutual affirmation and personal fulfillment, see Raymond A. Belliotti, *Good Sex: Perspectives on Sexual Ethics* (Lawrence: University Press of Kansas, 1993), 81–85.

33. Nagel, "Sexual Perversion," 44–46; Solomon, "Sex and Perversion," 279–86; Solomon, "Sexual Paradigms," 60–62.

34. Nagel, "Sexual Perversion," 50–51.

35. Solomon, "Sexual Paradigms," 62.

36. Solomon, "Sex and Perversion," 270.

37. For critiques of Nagel and Solomon, see Janice Moulton, "Sexual Behavior: Another Position," in Soble, *The Philosophy of Sex* (1991), 63–71; Soble, "Masturbation and Sexual Philosophy," 139–47; Ketchum, "The Good, the Bad and the Perverted," 139–50; Levy, "Perversion and the Unnatural," 171–72; Ruddick, "Better Sex," 288–89; Alan Goldman, "Plain Sex," in Soble, *The Philosophy of Sex* (1991), 80–83.

38. Goldman, "Plain Sex," 89–90; Gray, "Sex and Sexual Perversion," 167.

39. Gray, "Sex and Sexual Perversion," 166. For arguments that homosexuality may be adaptive to the species, see Ruse, "The Morality of Homosexuality," 380–81.

40. Levy, "Perversion and the Unnatural," 174–75.

41. Gray, "Sex and Sexual Perversion," 168.

42. Slote, "Inapplicable Concepts," 262.

43. Ibid.

44. Ibid., 265.

45. Kadish, "The Possibility of Perversion," 101, 98–104.

46. Ruse, "The Morality of Homosexuality," 384.

47. Ibid., 385; Kadish, "The Possibility of Perversion," 111, 112.

48. Ruddick, "Better Sex," 289; Moulton, "Sexual Behavior," 64.

49. Ruddick, "Better Sex," 288.

50. Moulton, "Sexual Behavior," 70. For other counterexamples to Ruddick's characterization, see Levy, "Perversion and the Unnatural," 172, and Ketchum, "The Good, the Bad and the Perverted," 150–51.

51. See Linda Williams's discussion of how performance artist Annie Sprinkle practices this form of sexual deconstruction in "A Provoking Agent: The Pornography and Performance of Annie Sprinkle," in Gibson and Gibson, *Dirty Looks*, 176–91; also see Lynne Segal's theorizing about "straight" sex as one of many "perverse" or "queer" alternatives, in *Straight Sex: Rethinking the Politics of Pleasure* (Berkeley: University of California Press, 1994).

52. For some fascinating contributions to this discussion, see Martine Rothblatt, *The Apartheid of Sex: A Manifesto on the Freedom of Gender* (New York: Crown, 1995); Jonathan

Ned Katz, *The Invention of Heterosexuality* (New York: Dutton, 1995); Marjorie Garber, *Vested Interests*; Ekins and King, *Blending Genders*; Judith Lorber, *Paradoxes of Gender* (New Haven: Yale University Press, 1994); Judith Butler, *Gender Trouble: Feminism and the Subversion of Identity* (New York: Routledge, 1990) and *Bodies That Matter: On the Discursive Limits of Sex* (New York: Routledge, 1993); Monique Wittig, *The Straight Mind and Other Essays* (Boston: Beacon Press, 1992); Anne McClintock, "Maid to Order: Commercial S/M and Gender Power," in Gibson and Gibson, *Dirty Looks*, 207–31; Patrick D. Hopkins's commentary on Honi Haber's "Gender Politics and the Cross-Dresser," paper and commentary presented at a symposium on the philosophy of sex and love at the Central Division meeting of the American Philosophical Association, Chicago, Illinois, April 1995; "Queer Theory: Lesbian and Gay Sexualities"; "More Gender Trouble: Feminism Meets Queer Theory," special issue, *differences: A Journal of Feminist Cultural Studies* 6 (summer–fall 1994); Lynn Cherny and Elizabeth Reba Wise, eds., *Wired Women: Gender and New Realities in Cyberspace* (Seattle: Seal Press, 1996); Jacob Hale, "Are Lesbians Women?," *Hypatia* 11 (spring 1996): 94–121.

53. Weeks, *Sexuality and Its Discontents*, 242.

54. On the lesbian community's ambivalence during the late 1960s about sacrificing a kind of "erotic secrecy" in order to be active lesbian feminists, see Snitow et al., "Introduction" in Snitow et al., *Powers of Desire*, 30, and Marotta, *The Politics of Homosexuality*.

55. For some observations about political correctness in discussions of feminist sexuality, see Muriel Dimen, "Politically Correct? Politically Incorrect?" in Vance, *Pleasure and Danger*, 138–48; also see Judy Butler, "Lesbian S & M: The Politics of Dis-illusion," in Linden et al., *Against Sadomasochism*, 171.

56. For feminist objections to the images and practices of dominant/submissive sex, see Kate Millett, "Beyond Politics?: Children and Sexuality," in Vance, *Pleasure and Danger*, 217–24; Andrea Dworkin, *Pornography: Men Possessing Women* (New York: E. P. Dutton, 1989); Laura Lederer, ed., *Take Back the Night: Women on Pornography* (New York: William Morrow, 1980); Catharine A. MacKinnon, *Feminism Unmodified: Discourses on Life and Law* (Cambridge: Harvard University Press, 1987); Kathleen Barry, "Sadomasochism: The New Backlash to Feminism," *Trivia* 1 (fall 1982): 77–92; Linden et al., *Against Sadomasochism*. For review of the cultural feminist position on sexual difference, see Steven Seidman, *Embattled Eros: Sexual Politics and Ethics in Contemporary America* (New York: Routledge, 1992), 97–106.

57. See Margaret Hunt's reference to Julia Penelope, acting as panelist at the "Feminism, Sexuality, and Power" conference, Mount Holyoke College, South Hadley, Massachusetts, 26–30 October 1986, in "Report of a Conference on Feminism, Sexuality and Power: The Elect Clash with the Perverse," in Samois, *Coming to Power*, 85.

58. For a discussion of the feminist issues surrounding man/boy love, see Pat Califia, "Man/Boy Love and the Lesbian Movement," in Tsang, *The Age Taboo*. For discussions of the psychological complexity of butch/femme roles, see Amber Hollibaugh and Cherríe Moraga, "What We're Rollin' Around in Bed With: Sexual Silences in Feminism," in Snitow et al., *Powers of Desire*, 394–405; Joan Nestle, "The Fem Question," and Esther Newton and Shirley Walton, "The Misunderstanding: Toward a More Precise Sexual Vocabulary," in Vance, *Pleasure and Danger*, 232–50; Joan Nestle, ed., *The Persistent Desire: A Femme-Butch Reader* (Boston: Alyson Publications, 1992). For arguments in favor of lesbian sadomasochism, see Pat Califia, "Feminism and Sadomasochism," *Heresies* #12 "Sex Issue" 3, no. 4 (1981): 30–34; Pat Califia, "Unraveling the Sexual Fringe: A Secret Side of Lesbian Sexuality," *The Advocate*, 27 December 1979; Califia, *Sapphistry*; Gayle Rubin and Pat Califia, "Talking about Sadomasochism: Fears, Facts, Fantasies," *Gay Community News*, 15 August 1981; Samois, *Coming to Power*; Irene Reti, ed., *Unleashing Feminism: Sadomasochism in the Gay 90s* (Santa Cruz, Calif.: HerBooks, 1993). For reviews of gay and feminist controversies surrounding sex-

ual difference, see Weeks, *Sexuality and Its Discontents*, chap. 9; Seidman, *Embattled Eros*, chaps. 3 and 4.

59. For more on gay male sadomasochism, see Andreas Spengler, "Manifest Sadomasochism of Males: Results of an Empirical Study," G. W. Levi Kamel and Thomas S. Weinberg, "Diversity in Sadomasochism: Four S & M Careers," and G. W. Levi Kamel, "Leathersex: Meaningful Aspects of Gay Sadomasochism," in *S & M: Studies in Sadomasochism*, ed. Thomas Weinberg and G. W. Levi Kamel (Buffalo, N.Y.: Prometheus Books, 1983), 57–72, 117–21, 162–74; Frederick Suppes's commentary on Patrick D. Hopkins's "Rethinking Sadomasochism: Feminism, Interpretation, and Simulation," paper and commentary presented at a symposium on philosophical perspectives on s/m sex at the Eastern Division meeting of the American Philosophical Association, Atlanta, Georgia, December 1993. For a fascinating psychoanalytic and literary treatment of the forms that specifically female perversions may take, see Louise J. Kaplan, *Female Perversions: The Temptation of Emma Bovary* (New York: Anchor Books/Doubleday, 1991), especially chaps. 1 and 6.

60. For claims that feminists should avoid legislating private sexual behavior despite the belief that lesbian s/m is antifeminist, see Jeanette Nichols, Darlene Pagano, and Margaret Rossoff, "Is Sadomasochism Feminist?: A Critique of the Samois Position," and Karen Sims and Rose Mason with Darlene Pagano, "Racism and Sadomasochism: A Conversation with Two Black Lesbians," in Linden et al., *Against Sadomasochism*, 100, 145.

61. For proponents of this view, see Diana E. H. Russell, "Sadomasochism: A Contra-Feminist Activity," and Susan Griffin, "Sadomasochism and the Erosion of Self: A Critical Reading of *Story of O*," in Linden et al., *Against Sadomasochism*, 176–201; also see Melinda Vadas, "Reply to Patrick Hopkins," *Hypatia* 10 (spring 1995): 159–61, whose criticism is that s/m sex is pleasurable only when constitutive of, and so dependent on, the actual occurrence of the harm simulated; and see Pat Califia's discussion of the position of Women against Violence and Pornography in the Media (WAVPM) in "A Personal View," 270. For a discussion of the public politics of s/m sex, see Lorena Leigh Saxe, "Sadomasochism and Exclusion," *Hypatia* 7 (fall 1992): 61–62, 65–68.

62. For example, see Saxe's discussion of respect in "Sadomasochism and Exclusion," 69, n. 3.

63. See Nichols et al., "Is Sadomasochism Feminist?," 140; Karen Rian, "Sadomasochism and the Social Construction of Desire," in Linden et al., *Against Sadomasochism*, 49.

64. See Russell, "Sadomasochism," 177; Dorchen Leidholdt, "When Women Defend Pornography," and Wendy Stock, "Toward a Feminist Praxis of Sexuality," in Leidholdt and Raymond, *The Sexual Liberals*, 129, 150–51; Pat Califia on Women against Violence and Pornography in the Media (WAVPM) in "A Personal View," 245, 260; also see Seidman, *Embattled Eros*, 118–19, 194.

65. Sarah Lucia Hoagland, "Sadism, Masochism, and Lesbian-Feminism," in Linden et al., *Against Sadomasochism*, 156; Valerie Heller, "Sexual Liberalism and Survivors of Sexual Abuse," in Leidholdt and Raymond, *The Sexual Liberals*, 159.

66. See Andrea Dworkin, "Resistance," in Leidholdt and Raymond, *The Sexual Liberals*, 138; Nichols et al., "Is Sadomasochism Feminist?," 140.

67. See Weeks, *Sexuality and Its Discontents*, 226–28; Marilyn Frye, "Critique [of Robert Ehman's "Adult-Child Sex"]," in Baker and Elliston, *Philosophy and Sex* (1984), 455, n. 1. For incest as "emotional extortion," see Heller, "Sexual Liberalism," 157.

68. See Armstrong, "Making an Issue of Incest," 49; Robert Ehman, "Adult-Child Sex," in Baker and Elliston, *Philosophy and Sex* (1984), 439.

69. Frye, "Critique," 453.

70. Newton and Walton, "The Misunderstanding," 247.

71. See Dimen on the dangers of political correctness, in "Politically Correct?," 141, and

Pat Califia's reference to "feminist mind police" in "A Personal View," 253; also see Rubin, "The Leather Menace," 225.

72. Nestle, "The Fem Question," 236.

73. Rubin, "The Leather Menace," 214.

74. See Califia, "A Personal View," 255–73; also see Rubin, "Thinking Sex," 304–6.

75. For arguments that the consent issue in feminist sexuality debates is problematic, see Saxe, "Sadomasochism and Exclusion," 61; Hunt, "Report of a Conference on Feminism, Sexuality and Power," 87–89; Ellen Willis, *No More Nice Girls: Countercultural Essays* (Hanover, N.H.: Wesleyan University Press, 1992), 12–13.

76. See Hollibaugh and Moraga, "What We're Rollin Around in Bed With," 398–400; Ann Cvetkovich, "Recasting Receptivity: Femme Sexualities," in *Lesbian Erotics*, ed. Karla Jay (New York: New York University Press, 1995), 125–46; Sue-Ellen Case, "Toward a Butch-Femme Aesthetic," *Discourse* 2 (fall 1988/winter 1989): 55–73. An excellent description of the sex radical aims of s/m can be found in Seidman, *Embattled Eros*, 116–18; also see Califia, "Feminism and Sadomasochism"; and Rubin and Califia, "Talking about Sadomasochism."

77. See McClintock, "Maid to Order," 210–11. For butch/femme roles as vehicles for woman-identified sex, see Hollibaugh and Moraga, "What We're Rollin Around in Bed With"; Nestle, "The Fem Question"; Nestle, *The Persistent Desire*; Newton and Walton, "The Misunderstanding." For s/m as a vehicle for a woman-identified sexuality, see Kitt, "Taking the Sting out of S/M," and Susan Farr, "The Art of Discipline: Creating Erotic Dramas of Play and Power," in Samois, *Coming to Power*, 60–63, 183–91. For the distinction in lesbian s/m between the replication of patriarchal sexual norms and the (mere) simulation of them, see Patrick D. Hopkins, "Rethinking Sadomasochism: Feminism, Interpretation, and Simulation," *Hypatia* 9 (winter 1994): 116–41, and "Simulation and Reproduction of Injustice: A Reply," *Hypatia* 10 (spring 1995): 162–70.

78. Nestle, "The Fem Question," 232, 235–36.

79. For example, see Sigmund Freud, "Three Essays on the Theory of Sexuality," in *The Standard Edition of the Complete Psychological Works of Sigmund Freud*, 24 vols., ed. James Strachey (London: Hogarth Press and the Institute of Psychoanalysis, 1953–74), vol. 7; Robert J. Stoller, *Sexual Excitement: Dynamics of Erotic Life* (New York: Simon & Schuster, 1980); Foucault, *The History of Sexuality* and *Power/Knowledge*.

80. See Hollibaugh and Moraga, "What We're Rollin Around in Bed With," 397; Rubin, "Thinking Sex," 277–79. For further discussion of Foucault's claim that history and culture, not biology, construct sexuality, see Lois McNay, "The Foucauldian Body and the Exclusion of Experience," *Hypatia* 6 (fall 1991): 125–39; Linda Singer, "True Confessions: Cixous and Foucault on Sexuality and Power," in *The Thinking Muse: Feminism and Modern French Philosophy*, ed. Jeffner Allen and Iris Marion Young (Bloomington: Indiana University Press, 1989), 136–55.

81. See Rubin, "The Leather Menace," 197–99; also see Weeks, *Sexuality and Its Discontents*, 226–27. For a discussion of how the internalization of culturally specific social norms narrows our conception of sexual identity, see Parveen Adams, "Of Female Bondage," in *Between Feminism and Psychoanalysis*, ed. Teresa Brennan (New York: Routledge, 1989), 247–65.

82. See Theo Sandfort, *The Sexual Aspects of Paedophile Relations: The Experience of Twenty-Five Boys* (Amsterdam: Pan/Spartacus, 1982); Ehman, "Adult-Child Sex," 436–39. For arguments in favor of man/boy love, see Tom O'Carroll, *Paedophilia: The Radical Case* (London: Peter Owen, 1980); interview by Guy Hocquenghem with David Thorstad in *Semiotext(e)* Special Large Type Series: "Loving Boys" (summer 1980).

83. See Weeks, *Sexuality and Its Discontents*, 227; also see Tom Reeves, "Loving Boys," in Tsang, *The Age Taboo*, 27–28.

84. See Weeks, *Sexuality and Its Discontents*, 230–31; also see Califia, "Man/Boy Love and the Lesbian Movement"; Tuppy Owens, *The Betrayal of Youth: Radical Perspectives on Childhood Sexuality, Intergenerational Sex and the Sexual Oppression of Children and Young People*, ed. Warren Middleton (London: CL Publications, 1986); Joan Nestle, *A Restricted Country* (Ithaca, N.Y.: Firebrand Books, 1987); Nettie Pollard, "The Small Matter of Children," in *Bad Girls and Dirty Pictures: The Challenge to Reclaim Feminism*, ed. Alison Assiter and Avedon Carol (London: Pluto Press, 1993), 105–11.

85. Cynthia Astuto and Pat Califia, "Being Weird Is Not Enough: How to Stay Healthy and Play Safe," in Samois, *Coming to Power*, 71. For further details on rules of dress and procedure, see Samois, ed., *What Color Is My Handkerchief?: A Lesbian S/M Sexuality Reader* (Berkeley: Samois, 1979).

86. Astuto and Califia, "Being Weird Is Not Enough," 69–72. For an honest and self-critical assessment of some of the difficulties in maintaining safe sex precautions in lesbian s/m sex, see Pat Califia, "Slipping," in *Melting Point* (Boston: Alyson Publications, 1993).

87. Rubin, "The Leather Menace," 204–5; also see Califia, "A Personal View," 251.

88. See Califia, "Unraveling the Sexual Fringe"; Weeks, *Sexuality and Its Discontents*, 237–38.

89. See Reeves, "Loving Boys."

90. For an excellent overview of the sex radical position on pedophilia, s/m, and other patterns of sexual difference, see Pat Califia, *Public Sex: The Culture of Radical Sex* (Pittsburgh: Cleis Press, 1994).

91. See McClintock, "Maid to Order," 224–28; Judy Butler, "The Politics of S & M: The Politics of Dis-illusion," in Linden et al., *Against Sadomasochism*, 172; Hoagland, "Sadism, Masochism, and Lesbian-Feminism," 158–60; Saxe, "Sadomasochism and Exclusion," 64; Julia Penelope, "The Illusion of Control: Sadomasochism and the Sexual Metaphors of Childhood," *Lesbian Ethics* 2, no. 3 (1987): 84–94.

92. See Nichols, "Is Sadomasochism Feminist?," 143.

93. Vadas, "Reply to Patrick Hopkins," 160.

94. Saxe, "Sadomasochism and Exclusion," 61–62; Griffin, "Sadomasochism and the Erosion of Self," 186–87; also see Sheila Jeffreys, "Sado-masochism: The Erotic Cult of Fascism," *Lesbian Ethics* 2, no. 1 (1986): 65–82; Bar On, "Feminism and Sadomasochism," 79–80.

95. See Judy Butler on the s/m practitioner's "fundamental faith in the rightness of desire," in "The Politics of S & M," 171.

96. See Stock, "Toward a Feminist Praxis of Sexuality," 154–55; Judy Butler, "The Politics of S & M," 173–74.

97. See Sims et al., "Racism and Sadomasochism"; also see Weeks, *Sexuality and Its Discontents*, 238.

98. Weeks, *Sexuality and Its Discontents*, 242.

99. Ibid., 225–26, 230–31. Ann Ferguson discusses the social and economic conditions that must be met in order to reconsider prevailing conservative attitudes toward adult/child sexuality in *Sexual Democracy: Women, Oppression, and Revolution* (Boulder, Colo.: Westview Press, 1991), 233.

100. For the essentialism implied in cultural feminist views of sexuality, see Alice Echols, "The Taming of the Id: Feminist Sexual Politics, 1968–1983," in Vance, *Pleasure and Danger*, 50–72. For the essentialism implied in sex radical views of sexuality, see Weeks, *Sexuality and Its Discontents*, 239–41. For the essentialism lurking in sociological and psychoanalytic theories of the relationship between sex and power, see Kathleen Barry, "On the History of Cultural Sadism," in Linden et al., *Against Sadomasochism*, 51–65.

101. For further discussion of the diversity in women's sexual preference, see Adrienne

Rich, "Compulsory Heterosexuality and Lesbian Existence," *Signs: Journal of Culture and Society* 5 (summer 1980): 631–60; Christine Overall, "Heterosexuality and Feminist Theory," *Canadian Journal of Philosophy* 20, no. 1 (March 1990): 9–17; Karin Baker, "Bisexual Feminist Politics: Because Bisexuality Is Not Enough," in *Closer to Home: Bisexuality and Feminism*, ed. Elizabeth Wise (Seattle: Seal Press, 1992), 255–67; Annie Sprinkle, "Beyond Bisexual," in *Bi Any Other Name: Bisexual People Speak Out*, ed. Loraine Hutchins and Lani Kaahumanu (Boston: Alyson Publications, 1991), 103–7. Excerpts from these articles can be found in *Living with Contradictions: Controversies in Feminist Social Ethics*, ed. Alison M. Jagger (Boulder, Colo.: Westview Press, 1994), 487–90, 499–510.

102. Dimen, "Politically Correct?," 147.

103. Califia, "Feminism and Sadomasochism"; Ruddick, "Better Sex," 298.

104. See Willis, *No More Nice Girls*, 14.

105. Hoagland, "Sadism, Masochism, and Lesbian-Feminism," 155; Sandra Bartky, *Femininity and Domination: Studies in the Phenomenology of Oppression* (New York: Routledge, 1990), 61; also see Saxe, "Sadomasochism and Exclusion," 61.

106. Marjorie Weinzweig, "Should a Feminist Choose a Marriage-Like Relationship?" *Hypatia* 1 (fall 1986): 147–58; Joyce Trebilcot, "Taking Responsibility for Sexuality," in Baker and Elliston, *Philosophy and Sex* (1984), 421–30.

107. Robin S. Dillon, "Care and Respect," in *Explorations in Feminist Ethics*, ed. Eve Browning Cole and Susan Coultrap-McQuin (Bloomington: Indiana University Press, 1992), 74.

108. Ibid., 74–75. Balancing an ethic of justice with an ethic of care is also a theme in Joan Tronto, *Moral Boundaries: A Political Argument for an Ethic of Care* (New York: Routledge, 1993).

109. Ibid., 75; also see Elizabeth Spelman, "On Treating Persons as Persons," *Ethics* 88 (1977): 150–61.

110. Dillon, "Care and Respect," 76–77.

111. See Belliotti, *Good Sex*, chap. 7, and Shrage, *Moral Dilemmas of Feminism: Prostitution, Adultery, and Abortion* (New York: Routledge, 1994), 174–79.

112. Weinzweig, "Should a Feminist Choose a Marriage-Like Relationship?," 156.

113. Ibid., 152–53. The importance of balancing care for the self and care for others is also cited in Joan Tronto, "Beyond Gender Difference to a Theory of Care," in *An Ethic of Care: Feminist and Interdisciplinary Perspectives*, ed. Mary Jeanne Larrabee (New York: Routledge, 1993), 249.

114. Trebilcot, "Taking Responsibility for Sexuality," 422, 428.

115. Webster, "The Forbidden," 395, 396.

116. Ibid., 395–97; also see Weeks, *Sexuality and Its Discontents*, 242–45.

Chapter 4

1. For example, see Part I, "Survivors of Pornography," in *Making Violence Sexy: Feminist Views on Pornography*, ed. Diana E. H. Russell (Buckingham, U.K.: Open University Press, 1993); Laura Lederer, "Then and Now: An Interview with a Former Pornography Model," in *Take Back the Night: Women on Pornography*, ed. Laura Lederer (New York: William Morrow, 1980), 57–70; Linda Lovelace, *Ordeal* (Secaucus, N.J.: Citadel Press, 1980); "Attorney General's Commission on Pornography: Final Report, 1986" (Washington: U.S. Department of Justice); "It's Not Outside Morality," by B, and "We Take It for All Women," by C, in *Prostitutes: Our Life*, ed. Claude Jaget (Bristol, U.K.: Falling Wall Press, 1980), 81–113; Kathleen Barry, *Female Sexual Slavery* (Englewood Cliffs, N.J.: Prentice Hall, 1979), 73–102; Florence Rush, "Child Pornography," in Lederer, *Take Back the Night*, 71–81.

2. See Martha O'Campo, "Pornography and Prostitution in the Philippines," in *Good Girls/Bad Girls: Feminists and Sex Trade Workers Face to Face*, ed. Laurie Bell (Toronto: Seal Press, 1987), 67–76; Saundra Pollack Sturdevant and Brenda Stoltzfus, *Let the Good Times Roll: Prostitution and the U.S. Military in Asia* (New York: New Press, 1993); Thanh-Dam Truong, *Sex, Money and Morality: Prostitution and Tourism in South-East Asia* (London: Zed Books, 1990).

3. Quoted in Catharine A. MacKinnon, *Feminism Unmodified: Discourses on Life and Law* (Cambridge: Harvard University Press, 1987), 180.

4. See Diana E. H. Russell, "Pornography and Rape: A Causal Model," in Russell, *Making Violence Sexy*, 142–45; MacKinnon, *Feminism Unmodified*, 183–84, 188–89; Patricia Hill Collins, "Pornography and Black Women's Bodies," and Alice Mayall and Diana E. H. Russell, "Racism in Pornography," in Russell, *Making Violence Sexy*, 97–104, 167–78; Voices M and K, in Kate Millett, "Prostitution: A Quartet of Female Voices," in *Woman in Sexist Society: Studies in Power and Powerlessness*, ed. Vivian Gornick and Barbara K. Moran (New York: Basic Books, 1971), 64–120; Priscilla Alexander, "Prostitution: A Difficult Issue for Feminists," in *Sex Work: Writings by Women in the Sex Industry*, ed. Frédérique Delacoste and Priscilla Alexander (Pittsburgh: Cleis Press, 1987), 201–2.

5. Evelina Giobbe, "Surviving Commercial Sexual Exploitation," in Russell, *Making Violence Sexy*, 40; also see J, in Millett, "Prostitution," 64–125; Lederer, "Then and Now," 57–70.

6. See Diana E. H. Russell, "Introduction," in Russell, *Making Violence Sexy*, 14–17; also see Sheldon Teitelbaum, "Cybersex," *Los Angeles Times Magazine*, 15 August 1993; Robert A. Jones, "Wanna Buy a Dirty CD-ROM?," *Los Angeles Times Magazine*, 19 March 1995; Gareth Branwyn, "Compu-Sex: Erotica for Cybernauts," in *Flame Wars: The Discourse of Cyberspace*, ed. Mark Dery (Durham, N.C.: Duke University Press, 1994), 203–35. According to John R. Levine and Carol Baroudi, the Internet newsgroup with the largest amount of traffic, measured in megabytes per day, is called "alt.binaries.pictures.erotica." The abbreviation "alt" stands for "alternative" newsgroup, one that is not part of the mainstream established newsgroup hierarchies requiring a formal charter and an on-line vote by its prospective readers and nonreaders. I wonder: is this newsgroup's "otherness" part of its allure? What would happen to its content and readership if it went mainstream? See *The Internet for Dummies*, 2d ed. (Foster City, Calif.: IDG Books, 1994), 136, 157.

7. MacKinnon, *Feminism Unmodified*, 137.

8. Susan Brownmiller, "Women Fight Back," in *Pornography: Private Right or Public Menace?*, ed. Robert M. Baird and Stuart E. Rosenbaum (Buffalo, N.Y.: Prometheus Books, 1991), 38 (also printed in Lederer, *Take Back the Night*); Robin Morgan, "Theory and Practice: Pornography and Rape," in Lederer, *Take Back the Night*, 139; MacKinnon, *Feminism Unmodified*, 183–86, 203; Diana E. H. Russell, *Sexual Exploitation: Rape, Child Sexual Abuse, and Workplace Harassment* (Beverly Hills, Calif.: Sage Publications, 1984).

9. See Judith Walkowitz, "The Politics of Prostitution," *Signs: Journal of Women in Culture and Society* 6, no. 1 (autumn 1980): 123–35, for the ways in which nineteenth-century feminist political goals were subverted by moral conservatives; also see Rosemarie Tong's discussion of *Miller v. California* (1973), which raises some of the difficulties with defining obscenity, in Rosemarie Tong, *Women, Sex, and the Law* (Savage, Md.: Rowman & Littlefield, 1984), 8–9; Donald Alexander Downs, *The New Politics of Pornography* (Chicago: University of Chicago Press, 1989).

10. See Gloria Steinem, "Erotica and Pornography: A Clear and Present Difference," in Baird and Rosenbaum, *Pornography*, 51–55 (also printed in Lederer, *Take Back the Night*); Eva Feder Kittay, "Pornography and the Erotics of Domination," in *Beyond Domination: New Perspectives on Women and Philosophy*, ed. Carol C. Gould (Totowa, N.J.: Rowman &

Littlefield, 1983), 145–85; Rosemarie Tong, "Feminism, Pornography, and Censorship," *Social Theory and Practice* 8, no. 1 (spring 1982): 1–17; Russell, "Introduction," 2–3. For work being done in lesbian erotica, see comments by Susie Bright (of *On Our Backs*), Nan Kinny and Debi Sundahl (of Blush Entertainment Productions), Marie Mason (of Hot Chixx), and author Katherine Forrest in Victoria A. Brownworth, "The Porn Boom," *Lesbian News* 18, no. 7 (February 1993): 42–43, 61–63. Less overtly sexist or less violent sexually explicit material has already found consumers in heterosexual women, as more women are choosing (with their dollars) which sex videos to bring home. See Brownworth, "The Porn Boom." For examples of erotic literature written by, and for, women, see Susie Bright, ed., *Herotica* (Burlingame, Calif.: Down There Press, 1988); Louise Thornton, Jan Sturtevant, and Amber Coverdale Sumrall, eds., *Touching Fire: Erotic Writings by Women* (New York: Carroll & Graf, 1989); Michele Slung, ed., *Slow Hand: Women Writing Erotica* (New York: HarperCollins, 1992); Lonnie Barbach, ed., *Pleasures: Women Write Erotica* (New York: HarperCollins, 1984); Laura Chester, ed., *Deep Down: The New Sensual Writing by Women* (Boston: Faber & Faber, 1989). Essays that combine erotic writing with feminist cultural criticism can be found in *Sexy Bodies: The Strange Carnalities of Feminism*, ed. Elizabeth Grosz and Elspeth Robyn (New York: Routledge, 1995).

11. Andrea Dworkin, *Pornography: Men Possessing Women* (New York: E. P. Dutton, 1989), xlii; also see Barry, *Female Sexual Slavery*, 174–85; MacKinnon, *Feminism Unmodified*, 148–49; A Southern Women's Writing Collective, "Sex Resistance in Heterosexual Arrangements," in *The Sexual Liberals and the Attack on Feminism*, ed. Dorchen Leidholdt and Janice G. Raymond (New York: Teachers College Press, 1990), 140–47.

12. MacKinnon, *Feminism Unmodified*, 160.

13. See Lorenne Clark, "Liberalism and Pornography," in *Pornography and Censorship: Philosophical, Scientific and Legal Studies*, ed. David Copp and Susan Wendell (Buffalo, N.Y.: Prometheus Books, 1983), 49–50, 56–57; Christine Boyle and Sheila Noonan, "Gender Neutrality, Prostitution, and Pornography," in Bell, *Good Girls/Bad Girls*, 45–47; Evelina Giobbe, "Confronting the Liberal Lies about Prostitution," in Leidholdt and Raymond, *The Sexual Liberals*, 75; Sarah Wynter, "WHISPER: Women Hurt in Systems of Prostitution Engaged in Revolt," in Delacoste and Alexander, *Sex Work*, 267–68. For a comprehensive survey of feminists' arguments against pornography, see Catherine Itzin, ed., *Pornography: Women, Violence, and Civil Liberties* (New York: Oxford University Press, 1993).

14. See Deirdre English, in Deirdre English, Amber Hollibaugh, and Gayle Rubin, "Talking Sex: A Conversation on Sexuality and Feminism," *Socialist Review* 11, no. 4 (1981): 61; Gayle Rubin, in ibid., 57, 60; Alison Assiter and Avedon Carol, "Introduction," and Gayle Rubin, "Misguided, Dangerous, and Wrong: An Analysis of Anti-Pornography Politics," in *Bad Girls and Dirty Pictures: The Challenge to Reclaim Feminism*, ed. Alison Assiter and Avedon Carol (London: Pluto Press, 1993), 15–16; 21–25; Camille Paglia, *Vamps and Tramps: New Essays* (New York: Vintage Books, 1994), 65; Paula Webster, "Pornography and Pleasure," *Heresies* #12 "Sex Issue" 3, no. 4 (1981): 48–51; Valerie Scott, Peggy Miller, and Ryan Hotchkiss, of the Canadian Organization for the Rights of Prostitutes (CORP), "Realistic Feminists," in Bell, *Good Girls/Bad Girls*, 217.

15. See COYOTE/National Task Force on Prostitution position statement, in Delacoste and Alexander, *Sex Work*, 290; Varda Burstyn, "Who the Hell Is 'We'?," in Bell, *Good Girls/Bad Girls*, 168. For an excellent contemporary history of the movement for prostitutes' rights as well as a discussion of the variety of prostitutes' lives, from victim to vamp, see Gail Pheterson, "Not Repeating History," in *A Vindication of the Rights of Whores*, ed. Gail Pheterson (Seattle: Seal Press, 1989), 3–30.

16. For examples of radical feminist positions that would reject a strong antipornography stance, see Deirdre English, "The Politics of Porn: Can Feminists Walk the Line?," *Mother*

Jones 5, no. 3 (April 1980): 20–23, 43–50; *Heresies* #12 "Sex Issue" 3, no. 4 (1981); English et al., "Talking Sex"; Assiter and Carol, *Bad Girls and Dirty Pictures*; Pamela Church Gibson and Roma Gibson, eds., *Dirty Looks: Women, Pornography, Power* (London: BFI Publishing, 1993); Lynne Segal and Mary McIntosh, eds., *Sex Exposed: Sexuality and the Pornography Debate* (New Brunswick, N.J.: Rutgers University Press, 1992). Liberal feminist Betty Friedan worries that "[t]he pornography issue is dividing the women's movement and giving the impression on college campuses that to be a feminist is to be against sex." See Betty Friedan, *The Second Stage* (New York: Summit Books, 1981), 357. Feminists of very different political perspectives from Friedan but who would agree with her on this point include Rene Denfeld, *The New Victorians: A Young Woman's Challenge to the Old Feminist Order* (New York: Warner Books, 1995), chap. 3, and Paglia, *Vamps and Tramps*, 56–67.

17. For arguments that pornography is both possible and desirable under communism, see Alan Soble, *Pornography, Marxism, Feminism, and the Future of Sexuality* (New Haven: Yale University Press, 1986), chap. 5.

18. The radical feminist organization Women against Pornography (WAP) founded by Susan Brownmiller defines pornography, like rape, in terms of violence against women. Catharine MacKinnon defines pornography in terms of a sexuality and gender hierarchy of dominance and submission; also see MacKinnon and Dworkin on the antipornography ordinances they wrote for Minneapolis and Indianapolis, citing porn as sex discrimination, in MacKinnon, *Feminism Unmodified*, 175–97, and Andrea Dworkin, *Pornography*, xxviii–xxxiv.

19. Caption quote from Larry Flynt, publisher of *Hustler* magazine (June 1978), cited in Kittay, "Pornography and the Erotics of Domination," 147; also see Rubin and English, in English et al., "Talking Sex," 57. For porn as parody, see Robert J. Stoller, *Porn: Myths for the Twentieth Century* (New Haven: Yale University Press, 1991), 219.

20. See Lovelace, *Ordeal*; also see Catherine A. MacKinnon, "Linda's Life and Andrea's Work," in MacKinnon, *Feminism Unmodified*, 127–33, and Gloria Steinem, "The Real Linda Lovelace," in Russell, *Making Violence Sexy*, 23–31. Compare these descriptions to Annie Sprinkle's experiences, "Feminism: 'Crunch Point,'" in Pheterson, *A Vindication of the Rights of Whores*, 146–47; also see Jane Smith, "Making Movies," and Nina Hartley, "Confessions of a Feminist Porno Star," in Delacoste and Alexander, *Sex Work*, 135–41, 142–44; International Committee for Prostitutes' Rights (ICPR), "International Committee for Prostitutes' Rights World Charter and World Whores' Congress Statement," in Delacoste and Alexander, *Sex Work*, 308–9.

21. Nina Lopez-Jones, "Workers: Introducing the English Collective of Prostitutes," in Delacoste and Alexander, *Sex Work*, 275.

22. See Wynter, "WHISPER," 269.

23. See Marie Arrington, "Under the Gun," in Bell, *Good Girls/Bad Girls*, 174–75. Wendy Chapkis notes that even a "pro-prostitution lobby" can fail to challenge class and status hierarchies within the profession. See Wendy Chapkis, "Paying for Pleasure," *Women's Review of Books* (April 1995), 19, reviewing "Sex Workers and Sex Work," special issue of *Social Text* 37 (winter 1993).

24. See the Commission on Obscenity and Pornography (1970), "The Effects of Explicit Sexual Materials," and "The Attorney General's Commission on Pornography: Final Report (1986)," in Baird and Rosenbaum, *Pornography*, 23–24, 41. Criticisms of these reports arise from both antipornography and sex radical sides of the debate. For example, see Tong, *Women, Sex and the Law*, 15–17; Rosemarie Tong, "Women, Pornography, and the Law," in *The Philosophy of Sex*, 2d ed., ed. Alan Soble (Savage, Md.: Rowman & Littlefield, 1991), 304; Irene Diamond, "Pornography and Repression: A Reconsideration," *Signs: Journal of Women in Culture and Society* 5, no. 4 (1980): 692–97; Carole S. Vance, "Negotiating Sex and Gender in the Attorney General's Commission on Pornography," in Segal and McIntosh, *Sex Exposed*,

29–49; Edward I. Donnerstein and Daniel G. Linz, "The Question of Pornography: It Is Not Sex, but Violence, That Is an Obscenity in Our Society," *Psychology Today* (December 1986), 56–59; Edward Donnerstein, Daniel Linz, and Steven Penrod, "Is It the Sex or Is It the Violence?," in their *The Question of Pornography: Research Findings and Policy Implications* (New York: Free Press, 1987), 108–36; James Check and Ted Guloien, reporting in *Pornography: Research Advances and Policy Considerations*, ed. Dolf Zillmann and Bryant Jennings (Hillsdale, N.J.: Lawrence Erlbaum, 1989), 159–84. Catharine MacKinnon speculates that the harm pornography does may be so pervasive that it is not measurable or causally identifiable by standard methods. See MacKinnon, *Feminism Unmodified*, 271–72, n. 53. For arguments for a causal connection between pornography and violence against women, see Russell, "Pornography and Rape," 120–50. For some criticisms of such models, see F. M. Christensen, *Pornography: The Other Side* (New York: Praeger, 1990), chaps. 7, 9, 10, and 11; Lynne Segal, "Does Pornography Cause Violence?: The Search for Evidence," in Gibson and Gibson, *Dirty Looks*, 5–21; Alison King, "Mystery and Imagination: The Case of Pornography Effects Studies," in Assiter and Carol, *Bad Girls and Dirty Pictures*, 57–87; Alan Soble, "Pornography and the Social Sciences," in Soble, *The Philosophy of Sex* (1991), 317–31.

25. For a description and critique of the 1983 Minneapolis Pornography Ordinance authored by MacKinnon and Dworkin, see Lisa Duggan, Nan Hunter, and Carole S. Vance, "False Promises: Feminist Antipornography Legislation in the U.S.," in *Women against Censorship*, ed. Varda Burstyn (Vancouver: Douglas & McIntyre, 1985), 130–51; also see Lisa Duggan and Nan D. Hunter, *Sex Wars: Sexual Dissent and Political Culture* (New York: Routledge, 1995). Arguments in favor of the ordinance as an extension of civil liberties for women can be found in Andrea Dworkin, *Pornography*, xxviii–xxxiv; MacKinnon, *Feminism Unmodified*, 175–79, 201–5; John Stoltenberg, "Pornography and Freedom," in Russell, *Making Violence Sexy*, 73–75.

26. Gail Pheterson, "Editor's Note," in Pheterson, *A Vindication of the Rights of Whores*, 149.

27. See Rachel West, "U.S. PROStitutes Collective," in Delacoste and Alexander, *Sex Work*, 279; Margaret Valentino and Mavis Johnson, "On the Game and On the Move," in Jaget, *Prostitutes*, 23–24; Alexander, "Prostitution," 195, 198–99; Pheterson, "Not Repeating History," 15–16; Cathy, "Unveiling," in Bell, *Good Girls/Bad Girls*, 89.

28. The increase in upper-income clubs with female dancers working as "independent contractors," even though their hours are fixed by club managers and their clothing and behavior restricted, has prompted questions about their wages and lack of benefits. See Alan Abrahamson, "Coverage of Exotic Entertainers Is Questioned," *Los Angeles Times*, 30 November 1992.

29. Rosemarie Tong notes that given the increase in male homosexual prostitutes and the limited increase in lesbian and heterosexual male prostitutes, we can say that "a considerate portion of prostitutes are men and a small minority of the customers are women." See *Women, Sex, and the Law*, 61–62, n. 1. Because my interest is in the degrading nature of women's sex work, the sex workers to which I will refer are women unless otherwise noted. However, there is some fascinating work to be done on the nature of the sex objectification of men in the sex trade. Some of the asymmetries between male and female sex workers are discussed later in this chapter; also see the interviews with Bill, Merlin, and Ron in Stoller, *Porn*, 29–63, 183–213; Jerry Butler, as told to Robert Rimmer and Catherine Tavel, *Raw Talent: The Adult Film Industry as Seen by Its Most Popular Male Star* (Buffalo, N.Y.: Prometheus Books, 1990); Linda Williams, *Hard Core: Power, Pleasure, and the "Frenzy of the Visible"* (Berkeley: University of California Press, 1989); Michael Kimmel, ed., *Men Confront Pornography* (New York: Crown, 1989).

30. See Judy Edelstein, "In the Massage Parlor," in Delacoste and Alexander, *Sex Work*, 65.

31. See Eva Rosta, "Feminism: 'Crunch Point,'" and "Statement on Prostitution and Feminism," in Pheterson, *A Vindication of the Rights of Whores*, 145, 194; Arrington, "Under the Gun," 174–75.

32. For an excellent overview of the variety within the sex industry, see Williams, *Hard Core*; Delacoste and Alexander, *Sex Work*, 20–182; Jaget, *Prostitutes*, 57–174; Nickie Roberts, ed., *The Front Line: Women in the Sex Industry Speak* (London: Grafton Books, 1986).

33. For example, see "Turning Out the Charter for the First World Whores' Congress, Amsterdam, February 14, 1985," in Pheterson, *A Vindication of the Rights of Whores*, 33–42; Participant 1, "From the Floor," and Margo St. James, "The Reclamation of Whores," in Bell, *Good Girls/Bad Girls*, 81–87, 181; Amber Cooke, a former stripper, says, "I'd rather be a whore than a Catholic." See Amber Cooke with Laurie Bell, "Sex Trade Workers and Feminists: Myths and Illusions," in Bell, *Good Girls/Bad Girls*, 202.

34. See Mary Johnson, "CABE and Strippers: A Delicate Union," in Bell, *Good Girls/Bad Girls*, 110; Pheterson, "Editor's Note," 149–50.

35. See Russell, "Introduction," 19; also see chapter 4, n. 20 in this book.

36. See Tong, "Feminism, Pornography, and Censorship," 2.

37. Andrea Dworkin, *Pornography*, 199–202; Rubin, "Misguided, Dangerous, and Wrong," 25, 35, and 166, nn. 40, 41, in Assiter and Carol, *Bad Girls*. Among Rubin's sources is Walter Kendrick's social history of pornography as a nineteenth-century invention named to describe sexually explicit Pompeiian artifacts acquired by affluent Neapolitan cognoscenti. See Walter Kendrick, *The Secret Museum: Pornography in Modern Culture* (New York: Viking Press, 1987).

38. Giobbe, "Confronting the Liberal Lies about Prostitution," 78–79.

39. Wynter, "WHISPER," 268, 269.

40. Russell, "Introduction," 18.

41. Stoller, *Porn*, 220.

42. Soble, *Pornography, Marxism, Feminism*, 134–35.

43. See Christobel MacKenzie, "The AntiSexism Campaign Invites You to Fight Sexism, Not Sex," in Assiter and Carol, *Bad Girls and Dirty Pictures*, 140–41; also see Alison Jaggar's discussion of the radical feminist analysis of prostitution, in "Prostitution," in Soble, *The Philosophy of Sex*, 270–74; K in Millett, "Prostitution"; Scott et al. (CORP), "Realistic Feminists," 211.

44. Frederick Engels, *The Origin of the Family, Private Property and the State* (New York: International Publishers, 1942), 63, also quoted in Jaggar, "Prostitution," 265.

45. J, in Millett, "Prostitution," 86.

46. See "Statement on Prostitution and Feminism," 193; St. James, "The Reclamation of Whores," 82; Cooke with Bell, "Sex Trade Workers and Feminists," 202; Pieke Biermann, "Feminism: 'Crunch Point,'" in Pheterson, *A Vindication of the Rights of Whores*, 170.

47. Pheterson, "Not Repeating History," 23; also see Tong, *Women, Sex, and the Law*, 38–39, 52.

48. This is the view of C, in "We Take It for All Women," 104.

49. See J, in Millett, "Prostitution"; Speaker 5, "'The Big Divide': Feminist Reactions to the Second World Whores' Congress," in Pheterson, *A Vindication of the Rights of Whores*, 181; Giobbe, "Confronting the Liberal Lies about Prostitution," 77.

50. Laurie Bell uses the expression "sex trade worker" in her anthology, as do many of the participants from the 1985 Toronto conference on pornography and prostitution on which her anthology *Good Girls/Bad Girls* is based.

51. Tracy Quan, Letter to the Editor, *New York Review of Books*, 5 November 1992.

52. Giobbe, "Confronting the Liberal Lies about Prostitution," 67; Diana E. H. Russell with Laura Lederer, "Questions We Get Asked Most Often," in Lederer, *Take Back the Night*, 24.

53. Helen E. Longino, "Pornography, Oppression, and Freedom: A Closer Look," in Baird and Rosenbaum, *Pornography*, 85 (also printed in Lederer, *Take Back the Night*); Andrea Dworkin, *Pornography*, xxxiii; Wynter, "WHISPER," 269.

54. Laurie Shrage, "Should Feminists Oppose Prostitution?," in *Feminism and Political Theory*, ed. Cass R. Sunstein (Chicago: University of Chicago Press, 1990), 197; also see 186–87, 198.

55. See Laurie Shrage, *Moral Dilemmas of Feminism: Prostitution, Adultery, and Abortion* (New York: Routledge, 1994), 94; also see her chaps., 4, 5, and 6.

56. See Rubin, "Misguided, Dangerous, and Wrong," 26–29; also see Paglia, *Vamps and Tramps*, 65; Fred R. Berger, "Pornography, Feminism, and Censorship," in *Philosophy and Sex*, 2d ed., ed. Robert Baker and Frederick Elliston (Buffalo, N.Y.: Prometheus Books, 1984), 333; Alan Soble, "Defamation and the Endorsement of Degradation," in Baird and Rosenbaum, *Pornography*, 100; English, "The Politics of Porn," 22.

57. Steinem, "Erotica and Pornography," 53.

58. Russell with Lederer, "Questions We Get Asked Most Often," 24.

59. Kittay, "Pornography and the Erotics of Domination," 148–49; Steinem, "Erotica and Pornography," 53.

60. For example, see Tong, "Women, Pornography, and the Law," 302; Harry Brod, "Pornography and the Alienation of Male Sexuality," in Soble, *The Philosophy of Sex*, 294.

61. Kittay, "Pornography and the Erotics of Domination," 154–55.

62. See Jonathan Gold, "Work on the Wild Side," *Los Angeles Times Magazine*, 8 August 1993; Anne McClintock, "Maid to Order: Commercial S/M and Gender Power," in Gibson and Gibson, *Dirty Looks*, 211–15, 217–19.

63. Soble, *Pornography, Marxism, Feminism*, 186. For discussions of how the context affects the content of pornography, see Ellen Willis, "Feminism, Moralism, and Pornography," in *Powers of Desire: The Politics of Sexuality*, ed. Ann Snitow, Christine Stansell, and Sharon Thompson (New York: Monthly Review Press, 1983), 463; also see English, "The Politics of Porn"; Webster, "Pornography and Pleasure"; Mariana Valverde, *Sex, Power and Pleasure* (Philadelphia: New Society Publishers, 1987), 121–45; Vance, "Negotiating Sex and Gender," 42–45; Linda Williams, "Pornographies On/scene, or Diff'rent Strokes for Diff'rent Folks," Carol Smart, "Unquestionably a Moral Issue: Rhetorical Devices and Regulatory Imperatives," and Harriet Gilbert, "So Long as It's Not Sex and Violence: Andrea Dworkin's *Mercy*," in Segal and McIntosh, *Sex Exposed*, 184–99, 216–29, 233–65; Theodore A. Gracyk, "Pornography as Representation: Aesthetic Considerations," in Baird and Rosenbaum, *Pornography*, 117–37; Berger, "Pornography, Feminism, and Censorship," 336–38; Ann Garry, "Pornography and Respect for Women," in Baker and Elliston, *Philosophy and Sex*, 325, n. 21; English et al., "Talking Sex," 57; Tong, *Women, Sex, and the Law*, 20; B. Ruby Rich, "Anti-Porn: Soft Issue, Hard World," *Village Voice* 20 (July 1982).

64. Longino, "Pornography, Oppression and Freedom," 85–87.

65. Judith M. Hill, "Pornography and Degradation," in Baird and Rosenbaum, *Pornography*, 64–65.

66. See Burstyn, "Who the Hell Is 'We'?," 168–72; Barbara Dority, "Feminist Moralism, 'Pornography,' and Censorship," in Baird and Rosenbaum, *Pornography*, 113; also see Ann Barr Snitow, "Mass Market Romance: Pornography for Women Is Different," in Snitow et al., *Powers of Desire*, 245–63; Rosalind Coward, "Sexual Violence and Sexuality," in *Sexuality: A Reader*, ed. Feminist Review (London: Virago, 1987), 307–25; Alisa L. Carse, "Pornography:

An Uncivil Liberty?," *Hypatia* 10 (winter 1995): 168, 170–71, 173–74; Helen Hazen, *Endless Rapture: Rape, Romance, and the Female Imagination* (New York: Scribner's, 1983).

67. Soble, "Defamation and the Endorsement of Degradation," 102; also see his critique of the claim that pornography is degrading to women, 99–101; also see Jeffrey Weeks, *Sexuality and Its Discontents: Meanings, Myths and Modern Sexualities* (New York: Routledge, 1985), 234–36; Kimmel, *Men Confront Pornography*; T. M. Scanlon, "Freedom of Expression and Categories of Expression," in Copp and Wendell, *Pornography and Censorship*, 139–65; Christensen, *Pornography*, 72–75; Dority, "Feminist Moralism," 114.

68. Christensen, *Pornography*, 80–88.

69. See Soble, *Pornography, Marxism, Feminism*, 78–85; Laura Kipnis, "She-Male Fantasies and the Aesthetics of Pornography," in Gibson and Gibson, *Dirty Looks*, 142.

70. See Anne McClintock, "Gonad the Barbarian and the Venus Flytrap: Portraying the Female and Male Orgasm," in Segal and McIntosh, *Sex Exposed*, 112–13.

71. Brod, "Pornography and the Alienation of Male Sexuality," 291–92.

72. See Andrea Dworkin, *Pornography*, xxxiii.

73. See Gilbert, "So Long as It's Not Sex and Violence," 219. Rita Manning and Theodore Gracyk also argue that the Dworkin/MacKinnon ordinance protects neither erotica nor sexually explicit moral realism from legal censure, since it does not require that the degradation depicted also be endorsed. See Rita C. Manning, "Redefining Obscenity," in Baird and Rosenbaum, *Pornography*, 154, and Gracyk, "Pornography as Representation," 129.

74. See Webster, "Pornography and Pleasure," 49; Rosta, "Feminism: 'Crunch Point,'" 146; Linda LeMoncheck, *Dehumanizing Women: Treating Persons as Sex Objects* (Totowa, N.J.: Rowman & Allanheld, 1985), 13–14; also see Tong (*Women, Sex, and the Law*, 43) who suggests that for a woman to sell her sexuality does not necessarily destroy her autonomy, but to condemn her for selling her sexuality may be a violation of that autonomy.

75. See Williams, "Pornographies On/scene," 235.

76. Russell, "Introduction," 6; Stoltenberg, "Pornography and Freedom," 76.

77. Garry, "Pornography and Respect for Women," 317–19; Robert Baker, "'Pricks' and 'Chicks': A Plea for Persons," in Baker and Elliston, *Philosophy and Sex*, 260–66; also see my criticisms of Garry and Baker on distinguishing degradation through objectification from degradation in sex, in *Dehumanizing Women*, 48–50.

78. See Carole Pateman, "Defending Prostitution: Charges against Ericsson," *Ethics* 93, no. 3 (April 1983): 561–65; also see Pateman's "Women and Consent," *Political Theory* 8, no. 2 (1980): 149–68.

79. See Naomi Wolf, *The Beauty Myth: How Images of Beauty Are Used against Women* (New York: Anchor Books/Doubleday, 1991), 132–42; Laura Lederer, "'Playboy Isn't Playing': An Interview with Judith Bat-Ada," in Lederer, *Take Back the Night*, 122–23, 128–29; MacKinnon, *Feminism Unmodified*, 260, n. 10; also see *Feminism Unmodified*, 85–92, and Russell, "Pornography and Rape."

80. Soble, *Pornography, Marxism, Feminism*, 156–57.

81. Dworkin, *Pornography*, 123; also see J, in Millett, "Prostitution," 94–96; C, in "We Take It for All Women," 103.

82. Dworkin, *Pornography*, xviii–xix, 109.

83. Christine Swanton, Viviane Robinson, and Jan Crosthwaite, "Treating Women as Sex-Objects," *Journal of Social Philosophy* 20, no. 3 (1989): 12.

84. Nancy Hartsock, *Money, Sex and Power* (New York: Longman, 1983), 172, 176–78; Robert J. Stoller, *Sexual Excitement: Dynamics of Erotic Life* (New York: Simon & Schuster, 1980), 6–8; Stoller, *Porn*, 219; Lynne Segal, "Sweet Sorrows, Painful Pleasures: Pornography and the Perils of Heterosexual Desire," in Segal and McIntosh, *Sex Exposed*, 69–70; Kittay, "Pornography and the Erotics of Domination," 157; also see Sheila Ruth, "Bodies and

Souls/Sex, Sin and the Senses in Patriarchy: A Study in Applied Dualism," *Hypatia* 2, no. 1 (winter 1987): 149–63.

85. McClintock, "Maid to Order," 211–15, 217–19, 227–28.

86. Brod, "Pornography and the Alienation of Male Sexuality," 285. For a discussion of men who "dismember" themselves under capitalism through a preoccupation with sexual performance, see Soble, *Pornography, Marxism, Feminism*, 61.

87. Jessica Benjamin, "Master and Slave: The Fantasy of Erotic Domination," in Snitow et al., *Powers of Desire*, 288. Avedon Carol argues that there is no evidence for the existence of snuff films. For Carol, their hyperbole and condemnation are merely tools by the moral right and antipornography feminists to associate porn with violence against women. See Avedon Carol, "Snuff: Believing the Worst," in Assiter and Carol, *Bad Girls and Dirty Pictures*, 126–30. For a contrasting view, see Beverly LaBelle, "*Snuff*—The Ultimate in Woman-Hating," in Lederer, *Take Back the Night*, 272–78.

88. MacKinnon, *Feminism Unmodified*, 157; also see Catharine A. MacKinnon, *Only Words* (Cambridge: Harvard University Press, 1993). For the conceptual distinction between "depiction" and "enactments" of activity, see Soble, *Pornography, Marxism, Feminism*, 128–30.

89. See Berger, "Pornography, Feminism, and Censorship," 335. Echoing my discussion of the complex dialectic between fantasy and reality in pornography, Judith Hill points out that the fiction in porn would not be successful if its subjects were not real people. See Hill, "Pornography and Degradation," 69.

90. Diana Russell, "On Pornography," *Chrysalis* 4 (1977): 12; MacKinnon, *Feminism Unmodified*, 150; also see Russell with Lederer, "Questions We Get Asked Most Often," 28; MacKinnon, *Only Words*.

91. Rubin, in English et al., "Talking Sex," 57.

92. See Kittay's discussion of men's "delicately balanced interactions with women," "Pornography and the Erotics of Domination," 169, and Segal, "Sweet Sorrows," 66–67; Vance, "Negotiating Sex and Gender," 44, and Elizabeth Cowrie, "Pornography and Fantasy: Psychoanalytic Perspectives," in Segal and McIntosh, *Sex Exposed*, 132–52; Soble, *Pornography, Marxism, Feminism*, 86–87; Stoller, *Porn*, 225. For criticism of pornography as catharsis, see Kittay, "Pornography and the Erotics of Domination," 171–72.

93. See Stoltenberg, "Pornography and Freedom," 71; Williams, "Pornographies On/scene," 244–45; also see Williams's discussion of gays and lesbians in heterosexual porn, as opposed to gay and lesbian porn, 244–62.

94. See Pateman, "Defending Prostitution," 365; Tong, *Women, Sex, and the Law*, 31, 58–59; LeMoncheck, *Dehumanizing Women*, 92–94; MacKinnon, *Feminism Unmodified*, 14.

95. John Stoltenberg, "You Can't Fight Homophobia and Protect the Pornographers at the Same Time—An Analysis of What Went Wrong in *Hardwick*," in Leidholdt and Raymond, *The Sexual Liberals*, 184–90; Stoltenberg, "Pornography and Freedom," 71; Susan G. Cole, "Pornography: What Do We Want?," in Bell, *Good Girls/Bad Girls*, 161; Bill's comments and Ron's comments, in Stoller's *Porn*, 35, 209–10. For a discussion of the asymmetry between male and female sex objects, see LeMoncheck, *Dehumanizing Women*, 86–94; also see Barbara Ehrenreich, Elizabeth Hess, and Gloria Jacobs, *Remaking Love: The Feminization of Sex* (New York: Anchor Books/Doubleday, 1986), 111–13; Andrea Dworkin, *Pornography*, 44–47.

96. See Kobena Mercer, "Just Looking for Trouble: Robert Mapplethorpe and Fantasies of Race," in Segal and McIntosh, *Sex Exposed*, 101–5; Isaac Julien and Kobena Mercer, "True Confessions: A Discourse on Images of Black Male Sexuality," in *Brother to Brother*, ed. Essex Hemphill (Boston: Alyson Publications, 1991); also see Janet R. Jakobsen, "Agency and Alliance in Public Discourses about Sexualities," *Hypatia* 10 (winter 1995): 140–42.

97. Margo St. James, "Feminism: 'Crunch Point,'" in Pheterson, *A Vindication of the*

Rights of Whores, 167; LeMoncheck, *Dehumanizing Women*, 26–30; also see Lederer, "Then and Now"; Lovelace, *Ordeal*.

98. See Scott et al. (CORP), "Realistic Feminists," 204–17; also see Lopez-Jones, "Workers"; West, "U.S. PROStitutes Collective"; Hartley, "Confessions of a Feminist Porno Star."

99. See Priscilla Alexander, "Prostitutes Are Being Scapegoated for Heterosexual AIDS," in Delacoste and Alexander, *Sex Work*, 248–63; Priscilla Alexander, "Update on HIV Infection and Prostitute Women," in Pheterson, *A Vindication of the Rights of Whores*, 132–37; Nina Lopez-Jones, "Prostitute Women and AIDS: Resisting the Virus of Repression," paper presented at the Women's Studies Seminar on Prostitution, Huntington Library, Pasadena, California, 13 March 1993; also see COYOTE/National Task Force on Prostitution position statement, 290; Hansje Verbeek and Terry van der Zijden, "The Red Thread: Whores' Movement in Holland," in Delacoste and Alexander, *Sex Work*, 300; "World Charter for Prostitutes' Rights," in Pheterson, *A Vindication of the Rights of Whores*, 41; Gail Pheterson, "The Social Consequences of Unchastity," in Delacoste and Alexander, *Sex Work*, 218; Clark, "Liberalism and Pornography"; Scott et al. (CORP), "Realistic Feminists," 205.

100. See Marjan Sax, "The Pink Thread," in Delacoste and Alexander, *Sex Work*, 301–4; also see chapter 4, n. 16 in this book. Annie Sprinkle describes how she uses sexually explicit stage performance traditionally labeled "objectifying" to define herself subversively as female sexual subject in *Post Porn Modernist* (Amsterdam: Torch Books, 1991); also see Linda Williams, "A Provoking Agent: The Pornography and Performance Art of Annie Sprinkle," in Gibson and Gibson, *Dirty Looks*, 176–91.

101. See C, in "We Take It for All Women," 102; St. James, "The Reclamation of Whores," 86; Scott et al. (CORP), "Realistic Feminists," 204–14.

102. See Sprinkle, "Feminism: 'Crunch Point,'" 146–47; Jane Smith, "Making Movies"; Hartley, "Confessions of a Feminist Porno Star"; Seph Weene, "Venus," *Heresies* #12 "Sex Issue" 3, no. 4 (1981): 36–38; Amber Cooke, "Stripping: Who Calls the Tune?," in Bell, *Good Girls/Bad Girls*, 92–99; Cathy, "Unveiling," 118–19. Linda Williams mentions the enthusiasm of lesbian performers in lesbian pornography, in "Pornographies On/scene," 253.

103. English, "The Politics of Porn," 22; also see Webster, "Pornography and Pleasure," 49; St. James, "The Reclamation of Whores"; Biermann, "Feminism: 'Crunch Point,'" 170; Gail Pheterson, "Feminism: 'Crunch Point,'" in Pheterson, *A Vindication of the Rights of Whores*, 150, 168; Valentino and Johnson, "On the Game and On the Move," 21. Bell quotes one sex worker as saying, "Feminism is incomplete without us," from Laurie Bell, "Introduction," in Bell, *Good Girls/Bad Girls*, 17.

104. Willis, "Feminism, Moralism, and Pornography," 462–63; Rubin, "Misguided, Dangerous, and Wrong," 25, 29–34; Soble, *Pornography, Marxism, Feminism*, 16–17, 19–20; Rubin, in English et al., "Talking Sex," 57, 60.

105. See Beatrice Faust, *Women, Sex, and Pornography* (New York: Macmillan, 1980).

106. See Rubin and English, in English et al., "Talking Sex"; Wendy McElroy, *XXX: A Woman's Right to Pornography* (New York: St. Martin's Press, 1995); Loretta Loach, "Bad Girls: Women Who Use Pornography," in Segal and McIntosh, *Sex Exposed*, 266–74; Walkowitz, "The Politics of Prostitution"; also see Judith Walkowitz, "Male Vice and Female Virtue: Feminism and the Politics of Prostitution in Nineteenth-Century Britain," in Snitow et al., *Powers of Desire*, 419–38; Brownworth, "The Porn Boom"; Smart, "Unquestionably a Moral Issue," 198.

107. Susan G. Cole, "Sexual Politics: Contradictions and Explosions," in Bell, *Good Girls/Bad Girls*, 35–36; Sprinkle, "Feminism: 'Crunch Point,'" 146–47.

108. Alexander, "Prostitution," 203–4, 206; also see St. James, "The Reclamation of

Whores," 84; Verbeek and van der Zijden, "The Red Thread," 300. For some conceptual and normative concerns about ascribing promiscuity to all prostitutes, see chapter 2, "Only a Numbers Game?"

109. Alexander, "Update on HIV Infection and Prostitute Women," 132–37; Alexander, "Prostitutes Are Being Scapegoated for Heterosexual AIDS," 248–63; Pheterson, "The Social Consequences of Unchastity," 226–27; also see Allen M. Brandt, *No Magic Bullet: A Social History of Venereal Disease in the United States since 1880* (New York: Oxford University Press, 1985).

110. Pheterson, "The Social Consequences of Unchastity," 215–17, 219–20; Cathy, "From the Floor," in Bell, *Good Girls/Bad Girls*, 119; Valentino and Johnson, "On the Game and On the Move," 26; St. James, "The Reclamation of Whores," 85; Tong, *Women, Sex, and the Law,* 56.

111. See Mercer, "Just Looking for Trouble," 94; Rubin, in English et al., "Talking Sex," 52–53; also see Biermann, "Feminism: 'Crunch Point,'" 169–70; Tong, *Women, Sex, and the Law,* 48; Walkowitz, "The Politics of Prostitution," 125; Valentino and Johnson, "On the Game and On the Move," 22; Scott et al. (CORP), "Realistic Feminists," 204–17; Marie Arrington, "Community Organizing," and Participant 1, "From the Floor," in Bell, *Good Girls/Bad Girls,* 106, 188; also see Valerie Jenness, *Making It Work: The Prostitutes' Rights Movement in Perspective* (New York: Aldene de Gruyter, 1993).

112. See *Los Angeles Times* front page stories, 9–11 August 1993; *People* magazine, 23 August 1993.

113. Such issues may be reflected in the affiliation of such organizations as the English Collective of Prostitutes with the International Wages for Housework Campaign. See Lopez-Jones, "Workers," 271; also see St. James, "The Reclamation of Whores," 82; Segal, "Sweet Sorrows," 86–87.

114. See Lopez-Jones, "Workers," 272.

115. Betty Friedan, quoted in Carla Freccero, "Notes of a Post–Sex Wars Theorizer," in *Conflicts in Feminism,* ed. Marianne Hirsch and Evelyn Fox Keller (New York: Routledge, 1990), 307; also see Participant 5, "From the Floor," in Bell, *Good Girls/Bad Girls,* 53; Alexander, "Prostitution," 198, 200, 205, 206; West, "U.S. PROStitutes Collective," 283; Valentino and Johnson, "On the Game and On the Move," 28; L, in Millett, "Prostitution"; Carol J. Clover, "Introduction," in Gibson and Gibson, *Dirty Looks,* 17.

116. Cooke with Bell, "Sex Trade Workers and Feminists," 202.

117. Statistics from Alexander, "Prostitution," 196–97; also see St. James, "The Reclamation of Whores," 81–82; Arrington, "Under the Gun," 174.

118. Alexander, "Prostitutes Are Being Scapegoated for Heterosexual AIDS," 258; Alexander, "Prostitution," 191–92, 196–98, 206–12; Tong, *Women, Sex, and the Law,* 57; St. James, "The Reclamation of Whores," 110–11.

119. See Scott et al. (CORP), "Realistic Feminists," 204; Alexander, "Prostitution," 189; Veronica Vera and Terry van der Zijden, "Feminism: 'Crunch Point,'" in Pheterson, *A Vindication of the Rights of Whores,* 148, 160–61; Cooke with Bell, "Sex Trade Workers and Feminists," 197, 201; Robin Abcarian, "In the Parallel Universe, Posing for *Playboy* Is . . . OK," *Los Angeles Times,* 14 May 1995; also see Flori Lille and Margot Alvarez, "Feminism: 'Crunch Point,'" in Pheterson, *A Vindication of the Rights of Whores,* 161–63.

120. See Cooke with Bell, "Sex Trade Workers and Feminists," 193–95; Pheterson, "Not Repeating History," 27.

121. Pat Califia, "Feminism and Sadomasochism," *Heresies* #12 "Sex Issue," 3, no. 4 (1981): 32; Catharine A. MacKinnon, "Sexuality, Pornography, and Method: 'Pleasure under Patriarchy,'" in Sunstein, *Feminism and Political Theory,* 219, 222; also see 216–17, 223.

122. MacKinnon, "Sexuality, Pornography, and Method," 233; Candida Royalle, quoted in

Denfeld, *The New Victorians*, 117; also see "World Charter for Prostitutes' Rights" and Pheterson, "Feminism: 'Crunch Point,'" 41, 154.

123. Carse, "Pornography," 170; also see Burstyn, *Women against Censorship*; Duggan and Hunter, *Sex Wars*; Robin Gorna, "Delightful Visions: From Anti-Porn to Eroticizing Safer Sex," in Segal and McIntosh, *Sex Exposed*, 169–83; Tong, "Women, Pornography, and the Law," 310–11; Tong, *Women, Sex, and the Law*, 6–7; Susan G. Cole, "A View from Another Country," in Leidholdt and Raymond, *The Sexual Liberals*, 194–95; Wendy Kaminer, "Pornography and the First Amendment: Prior Restraints and Private Action," in Lederer, *Take Back the Night*, 241–47; Boyle and Noonan, "Gender Neutrality, Prostitution and Pornography," 46–47.

124. See Joan Nestle, "Lesbians and Prostitutes: A Historical Sisterhood," in Bell, *Good Girls/Bad Girls*, 131–45; Gillian Rodgerson, "Lesbian Erotic Explorations," in Segal and McIntosh, *Sex Exposed*, 275–79; Gorna, "Delightful Visions," 180–81; Loach, "Bad Girls," 266–74; also see Brownworth, "The Porn Boom"; Lisa Henderson, "Lesbian Pornography: Cultural Transgression and Sexual Demystification," in *New Lesbian Criticism: Literary and Cultural Readings*, ed. Sally Munt (New York: Columbia University Press, 1992), 173–91. For a fascinating discussion of lesbian and bisexual pornography, see Williams, "Pornographies On/scene," 251–62.

125. See Tong, *Women, Sex, and the Law*, 24, and Pateman, "Defending Prostitution," 562. Catharine MacKinnon remarks, "Perhaps a human being, for gender purposes, is someone who controls the social definition of sexuality." *Feminism Unmodified*, 158.

126. MacKinnon, *Feminism Unmodified*, 193. The organization known as Lesbians of Colour contend that pornography has a political history as a tool for the control of slaves, Catholics, and Jews. See Lesbians of Colour, "Racism in Pornography," in Bell, *Good Girls/Bad Girls*, 62; also see Andrea Dworkin, *Pornography*, xxxvi.

127. Valerie Scott, "From the Floor," in Bell, *Good Girls/Bad Girls*, 121.

128. McClintock, "Gonad the Barbarian," 113.

129. See Speakers 1, 4, and 11, "'The Big Divide': Feminist Reactions," in Pheterson, *A Vindication of the Rights of Whores*, 178, 179, 190; Cole, "Sexual Politics," 35–36.

130. Alice Walker, "Coming Apart," in Lederer, *Take Back the Night*, 95–100; Mayall and Russell, "Racism in Pornography," 177.

131. Lopez-Jones, "Workers," 276.

132. See Tracey A. Gardner, "Racism in Pornography and the Women's Movement," in Lederer, *Take Back the Night*, 105–14; Walker, "Coming Apart"; Lesbians of Colour, "Racism in Pornography"; Collins, "Pornography and Black Women's Bodies"; Mayall and Russell, "Racism in Pornography"; also see Alexander, "Prostitution," 196.

133. See Arrington, "Under the Gun," 174.

134. Quoted in Lederer, "Then and Now," 68.

135. Diamond, "Pornography and Repression," 701.

136. Cooke with Bell, "Sex Trade Workers and Feminists," 199.

137. Ibid., 198–201; also see Biermann, "Feminism: 'Crunch Point,'" 169–70, 172.

138. See Soble, *Pornography, Marxism, Feminism*, 22–37, 103–49.

139. Stoller, *Porn*, 223; also see Lynda Nead, "The Female Nude: Pornography, Art, and Sexuality," in Segal and McIntosh, *Sex Exposed*, 293–94.

140. For example, see Kimmel, *Men Confront Pornography*; Stoltenberg, "Pornography and Freedom"; Van F. White, "Pornography and Pride," and Martin Duphresne, "Getting Off on Sexploitation," in Russell, *Making Violence Sexy*, 105–6, 107–10.

141. See Russell, *Sexual Exploitation*; Barry, *Female Sexual Slavery*, 45–136; see also chapter 5 in this book.

142. Clover, "Introduction," 3–4; Denfeld, *The New Victorians*, 103–4, 108.

143. A similar theme is adopted by Mariana Valverde in "Too Much Heat, Not Enough Light," in Bell, *Good Girls/Bad Girls*, 32; also see Valverde, *Sex, Power, and Pleasure*, 34–46. Lynne Segal challenges antipornography feminists both to refuse men's sexual objectification of women and to construct a woman-identified sexual subjectivity, in the section entitled "My Generation" from *Straight Sex: Rethinking the Politics of Pleasure* (Berkeley: University of California Press, 1994).

Chapter 5

1. This is not to deny the existence of pervasive and often brutal violence against women worldwide. See Marilyn French, *The War against Women* (New York: Ballentine Books, 1992), 179–207. Those who characterize sexual violence against women as epidemic in the United States include Florence Rush, *The Best-Kept Secret: The Sexual Abuse of Children* (Blue Ridge Summit, Penn.: TAB Books, 1980), 5; Diana E. H. Russell, *Sexual Exploitation: Rape, Child Sexual Abuse, and Workplace Harassment* (Newbury Park, Calif.: Sage Publications, 1984), 62. For recent feminist overviews and critical discussion of women's sexual victimization, also see Diana E. H. Russell, *Rape in Marriage* (New York: Macmillan, 1982) and *The Secret Trauma* (New York: Basic Books, 1986); Jill Radford and Diana E. H. Russell, *Femicide: The Politics of Woman Killing* (New York: Macmillan, 1990); Lenore Walker, *The Battered Woman Syndrome* (New York: Springer Publishing, 1984); Kersti Yllö and Michele Bograd, eds., *Feminist Perspectives on Wife Abuse* (Newbury Park, Calif.: Sage Publications, 1988); Judith Lewis Herman, *Father-Daughter Incest* (Cambridge: Harvard University Press, 1981); Louise Armstrong, *Kiss Daddy Goodnight* (New York: Hawthorn Press, 1978) and *Kiss Daddy Goodnight: Ten Years Later* (New York: Pocket Books, 1987).

2. See Russell, *Sexual Exploitation*, 143, 253, 265; Barrie Levy, ed., *Dating Violence: Young Women in Danger* (Seattle: Seal Press, 1991), 8; Julie A. Allison and Lawrence S. Wrightsman, *Rape: The Misunderstood Crime* (Newbury Park, Calif.: Sage Publications, 1993), ix, 34; French, *The War against Women*, 194; Del Martin, *Battered Wives* (Volcano, Calif.: Volcano Press, 1976, 1981), 19–20; Rush, *The Best-Kept Secret*, 2; Larry L. Tifft, *Battering of Women: The Failure of Intervention and the Case for Prevention* (Boulder, Colo.: Westview Press, 1993), 12.

3. For example, see Russell, *Sexual Exploitation*; French, *The War against Women*; Susan Schechter, *Women and Male Violence: The Visions and Struggles of the Battered Women's Movement* (Boston: South End Press, 1982). For arguments that men are violated and victimized to a far greater extent than feminists allow and that the power of patriarchy to victimize women is overblown and overstated, see Warren Farrell, *The Myth of Male Power* (New York: Simon & Schuster, 1993); also see Alan M. Dershowitz, "Wives Also Kill Husbands—Quite Often," *Los Angeles Times*, 21 July 1994; Cathy Young, "The Sexist Violence against Women Act," *Wall Street Journal*, 23 March 1994; Christina Hoff Sommers, *Who Stole Feminism?: How Women Have Betrayed Women* (New York: Simon & Schuster, 1994), chaps. 1, 9, 10, and 11; Katie Roiphe, *The Morning After: Sex, Fear, and Feminism on Campus* (Boston: Little, Brown, 1993), 8–112.

4. French, *The War against Women*, 195. As late as 1991, it was easier to convict a car thief than a rapist, and officers were more likely to arrest a man for parking tickets than for beating his wife. See Ola W. Barnett and Alyce D. LaViolette, *It Could Happen to Anyone: Why Battered Women Stay* (Newbury Park, Calif.: Sage Publications, 1993), 37.

5. See Louise Armstrong, "Making an Issue of Incest," and Ann Jones, "Family Matters," in *The Sexual Liberals and the Attack on Feminism*, ed. Dorchen Leidholdt and Janice G. Raymond (New York: Teachers College Press, 1990), 49, 63.

6. For a variety of feminist analyses of women's sexual victimization from this perspective, see Susan Brownmiller, *Against Our Will: Men, Women, and Rape* (New York: Bantam Books,

1975); Diana E. H. Russell, *The Politics of Rape* (New York: Stein & Day, 1975); Susan Griffin, "Rape: The All-American Crime," *Ramparts* (September 1971), reprinted in *Feminism and Philosophy*, ed. Mary Vetterling-Braggin, Frederick A. Elliston, and Jane English (Totowa, N.J.: Littlefield, Adams, 1978), 313–32; Kathleen Barry, *Female Sexual Slavery* (Englewood Cliffs, N.J.: Prentice Hall, 1979); Catharine A. MacKinnon, *Sexual Harassment of Working Women* (New Haven: Yale University Press, 1979) and *Feminism Unmodified: Discourses on Life and Law* (Cambridge: Harvard University Press, 1987); Schechter, *Women and Male Violence*; Allison and Wrightsman, *Rape*; Martin, *Battered Wives*; Tifft, *Battering of Women*; Barnett and LaViolette, *It Could Happen to Anyone*; Rush, *The Best-Kept Secret*; Armstrong, *Kiss Daddy Goodnight*; Russell, *Sexual Exploitation*; French, *The War against Women*; Sandra Butler, *Conspiracy of Silence: The Trauma of Incest* (Volcano, Calif.: Volcano Press, 1978, 1985); Judith Lewis Herman, *Trauma and Recovery* (New York: Basic Books, 1992); Valerie Heller, "Sexual Liberalism and Survivors of Sexual Abuse," in Leidholdt and Raymond, *The Sexual Liberals*, 157–61; R. Emerson Dobash and Russell Dobash, *Violence against Wives: A Case against the Patriarchy* (New York: Free Press, 1979).

7. Christina Sommers, Camille Paglia, Katie Roiphe, and Rene Denfeld are examples of contemporary feminists with diverse philosophical views about sex and sexuality; yet they share a skepticism of the ways in which radical feminism characterizes the sexual intimidation of the modern American woman. See Sommers, *Who Stole Feminism?*, chaps. 1, 9, 10, and 11; Christina Sommers, "Feminist Philosophers Are Oddly Unsympathetic to the Women They Claim to Represent," *Chronicle of Higher Education*, 11 October 1989, and "Do These Feminists Like Women?," *Journal of Social Philosophy* 21 (fall/winter 1990): 66–74; Camille Paglia, *Sex, Art, and American Culture* (New York: Vintage Books, 1992), 46–74, and *Vamps and Tramps: New Essays* (New York: Vintage Books, 1994), 24–67, 188–90, 250–76; Roiphe, *The Morning After*, 8–112; Rene Denfeld, *The New Victorians: A Young Woman's Challenge to the Old Feminist Order* (New York: Warner Books, 1995), 1–21, 58–89. A discussion and critique of these authors' views are included in this chapter.

8. Marilyn Frye, *The Politics of Reality: Essays in Feminist Theory* (Trumansburg, N.Y.: Crossing Press, 1983), 7.

9. See especially Brownmiller, *Against Our Will*, and Griffin, "Rape"; Schechter, *Women and Male Violence*; Tifft, *Battering of Women*; Denise Ganache, "Domination and Control: The Social Context of Dating Violence," in Levy, *Dating Violence*, 69–83; also see Lorenne M. G. Clark and Debra J. Lewis, "Rapists and Other Normal Men," in their *Rape: The Price of Coercive Sexuality* (Toronto: Canadian Women's Educational Press, 1977); Susan Rae Peterson, "Coercion and Rape: The State as a Male Protection Racket," in Vetterling-Braggin et al., *Feminism and Philosophy*, 365–66; MacKinnon, *Feminism Unmodified*, 81–84, 85–92.

10. See Peterson, "Coercion and Rape," 368–70. For discussion of the gender politics of masculinity, see Harry Brod, ed., *The Making of Masculinities: The New Men's Studies* (Boston: Allen & Unwin, 1987); Larry May and Robert Strikwerda, eds., *Rethinking Masculinity: Philosophical Explorations in Light of Feminism* (Lanham, Md.: Rowman & Littlefield, 1992); Kenneth Clatterbaugh, ed., *Contemporary Perspectives on Masculinity: Men, Women, and Politics in Modern Society*, 2d ed. (Boulder, Colo.: Westview Press, 1996).

11. It is an interesting statistic that three-quarters or more of the sexual abuse of boys may be perpetrated by men, not women, whereas 95 percent of the sexual abuse of girls may be perpetrated by men. See Russell, *Sexual Exploitation*, 228–31, for speculations as to why sexual abuse perpetrated by women is relatively rare. For more on the sexual abuse of boys, see Mike Lew, *Victims No Longer: Men Recovering from Incest and Other Sexual Child Abuse* (New York: HarperCollins, 1988); Mic Hunter, *Abused Boys: The Neglected Victims of Sexual Abuse* (New York: Fawcett Columbine, 1990).

12. Ellen Frankel Paul, "Bared Buttocks and Federal Cases," in *Sexual Harassment: Con-*

frontations and Decisions, ed. Edmund Wall (Buffalo, N.Y.: Prometheus Books, 1992), 152–54; Rosemarie Tong, *Women, Sex, and the Law* (Savage, Md.: Rowman & Littlefield, 1984), 71.

13. See Edmund Wall, "Introduction," and "The Definition of Sexual Harassment," in Wall, *Sexual Harassment,* 11–12, 75.

14. See Nancy Tuana, "Sexual Harassment in Academe: Issues of Power and Coercion," in Wall, *Sexual Harassment,* 54–56.

15. See Stephanie Riger, "Gender Dilemmas in Sexual Harassment Policies and Procedures," in Wall, *Sexual Harassment,* 199–200; Susan L. Webb, *Step Forward: Sexual Harassment in the Workplace/What You Need to Know!* (New York: MasterMedia Limited, 1991), 25–35; MacKinnon, *Sexual Harassment,* 32.

16. See John H. Bogart, "On the Nature of Rape," in *Philosophical Perspectives on Sex and Love,* ed. Robert M. Stewart (New York: Oxford University Press, 1995), 169–73.

17. See Martin Eskenazi and David Gallen, *Sexual Harassment: Know Your Rights!* (New York: Carroll & Graf, 1992); William Petrocelli and Barbara Kate Repa, *Sexual Harassment on the Job* (Berkeley: Nolo Press, 1992); William L. Woerner and Sharon L. Oswald, "Sexual Harassment in the Workplace: A View through the Eyes of the Courts," in Wall, *Sexual Harassment,* 171–81; Riger, "Gender Dilemmas," 199–200.

18. See Tong, *Women, Sex, and the Law,* 125–26; Russell, *Rape in Marriage,* 101. For the practical and theoretical advantages and disadvantages of subsuming rape under crimes of assault, see Tong, *Women, Sex, and the Law,* 112–19; also see Allison and Wrightsman, *Rape,* 87–97.

19. See David B. Sugarman and Gerald T. Hotaling, "Dating Violence: A Review of Contextual and Risk Factors," in Levy, *Dating Violence,* 100–18; also see B. R. Burkhart and M. E. Fromuth, "Individual and Social Psychological Understanding of Sexual Coercion," in their *Sexual Coercion: A Sourcebook on Its Nature, Causes, and Prevention* (Lexington, Mass.: Lexington Press, 1991).

20. See Russell, *Sexual Exploitation,* 177, 189, 251–52; Sandra Butler, *Conspiracy of Silence,* 16.

21. Sandra Lee Bartky, *Femininity and Domination: Studies in the Phenomenology of Oppression* (New York: Routledge, 1990), 17.

22. For example, see Allison and Wrightsman, *Rape,* chaps. 2, 3, 4, and 5; Webb, *Step Forward,* chap. 2.

23. See French, *The War against Women,* 136.

24. See Wall, "The Definition of Sexual Harassment," 74; MacKinnon, *Sexual Harassment,* 171–72.

25. See Tuana, "Sexual Harassment in Academe," 51; Eskenazi and Gallen, *Sexual Harassment,* 14; MacKinnon, *Sexual Harassment,* 27; Tong, *Women, Sex, and the Law,* 66.

26. For some of the variety and complexity in African American women's reactions to, and experiences of, sexual harassment, see Geneva Smitherman, ed., *African American Women Speak Out on Anita Hill–Clarence Thomas* (Detroit: Wayne State University Press, 1995). On the illusion of objectivity in legal tests of reasonableness, see Nancy S. Ehrenreich, "Pluralist Myths and Powerless Men: The Ideology of Reasonableness in Sexual Harassment Law," in Wall, *Sexual Harassment,* esp. 246–48; also see Tong, *Women, Sex, and the Law,* 165–66.

27. MacKinnon, *Sexual Harassment,* 51–54.

28. See Tong, *Women, Sex, and the Law,* 186, 188–89; Celia Kitzinger, "Anti-Lesbian Harassment," in *Rethinking Sexual Harassment,* ed. Clare Brant and Yun Lee Too (London: Pluto Press, 1994), 125–47.

29. MacKinnon, *Sexual Harassment,* 156–58, 173; MacKinnon, *Feminism Unmodified,* 46–62, 85–92.

30. Judith Lewis Herman, *Trauma and Recovery,* 53. In another part of the same work

(p. 57), Herman refers to rape as the "physical, psychological, and moral violation of the person" intentionally designed to produce psychological trauma. Carolyn M. Shafer and Marilyn Frye, "Rape and Respect," in Vetterling-Braggin et al., *Feminism and Philosophy*, 339; Bogart, "On the Nature of Rape," 172; Jacquelyn Dowd Hall, "'The Mind That Burns in Each Body': Women, Rape, and Racial Violence," in *Powers of Desire: The Politics of Sexuality*, ed. Ann Snitow, Christine Stansell, and Sharon Thompson (New York: Monthly Review Press, 1983), 342.

31. MacKinnon, *Feminism Unmodified*, 87–88, 92.

32. See Pamela Foa, "What's Wrong with Rape?," in Vetterling-Braggin et al., *Feminism and Philosophy*, 351–52.

33. See Tong, *Women, Sex, and the Law*, 90, 92; Griffin, "Rape," 326–27; Brownmiller, *Against Our Will*, 447, 450.

34. See Tong, *Women, Sex, and the Law*, 94–96; Allison and Wrightsman, *Rape*, 89–92. Catharine MacKinnon notes, "[O]nly male ideas of what sexually violates us as women, are illegal" (*Feminism Unmodified*, 90).

35. See Tong, *Women, Sex, and the Law*, 94, 106–9; Allison and Wrightsman, *Rape*, 55, 171–74; Kathryn Larsen, *Life after Rape: Survivors Speak Healing Words for All* (Louisville, Ky.: Butler Book Publishing Services, 1990), 25, 34. For testimonials of the profound long-term effects of rape on the lives of rape victims, see Larsen, *Life After Rape*, and Cynthia Carasella, ed., *Who's Afraid of the Dark?: A Forum of Truth, Support, and Assurance for Those Affected by Rape* (New York: HarperCollins, 1995).

36. Allison and Wrightsman, *Rape*, 52, 122, 125, 138–44, 194; French, *The War against Women*, 193, 194; Larsen, *Life after Rape*, 26, 28, 56; Martin, *Battered Wives*, 72–86.

37. See Allison and Wrightsman, *Rape*, 208–18; Tong, *Women, Sex, and the Law*, 115–16; MacKinnon, *Feminism Unmodified*, 86–88, 91.

38. See Tong, *Women, Sex, and the Law*, 107; Griffin, "Rape," 320.

39. Russell, *Sexual Exploitation*, 117–19; Allison and Wrightsman, *Rape*, 12–13, 29–33, 77–84; MacKinnon, *Feminism Unmodified*, 85–92; Py Bateman, "The Context of Date Rape," in Levy, *Dating Violence*, 95.

40. See Tong, *Women, Sex, and the Law*, 189–90; Martin, *Battered Wives*, 66; also see Larry Lobel, ed., *Naming the Violence: Speaking Out about Lesbian Battering* (Seattle: Seal Press, 1986).

41. See Tong, *Women, Sex, and the Law*, 166–69; MacKinnon, *Feminism Unmodified*, 82; Griffin, "Rape," 324, 327–29; Allison and Wrightsman, *Rape*, 52–54; Hall, "'The Mind That Burns in Each Body,'" 328–49; Tracey A. Gardner, "Racism in Pornography and the Women's Movement," in *Take Back the Night: Women on Pornography*, ed. Laura Lederer (New York: William Morrow, 1980), 105–14; Angela Davis, *Women, Race and Class* (New York: Random House, 1983), 172–201; Valerie Smith, "Split Affinities: The Case of Interracial Rape," in *Conflicts in Feminism*, ed. Marianne Hirsch and Evelyn Fox Keller (New York: Routledge, 1990), 271–87.

42. See Barrie Levy, "Introduction," in Levy, *Dating Violence*, 6; Ganache, "Domination and Control," 72; Schechter, *Women and Male Violence*, 232–38; Tong, *Women, Sex, and the Law*, 170–72; also see Evelyn C. White, "The Abused Black Woman: Challenging a Legacy of Pain," in Levy, *Dating Violence*, 84–93, and *Chain Chain Change: For Black Women Dealing with Physical and Emotional Abuse* (Seattle: Seal Press, 1985).

43. Tong, *Women, Sex, and the Law*, 125; Barnett and LaViolette, *It Could Happen to Anyone*, xx–xxiii, 62; also see Tifft, *Battering of Women*, 13, 16, 19, 51–53; Levy, "Introduction," 6–11; Elizabeth A. Stanko, *Intimate Intrusions: Women's Experience of Male Violence* (London: Routledge & Kegan Paul, 1985).

44. See Tong, *Women, Sex, and the Law*, 135, 138; Barnett and LaViolette, *It Could Happen to Anyone*, 40–43, 59–61, 63, 109–10; Kathleen H. Hofeller, *Battered Women, Shattered Lives*

(Saratoga, Calif.: R & E Publishers, 1983), 30–31, 70–75; Leslie Berger, "New Line in Battle over Batterers," *Los Angeles Times*, 13 October 1993; also see Ann Jones, *Women Who Kill* (New York: Holt, Rinehart & Winston, 1980).

45. See Tong, *Women, Sex, and the Law*, 127–28; Levy, "Introduction," 16; also see Ganache, "Domination and Control," 69; Hofeller, *Battered Women*, 49–66; Martin, *Battered Wives*, 25–43.

46. MacKinnon, *Feminism Unmodified*, 160; also see Martin, *Battered Wives*, 69.

47. Ganache, "Domination and Control," 78–79.

48. On the failure of women to report their abuse, see Hofeller, *Battered Women*, 94–95. On lesbian battering, see Lobel, *Naming the Violence*; Suzanne Pharr, *Homophobia: A Weapon of Sexism* (Little Rock, Ark.: Chardon Press, 1988); Minnesota Coalition for Battered Women (MCBW), *Confronting Lesbian Battering: A Manual for the Battered Women's Movement* (St. Paul, Minn.: MCBW, 1990).

49. See Ganache, "Domination and Control," 78–79, 81–83; Levy, "Introduction," 13.

50. See Walker, *The Battered Woman Syndrome*; Barnett and LaViolette, *It Could Happen to Anyone*, 94–101; Judith Lewis Herman, *Trauma and Recovery*, 74–95.

51. Rush, *The Best-Kept Secret*, 2.

52. Sandra Butler, *Conspiracy of Silence*, 32.

53. See Larsen, *Life after Rape*, 63–74; Russell, *Sexual Exploitation*, 185–87; Sandra Butler, *Conspiracy of Silence*, 5–6.

54. See Russell, *Sexual Exploitation*, 153–60, 228–31, 237–38; Sandra Butler, *Conspiracy of Silence*, 58–59, 64–67, 73–74, 79–93.

55. See Rush, *The Best-Kept Secret*, 13–15, 158–69.

56. See Russell, *Sexual Exploitation*, 169–70, 178; Sandra Butler, *Conspiracy of Silence*, 45; Armstrong, "Making an Issue of Incest," 43–44, 54.

57. For example, see the studies by David Finkelhor in *Sexually Victimized Children* (New York: Free Press, 1979); Judith Lewis Herman, *Father-Daughter Incest*; Russell, *Sexual Exploitation*, 173–76, 215–31. On racism and child sexual abuse convictions, see Russell, *Sexual Exploitation*, 174.

58. Larsen, *Life after Rape*, 74; also see Armstrong, "Making an Issue of Incest," 54; Heller, "Sexual Liberalism," 160.

59. Rush, *The Best-Kept Secret*, 9.

60. See Judith Lewis Herman and L. Hirschman, "Father-Daughter Incest," *Signs: Journal of Women in Culture and Society* 2 (1977): 735–56; Judith Lewis Herman, *Trauma and Recovery*, 28–32, 109.

61. See Sandra Butler, *Conspiracy of Silence*, 109–11, 94–125; Armstrong, "Making an Issue of Incest"; Janis Tyler Johnson, *Mothers of Incest Survivors: Another Side of the Story* (Bloomington: Indiana University Press, 1992).

62. Tom Reeves, quoted in Jeffrey Weeks, *Sexuality and Its Discontents: Meanings, Myths and Modern Sexualities* (New York: Routledge, 1985), 227.

63. See Sandra Butler, *Conspiracy of Silence*, 4–5; Rush, *The Best-Kept Secret*, 183–92.

64. Robin Morgan, *The Demon Lover: On the Sexuality of Terrorism* (New York: W. W. Norton, 1989), 23–24, 44, 49–50, 288–320.

65. Bat-Ami Bar On, "Why Terrorism Is Morally Problematic," in *Feminist Ethics*, ed. Claudia Card (Lawrence: University Press of Kansas, 1991), 107–25; Brownmiller, *Against Our Will*, 229. For more analyses on the concept of terrorism, see Michael Walzer, *Just and Unjust Wars: A Moral Argument with Historical Illustrations* (New York: Basic Books, 1977), 197–206; Grant Wardlaw, "The Problem of Defining Terrorism," in his *Political Terrorism: Theory, Tactics, and Counter-Measures* (Cambridge: Cambridge University Press, 1982), 3–17; Carl Wellman, "On Terrorism Itself," *Journal of Value Inquiry* 13 (1979): 250–58.

66. See Tong, *Women, Sex, and the Law,* 70; Wall, "Introduction," 13; Tuana, "Sexual Harassment in Academe," 51.

67. Bartky, *Femininity and Domination,* 18; also see Bar On, "Why Terrorism Is Morally Problematic," 113.

68. See Amber Coverdale Sumrall and Dena Taylor, eds., *Sexual Harassment: Women Speak Out* (Freedom, Calif.: Crossing Press, 1992); Woerner and Oswald, "Sexual Harassment in the Workplace."

69. Griffin, "Rape," 331; Brownmiller, *Against Our Will,* 228, 439, 447; Allison and Wrightsman, *Rape,* 134; also see Russell, *Sexual Exploitation,* 167, who cites the U.S. statistic that one out of every ten female homicides is a rape/murder.

70. Hall, "'The Mind That Burns in Each Body,'" 339.

71. Barry, *Female Sexual Slavery,* 36; also see Larsen, *Life after Rape,* 25, 33.

72. See Russell, *Sexual Exploitation,* 70; also see 69–71, 71–76, and Allison and Wrightsman, *Rape,* 48–49, for a more general discussion of the rape of men by heterosexual and homosexual men. For a discussion of the relevant differences between a female versus male "rape mentality" under conditions of institutionalized male dominance, see Linda LeMoncheck, *Dehumanizing Women: Treating Persons as Sex Objects* (Totowa, N.J.: Rowman & Allanheld, 1985), 88–89.

73. See MacKinnon, *Feminism Unmodified,* 82; Allison and Wrightsman, *Rape,* 2, 171–94; Judith Lewis Herman, *Trauma and Recovery,* 50.

74. Ann Jones, "Family Matters," 64; Barnett and LaViolette, *It Could Happen to Anyone,* viii, xx–xxi; also see Schechter, *Women and Male Violence,* 17, 170–74.

75. See Judith Lewis Herman, *Trauma and Recovery,* 90–91; Barnett and LaViolette, *It Could Happen to Anyone,* 50, 52–59, 103–7; Martin, *Battered Wives,* 76–79; Tong, *Women, Sex, and the Law,* 125–26, 143; Hofeller, *Battered Women,* 15–18, 44, 98; also see the testimonials in the section entitled "Teens and Parents Tell Their Stories" in Levy, *Dating Violence,* 21–66.

76. See Dee L. R. Graham and Edna I. Rawlings, "Bonding with Abusive Dating Partners: Dynamics of Stockholm Syndrome," in Levy, *Dating Violence,* 119–35; Barnett and LaViolette, *It Could Happen to Anyone,* 82–89; Frye, *The Politics of Reality,* 61–76; also see F. M. Ochberg and D. A. Soskin, eds., *Victims of Terrorism* (Boulder, Colo.: Westview Press, 1982).

77. Barnett and LaViolette, *It Could Happen to Anyone,* xxvi, 107–11; also see Hofeller, *Battered Women,* 48; Walker, *The Battered Woman Syndrome;* Steven Morgan, *Conjugal Terrorism: A Psychological and Community Treatment Model of Wife Abuse* (Palo Alto, Calif.: R & E Research Associates, 1981).

78. See Butler, *Conspiracy of Silence,* 32–34, 66–67; Russell, *Sexual Exploitation,* 184; Judith Lewis Herman, *Trauma and Recovery,* 33–50, 86–95; Larsen, *Life after Rape,* 65.

79. Judith Lewis Herman, *Trauma and Recovery,* 33–47, 56. Such symptoms apply to adult victims of rape and woman battering as well; also see Heller, "Sexual Liberalism," 160–61; Rush, *The Best-Kept Secret,* 81.

80. Barry, *Female Sexual Slavery,* 73–82; also see Frye, *The Politics of Reality,* 61–76; Armstrong, "Making an Issue of Incest," 44–49; Sandra Butler, *Conspiracy of Silence,* 120; Rush, *The Best-Kept Secret,* 162.

81. Paul, "Bared Buttocks," 154–55.

82. See Ehrenreich, "Pluralist Myths and Powerless Men," 238–39.

83. See Tong, *Women, Sex, and the Law,* 68–71; Wall, "The Definition of Sexual Harassment," 69–85; Larry May and John C. Hughes, "Is Sexual Harassment Coercive?," in Wall, *Sexual Harassment,* 61–68; Tuana, "Sexual Harassment in Academe," 54–56.

84. See MacKinnon, *Sexual Harassment,* 49, and *Feminism Unmodified,* 112, 114; Tuana, "Sexual Harassment in Academe," 51. For extended discussions of sexual harassment on campus, see Billie Wright Dziech and Linda Weiner, *The Lecherous Professor,* 2d ed. (Urbana:

University of Illinois Press, 1990); Michele A. Paludi, ed., *Ivory Power: Sexual Harassment on Campus* (Albany: State University of New York Press, 1990).

85. MacKinnon, *Sexual Harassment*, 25, 173.

86. For example, see Tong, *Women, Sex, and the Law*, 68–71.

87. See Russell, *Sexual Exploitation*, 274–76.

88. See Tuana, "Sexual Harassment in Academe," 57–58. For overviews of the role of gender and organizational power in sexual harassment, see Barbara A. Gutek, *Sex and the Workplace* (San Francisco: Jossey-Bass, 1985); Dziech and Weiner, *The Lecherous Professor*; Paludi, *Ivory Power*; National Council for Research on Women, *Sexual Harassment: Research and Resources*, 3d ed., written by Deborah L. Siegel and revised by Marina Budhos (New York: National Council for Research on Women, 1995). For discussions of sexual harassment understood as a function of both cultural context and individual experience, see Smitherman, *African American Women Speak Out on Anita Hill–Clarence Thomas*; Brant and Too, *Rethinking Sexual Harassment*; Linda LeMoncheck, "Taunted and Tormented or Savvy and Seductive?: Feminist Discourse on Sexual Harassment," and "Response," in *Sexual Harassment: A Debate*, Linda LeMoncheck and Mane Hajdin (Lanham, Md.: Rowman & Littlefield, 1997).

89. See Tong, *Women, Sex, and the Law*, 91; Bogart, "On the Nature of Rape," 168–80.

90. For changes in evidentiary rules for rape, see Allison and Wrightsman, *Rape*, 199–216. For an excellent discussion of what current rape law reform really means in practice and how victims and defendants fare, see Linda A. Fairstein, *Sexual Violence: Our War against Rape* (New York: Berkley Publishing Group, 1995) and *Sexual Violence: Twenty Years in New York's Sex Crimes Prosecution Unit* (New York: William Morrow, 1993); also see Robin Abcarian, "When a Woman Just Says 'No,'" *Los Angeles Times*, 8 June 1994; René Lynch, "Rapists May Strike Again, and Again, Experts Say," *Los Angeles Times*, 29 May 1994.

91. See Tong, *Women, Sex, and the Law*, 97–104; Allison and Wrightsman, *Rape*, 65; also see MacKinnon, *Feminism Unmodified*, 83–84; Russell, *Sexual Exploitation*, 138–39.

92. See Griffin, "Rape," 315–19; Brownmiller, *Against Our Will*, 346–47; Abcarian, "When a Woman Just Says 'No.'"

93. MacKinnon, *Feminism Unmodified*, 88–89; Russell, *Sexual Exploitation*, 122, 161–64; Allison and Wrightsman, *Rape*, 22.

94. See Bateman, "The Context of Date Rape," 98; Russell, *Sexual Exploitation*, 138; also see Allison and Wrightsman, *Rape*, 71–74; Robert Rosenfeld, "The Burden of Initiation," and Louisa Moon, "Prostitution and Date Rape: The Commodification of 'Consent,'" papers presented at a symposium on the philosophy of sex and love at the Eastern Division meeting of the American Philosophical Association, Boston, Massachusetts, December 1994.

95. Peterson, "Coercion and Rape," 360–61, 367; also see Frye, *The Politics of Reality*, 2–7, 54–57.

96. Frye, *The Politics of Reality*, 56–57.

97. See Russell, *Sexual Exploitation*, 117, 119.

98. See Frye, *The Politics of Reality*, 3. Russell claims that such contradictions create the kind of sexual misunderstandings and hostility extremely conducive to rape. *Sexual Exploitation*, 164; also see Bateman, "The Context of Dating Violence," 97–99.

99. See Allison and Wrightsman, *Rape*, 14–15, 26–27, 61–64, 78–82. For feminist commentary on the ways women are socialized to see nothing wrong with men forcing them into sex, see Paola Tabet, "Hands, Tools, Weapons," *Feminist Issues* 2 (1982): 3–62, and "Imposed Reproduction: Maimed Sexuality," *Feminist Issues* 7 (1987): 3–31. For a discussion of how psychoanalytic theory perpetuates rape myths, see Brownmiller, *Against Our Will*, 350–64.

100. See Frye, *The Politics of Reality*, 61–72. The contention that such seasoning is a fundamental goal and reality of patriarchy is reiterated in Barry, *Female Sexual Slavery*, 78–82,

and Sonia Johnson, "Taking Our Eyes off the Guys," in Leidholdt and Raymond, *The Sexual Liberals*, 56–60.

101. Frye, *The Politics of Reality*, 73–74; also see Graham and Rawlings, "Bonding with Abusive Dating Partners"; Barnett and LaViolette, *It Could Happen to Anyone*, 82–88, 103–7; Tifft, *Battering of Women*, 50–56; Ganache, "Domination and Control," 74; Bateman, "The Context of Dating Violence," 98.

102. See French, *The War against Women*, 189–90; Schechter, *Women and Male Violence*, 3; Martin, *Battered Wives*, 20–21, 279–80; also see Tong, *Women, Sex, and the Law*, 124; Hofeller, *Battered Women*, 2–3.

103. See Tong, *Women, Sex, and the Law*, 136–37, 140, 144, 169–72; Hofeller, *Battered Women*, 18–19, 69–70, 94–95, 97; Barnett and LaViolette, *It Could Happen to Anyone*, xix, 1–9, 16–21, 31–37; Schechter, *Women and Male Violence*, 24; also see White, "The Abused Black Woman," 92–93.

104. See Tong, *Women, Sex, and the Law*, 145–49; Schechter, *Women and Male Violence*, 170–74; Martin, *Battered Wives*, 57–59, 270–71.

105. See Russell, *Sexual Exploitation*, 172; also see Finkelhor, *Sexually Victimized Children*, 2, quoted in Russell with her analysis, in *Sexual Exploitation*, 266–68; also see Rush, *The Best-Kept Secret*, 2; Kate Millett, "Beyond Politics?: Children and Sexuality," in *Pleasure and Danger: Exploring Female Sexuality*, ed. Carole S. Vance (London: Pandora Press, 1989), 222–23.

106. See Sandra Butler, *Conspiracy of Silence*, 4, 46–48, 94–125; Judith Lewis Herman, *Father-Daughter Incest*, 27, quoted in Russell, *Sexual Exploitation*, 248; Rush, *The Best-Kept Secret*, 147.

107. See Russell, *Sexual Exploitation*, 228–31. Judith Lewis Herman points out that the majority of child sexual abuse victims do not become perpetrators. See *Trauma and Recovery*, 113, 114.

108. See Russell, *Sexual Exploitation*, 242–43, 263–64; Armstrong, "Making an Issue of Incest," 44, 51–52; Sandra Butler, *Conspiracy of Silence*, 90–91; Rush, *The Best-Kept Secret*, 99, 134–41, 162–64, 193–94.

109. Rush, *The Best-Kept Secret*, 104, 14–15, 80, 138, 143, 145; Armstrong, "Making an Issue of Incest," 51; Sandra Butler, *Conspiracy of Silence*, 9–11, 34–36, 211–12; Judith Lewis Herman, *Trauma and Recovery*, 10–20. For some of the ways in which adults' recovered memories of their childhood abuse are meeting with resistance and backlash, see Louise Armstrong, *Rocking the Cradle of Sexual Politics: What Happened When Women Said Incest* (Reading, Mass.: Addison-Wesley, 1994).

110. For example, see Barry, *Female Sexual Slavery*; MacKinnon, *Feminism Unmodified*; Andrea Dworkin, *Right-Wing Women* (New York: Perigee Books, 1983). For an analysis of sex objectification in terms of treating persons as less than moral equals, see LeMoncheck, *Dehumanizing Women*, 26–38.

111. See Ronald K. L. Collins, "Bikini Team: Sexism for the Many," *Los Angeles Times*, 15 November 1991; also see Russell, *Sexual Exploitation*, 275–76; MacKinnon, *Sexual Harassment*, 51.

112. See Nancy Tuana's examples of a professor's crude female drawings, sexist remarks, and ogling female students in class, in "Sexual Harassment in Academe," 57–59; also see Stephanie Riger, who comments that since men typically have more power in organizations, their definition of what counts as sexual harassment is likely to predominate ("Gender Dilemmas," 201); MacKinnon, *Sexual Harassment*, 47–48.

113. MacKinnon, *Feminism Unmodified*, 112; *Sexual Harassment*, 29, 158.

114. Larsen, *Life after Rape*, 13; Brownmiller, *Against Our Will*; Susan Griffin, *Rape: The Power of Consciousness* (San Francisco: Harper & Row, 1979); Tong, *Women, Sex, and the Law*,

90; Peterson, "Coercion and Rape," 362; Shafer and Frye, "Rape and Respect," 341; Bogart, "On the Nature of Rape," 172; Foa, "What's Wrong with Rape?," 350–52.

115. See French, *The War against Women*, 192, 195; also see Russell, *Sexual Exploitation*, 163; Levy, "Introduction," 4–5.

116. See Bar On, "Why Terrorism Is Morally Problematic," 116; Tifft, *Battering of Women*, 50–56, 91–94, and 177, n. 16; also see Tong, *Women, Sex, and the Law*, 126.

117. See Jessica Benjamin, "Master and Slave: The Fantasy of Erotic Domination," in Snitow et al., *Powers of Desire*, 284–85, 288, 292; also see Tifft, *Battering of Women*, 54–56.

118. See Frye, *The Politics of Reality*, 60; Hofeller, *Battered Women*, 19–20; Martin, *Battered Wives*, 8, 85, 273–74; Barnett and LaViolette, *It Could Happen to Anyone*, 1–5; Schechter, *Women and Male Violence*, 231.

119. White, "The Abused Black Woman," 91–92; Martin, *Battered Wives*, 27, 36.

120. David Finkelhor, *Child Sexual Abuse: New Theory and Research* (New York: Free Press, 1984), quoted in Russell, *Sexual Exploitation*, 261; also see Russell, *Sexual Exploitation*, 248–49; Armstrong, *Kiss Daddy Goodnight*, 234–35; Heller, "Sexual Liberalism," 159–60.

121. See Judith Lewis Herman, *Trauma and Recovery*, 105, 109; Sandra Butler, *Conspiracy of Silence*, 142; Rush, *The Best-Kept Secret*, 146; Armstrong, "Making an Issue of Incest," 50; Johnson, "Taking Our Eyes off the Guys," 56–57.

122. See Larsen, *Life after Rape*, 65, 70; Judith Lewis Herman, *Trauma and Recovery*, 51–56, 111; Heller, "Sexual Liberalism," 160; Sandra Butler, *Conspiracy of Silence*, 48; Russell, *Sexual Exploitation*, 55.

123. For example, compare the political liberalism of Christina Sommers in "Do These Feminists Like Women?" to Camille Paglia's sexual libertarian stance in "Madonna II: Venus of the Radio Waves," in *Sex, Art, and American Culture*, 6–13. Broad similarities in critical stance can also be found in Denfeld, *The New Victorians*, 1–21, 25–89; Roiphe, *The Morning After*, 8–112; Christina Sommers, "Philosophers against the Family," in *Person to Person*, ed. George Graham and Hugh LaFollette (Philadelphia: Temple University Press, 1989), 82–105; Sommers, *Who Stole Feminism?*, chaps. 1, 9, 10, and 11; Paglia, *Sex, Art, and American Culture*, 49–74; Paglia, *Vamps and Tramps*, 24–56, 188–90, 250–76.

124. Paul, "Bared Buttocks," 156.

125. See Riger, "Gender Dilemmas," 202, citing J. B. Pryor and J. D. Day, "Interpretations of Sexual Harassment: An Attributional Analysis," *Sex Roles* 18 (1988): 405–17.

126. See Paglia, in *Sex, Art, and American Culture*, 47.

127. Paul, "Bared Buttocks," 156–57; Paglia, *Sex, Art, and American Culture*, 47; also see Paglia, *Vamps and Tramps*, 45–56, 188–90.

128. Kate Walsh, "The Hill on Hillary: What a Bright Girl," *Wall Street Journal*, 5 November 1993; Paglia, *Vamps and Tramps*, 51.

129. See Russell, *Sexual Exploitation*, 279–80; Paglia, *Vamps and Tramps*, 49.

130. J. P. Minson, "Social Theory and Legal Argument: Catharine MacKinnon on Sexual Harassment," in Wall, *Sexual Harassment*, 166–67 and 169, n. 26. For sexual harassment policy guidelines for businesses and academia, see Eskenazi and Gallen, *Sexual Harassment*, 101–5, 108–16; also see Webb, *Step Forward*, 40–51; Petrocelli and Repa, *Sexual Harassment on the Job*, chap. 4; National Council for Research on Women, *Sexual Harassment*, 39–44. For problems with informal dispute-resolution procedures, see Riger, "Gender Dilemmas," 205–7.

131. Roiphe, *The Morning After*, 85–112, 162–63.

132. Ibid., 60–84.

133. Paglia, *Vamps and Tramps*, 251; also see Paglia, *Sexual Personae: Art and Decadence from Nefertiti to Emily Dickinson* (New Haven: Yale University Press, 1990), 1–5.

134. Paglia, *Sex, Art, and American Culture*, 51, 53–54; also see *Vamps and Tramps*, 24–38, 250–76.

135. Quoted in Martin, *Battered Wives*, 150; also see Erik Larson, "Paxton Quigley Shows Her Women Students How to Shoot a Man," *Wall Street Journal*, 4 February 1993; Paxton Quigley, *Armed and Female: Twelve Million Americans Own Guns, Should You?* (New York: St. Martin's Press, 1990).

136. Nigella Lawson, "Rape Is Horrible but Women Are Also Accountable for Their Actions," *Los Angeles Times*, 24 October 1993, excerpted from her article in the *Evening Standard* (London), 20 October 1993.

137. Paglia, *Sex, Art, and American Culture*, 62–65, 74.

138. See Tong, *Women, Sex, and the Law*, 91–92, 109–10, 117–18; H. E. Baber, "How Bad Is Rape?," in *The Philosophy of Sex*, 2d ed., ed. Alan Soble (Savage, Md.: Rowman & Littlefield, 1991), 246–49, 255–56; also see Victor J. Seidler, "Men, Feminism, and Power," in May and Strikwerda, *Rethinking Masculinity*, 209–20.

139. See Roiphe, *The Morning After*, 29–50.

140. See Young, "The Sexist Violence against Women Act"; also see Allison and Wrightsman, *Rape*, 232. On rape prevention and its limitations, see Allison and Wrightsman, *Rape*, 242–59. For an excellent analysis of the consequences of an overemphasis on men's victimization of women (here referred to as "victimism") from a feminist committed to, not critical of, the view that women are sexually oppressed under patriarchy, see Barry, *Female Sexual Slavery*, 37–39; also see Naomi Wolf's distinction between "victim feminism" and "power feminism" in her *Fire with Fire: The New Female Power and How to Use It* (New York: Ballentine Books, 1994), 135–51.

141. See Sommers, *Who Stole Feminism?*, 188–226; Roiphe, *The Morning After*, 51–84.

142. See Barnett and LaViolette, *It Could Happen to Anyone*, 108; Tong, *Women, Sex, and the Law*, 145–46.

143. Paglia, *Vamps and Tramps*, 42–45, 368. The study of "victimology" includes what has been called "victim precipitation theory," which looks at the ways in which victims of violence unconsciously encourage or provoke abuse that they consciously resent. However, many feminists are skeptical of whether such theories take into account the ways in which women can be falsely represented as manipulative and masochistic agents of our own demise. For an overview of psychotherapy for battered women, and its risks, see Martin, *Battered Wives*, 154–59.

144. Sommers, *Who Stole Feminism?*, chap. 9.

145. See Sommers, "Do These Feminists Like Women?" and "Feminist Philosophers Are Oddly Unsympathetic to the Women They Claim to Represent"; also see Sommers, *Who Stole Feminism?*, chaps. 1 and 12; Janet Radcliffe Richards, *The Sceptical Feminist: A Philosophical Enquiry* (Boston: Routledge & Kegan Paul, 1980), chaps. 5 and 10.

146. See Denfeld, *The New Victorians*, 25–57; Sommers, *Who Stole Feminism?*, 19–40.

147. White, "The Abused Black Woman"; also see Cornel West, *Race Matters* (Boston: Beacon Press, 1993).

148. For examples of women's efforts around the world to liberate themselves from male oppression, see French, *The War against Women*, 200–207; also see Robin Morgan, ed., *Sisterhood Is Global* (Garden City, N.Y.: Doubleday, 1984); Amrita Basú, *The Challenge of Local Feminisms: Women's Movements in Global Perspective* (Boulder, Colo.: Westview Press, 1995); Lourdes Torres and Chandra Mohanty, eds., *Third World Women and the Politics of Feminism* (Bloomington: Indiana University Press, 1991). On survival tactics for the battered woman, see Martin, *Battered Wives*, 148–73. On responses to woman battering which aim at reducing her "victim" status, see Barnett and LaViolette, *It Could Happen to Anyone*, 112–31.

149. Sonia Johnson, "Taking Our Eyes off the Guys."

150. See Brownmiller, *Against Our Will*, 449; also see MacKinnon, *Feminism Unmodified*, 85–92, 103–16.

151. In fact, Allison and Wrightsman report that women continue to get contradictory advice about whether and how to resist rape (*Rape*, 246); also see Abcarian, "When a Woman Just Says 'No.'"

152. Robin Morgan, *The Demon Lover*, 322.

153. Frye, *The Politics of Reality*, 76; also see 74–76, 81–82.

154. See Rush, *The Best-Kept Secret*, 142–49; Sandra Butler, *Conspiracy of Silence*, 34, 58–59; Judith Lewis Herman, *Trauma and Recovery*, 41, 59, 69.

155. Judith Lewis Herman, *Trauma and Recovery*, 7–8, 65, 73, 207–11.

156. Barry, *Female Sexual Slavery*, 39–42.

157. Heller, "Sexual Liberalism," 158.

158. For some of the ways in which an ethic of justice is limited in its failure to obligate persons to care about the morally appropriate projects of intimate others, see Jasminka Udovicki, "Justice and Care in Close Relationships," *Hypatia* 8 (summer 1993): 48–60; John Hardwig, "Should Women Think in Terms of Rights?," in *Feminism and Political Theory*, ed. Cass R. Sunstein (Chicago: University of Chicago Press, 1990), 53–67; also see Marilyn Friedman, "The Social Self and the Partiality Debates," in Card, *Feminist Ethics*, 161–79.

159. For a fuller elaboration on an ethic of care, see Nel Noddings, *Caring: A Feminine Approach to Ethics and Moral Education* (Berkeley: University of California Press, 1984); Rita C. Manning, *Speaking from the Heart: A Feminist Perspective on Ethics* (Lanham, Md.: Rowman & Littlefield, 1992); Mary Jeanne Larrabee, ed., *An Ethic of Care: Feminist and Interdisciplinary Perspectives* (New York: Routledge, 1993). For a discussion of how an ethic of justice based on abstract principles of fairness and claims of competing rights may be part of a male-biased moral psychology, see Carol Gilligan, *In a Different Voice: Psychological Theory and Women's Development* (Cambridge: Harvard University Press, 1982). For some perspectives on how an ethic of justice and an ethic of care can work in tandem, see Annette Baier, "What Do Women Want in a Moral Theory?," *Nous* 19 (1985): 53–63; Owen Flanagan and Kathryn Jackson, "Justice, Care and Gender: The Kohlberg-Gilligan Debate Revisited," in Sunstein, *Feminism and Political Theory*, 37–52; Joan Tronto, "Beyond Gender Difference to a Theory of Care," in Larrabee, *An Ethic of Care*, 240–57.

160. See Linda LeMoncheck, "Taunted and Tormented or Savvy and Seductive?"; also see Riger, "Gender Dilemmas," 201–7; E. G. C. Collins and T. B. Blodgett, "Sexual Harassment . . . Some See It . . . Some Won't," *Harvard Business Review* (March/April 1981): 82–93; MacKinnon, *Feminism Unmodified*, 107; Webb, *Step Forward*, 16–17; Ehrenreich, "Pluralist Myths and Powerless Men," 243. For the ways in which an ethic of care can enhance our understanding of the complaints of women who are treated as sex objects, see Linda LeMoncheck, "Feminist Politics and Feminist Ethics: Treating Women as Sex Objects," in Stewart, *Philosophical Perspectives on Sex and Love*, 29–38.

161. Foa, "What's Wrong with Rape?," 357–58.

162. Lawrence Blum, "Compassion," in *Explaining Emotions*, ed. Amelie Rorty (Berkeley: University of California Press, 1980), 513; Tom Regan, "Cruelty, Kindness, and Unnecessary Suffering," *Philosophy* 55 (October 1980): 536, both quoted in Bar On, "Why Terrorism Is Morally Problematic," 118.

163. For example, see Diana E. H. Russell, "Introduction," in Martin, *Battered Wives*, xii, and Tifft, *Battering of Women*, 93, 166–70.

164. See Seidler, "Men, Feminism, and Power," 210, 218–19; also see Allison and Wrightsman, *Rape*, 74–84.

165. Morgan, *The Demon Lover*, 347.

166. Ibid., 341–42; Udovicki, "Justice and Care in Close Relationships," 54–57. For further discussion of how a feminist sexual ethic encourages transforming the notion of power, see LeMoncheck, "Taunted and Tormented or Savvy and Seductive?"

Conclusion

1. Raymond A. Belliotti, *Good Sex: Perspectives on Sexual Ethics* (Lawrence: University Press of Kansas, 1993), 183.

2. Publications that highlight such debates include Naomi Schor and Elizabeth Weed, eds., *The Essential Difference* (Bloomington: Indiana University Press, 1994); Jeffner Allen and Iris Marion Young, eds., *The Thinking Muse: Feminism and Modern French Philosophy* (Bloomington: Indiana University Press, 1989); Nancy Fraser and Sandra Lee Bartky, eds., *Revaluing French Feminism: Critical Essays on Difference, Agency, and Culture* (Bloomington: Indiana University Press, 1992); Louise M. Antony and Charlotte Witt, eds., *A Mind of One's Own: Feminist Essays on Reason and Objectivity* (Boulder, Colo.: Westview Press, 1993); "Analytic Feminism," special issue, *Hypatia* 10 (summer 1995); Marilyn R. Schuster and Susan R. Van Dyne, eds., *Women's Place in the Academy: Transforming the Liberal Arts Curriculum* (Totowa, N.J.: Rowman & Allanheld, 1985); Mary K. Tetreault and Frances A. Maher, *Feminist Classroom: An Inside Look at How Professors and Students Are Transforming Higher Education for a Diverse Society* (New York: Basic Books, 1994); Ann Diller, Barbara Houston, Kathryn Pauly Morgan, and Maryann Ayim, eds., *The Gender Question in Education: Theory, Pedagogy, and Politics* (Boulder, Colo.: Westivew Press, 1996); Daphne Patai and Noretta Koertge, *Professing Feminism: Cautionary Tales from the Strange World of Women's Studies* (New York: Basic Books, 1994); Teresa Brennan, ed., *Between Feminism and Psychoanalysis* (New York: Routledge, 1989); Rita Arditti, Renate Duelli Klein, and Shelley Minden, eds., *Test-Tube Women: What Future for Motherhood?* (London: Pandora Press, 1989); Michelle Stanworth, ed., *Reproductive Technologies: Gender, Motherhood and Medicine* (Minneapolis: University of Minnesota Press, 1987); "More Gender Trouble: Feminism Meets Queer Theory," special issue, *differences: A Journal of Feminist Cultural Studies* 6 (summer–fall 1994).

Select Bibliography

Anthologies

Alexander, M. Jacqui, and Chandra Talpade Mohanty, eds., *Feminist Genealogies, Colonial Legacies, Democratic Futures*. New York: Routledge, 1996.

Allen, Jeffner, and Iris Marion Young, eds. *The Thinking Muse: Feminism and Modern French Philosophy*. Bloomington: Indiana University Press, 1989.

Anzaldúa, Gloria, ed. *Making Face, Making Soul—Haciendo Caras: Creative and Critical Perspectives by Women of Color*. San Francisco: Aunt Lute Press, 1990.

Arthur, John, and Amy Shapiro, eds., *Color, Class, Identity: The New Politics of Race*. Boulder, Colo.: Westview Press, 1996.

Assiter, Alison, and Avedon Carol, eds. *Bad Girls and Dirty Pictures: The Challenge to Reclaim Feminism*. London: Pluto Press, 1993.

Baird, Robert M., and Stuart E. Rosenbaum, eds. *Pornography: Private Right or Public Menace?* Buffalo, N.Y.: Prometheus Books, 1991.

Baker, Robert, and Frederick Elliston, eds. *Philosophy and Sex*. Buffalo, N.Y.: Prometheus Books, 1975; 2d ed., 1984.

Barbach, Lonnie, ed. *Pleasures: Women Write Erotica*. New York: HarperCollins, 1984.

Basú, Amrita, ed. *The Challenge of Local Feminisms: Women's Movements in Global Perspective*. Boulder, Colo.: Westview Press, 1995.

Bell, Laurie, ed. *Good Girls/Bad Girls: Feminists and Sex Trade Workers Face to Face*. Toronto: Seal Press, 1987.

Brant, Clare, and Yun Lee Too, eds. *Rethinking Sexual Harassment*. London: Pluto Press, 1994.

Brennan, Teresa, ed. *Between Feminism and Psychoanalysis*. New York: Routledge, 1989.

Bright, Susie, ed. *Herotica*. Burlingame, Calif.: Down There Press, 1988.

Brod, Harry, ed. *The Making of Masculinities: The New Men's Studies*. Boston: Allen & Unwin, 1987.

Burstyn, Varda, ed. *Women against Censorship*. Vancouver: Douglas & McIntyre, 1985.

Carasella, Cynthia, ed. *Who's Afraid of the Dark?: A Forum of Truth, Support, and Assurance for Those Affected by Rape*. New York: HarperCollins, 1995.

Card, Claudia, ed. *Feminist Ethics*. Lawrence: University Press of Kansas, 1991.

Cherny, Lynn, and Elizabeth Reba Wise, eds. *Wired Women: Gender and New Realities in Cyberspace*. Seattle: Seal Press, 1996.

Chester, Laura, ed. *Deep Down: The New Sensual Writing by Women*. Boston: Faber & Faber, 1989.

Clatterbaugh, Kenneth, ed. *Contemporary Perspectives on Masculinity: Men, Women, and Politics in Modern Society*, 2d ed. Boulder, Colo.: Westview Press, 1996.

Cole, Eve Browning, and Susan Coultrap-McQuin, eds. *Explorations in Feminist Ethics*. Bloomington: Indiana University Press, 1992.

Copp, David, and Susan Wendell, eds. *Pornography and Censorship: Scientific, Philosophical, and Legal Studies*. Buffalo, N.Y.: Prometheus Books, 1983.

Delacoste, Frédérique, and Priscilla Alexander, eds. *Sex Work: Writings by Women in the Sex Industry*. Pittsburgh: Cleis Press, 1987.

Diamond, Irene, and Lee Quinby, eds. *Feminism and Foucault*. Boston: Northeastern University Press, 1988.

Diller, Ann, Barbara Houston, Kathryn Pauly Morgan, and Maryann Ayim, eds. *The Gender Question in Education: Theory, Pedagogy, and Politics*. Boulder, Colo.: Westview Press, 1996.

Ekins, Richard, and David King, eds. *Blending Genders*. New York: Routledge, 1996.

Fee, Elizabeth, and Daniel Fox, eds. *AIDS: The Burden of History*. Berkeley: University of California Press, 1988.

Fraser, Nancy, and Sandra Lee Bartky, eds. *Revaluing French Feminism: Critical Essays on Difference, Agency, and Culture*. Bloomington: Indiana University Press, 1992.

Garry, Ann, and Marilyn Pearsall, eds. *Women, Knowledge, and Reality*. Boston: Unwin Hyman, 1989.

Gibson, Pamela Church, and Roma Gibson, eds. *Dirty Looks: Women, Pornography, Power*. London: BFI Publishing, 1993.

Gould, Carol C., ed. *Beyond Domination: New Perspectives on Women and Philosophy*. Totowa, N.J.: Rowman & Littlefield, 1983.

Grosz, Elizabeth, and Elspeth Robyn, eds. *Sexy Bodies: The Strange Carnalities of Feminism*. New York: Routledge, 1995.

Harding, Sandra, and Merrill Hintikka, eds. *Discovering Reality: Feminist Perspectives on Epistemology, Metaphysics, Methodology, and Philosophy of Science*. Dordrecht, Holland: D. Reidel, 1983.

Hirsch, Marianne, and Evelyn Fox Keller, eds. *Conflicts in Feminism*. New York: Routledge, 1990.

Hull, Gloria T., Patricia Bell Scott, and Barbara Smith, eds. *All the Women Are White, All the Blacks Are Men, but Some of Us Are Brave: Black Women's Studies*. Old Westbury, N.Y.: Feminist Press, 1982.

Hutchins, Loraine, and Lani Kaahumanu, eds. *Bi Any Other Name: Bisexual People Speak Out*. Boston: Alyson Publications, 1991.

Itzin, Catherine, ed. *Pornography: Women, Violence, and Civil Liberties*. New York: Oxford University Press, 1993.

Jaget, Claude, ed. *Prostitutes: Our Life.* Bristol, U.K.: Falling Wall Press, 1980.

Jaggar, Alison M., ed. *Living with Contradictions: Controversies in Feminist Social Ethics.* Boulder, Colo.: Westview Press, 1994.

Jay, Karla, ed. *Lesbian Erotics.* New York: New York University Press, 1995.

Kimmel, Michael, ed. *Men Confront Pornography.* New York: Crown, 1989.

Kittay, Eva Feder, and Diana T. Meyers, eds. *Women and Moral Theory.* Savage, Md.: Rowman & Littlefield, 1987.

Koedt, Anne, Ellen Levine, and Anita Rapone, eds. *Radical Feminism.* New York: Quadrangle Books, 1973.

Larrabee, Mary Jeanne, ed. *An Ethic of Care: Feminist and Interdisciplinary Perspectives.* New York: Routledge, 1993.

Lederer, Laura, ed. *Take Back the Night: Women on Pornography.* New York: William Morrow, 1980.

Leidholdt, Dorchen, and Janice G. Raymond, eds. *The Sexual Liberals and the Attack on Feminism.* New York: Teachers College Press, 1990.

Levy, Barrie, ed. *Dating Violence: Young Women in Danger.* Seattle: Seal Press, 1991.

Linden, Robin Ruth, Darlene R. Pagano, Diana E. H. Russell, and Susan Leigh Star, eds. *Against Sadomasochism: A Radical Feminist Analysis.* San Francisco: Frog in the Well, 1982.

Lobel, Larry, ed. *Naming the Violence: Speaking Out about Lesbian Battering.* Seattle: Seal Press, 1986.

MacNaron, Toni A. H., and Yarrow Morgan, eds. *Voices in the Night: Women Speaking about Incest.* Minneapolis: Cleis Press, 1981.

Marks, Elaine, and Isabelle de Courtivron, eds. *New French Feminisms.* New York: Schocken Books, 1981.

May, Larry, and Robert Strikwerda, eds. *Rethinking Masculinity: Philosophical Explorations in Light of Feminism.* Lanham, Md.: Rowman & Littlefield, 1992.

Moraga, Cherríe, and Gloria Anzaldúa, eds. *This Bridge Called My Back: Writings by Radical Women of Color.* Watertown, Mass.: Persephone Press, 1981.

Morgan, Robin, ed. *Sisterhood Is Global.* Garden City, N.Y.: Doubleday, 1984.

Morton, Donald, ed. *The Material Queer: A LesBiGay Cultural Studies Reader.* Boulder, Colo.: Westview Press, 1996.

Nestle, Joan, ed. *The Persistent Desire: A Femme-Butch Reader.* Boston: Alyson Publications, 1992.

Nicholson, Linda J., ed. *Feminism/Postmodernism.* New York: Routledge, 1990.

Ochberg, F. M., and D. A. Soskin, eds. *Victims of Terrorism.* Boulder, Colo.: Westview Press, 1982.

Ortner, Sheryl, and Harriet Whitehead, eds. *Sexual Meanings: The Cultural Construction of Gender and Sexuality.* New York: Cambridge University Press, 1981.

Paludi, Michele A., ed. *Ivory Power: Sexual Harassment on Campus.* Albany: State University of New York Press, 1990.

Pheterson, Gail, ed. *A Vindication of the Rights of Whores.* Seattle: Seal Press, 1989.

Philips, Eileen, ed. *The Left and the Erotic.* London: Lawrence & Wishart, 1983.

Reti, Irene, ed. *Unleashing Feminism: Sadomasochism in the Gay 90s.* Santa Cruz, Calif.: HerBooks, 1993.

Roberts, Nickie, ed. *The Front Line: Women in the Sex Industry Speak.* London: Grafton Books, 1986.

Russell, Diana E. H., ed. *Making Violence Sexy: Feminist Views on Pornography.* Buckingham, U.K.: Open University Press, 1993.

Ruth, Sheila, ed. *Issues in Feminism: An Introduction to Women's Studies.* Mountain View, Calif.: Mayfield Publishing Company, 1990.

Samois, ed. *Coming to Power: Writings and Graphics on Lesbian S/M.* Boston: Alyson Publications, 1987.

——. *What Color Is My Handkerchief?: A Lesbian S/M Sexuality Reader.* Berkeley: Samois, 1979.

Schneider, Beth E., and Nancy E. Stoller, eds. *Women Resisting AIDS: Feminist Strategies of Empowerment.* Philadelphia: Temple University Press, 1995.

Segal, Lynne, and Mary McIntosh, eds. *Sex Exposed: Sexuality and the Pornography Debate.* New Brunswick, N.J.: Rutgers University Press, 1992.

Slung, Michele, ed. *Slow Hand: Women Writing Erotica.* New York: HarperCollins, 1992.

Smith, Barbara, ed. *Homegirls: A Black Feminist Anthology.* New York: Kitchen Table: Women of Color Press, 1983.

Smitherman, Geneva, ed. *African American Women Speak Out on Anita Hill–Clarence Thomas.* Detroit: Wayne State University Press, 1995.

Snitow, Ann, Christine Stansell, and Sharon Thompson, eds. *Powers of Desire: The Politics of Sexuality.* New York: Monthly Review Press, 1983.

Soble, Alan, ed. *The Philosophy of Sex: Contemporary Readings.* Savage, Md.: Rowman & Littlefield, 1980; 2d ed., 1991.

Solomon, Robert C., and Kathleen M. Higgins, eds. *The Philosophy of (Erotic) Love.* Lawrence: University Press of Kansas: 1991.

Stein, Arlene, ed. *Sisters, Sexperts, Queers: Beyond the Lesbian Nation.* New York: Plume Books, 1993.

Stewart, Robert M., ed. *Philosophical Perspectives on Sex and Love.* New York: Oxford University Press, 1995.

Suleiman, Susan, ed. *The Female Body in Western Culture.* Cambridge: Harvard University Press, 1986.

Sumrall, Amber Coverdale, and Dena Taylor, eds. *Sexual Harassment: Women Speak Out.* Freedom, Calif.: Crossing Press, 1992.

Sunstein, Cass R., ed. *Feminism and Political Theory.* Chicago: University of Chicago Press, 1990.

Thornton, Louise, Jan Sturtevant, and Amber Coverdale Sumrall, eds. *Touching Fire: Erotic Writings by Women.* New York: Carroll & Graf, 1989.

Torres, Lourdes, and Chandra Mohanty, eds. *Third World Women and the Politics of Feminism.* Bloomington: Indiana University Press, 1991.

Tsang, Daniel, ed. *The Age Taboo: Gay Male Sexuality, Power and Consent.* Boston: Alyson Publications, 1981.

Vance, Carole S., ed. *Pleasure and Danger: Exploring Female Sexuality.* London: Pandora Press, 1989.

Verene, D. P., ed. *Sexual Love and Western Morality.* New York: Harper Torchbooks, 1972.

Wall, Edmund, ed. *Sexual Harassment: Confrontations and Decisions.* Buffalo, N.Y.: Prometheus Books, 1992.

Weinberg, Thomas, and G. W. Levi Kamel, eds. *S & M: Studies in Sadomasochism.* Buffalo, N.Y.: Prometheus Books, 1983.

Wise, Elizabeth Reba, ed. *Closer to Home: Bisexuality and Feminism.* Seattle: Seal Press, 1992.

Ylló, Kersti, and Michele Bograd, eds. *Feminist Perspectives on Wife Abuse.* Newbury Park, Calif.: Sage Publications, 1988.

Zillmann, Dolf, and Bryant Jennings, eds. *Pornography: Research Advances and Policy Considerations.* Hillsdale, N.J.: Lawrence Erlbaum, 1989.

Books and Articles

Abcarian, Robin. "In the Parallel Universe, Posing for *Playboy* Is . . . OK." *Los Angeles Times,* 14 May 1995.

——. "When a Woman Just Says 'No.'" *Los Angeles Times,* 8 June 1994.

Abrahamson, Alan. "Coverage of Exotic Entertainers Is Questioned." *Los Angeles Times,* 30 November 1992.

Adams, Jad. *AIDS: The HIV Myth.* New York: St. Martin's Press, 1989.

Adams, Parveen. "Of Female Bondage." In *Between Feminism and Psychoanalysis,* edited by Teresa Brennan, 247–65. New York: Routledge, 1989.

Alcoff, Linda. "Cultural Feminism versus Post-Structuralism: The Identity Crisis in Feminist Theory." In *Feminist Theory in Practice and Process,* edited by Micheline R. Malson, Jean F. O'Barr, Sarah Westphal-Wihl, and Mary Wyer, 295–326. Chicago: University of Chicago Press, 1989.

Alexander, Priscilla. "Prostitutes Are Being Scapegoated for Heterosexual AIDS." In *Sex Work: Writings by Women in the Sex Industry,* edited by Frédérique Delacoste and Priscilla Alexander, 248–63. Pittsburgh: Cleis Press, 1987.

——. "Prostitution: A Difficult Issue for Feminists." In *Sex Work: Writings by Women in the Sex Industry,* edited by Frédérique Delacoste and Priscilla Alexander, 184–214. Pittsburgh: Cleis Press, 1987.

——. "Update on HIV Infection and Prostitute Women." In *A Vindication of the Rights of Whores,* edited by Gail Pheterson, 132–40. Seattle: Seal Press, 1989.

Allison, Dorothy. "Public Silence, Private Terror." In *Pleasure and Danger: Exploring Female Sexuality,* edited by Carole S. Vance, 103–14. London: Pandora Press, 1989.

Allison, Julie A., and Lawrence S. Wrightsman. *Rape: The Misunderstood Crime.* Newbury Park, Calif.: Sage Publications, 1993.

Altman, Dennis. "AIDS: The Politicization of an Epidemic." *Socialist Review* 14 (November–December 1984): 93–109.

——. *AIDS and the Mind of America.* New York: Doubleday, 1985.

Anzaldúa, Gloria. *Borderlands/La Frontera: The New Mestiza.* San Francisco: Spinsters/Aunt Lute, 1987.

Armstrong, Louise. *Kiss Daddy Goodnight.* New York: Hawthorn Press, 1978.

——. *Kiss Daddy Goodnight: Ten Years Later.* New York: Pocket Books, 1987.

——. "Making an Issue of Incest." In *The Sexual Liberals and the Attack on Feminism,* edited by Dorchen Leidholdt and Janice G. Raymond, 43–55. New York: Teachers College Press, 1990.

——. *Rocking the Cradle of Sexual Politics: What Happened When Women Said Incest.* Reading, Mass.: Addison-Wesley, 1994.

Arrington, Marie. "Under the Gun." In *Good Girls/Bad Girls: Feminists and Sex Trade Workers Face to Face,* edited by Laurie Bell, 173–78. Toronto: Seal Press, 1987.

Astuto, Cynthia, and Pat Califia. "Being Weird Is Not Enough: How to Stay Healthy and Play Safe." In *Coming to Power: Writings and Graphics on Lesbian S/M,* edited by Samois, 69–80. Boston: Alyson Publications, 1987.

Atkinson, Ti-Grace. *Amazon Odyssey.* New York: Links, 1974.

Attorney General's Commission on Pornography: Final Report, 1986. Washington: U.S. Department of Justice.

Baber, H. E. "How Bad Is Rape?" In *The Philosophy of Sex,* 2d ed., edited by Alan Soble, 243–58. Savage, Md.: Rowman & Littlefield, 1991.

Baier, Annette. "What Do Women Want in a Moral Theory?" *Nous* 19 (1985): 53–63.

Baker, Karin. "Bisexual Feminist Politics: Because Bisexuality Is Not Enough." In *Closer to Home: Bisexuality and Feminism*, edited by Elizabeth Reba Wise, 255–67. Seattle: Seal Press, 1992.

Baker, Robert. "'Pricks' and 'Chicks': A Plea for Persons." In *Philosophy and Sex*, 2d ed., edited by Robert Baker and Frederick Elliston, 249–67. Buffalo, N.Y.: Prometheus Books, 1984.

Barnett, Ola W., and Alyce D. LaViolette. *It Could Happen to Anyone: Why Battered Women Stay*. Newbury Park, Calif.: Sage Publications, 1993.

Bar On, Bat-Ami. "Feminism and Sadomasochism: Self-Critical Notes." In *Against Sadomasochism: A Radical Feminist Analysis*, edited by Robin Ruth Linden, Darlene R. Pagano, Diana E. H. Russell, and Susan Leigh Star, 72–82. San Francisco: Frog in the Well, 1982.

——. "Why Terrorism Is Morally Problematic." In *Feminist Ethics*, edited by Claudia Card, 107–25. Lawrence: University Press of Kansas, 1991.

Barry, Kathleen. *Female Sexual Slavery*. Englewood Cliffs, N.J.: Prentice Hall, 1979.

——. "On the History of Cultural Sadism." In *Against Sadomasochism: A Radical Feminist Analysis*, edited by Robin Ruth Linden, Darlene R. Pagano, Diana E. H. Russell, and Susan Leigh Star, 51–65. San Francisco: Frog in the Well, 1982.

——. "Sadomasochism: The New Backlash to Feminism." *Trivia* 1 (fall 1982): 77–92.

Bartky, Sandra Lee. *Femininity and Domination: Studies in the Phenomenology of Oppression*. New York: Routledge, 1990.

Bateman, Py. "The Context of Date Rape." In *Dating Violence: Young Women in Danger*, edited by Barrie Levy, 94–99. Seattle: Seal Press, 1991.

Belenky, Mary Field, Blythe McVicker Clinchy, Nancy Rule Goldberger, and Jill Mattuck Tarule. *Women's Ways of Knowing: The Development of Self, Voice, and Mind*. New York: Basic Books, 1986.

Bell, Shannon. "Feminist Ejaculations." In *The Hysterical Male: New Feminist Theory*, edited by Arthur and Marilouise Kroker, 155–69. New York: St. Martin's Press, 1991.

——. *Reading, Writing, and Rewriting the Prostitute Body*. Bloomington: Indiana University Press, 1994.

Belliotti, Raymond A. *Good Sex: Perspectives on Sexual Ethics*. Lawrence: University Press of Kansas, 1993.

Benjamin, Jessica. "Master and Slave: The Fantasy of Erotic Domination." In *Powers of Desire: The Politics of Sexuality*, edited by Ann Snitow, Christine Stansell, and Sharon Thompson, 280–99. New York: Monthly Review Press, 1983.

Berger, Fred R. "Pornography, Feminism, and Censorship." In *Philosophy and Sex*, 2d ed., edited by Robert Baker and Frederick Elliston, 327–51. Buffalo, N.Y.: Prometheus Books, 1984.

Berger, Leslie. "New Line in Battle over Batterers." *Los Angeles Times*, 13 October 1993.

Bernstein, Richard. *Beyond Objectivism and Relativism*. Philadelphia: University of Pennsylvania Press, 1983.

"'The Big Divide': Feminist Reactions to the Second World Whores' Congress." In *A Vindication of the Rights of Whores*, edited by Gail Pheterson, 173–91. Seattle: Seal Press, 1989.

Blum, Lawrence. "Compassion." In *Explaining Emotions*, edited by Amelie Rorty, 507–17. Berkeley: University of California Press, 1980.

——. *Friendship, Altruism and Morality*. London: Routledge & Kegan Paul, 1980.

Bogart, John H. "On the Nature of Rape." In *Philosophical Perspectives on Sex and Love*, edited by Robert M. Stewart, 168–80. New York: Oxford University Press, 1995.

Bordo, Susan. "Feminism, Postmodernism, and Gender-Scepticism." In *Feminism/ Postmodernism*, edited by Linda J. Nicholson, 133–56. New York: Routledge, 1990.

Boyle, Christine, and Sheila Noonan. "Gender Neutrality, Prostitution, and Pornography." In

Good Girls/Bad Girls: Feminists and Sex Trade Workers Face to Face, edited by Laurie Bell, 37–47. Toronto: Seal Press, 1987.

Brandt, Allen M. *No Magic Bullet: A Social History of Venereal Disease in the United States since 1880.* New York: Oxford University Press, 1985.

Branwyn, Gareth. "Compu-Sex: Erotica for Cybernauts." In *Flame Wars: The Discourse of Cyberspace*, edited by Mark Dery, 203–35. Durham, N.C.: Duke University Press, 1994.

Bright, Susie. *Susie Sexpert's Lesbian Sex World.* Pittsburgh: Cleis Press, 1990.

Brod, Harry. "Pornography and the Alienation of Male Sexuality." In *The Philosophy of Sex*, 2d ed., edited by Alan Soble, 281–99. Savage, Md.: Rowman & Littlefield, 1991.

Brownmiller, Susan. *Against Our Will: Men, Women, and Rape.* New York: Bantam Books, 1975.

———. "Women Fight Back." In *Pornography: Private Right or Public Menace?*, edited by Robert M. Baird and Stuart E. Rosenbaum, 36–39. Buffalo, N.Y.: Prometheus Books, 1991.

Brownworth, Victoria A. "The Porn Boom." *Lesbian News* 18, no. 7 (February 1993): 42–43, 61–63.

Bunch, Charlotte. "A Global Perspective on Feminist Ethics and Diversity." In *Explorations in Feminist Ethics*, edited by Eve Browning Cole and Susan Coultrap-McQuin, 176–85. Bloomington: Indiana University Press, 1992.

Burgess, Ann W., and Lynda L. Holstrom. *Rape: Crisis and Recovery.* Bowie, Md.: Robert J. Brady Co., 1979.

Burkhart, B. R., and M. E. Fromuth. *Sexual Coercion: A Sourcebook on Its Nature, Causes, and Prevention.* Lexington, Mass.: Lexington Press, 1991.

Burstyn, Varda. "Who the Hell Is 'We'?" In *Good Girls/Bad Girls: Feminists and Sex Trade Workers Face to Face*, edited by Laurie Bell, 163–72. Toronto: Seal Press, 1987.

Butler, Jerry, as told to Robert Rimmer and Catherine Tavel. *Raw Talent: The Adult Film Industry as Seen by Its Most Popular Male Star.* Buffalo, N.Y.: Prometheus Books, 1990.

Butler, Judith. *Bodies That Matter: On the Discursive Limits of Sex.* New York: Routledge, 1993.

———. *Gender Trouble: Feminism and the Subversion of Identity.* New York: Routledge, 1990.

Butler, Judy. "Lesbian S & M: The Politics of Dis-illusion." In *Against Sadomasochism: A Radical Feminist Analysis*, edited by Robin Ruth Linden, Darlene R. Pagano, Diana E. H. Russell, and Susan Leigh Star, 169–75. San Francisco: Frog in the Well, 1982.

Butler, Sandra. *Conspiracy of Silence: The Trauma of Incest.* Volcano, Calif.: Volcano Press, 1978, 1985.

Califia, Pat. "Feminism and Sadomasochism." *Heresies #12* "Sex Issue" 3, no. 4 (1981): 30–34.

———. *Macho Sluts: Erotic Fiction.* Boston: Alyson Publications, 1988.

———. "Man/Boy Love and the Lesbian Movement." In *The Age Taboo: Gay Male Sexuality, Power and Consent*, edited by Daniel Tsang. Boston: Alyson Publications, 1981.

———. *Melting Point.* Boston: Alyson Publications, 1993.

———. "A Personal View of the History of the Lesbian S/M Community and Movement in San Francisco." In *Coming to Power: Writings and Graphics on Lesbian S/M*, edited by Samois, 245–82. Boston: Alyson Publications, 1987.

———. *Public Sex: The Culture of Radical Sex.* Pittsburgh: Cleis Press, 1994.

———. *Sapphistry: The Book of Lesbian Sexuality.* 2d ed. Tallahassee, Fla.: Naiad Press, 1983.

———. "Unraveling the Sexual Fringe: A Secret Side of Lesbian Sexuality." *The Advocate*, 27 December 1979.

Carol, Avedon. "Snuff: Believing the Worst." In *Bad Girls and Dirty Pictures: The Challenge to Reclaim Feminism*, edited by Alison Assiter and Avedon Carol, 126–30. London: Pluto Press, 1993.

Carse, Alisa L. "Pornography: An Uncivil Liberty?" *Hypatia* 10 (winter 1995): 155–82.

Carter, Angela. *The Sadeian Woman: The Ideology of Pornography*. New York: Pantheon, 1978.

Case, Sue-Ellen. "Toward a Butch-Femme Aesthetic." *Discourse* 2 (fall 1988/winter 1989): 55–73.

Chapkis, Wendy. "Paying for Pleasure." *Women's Review of Books* (April 1995).

Chiaramonte, Lee. "Lesbian Safety and AIDS: The Very Last Fairytale." *Visibilities* (January/February 1988).

Christensen, F. M. *Pornography: The Other Side*. New York: Praeger, 1990.

Clark, Lorenne. "Liberalism and Pornography." In *Pornography and Censorship: Philosophical, Scientific and Legal Studies*, edited by David Copp and Susan Wendell, 45–59. Buffalo, N.Y.: Prometheus Books, 1983.

Clark, Lorenne M. G., and Debra J. Lewis. *Rape: The Price of Coercive Sexuality*. Toronto: Canadian Women's Educational Press, 1977.

Code, Lorraine B. "Is the Sex of the Knower Epistemologically Significant?" *Metaphilosophy* 12 (July–October 1981): 267–76.

———. *What Can She Know?: Feminist Theory and the Construction of Knowledge*. Ithaca, N.Y.: Cornell University Press, 1991.

Cole, Susan G. "Pornography: What Do We Want?" In *Good Girls/Bad Girls: Feminists and Sex Trade Workers Face to Face*, edited by Laurie Bell, 157–62. Toronto: Seal Press, 1987.

———. "Sexual Politics: Contradictions and Explosions." In *Good Girls/Bad Girls: Feminists and Sex Trade Workers Face to Face*, edited by Laurie Bell, 33–36. Toronto: Seal Press, 1987.

Collins, E. G. C., and T. B. Blodgett. "Sexual Harassment . . . Some See It . . . Some Won't." *Harvard Business Review* (March/April 1981): 82–93.

Collins, Patricia Hill. *Black Feminist Thought*. New York: Unwin Hyman, 1990.

———. "Pornography and Black Women's Bodies." In *Making Violence Sexy: Feminist Views on Pornography*, edited by Diana E. H. Russell, 97–104. Buckingham, U.K.: Open University Press, 1993.

Commission on Obscenity and Pornography (1970). "The Effects of Explicit Sexual Materials." In *Pornography: Private Right or Public Menace?*, edited by Robert M. Baird and Stuart E. Rosenbaum, 19–25. Buffalo, N.Y.: Prometheus Books, 1991.

Connor, Steve, and Sharon Kingman. *The Search for the Virus*. New York: Penguin, 1988.

Cooke, Amber. "Stripping: Who Calls the Tune?" In *Good Girls/Bad Girls: Feminists and Sex Trade Workers Face to Face*, edited by Laurie Bell, 92–99. Toronto: Seal Press, 1987.

Cooke, Amber, with Laurie Bell. "Sex Trade Workers and Feminists: Myths and Illusions." In *Good Girls/Bad Girls: Feminists and Sex Trade Workers Face to Face*, edited by Laurie Bell, 190–203. Toronto: Seal Press, 1987.

Corea, Gena. *The Invisible Epidemic*. New York: HarperCollins, 1993.

Coward, Rosalind. "Sexual Violence and Sexuality." In *Sexuality: A Reader*, edited by Feminist Review, 307–25. London: Virago, 1987.

Cowrie, Elizabeth. "Pornography and Fantasy: Psychoanalytic Perspectives." In *Sex Exposed: Sexuality and the Pornography Debate*, edited by Lynne Segal and Mary McIntosh, 132–52. New Brunswick, N.J.: Rutgers University Press, 1992.

COYOTE/National Task Force on Prostitution. Position statement. In *Sex Work: Writings by Women in the Sex Industry*, edited by Frédérique Delacoste and Priscilla Alexander, 290–96. Pittsburgh: Cleis Press, 1987.

Craft, Christine. *Too Old, Too Ugly and Not Deferential to Men*. New York: Dell, 1988.

Creet, Julia. "Daughter of the Movement: The Psychodynamics of Lesbian S/M Fantasy." *differences: A Journal of Feminist Cultural Studies* 3 (summer 1991): 135–59.

Cvetkovich, Ann. "Recasting Receptivity: Femme Sexualities." In *Lesbian Erotics*, edited by Karla Jay, 125–46. New York: New York University Press, 1995.

Daly, Mary. *Gyn/Ecology: The Metaethics of Radical Feminism.* Boston: Beacon Press, 1978.

———. *Pure Lust: Elemental Feminist Philosophy.* Boston: Beacon Press, 1984.

———. *Webster's First New Intergalactic Wickedary of the English Language.* Edited by Jane Caputi. Boston: Beacon Press, 1987.

Davis, Angela. *Women, Race and Class.* New York: Random House, 1983.

De Beauvoir, Simone. *The Second Sex.* Translated and edited by H. M. Parshley. New York: Vintage Books, 1974.

De Lauretis, Teresa. "Feminist Studies/Critical Studies: Issues, Terms, and Contexts." In *Feminist Studies/Critical Studies*, edited by Teresa de Lauretis. Bloomington: Indiana University Press, 1986.

Denfeld, Rene. *The New Victorians: A Young Woman's Challenge to the Old Feminist Order.* New York: Warner Books, 1995.

Dershowitz, Alan M. "Wives Also Kill Husbands—Quite Often." *Los Angeles Times*, 21 July 1994.

Diamond, Irene. "Pornography and Repression: A Reconsideration." *Signs: Journal of Women in Culture and Society* 5, no. 4 (1980): 686–701.

differences: A Journal of Feminist Cultural Studies "Queer Theory: Lesbian and Gay Sexualities" 3 (winter 1991).

differences: A Journal of Feminist Cultural Studies "More Gender Trouble: Feminism Meets Queer Theory" 6 (summer–fall 1994).

Dillon, Robin S. "Care and Respect." In *Explorations in Feminist Ethics*, edited by Eve Browning Cole and Susan Coultrap-McQuin, 69–81. Bloomington: Indiana University Press, 1992.

Dimen, Muriel. "Politically Correct? Politically Incorrect?" In *Pleasure and Danger: Exploring Female Sexuality*, edited by Carole S. Vance, 138–48. London: Pandora Press, 1989.

Dobash, R. Emerson, and Russell Dobash. *Violence against Wives: A Case against the Patriarchy.* New York: Free Press, 1979.

Donnerstein, Edward, and Daniel Linz. Paper presented to the Attorney General's Commission on Pornography, Houston, Texas, 1985.

Donnerstein, Edward, Daniel Linz, and Steven Penrod. "Is It the Sex or Is It the Violence?" In their *The Question of Pornography: Research Findings and Policy Implications*, 108–36. New York: Free Press, 1987.

Dority, Barbara. "Feminist Moralism, 'Pornography,' and Censorship." In *Pornography: Private Right or Public Menace?*, edited by Robert M. Baird and Stuart E. Rosenbaum, 111–16. Buffalo, N.Y.: Prometheus Books, 1991.

Downs, Donald Alexander. *The New Politics of Pornography.* Chicago: University of Chicago Press, 1989.

DuBois, Ellen Carol, and Linda Gordon. "Seeking Ecstasy on the Battlefield: Danger and Pleasure in Nineteenth-Century Feminist Sexual Thought." In *Pleasure and Danger: Exploring Female Sexuality*, edited by Carole S. Vance, 31–49. London: Pandora Press, 1989.

Duesberg, Peter. "HIV and AIDS, Correlation but Not Causation." *Proceedings of the National Academy of Sciences USA* 86 (February 1989): 755–64.

Duggan, Lisa, and Nan D. Hunter. *Sex Wars: Sexual Dissent and Political Culture.* New York: Routledge, 1995.

Duggan, Lisa, Nan Hunter, and Carole S. Vance. "False Promises: Feminist Antipornography

Legislation in the U.S." In *Women against Censorship*, edited by Varda Burstyn, 130–51. Vancouver: Douglas & McIntyre, 1985.

Dworkin, Andrea. *Our Blood: Prophesies and Discourses on Sexual Politics*. New York: G. P. Putnam, 1981.

——. *Pornography: Men Possessing Women*. New York: E. P. Dutton, 1989.

——. "Resistance." In *The Sexual Liberals and the Attack on Feminism*, edited by Dorchen Leidholdt and Janice G. Raymond, 136–39. New York: Teachers College Press, 1990.

Dworkin, Ronald. "Pornography, Feminism, and Liberty." In *Pornography: Private Right or Public Menace?*, edited by Robert M. Baird and Stuart E. Rosenbaum, 164–73. Buffalo, N.Y.: Prometheus Books, 1991.

Dziech, Billie Wright, and Linda Weiner. *The Lecherous Professor*. 2d ed. Urbana: University of Illinois Press, 1990.

Eberle, Paul, and Shirley Eberle. *The Politics of Child Abuse*. New Jersey: Lyle Stuart, 1986.

Echols, Alice. *Daring to Be Bad*. Minneapolis: University of Minnesota Press, 1990.

——. "The New Feminism of Yin and Yang." In *Powers of Desire: The Politics of Sexuality*, edited by Ann Snitow, Christine Stansell, and Sharon Thompson, 439–59. New York: Monthly Review Press, 1983.

——. "The Taming of the Id: Feminist Sexual Politics, 1968–1983." In *Pleasure and Danger: Exploring Female Sexuality*, edited by Carole S. Vance, 50–72. London: Pandora Press, 1989.

Edelstein, Judy. "In the Massage Parlor." In *Sex Work: Writings by Women in the Sex Industry*, edited by Frédérique Delacoste and Priscilla Alexander, 62–69. Pittsburgh: Cleis Press, 1987.

Ehman, Robert. "Adult-Child Sex." In *Philosophy and Sex*, 2d ed., edited by Robert Baker and Frederick Elliston, 431–46. Buffalo, N.Y.: Prometheus Books, 1984.

Ehrenreich, Barbara, and Deirdre English. *For Her Own Good: 150 Years of the Experts' Advice to Women*. Garden City, N.Y.: Anchor Books/Doubleday, 1978.

Ehrenreich, Barbara, Elizabeth Hess, and Gloria Jacobs. *Remaking Love: The Feminization of Sex*. New York: Anchor Books/Doubleday, 1986.

Ehrenreich, Nancy S. "Pluralist Myths and Powerless Men: The Ideology of Reasonableness in Sexual Harassment Law." In *Sexual Harassment: Confrontations and Decisions*, edited by Edmund Wall, 229–60. Buffalo, N.Y.: Prometheus Books, 1992.

Ellis, A. "Casual Sex." *International Journal of Moral and Social Studies* 1 (summer 1986): 157–69.

Elliston, Frederick. "In Defense of Promiscuity." In *Philosophy and Sex*, edited by Robert Baker and Frederick Elliston, 222–43. Buffalo, N.Y.: Prometheus Books, 1975.

Engels, Frederick. *The Origin of the Family, Private Property and the State*. New York: International Publishers, 1942.

English, Deirdre. "The Fear That Feminism Will Free Men First." In *Powers of Desire: The Politics of Sexuality*, edited by Ann Snitow, Christine Stansell, and Sharon Thompson, 477–83. New York: Monthly Review Press, 1983.

——. "The Politics of Porn: Can Feminists Walk the Line?" *Mother Jones* 5, no. 3 (April 1980): 20–23, 43–50.

English, Deirdre, Amber Hollibaugh, and Gayle Rubin. "Talking Sex: A Conversation on Sexuality and Feminism." *Socialist Review* 11, no. 4 (1981): 43–62.

Eskenazi, Martin, and David Gallen. *Sexual Harassment: Know Your Rights!* New York: Carroll & Graf, 1992.

Espin, Oliva M. "Influences on Sexuality in Hispanic/Latin Women." In *Pleasure and Danger: Exploring Female Sexuality*, edited by Carole S. Vance, 149–64. London: Pandora Press, 1989.

Estes, Clarissa Pinkola. *Women Who Run with the Wolves: Myths and Stories of the Wild Woman Archetype*. New York: Ballantine Books, 1992.

Fairstein, Linda A. *Sexual Violence: Our War against Rape*. New York: Berkley Publishing Group, 1995.

———. *Sexual Violence: Twenty Years in New York's Sex Crimes Prosecution Unit*. New York: William Morrow, 1993.

Farr, Susan. "The Art of Discipline: Creating Erotic Dramas of Play and Power." In *Coming to Power: Writings and Graphics on Lesbian S/M*, edited by Samois, 183–91. Boston: Alyson Publications, 1987.

Farrell, Warren. *The Myth of Male Power*. New York: Simon & Schuster, 1993.

Faust, Beatrice. *Women, Sex, and Pornography*. New York: Macmillan, 1980.

"Feminism 'Crunch Point.'" In *A Vindication of the Rights of Whores*, edited by Gail Pheterson, 144–72. Seattle: Seal Press, 1989.

Ferguson, Ann. "On Conceiving Motherhood and Sexuality: A Feminist Materialist Approach." In *Mothering: Essays in Feminist Theory*, edited by Joyce Trebilcot, 153–82. Savage, Md.: Rowman & Littlefield, 1983.

———. *Sexual Democracy: Women, Oppression, and Revolution*. Boulder, Colo.: Westview Press, 1991.

Ferguson, Ann, Ilene Philipson, Irene Diamond, Lee Quinby, Carole S. Vance, and Ann Barr Snitow. "Forum: The Feminist Sexuality Debates." *Signs: Journal of Women in Culture and Society* 10 (autumn 1984): 106–35.

Finkelhor, David. *Child Sexual Abuse: New Theory and Research*. New York: Free Press, 1984.

———. *Sexually Victimized Children*. New York: Free Press, 1979.

Firestone, Shulamith. *The Dialectic of Sex: The Case for Feminist Revolution*. New York: Bantam Books, 1970.

Fisher, Helen E. *Anatomy of Love: The Natural History of Monogamy, Adultery and Divorce*. New York: W. W. Norton, 1992.

Flanagan, Owen, and Kathryn Jackson. "Justice, Care and Gender: The Kohlberg-Gilligan Debate Revisited." In *Feminism and Political Theory*, edited by Cass R. Sunstein, 37–52. Chicago: University of Chicago Press, 1990.

Flax, Jane. "Postmodernism and Gender Relations in Feminist Theory." In *Feminist Theory in Practice and Process*, edited by Micheline R. Malson, Jean F. O'Barr, Sarah Westphal-Wihl, and Mary Wyer, 51–73. Chicago: University of Chicago Press, 1989.

Foa, Pamela. "What's Wrong with Rape?" In *Feminism and Philosophy*, edited by Mary Vetterling-Braggin, Frederick A. Elliston, and Jane English, 347–59. Totowa, N.J.: Littlefield, Adams, 1978.

Foucault, Michel. *The History of Sexuality: Volume I, an Introduction*. Translated by Robert Huxley. New York: Vintage Books, 1980.

———. *Power/Knowledge*. Edited by Colin Gordon. New York: Pantheon, 1980.

Freccero, Carla. "Notes of a Post–Sex Wars Theorizer." In *Conflicts in Feminism*, edited by Marianne Hirsch and Evelyn Fox Keller, 305–25. New York: Routledge, 1990.

Freud, Sigmund. "'Civilized' Sexual Morality and Nervous Illness." In *The Philosophy of (Erotic) Love*, edited by Robert C. Solomon and Kathleen M. Higgins, 153–76. Lawrence: University Press of Kansas, 1991.

———. "Three Essays on the Theory of Sexuality." In *The Standard Edition of the Complete Psychological Works of Sigmund Freud*, 24 vols. Edited by James Strachey, vol. 7. London: Hogarth Press and the Institute of Psychoanalysis, 1953–74.

Friday, Nancy. *My Secret Garden*. New York: Pocket Books, 1974.

Friedan, Betty. *The Feminine Mystique*. New York: Dell, 1974.

———. *The Second Stage*. New York: Summit Books, 1981.

Friedman, Marilyn. "Beyond Caring: The De-moralization of Gender." In *An Ethic of Care: Feminist and Interdisciplinary Perspectives*, edited by Mary Jeanne Larrabee, 258–73. New York: Routledge, 1993.

———. "Does Sommers Like Women? More on Liberalism, Gender Hierarchy, and Scarlett O'Hara." *Journal of Social Philosophy* 21 (fall/winter 1990): 75–90.

———. "The Social Self and the Partiality Debates." In *Feminist Ethics*, edited by Claudia Card, 161–79. Lawrence: University Press of Kansas, 1991.

———. "'They Lived Happily Ever After': Sommers on Women and Marriage." *Journal of Social Philosophy* 21 (fall/winter 1990): 57–65.

Frye, Marilyn. "Critique [of Robert Ehman's "Adult-Child Sex"]". In *Philosophy and Sex*, 2d ed., edited by Robert Baker and Frederick Elliston, 447–55. Buffalo, N.Y.: Prometheus Books, 1984.

———. *The Politics of Reality: Essays in Feminist Theory*. Trumansburg, N.Y.: Crossing Press, 1983.

Ganache, Denise. "Domination and Control: The Social Context of Dating Violence." In *Dating Violence: Young Women in Danger*, edited by Barrie Levy, 69–83. Seattle: Seal Press, 1991.

Garber, Marjorie. "Spare Parts: The Surgical Construction of Gender." *differences: A Journal of Feminist Cultural Studies* 1, no. 3 (1989): 137–59.

———. *Vested Interests: Cross-Dressing and Cultural Anxiety*. New York: Routledge, 1992.

———. *Vice Versa: Bisexuality and the Eroticism of Everyday Life*. New York: Simon & Schuster, 1995.

Gardner, Tracey A. "Racism in Pornography and the Women's Movement." In *Take Back the Night: Women on Pornography*, edited by Laura Lederer, 105–14. New York: William Morrow, 1980.

Garry, Ann. "Pornography and Respect for Women." In *Philosophy and Sex*, 2d ed., edited by Robert Baker and Frederick Elliston, 312–26. Buffalo, N.Y.: Prometheus Books, 1984.

Gilbert, Harriet. "So Long as It's Not Sex and Violence: Andrea Dworkin's *Mercy*." In *Sex Exposed: Sexuality and the Pornography Debate*, edited by Lynne Segal and Mary McIntosh, 233–65. New Brunswick, N.J.: Rutgers University Press, 1992.

Gilligan, Carol. *In a Different Voice: Psychological Theory and Women's Development*. Cambridge: Harvard University Press, 1982.

Giobbe, Evelina. "Confronting the Liberal Lies about Prostitution." In *The Sexual Liberals and the Attack on Feminism*, edited by Dorchen Leidholdt and Janice G. Raymond, 67–81. New York: Teachers College Press, 1990.

———. "Surviving Commercial Sexual Exploitation." In *Making Violence Sexy: Feminist Views on Pornography*, edited by Diana E. H. Russell, 37–41. Buckingham, U.K.: Open University Press, 1993.

Goldman, Alan. "Plain Sex." In *The Philosophy of Sex*, 2d ed., edited by Alan Soble, 73–92. Savage, Md.: Rowman & Littlefield, 1991.

Gorna, Robin. "Delightful Visions: From Anti-Porn to Eroticizing Safer Sex." In *Sex Exposed: Sexuality and the Pornography Debate*, edited by Lynne Segal and Mary McIntosh, 169–83. New Brunswick, N.J.: Rutgers University Press, 1992.

Gracyk, Theodore A. "Pornography as Representation: Aesthetic Considerations." In *Pornography: Private Right or Public Menace?*, edited by Robert M. Baird and Stuart E. Rosenbaum, 117–37. Buffalo, N.Y.: Prometheus Books, 1991.

Graham, Dee L. R., and Edna I. Rawlings. "Bonding with Abusive Dating Partners: Dynamics of Stockholm Syndrome." In *Dating Violence: Young Women in Danger*, edited by Barrie Levy, 119–35. Seattle: Seal Press, 1991.

Gray, Robert. "Sex and Sexual Perversion." In *The Philosophy of Sex*, edited by Alan Soble, 158–68. Totowa, N.J.: Littlefield, Adams, 1980.

Greenfeld, Karl Taro. "The Broken Dreams of the Blond Geishas." *Los Angeles Times Magazine*, 8 November 1992.

Greer, Germaine. *The Female Eunuch*. New York: Bantam Books, 1972.

Gregory, Paul. "Against Couples." *Journal of Applied Philosophy* 1, no. 2 (1984): 263–68.

Griffin, Susan. *Pornography and Silence*. New York: Harper & Row, 1981.

———. "Rape: The All-American Crime." *Ramparts* (September 1971). Reprinted in *Feminism and Philosophy*, edited by Mary Vetterling-Braggin, Frederick A. Elliston, and Jane English, 313–32. Totowa, N.J.: Littlefield, Adams, 1978.

———. *Rape: The Power of Consciousness*. San Francisco: Harper & Row, 1979.

———. "Sadomasochism and the Erosion of Self: A Critical Reading of *Story of O*." In *Against Sadomasochism: A Radical Feminist Analysis*, edited by Robin Ruth Linden, Darlene R. Pagano, Diana E. H. Russell, and Susan Leigh Star, 183–201. San Francisco: Frog in the Well, 1982.

———. *Women and Nature: The Roaring inside Her*. New York: Harper & Row, 1978.

Gutek, Barbara A. *Sex and the Workplace*. San Francisco: Jossey-Bass, 1985.

Hale, Jacob. "Are Lesbians Women?" *Hypatia* 11 (spring 1996): 94–121.

Hall, Jacquelyn Dowd. "'The Mind That Burns in Each Body': Women, Rape, and Racial Violence." In *Powers of Desire: The Politics of Sexuality*, edited by Ann Snitow, Christine Stansell, and Sharon Thompson, 328–49. New York: Monthly Review Press, 1983.

Hammonds, Evelynn. "Black (W)holes and the Geometry of Black Female Sexuality." *differences: A Journal of Feminist Cultural Studies* 6 (summer–fall 1994): 126–45.

Harding, Sandra. "The Instability of the Analytical Categories of Feminist Theory." In *Feminist Theory in Practice and Process*, edited by Micheline R. Malson, Jean F. O'Barr, Sarah Westphal-Wihl, and Mary Wyer, 15–34. Chicago: University of Chicago Press, 1989.

———. *The Science Question in Feminism*. Ithaca, N.Y.: Cornell University Press, 1986.

———. *Whose Science? Whose Knowledge?: Thinking from Women's Lives*. Ithaca, N.Y.: Cornell University Press, 1991.

Hardwig, John. "Should Women Think in Terms of Rights?" In *Feminism and Political Theory*, edited by Cass R. Sunstein, 53–67. Chicago: University of Chicago Press, 1990.

Hartley, Nina. "Confessions of a Feminist Porno Star." In *Sex Work: Writings by Women in the Sex Industry*, edited by Frédérique Delacoste and Priscilla Alexander, 142–44. Pittsburgh: Cleis Press, 1987.

Hartsock, Nancy. *Money, Sex and Power*. New York: Longman, 1983.

Hawkesworth, Mary. "Knowers, Knowing, Known: Feminist Theory and Claims of Truth." In *Feminist Theory in Practice and Process*, edited by Micheline R. Malson, Jean F. O'Barr, Sarah Westphal-Wihl, and Mary Wyer, 327–51. Chicago: University of Chicago Press, 1989.

Hazen, Helen. *Endless Rapture: Rape, Romance, and the Female Imagination*. New York: Scribner's, 1983.

Hekman, Susan. *Gender and Knowledge: Elements of a Postmodern Feminism*. Boston: Northeastern University Press, 1990.

Heller, Valerie. "Sexual Liberalism and Survivors of Sexual Abuse." In *The Sexual Liberals and the Attack on Feminism*, edited by Dorchen Leidholdt and Janice G. Raymond, 157–61. New York: Teachers College Press, 1990.

Henderson, Lisa. "Lesbian Pornography: Cultural Transgression and Sexual Demystification." In *New Lesbian Criticism: Literary and Cultural Readings*, edited by Sally Munt, 173–91. New York: Columbia University Press, 1992.

Heresies #12 "Sex Issue" 3, no. 4 (1981).

Herman, Barbara. "Could It Be Worth Thinking about Kant on Sex and Marriage?" In *A Mind of One's Own: Feminist Essays on Reason and Objectivity*. Boulder, Colo.: Westview Press, 1993.

Herman, Judith Lewis. *Father-Daughter Incest*. Cambridge: Harvard University Press, 1981.

——. *Trauma and Recovery*. New York: Basic Books, 1992.

Heyn, Dalma. *The Erotic Silence of the American Wife*. New York: Turtle Bay Books, 1992.

Hill, Judith M. "Pornography and Degradation." In *Pornography: Private Right or Public Menace?*, edited by Robert M. Baird and Stuart E. Rosenbaum, 62–75. Buffalo, N.Y.: Prometheus Books, 1991.

Hill, Thomas E., Jr. *Autonomy and Self-Respect*. Cambridge: Cambridge University Press, 1991.

Hirsch, Marianne, and Evelyn Fox Keller. "Conclusion: Practicing Conflict in Feminist Theory." In *Conflicts in Feminism*, edited by Marianne Hirsch and Evelyn Fox Keller, 370–85. New York: Routledge, 1990.

Hoagland, Sarah Lucia. *Lesbian Ethics: Toward New Value*. Palo Alto, Calif.: Institute of Lesbian Studies, 1988.

——. "Sadism, Masochism, and Lesbian Feminism." In *Against Sadomasochism: A Radical Feminist Analysis*, edited by Robin Ruth Linden, Darlene R. Pagano, Diana E. H. Russell, and Susan Leigh Star, 153–63. San Francisco: Frog in the Well, 1982.

Hofeller, Kathleen H. *Battered Women, Shattered Lives*. Saratoga, Calif.: R & E Publishers, 1983.

Hollibaugh, Amber. "Desire for the Future: Radical Hope in Passion and Pleasure." In *Pleasure and Danger: Exploring Female Sexuality*, edited by Carole S. Vance, 401–10. London: Pandora Press, 1989.

Hollibaugh, Amber, and Cherríe Moraga. "What We're Rollin Around in Bed With: Sexual Silences in Feminism." In *Powers of Desire: The Politics of Sexuality*, edited by Ann Snitow, Christine Stansell, and Sharon Thompson, 394–405. New York: Monthly Review Press, 1983.

hooks, bell. *Feminist Theory from Margin to Center*. Boston: South End Press, 1984.

——. *Talking Back: Thinking Feminist, Thinking Black*. Boston: South End Press, 1989.

Hopkins, Patrick D. Commentary on Honi Haber, "Gender Politics and the Cross-Dresser." Paper and commentary presented at a symposium on the philosophy of sex and love at the Central Division meeting of the American Philosophical Association, Chicago, Illinois, April 1995.

——. "Gender Treachery: Homophobia, Masculinity, and Threatened Identities." In *Free Spirits: Feminist Philosophers on Culture*, edited by Kate Mehuron and Gary Percesepe, 419–32, 518–20. Englewood Cliffs, N.J.: Prentice Hall, 1995.

——. "Rethinking Sadomasochism: Feminism, Interpretation, and Simulation." *Hypatia* 9 (winter 1994): 116–41.

——. "Simulation and Reproduction of Injustice: A Reply." *Hypatia* 10 (spring 1995): 162–70.

Hunt, Margaret. "Report of a Conference on Feminism, Sexuality and Power: The Elect Clash with the Perverse." In *Coming to Power: Writings and Graphics on Lesbian S/M*, edited by Samois, 81–89. Boston: Alyson Publications, 1987.

Hunter, Mic. *Abused Boys: The Neglected Victims of Sexual Abuse*. New York: Fawcett Columbine, 1990.

Hurtado, Aída. *The Color of Privilege: Three Blasphemies on Race and Feminism*. Ann Arbor: University of Michigan Press, 1996.

International Committee for Prostitutes' Rights. European Parliament, Brussels, 1–3 October 1986. "Statement on Prostitution and Feminism." In *A Vindication of the Rights of Whores*, edited by Gail Pheterson, 192–97. Seattle: Seal Press, 1989.

Irigaray, Luce. *This Sex Which Is Not One*. Translated by Catherine Porter with Carolyn Burke. Ithaca, N.Y.: Cornell University Press, 1985.

Iwao, Sumiko. *The Japanese Woman's Traditional Image and Changing Reality*. New York: Free Press, 1993.

Jaggar, Alison M. *Feminist Politics and Human Nature*. Totowa, N.J.: Rowman & Allanheld, 1983.

———. "Prostitution." In *The Philosophy of Sex*, 2d ed., edited by Alan Soble, 259–80. Savage, Md.: Rowman & Littlefield, 1991.

Jakobsen, Janet R. "Agency and Alliance in Public Discourses about Sexualities." *Hypatia* 10 (winter 1995): 133–54.

Jeffreys, Sheila. "Eroticizing Women's Subordination." In *The Sexual Liberals and the Attack on Feminism*, edited by Dorchen Leidholdt and Janice G. Raymond, 132–35. New York: Teachers College Press, 1990.

———. "Sado-masochism: The Erotic Cult of Fascism." *Lesbian Ethics* 2, no. 1 (1986): 65–82.

Jenness, Valerie. *Making It Work: The Prostitutes' Rights Movement in Perspective*. New York: Aldene de Gruyter, 1993.

Johnson, Charles. *Being and Race*. Bloomington: Indiana University Press, 1988.

Johnson, Janis Tyler. *Mothers of Incest Survivors: Another Side of the Story*. Bloomington: Indiana University Press, 1992.

Johnson, Sonia. "Taking Our Eyes off the Guys." In *The Sexual Liberals and the Attack on Feminism*, edited by Dorchen Leidholdt and Janice G. Raymond, 56–60. New York: Teachers College Press, 1990.

Jones, Ann. "Family Matters." In *The Sexual Liberals and the Attack on Feminism*, edited by Dorchen Leidholdt and Janice G. Raymond, 61–66. New York: Teachers College Press, 1990.

———. *Women Who Kill*. New York: Holt, Rinehart & Winston, 1980.

Jones, Robert A. "Wanna Buy a Dirty CD-ROM?" *Los Angeles Times Magazine*, 19 March 1995.

Julien, Isaac, and Kobena Mercer. "True Confessions: A Discourse on Images of Black Male Sexuality." In *Brother to Brother*, edited by Essex Hemphill, 167–83. Boston: Alyson Publications, 1991.

Kadish, Mortimer R. "The Possibility of Perversion." In *The Philosophy of Sex*, 2d ed., edited by Alan Soble, 93–116. Savage, Md.: Rowman & Littlefield, 1991.

Kaminer, Wendy. "Pornography and the First Amendment: Prior Restraints and Private Action." In *Take Back the Night: Women on Pornography*, edited by Laura Lederer, 241–47. New York: William Morrow, 1980.

Kaplan, E. Ann. "Is the Gaze Male?" In *Powers of Desire: The Politics of Sexuality*, edited by Ann Snitow, Christine Stansell, and Sharon Thompson, 309–27. New York: Monthly Review Press, 1983.

Kaplan, Louise J. *Female Perversions: The Temptation of Emma Bovary*. New York: Anchor Books/Doubleday, 1991.

Katz, Jonathan Ned. *The Invention of Heterosexuality*. New York: Dutton, 1995.

Kendrick, Walter. *The Secret Museum: Pornography in Modern Culture*. New York: Viking Press, 1987.

Ketchum, Sara Ann. "The Good, the Bad and the Perverted: Sexual Paradigms Revisited." In *The Philosophy of Sex*, edited by Alan Soble, 139–57. Totowa, N.J.: Rowman & Littlefield, 1980.

Kierkegaard, Søren. "The Immediate Stages of the Erotic." In *Either/Or*, vol. 1. Translated by David F. Swenson and Lillian Marvin Swenson, 86–102. Princeton: Princeton University Press, 1944, 1959.

King, Alison. "Mystery and Imagination: The Case of Pornography Effects Studies." In *Bad Girls and Dirty Pictures: The Challenge to Reclaim Feminism*, edited by Alison Assiter and Avedon Carol, 57–87. London: Pluto Press, 1993.

King, Katie. "Producing Sex, Theory, and Culture: Gay/Straight Remappings in Contemporary Feminism." In *Conflicts in Feminism*, edited by Marianne Hirsch and Evelyn Fox Keller, 82–101. New York: Routledge, 1990.

Kipnis, Laura. "She-Male Fantasies and the Aesthetics of Pornography." In *Dirty Looks: Women, Pornography, Power*, edited by Pamela Church Gibson and Roma Gibson, 124–43. London: BFI Publishing, 1993.

Kittay, Eva Feder. "Pornography and the Erotics of Domination." In *Beyond Domination: New Perspectives on Women and Philosophy*, edited by Carol C. Gould, 145–85. Totowa, N.J.: Rowman & Littlefield, 1983.

Kitzinger, Celia. "Anti-Lesbian Harassment." In *Rethinking Sexual Harassment*, edited by Clare Brant and Yun Lee Too, 125–47. London: Pluto Press, 1994.

Koedt, Anne. "The Myth of the Vaginal Orgasm." In *Radical Feminism*, edited by Anne Koedt, Ellen Levine, and Anita Rapone, 198–207. New York: Quadrangle Books, 1973.

LaBelle, Beverly. "*Snuff*—The Ultimate in Woman-Hating." In *Take Back the Night: Women on Pornography*, edited by Laura Lederer, 272–78. New York: William Morrow, 1980.

Larsen, Kathryn. *Life after Rape: Survivors Speak Healing Words for All*. Louisville, Ky.: Butler Book Publishing Services, 1990.

Larson, Erik. "Paxton Quigley Shows Her Women Students How to Shoot a Man." *Wall Street Journal*, 4 February 1993.

Lawson, Nigella. "Rape Is Horrible but Women Are Also Accountable for Their Actions." *Los Angeles Times*, 24 October 1993. Excerpted from the *Evening Standard* (London), 20 October 1993.

Lederer, Laura. "'Playboy Isn't Playing': An Interview with Judith Bat-Ada." In *Take Back the Night: Women on Pornography*, edited by Laura Lederer, 121–33. New York: William Morrow, 1980.

———. "Then and Now: An Interview with a Former Pornography Model." In *Take Back the Night: Women on Pornography*, edited by Laura Lederer, 57–70. New York: William Morrow, 1980.

Leidholdt, Dorchen. "When Women Defend Pornography." In *The Sexual Liberals and the Attack on Feminism*, edited by Dorchen Leidholdt and Janice G. Raymond, 125–31. New York: Teachers College Press, 1990.

LeMoncheck, Linda. *Dehumanizing Women: Treating Persons as Sex Objects*. Totowa, N.J.: Rowman & Allanheld, 1985.

———. "Feminist Politics and Feminist Ethics: Treating Women as Sex Objects." In *Philosophical Perspectives on Sex and Love*, edited by Robert M. Stewart, 29–38. New York: Oxford University Press, 1995.

LeMoncheck, Linda, and Mane Hajdin. *Sexual Harassment: A Debate*. Lanham, Md.: Rowman & Littlefield, 1997.

Lesbians of Colour. "Racism in Pornography." In *Good Girls/Bad Girls: Feminists and Sex Trade Workers Face to Face*, edited by Laurie Bell, 58–66. Toronto: Seal Press, 1987.

Levy, Donald. "Perversion and the Unnatural as Moral Categories." In *The Philosophy of Sex*, edited by Alan Soble, 169–89. Totowa, N.J.: Littlefield, Adams, 1980.

Lew, Mike. *Victims No Longer: Men Recovering from Incest and Other Sexual Child Abuse*. New York: HarperCollins, 1988.

Lloyd, Genevieve. *The Man of Reason: "Male" and "Female" in Western Philosophy*. Minneapolis: University of Minnesota Press, 1986.

Loach, Loretta. "Bad Girls: Women Who Use Pornography." In *Sex Exposed: Sexuality and the Pornography Debate*, edited by Lynne Segal and Mary McIntosh, 266–74. New Brunswick, N.J.: Rutgers University Press, 1992.

Longino, Helen E. "Pornography, Oppression, and Freedom: A Closer Look." In *Pornography: Private Right or Public Menace?*, edited by Robert M. Baird and Stuart E. Rosenbaum, 84–95. Buffalo, N.Y.: Prometheus Books, 1991.

Lopez-Jones, Nina. "Prostitute Women and AIDS: Resisting the Virus of Repression." Paper presented at the Women's Studies Seminar on Prostitution. Huntington Library, Pasadena, California, 13 March 1993.

———. "Workers: Introducing the English Collective of Prostitutes." In *Sex Work: Writings by Women in the Sex Industry*, edited by Frédérique Delacoste and Priscilla Alexander, 271–78. Pittsburgh: Cleis Press, 1987.

Lorber, Judith. *Paradoxes of Gender*. New Haven: Yale University Press, 1994.

Lorde, Audre. "Uses of the Erotic: The Erotic as Power." In *Sister Outsider: Essays and Speeches by Audre Lorde*, 53–59. Freedom, Calif.: Crossing Press, 1984.

Lovelace, Linda. *Ordeal*. Secaucus, N.J.: Citadel Press, 1980.

Lugones, María C. "On the Logic of Pluralist Feminism." In *Feminist Ethics*, edited by Claudia Card, 35–44. Lawrence: University Press of Kansas, 1991.

———. "Playfulness, 'World'-Traveling, and Loving Perception." In *Women, Knowledge, and Reality*, edited by Ann Garry and Marilyn Pearsall, 275–90. Boston: Unwin Hyman, 1989.

Lugones, María C., and Elizabeth V. Spelman. "Have We Got a Theory for You! Feminist Theory, Cultural Imperialism and the Demand for 'The Woman's Voice.'" In *Women and Values*, edited by Marilyn Pearsall, 19–31. Belmont, Calif.: Wadsworth Publishing Co., 1986.

Lynch, René. "Rapists May Strike Again, and Again, Experts Say." *Los Angeles Times*, 29 May 1994.

MacKenzie, Christobel. "The AntiSexism Campaign Invites You to Fight Sexism, Not Sex." In *Bad Girls and Dirty Pictures: The Challenge to Reclaim Feminism*, edited by Alison Assiter and Avedon Carol, 139–45. London: Pluto Press, 1993.

MacKinnon, Catharine A. "Feminism, Marxism, Method, and the State: Agenda for Theory." *Signs: Journal of Women in Culture and Society* 7, no. 3 (spring 1982): 515–44.

———. *Feminism Unmodified: Discourses on Life and Law*. Cambridge: Harvard University Press, 1987.

———. *Only Words*. Cambridge: Harvard University Press, 1993.

———. *Sexual Harassment of Working Women*. New Haven: Yale University Press, 1979.

———. "Sexuality, Pornography, and Method: 'Pleasure under Patriarchy.'" In *Feminism and Political Theory*, edited by Cass R. Sunstein, 207–39. Chicago: University of Chicago Press, 1990.

Malamuth, Neil, and Edward Donnerstein. *Pornography and Sexual Aggression*. New York: Academic Press, 1984.

Manning, Rita C. "Redefining Obscenity." In *Pornography: Private Right or Public Menace?*, edited by Robert M. Baird and Stuart E. Rosenbaum, 153–63. Buffalo, N.Y.: Prometheus Books, 1991.

———. *Speaking from the Heart: A Feminist Perspective on Ethics*. Lanham, Md.: Rowman & Littlefield, 1992.

Martin, Del. *Battered Wives*. Volcano, Calif.: Volcano Press, 1976, 1981.

May, Larry, and John C. Hughes. "Is Sexual Harassment Coercive?" In *Sexual Harassment: Confrontations and Decisions*, edited by Edmund Wall, 61–68. Buffalo, N.Y.: Prometheus Books, 1992.

Mayall, Alice, and Diana E. H. Russell. "Racism in Pornography." In *Making Violence Sexy: Feminist Views on Pornography*, edited by Diana E. H. Russell, 167–78. Buckingham, U.K.: Open University Press, 1993.

McClintock, Anne. "Gonad the Barbarian and the Venus Flytrap: Portraying the Female and Male Orgasm." In *Sex Exposed: Sexuality and the Pornography Debate*, edited by Lynne Segal and Mary McIntosh, 111–31. New Brunswick, N.J.: Rutgers University Press, 1992.

———."Maid to Order: Commercial S/M and Gender Power." In *Dirty Looks: Women, Pornography, Power*, edited by Pamela Church Gibson and Roma Gibson, 207–31. London: BFI Publishing, 1993.

———. "Screwing the System: Sexwork, Race and the Law." *Boundary* 11 (fall 1992): 70–95.

McElroy, Wendy. *XXX: A Woman's Right to Pornography*. New York: St. Martin's Press, 1995.

McMurtry, John. "Monogamy: A Critique." In *Philosophy and Sex*, 2d ed., edited by Robert Baker and Frederick Elliston, 107–18. Buffalo, N.Y.: Prometheus Books, 1984.

McNay, Lois. "The Foucauldian Body and the Exclusion of Experience." *Hypatia* 6 (fall 1991): 125–39.

Mercer, Kobena. "Just Looking for Trouble: Robert Mapplethorpe and Fantasies of Race." In *Sex Exposed: Sexuality and the Pornography Debate*, edited by Lynne Segal and Mary McIntosh, 92–110. New Brunswick, N.J.: Rutgers University Press, 1992.

Millett, Kate. "Beyond Politics?: Children and Sexuality." In *Pleasure and Danger: Exploring Female Sexuality*, edited by Carole S. Vance, 217–24. London: Pandora Press, 1989.

———. "Prostitution: A Quartet of Female Voices." In *Woman in Sexist Society: Studies in Power and Powerlessness*, edited by Vivian Gornick and Barbara K. Moran, 6–125. New York: Basic Books, 1971.

———. *Sexual Politics*. Garden City, N.Y.: Doubleday, 1970.

Minnesota Coalition for Battered Women (MCBW). *Confronting Lesbian Battering: A Manual for the Battered Women's Movement*. St. Paul, Minn.: MCBW, 1990.

Minot, Susan. *Lust and Other Stories*. New York: Washington Square Press/Pocket Books, 1990.

Minson, J. P. "Social Theory and Legal Argument: Catharine MacKinnon on Sexual Harassment." In *Sexual Harassment: Confrontations and Decisions*, edited by Edmund Wall, 159–69. Buffalo, N.Y.: Prometheus Books, 1992.

Moon, Louisa. "Prostitution and Date Rape: The Commodification of 'Consent.'" Paper presented at a symposium on the philosophy of sex and love at the Eastern Division meeting of the American Philosophical Association, Boston, Massachusetts, December 1994.

Morgan, Kathryn Pauly. "Romantic Love, Altruism, and Self-Respect: An Analysis of Beauvoir." In *The Philosophy of (Erotic) Love*, edited by Robert C. Solomon and Kathleen M. Higgins, 391–414. Lawrence: University Press of Kansas, 1991.

Morgan, Robin. *The Demon Lover: On the Sexuality of Terrorism*. New York: W. W. Norton, 1989.

———. "Theory and Practice: Pornography and Rape." In *Take Back the Night: Women on Pornography*, edited by Laura Lederer, 134–40. New York: William Morrow, 1980.

Morgan, Steven. *Conjugal Terrorism: A Psychological and Community Treatment Model of Wife Abuse*. Palo Alto, Calif.: R & E Research Associates, 1981.

Morton, Patricia. *The Historical Assault on Afro-American Women*. Westport, Conn.: Greenwood Press, 1991.

Moulton, Janice. "Sexual Behavior: Another Position." In *The Philosophy of Sex: Contemporary Readings*, 2d ed., edited by Alan Soble, 63–71. Savage, Md.: Rowman & Littlefield, 1991.

Nagel, Thomas. "Sexual Perversion." In *The Philosophy of Sex*, 2d ed., edited by Alan Soble, 39–51. Savage, Md.: Rowman & Littlefield, 1991.

———. *The View from Nowhere*. Oxford: Oxford University Press, 1986.

National Council for Research on Women. *Sexual Harassment: Research and Resources*, 3d ed. Written by Deborah L. Siegel and revised by Marina Budhos. New York: National Council for Research on Women, 1995.

Nead, Lynda. "The Female Nude: Pornography, Art, and Sexuality." In *Sex Exposed: Sexuality and the Pornography Debate*, edited by Lynne Segal and Mary McIntosh, 280–94. New Brunswick, N.J.: Rutgers University Press, 1992.

Nestle, Joan. "The Fem Question." In *Pleasure and Danger: Exploring Female Sexuality*, edited by Carole S. Vance, 232–41. London: Pandora Press, 1989.

———. "Lesbians and Prostitutes: A Historical Sisterhood." In *Good Girls/Bad Girls: Feminists and Sex Trade Workers Face to Face*, edited by Laurie Bell, 131–45. Toronto: Seal Press, 1987.

———. *A Restricted Country*. Ithaca, N.Y.: Firebrand Books, 1987.

Neu, Jerome. "What Is Wrong with Incest?" In *Today's Moral Problems*, 3d ed., edited by Richard Wasserstrom, 220–30. New York: Macmillan, 1985.

Newton, Esther, and Shirley Walton. "The Misunderstanding: Toward a More Precise Sexual Vocabulary." In *Pleasure and Danger: Exploring Female Sexuality*, edited by Carole S. Vance, 242–50. London: Pandora Press, 1989.

Nichols, Jeanette, Darlene Pagano, and Margaret Rossoff. "Is Sadomasochism Feminist?: A Critique of the Samois Position." In *Against Sadomasochism: A Radical Feminist Analysis*, edited by Robin Ruth Linden, Darlene R. Pagano, Diana E. H. Russell, and Susan Leigh Star, 137–46. San Francisco: Frog in the Well, 1982.

Noddings, Nel. *Caring: A Feminine Approach to Ethics and Moral Education*. Berkeley: University of California Press, 1984.

Nozick, Robert. "Love's Bond." In *The Philosophy of (Erotic) Love*, edited by Robert C. Solomon and Kathleen M. Higgins, 417–32. Lawrence: University Press of Kansas, 1991.

O'Campo, Martha. "Pornography and Prostitution in the Philippines." In *Good Girls/Bad Girls: Feminists and Sex Trade Workers Face to Face*, edited by Laurie Bell, 67–76. Toronto: Seal Press, 1987.

O'Carroll, Tom. *Paedophilia: The Radical Case*. London: Peter Owen, 1980.

Omolade, Barbara. "Hearts of Darkness." In *Powers of Desire: The Politics of Sexuality*, edited by Ann Snitow, Christine Stansell, and Sharon Thompson, 350–67. New York: Monthly Review Press, 1983.

Overall, Christine. "Heterosexuality and Feminist Theory." *Canadian Journal of Philosophy* 20, no. 1 (March 1990): 9–17.

Owens, Tuppy. *The Betrayal of Youth: Radical Perspectives on Childhood Sexuality, Intergenerational Sex and the Sexual Oppression of Children and Young People*. Edited by Warren Middleton. London: CL Publications, 1986.

Paglia, Camille. *Sex, Art, and American Culture*. New York: Vintage Books, 1992.

———. *Sexual Personae: Art and Decadence from Nefertiti to Emily Dickinson*. New Haven: Yale University Press, 1990.

———. *Vamps and Tramps: New Essays*. New York: Vintage Books, 1994.

Pateman, Carole. "Defending Prostitution: Charges against Ericsson." *Ethics* 93, no. 3 (April 1983): 561–65.

———. "Women and Consent." *Political Theory* 8, no. 2 (1980): 149–68.

Patton, Cindy. *Inventing AIDS*. New York: Routledge, 1991.

———. *Sex and Germs*. Boston: South End Press, 1985.

Paul, Ellen Frankel. "Bared Buttocks and Federal Cases." In *Sexual Harassment: Confrontations and Decisions*, edited by Edmund Wall, 151–57. Buffalo, N.Y.: Prometheus Books, 1992.

Penelope, Julia. "The Illusion of Control: Sadomasochism and the Sexual Metaphors of Childhood." *Lesbian Ethics* 2, no. 3 (1987): 84–94.

Peterson, Susan Rae. "Coercion and Rape: The State as a Male Protection Racket." In *Feminism and Philosophy*, edited by Mary Vetterling-Braggin, Frederick A. Elliston, and Jane English, 360–71. Totowa, N.J.: Littlefield, Adams, 1978.

Petrocelli, William, and Barbara Kate Repa. *Sexual Harassment on the Job.* Berkeley: Nolo Press, 1992.

Pharr, Suzanne. *Homophobia: A Weapon of Sexism.* Little Rock, Ark.: Chardon Press, 1988.

Pheterson, Gail. "Not Repeating History." In *A Vindication of the Rights of Whores,* edited by Gail Pheterson, 3–30. Seattle: Seal Press, 1989.

———. "The Social Consequences of Unchastity." In *Sex Work: Writings by Women in the Sex Industry,* edited by Frédérique Delacoste and Priscilla Alexander, 215–30. Pittsburgh: Cleis Press, 1987.

Pollard, Nettie. "The Small Matter of Children." In *Bad Girls and Dirty Pictures: The Challenge to Reclaim Feminism,* edited by Alison Assiter and Avedon Carol, 105–11. London: Pluto Press, 1993.

Pryor, J. B., and J. D. Day. "Interpretations of Sexual Harassment: An Attributional Analysis." *Sex Roles* 18 (1988): 405–17.

Quigley, Paxton. *Armed and Female: Twelve Million Americans Own Guns, Should You?* New York: St. Martin's Press, 1990.

Radford, Jill, and Diana E. H. Russell. *Femicide: The Politics of Woman Killing.* New York: Macmillan, 1990.

Rapaport, Elizabeth. "On the Future of Love: Rousseau and the Radical Feminists." In *The Philosophy of (Erotic) Love,* edited by Robert C. Solomon and Kathleen M. Higgins, 372–90. Lawrence: University Press of Kansas, 1991.

Raymond, Janice G. *The Transsexual Empire.* Boston: Beacon Press, 1979.

Reeves, Tom. "Loving Boys." In *The Age Taboo: Gay Male Sexuality, Power and Consent,* edited by Daniel Tsang. Boston: Alyson Publications, 1981.

Rian, Karen. "Sadomasochism and the Social Construction of Desire." In *Against Sado-masochism: A Radical Feminist Analysis,* edited by Robin Ruth Linden, Darlene R. Pagano, Diana E. H. Russell, and Susan Leigh Star, 45–50. San Francisco: Frog in the Well, 1982.

Rich, Adrienne. "Compulsory Heterosexuality and Lesbian Existence." *Signs: Journal of Culture and Society* 5 (summer 1980): 631–60.

———. *Of Woman Born: Motherhood as Experience and Institution.* New York: Bantam Books, 1977.

Rich, B. Ruby. "Anti-Porn: Soft Issue, Hard World." *Village Voice* 20 (July 1982).

———. "Feminism and Sexuality in the 1980's." *Feminist Studies* 12, no. 3 (1986): 525–61.

Richards, Janet Radcliffe. *The Sceptical Feminist: A Philosophical Enquiry.* Boston: Routledge & Kegan Paul, 1980.

Riger, Stephanie. "Gender Dilemmas in Sexual Harassment Policies and Procedures." In *Sexual Harassment: Confrontations and Decisions,* edited by Edmund Wall, 197–215. Buffalo, N.Y.: Prometheus Books, 1992.

Rodgerson, Gillian. "Lesbian Erotic Explorations." In *Sex Exposed: Sexuality and the Pornography Debate,* edited by Lynne Segal and Mary McIntosh, 275–79. New Brunswick, N.J.: Rutgers University Press, 1992.

Rodriguez, Cecilia, and Marjorie Miller. "Muy Macho." *Los Angeles Times Magazine,* 6 December 1992.

Roiphe, Katie. *The Morning After: Sex, Fear, and Feminism on Campus.* Boston: Little, Brown, 1993.

Rosenfeld, Robert. "The Burden of Initiation." Paper presented at a symposium on the philosophy of sex and love at the Eastern Division meeting of the American Philosophical Association, Boston, Massachusetts, December 1994.

Rothblatt, Martine. *The Apartheid of Sex: A Manifesto on the Freedom of Gender.* New York: Crown, 1995.

Rubin, Gayle. "The Leather Menace: Comments on Politics and S/M." In *Coming to Power: Writings and Graphics on Lesbian S/M*, edited by Samois, 194–229. Boston: Alyson Publications, 1987.

———. "Misguided, Dangerous, and Wrong: An Analysis of Anti-Pornography Politics." In *Bad Girls and Dirty Pictures: The Challenge to Reclaim Feminism*, edited by Alison Assiter and Avedon Carol, 18–40. London: Pluto Press, 1993.

———. "Thinking Sex: Notes for a Radical Theory of the Politics of Sexuality." In *Pleasure and Danger: Exploring Female Sexuality*, edited by Carole S. Vance, 267–319. London: Pandora Press, 1989.

Rubin, Gayle, and Pat Califia. "Talking about Sadomasochism: Fears, Facts, Fantasies." *Gay Community News*, 15 August 1981.

Ruddick, Sara. "Better Sex." In *Philosophy and Sex*, 2d ed., edited by Robert Baker and Frederick Elliston, 280–99. Buffalo, N.Y.: Prometheus Books, 1984.

Ruse, Michael. "The Morality of Homosexuality." In *Philosophy and Sex*, 2d ed., edited by Robert Baker and Frederick Elliston, 370–90. Buffalo, N.Y.: Prometheus Books, 1984.

Rush, Florence. *The Best-Kept Secret: The Sexual Abuse of Children*. Blue Ridge Summit, Penn.: TAB Books, 1980.

———. "Child Pornography." In *Take Back the Night: Women on Pornography*, edited by Laura Lederer, 71–81. New York: William Morrow, 1980.

Russell, Diana E. H. *The Politics of Rape*. New York: Stein & Day, 1975.

———. "Pornography and Rape: A Causal Model." In *Making Violence Sexy: Feminist Views on Pornography*, edited by Diana E. H. Russell, 120–50. Buckingham, U.K.: Open University Press, 1993.

———. *Rape in Marriage*. New York: Macmillan, 1982.

———. "Sadomasochism: A Contra-Feminist Activity." In *Against Sadomasochism: A Radical Feminist Analysis*, edited by Robin Ruth Linden, Darlene R. Pagano, Diana E. H. Russell, and Susan Leigh Star, 176–83. San Francisco: Frog in the Well, 1982.

———. *The Secret Trauma*. New York: Basic Books, 1986.

———. *Sexual Exploitation: Rape, Child Sexual Abuse, and Workplace Harassment*. Newbury Park, Calif.: Sage Publications, 1984.

Russell, Diana E. H., with Laura Lederer. "Questions We Get Asked Most Often." In *Take Back the Night: Women on Pornography*, edited by Laura Lederer, 23–29. New York: William Morrow, 1980.

Ruth, Sheila. "Bodies and Souls/Sex, Sin and the Senses in Patriarchy: A Study in Applied Dualism." *Hypatia* 2, no. 1 (winter 1987): 149–63.

Sack, Fleur, and Anne Streeter. *Romance to Die For: The Startling Truth about Women, Sex, and AIDS*. Deerfield Beach, Fla.: Health Communications, Inc., 1992.

Sandfort, Theo. *The Sexual Aspects of Paedophile Relations: The Experience of Twenty-Five Boys*. Amsterdam: Pan/Spartacus, 1982.

Sawicki, Jana. *Disciplining Foucault*. New York: Routledge, 1991.

Sax, Marjan. "The Pink Thread." In *Sex Work: Writings by Women in the Sex Industry*, edited by Frédérique Delacoste and Priscilla Alexander, 301–4. Pittsburgh: Cleis Press, 1987.

Saxe, Lorena Leigh. "Sadomasochism and Exclusion." *Hypatia* 7 (fall 1992): 59–72.

Scanlon, T. M. "Freedom of Expression and Categories of Expression." In *Pornography and Censorship: Scientific, Philosophical and Legal Studies*, edited by David Copp and Susan Wendell, 139–65. Buffalo, N.Y.: Prometheus Books, 1983.

Schechter, Susan. *Women and Male Violence: The Visions and Struggles of the Battered Women's Movement*. Boston: South End Press, 1982.

Scheman, Naomi. *Engenderings: Constructions of Knowledge, Authority, and Privilege*. New York: Routledge, 1993.

Scott, Valerie, Peggy Miller, and Ryan Hotchkiss, of the Canadian Organization for the Rights of Prostitutes (CORP). "Realistic Feminists." In *Good Girls/Bad Girls: Feminists and Sex Trade Workers Face to Face*, edited by Laurie Bell, 204–17. Toronto: Seal Press, 1987.

Scruton, Roger. *Sexual Desire*. New York: Free Press, 1986.

Segal, Lynne. "Does Pornography Cause Violence?: The Search for Evidence." In *Dirty Looks: Women, Pornography, Power*, edited by Pamela Church Gibson and Roma Gibson, 5–21. London: BFI Publishing, 1993.

——. *Straight Sex: Rethinking the Politics of Pleasure*. Berkeley: University of California Press, 1994.

——. "Sweet Sorrows, Painful Pleasures: Pornography and the Perils of Heterosexual Desire." In *Sex Exposed: Sexuality and the Pornography Debate*, edited by Lynne Segal and Mary McIntosh, 65–91. New Brunswick, N.J.: Rutgers University Press, 1992.

Seidler, Victor J. "Men, Feminism, and Power." In *Rethinking Masculinity: Philosophical Explorations in Light of Feminism*, edited by Larry May and Robert Strikwerda, 209–20. Lanham, Md.: Rowman & Littlefield, 1992.

Seidman, Steven. *Embattled Eros: Sexual Politics and Ethics in Contemporary America*. New York: Routledge, 1992.

Shafer, Carolyn M., and Marilyn Frye. "Rape and Respect." In *Feminism and Philosophy*, edited by Mary Vetterling-Braggin, Frederick A. Elliston, and Jane English, 333–46. Totowa, N.J.: Littlefield, Adams, 1978.

Shrage, Laurie. "Is Sexual Desire Raced?: The Social Meaning of Interracial Prostitution." *Journal of Social Philosophy* 23 (spring 1992): 42–51.

——. *Moral Dilemmas of Feminism: Prostitution, Adultery, and Abortion*. New York: Routledge, 1994.

——. "Should Feminists Oppose Prostitution?" In *Feminism and Political Theory*, edited by Cass R. Sunstein, 185–99. Chicago: University of Chicago Press, 1990.

Sims, Karen, and Rose Mason, with Darlene Pagano. "Racism and Sadomasochism: A Conversation with Two Black Lesbians." In *Against Sadomasochism: A Radical Feminist Analysis*, edited by Robin Ruth Linden, Darlene R. Pagano, Diana E. H. Russell, and Susan Leigh Star, 99–105. San Francisco: Frog in the Well, 1982.

Simson, Rennie. "The Afro-American Female: The Historical Context of the Construction of Sexual Identity." In *Powers of Desire: The Politics of Sexuality*, edited by Ann Snitow, Christine Stansell, and Sharon Thompson, 229–35. New York: Monthly Review Press, 1983.

Singer, Linda. "True Confessions: Cixous and Foucault on Sexuality and Power." In *The Thinking Muse: Feminism and Modern French Philosophy*, edited by Jeffner Allen and Iris Marion Young, 136–55. Bloomington: Indiana University Press, 1989.

Slote, Michael. "Inapplicable Concepts and Sexual Perversion." In *Philosophy and Sex*, edited by Robert Baker and Frederick Elliston, 261–67. Buffalo, N.Y.: Prometheus Books, 1975.

Smart, Carol. "Unquestionably a Moral Issue: Rhetorical Devices and Regulatory Imperatives." In *Sex Exposed: Sexuality and the Pornography Debate*, edited by Lynne Segal and Mary McIntosh, 216–29. New Brunswick, N.J.: Rutgers University Press, 1992.

Smith, Jane. "Making Movies." In *Sex Work: Writings by Women in the Sex Industry*, edited by Frédérique Delacoste and Priscilla Alexander, 135–41. Pittsburgh: Cleis Press, 1987.

Smith, Valerie. "Split Affinities: The Case of Interracial Rape." In *Conflicts in Feminism*, edited by Marianne Hirsch and Evelyn Fox Keller, 271–87. New York: Routledge, 1990.

Snitow, Ann Barr. "Mass Market Romance: Pornography for Women Is Different." In *Powers of Desire: The Politics of Sexuality*, edited by Ann Snitow, Christine Stansell, and Sharon Thompson, 245–63. New York: Monthly Review Press, 1983.

Soble, Alan. "Defamation and the Endorsement of Degradation." In *Pornography: Private*

Right or Public Menace?, edited by Robert M. Baird and Stuart E. Rosenbaum, 96–107. Buffalo, N.Y.: Prometheus Books, 1991.

———. "Masturbation and Sexual Philosophy." In *The Philosophy of Sex*, 2d ed., edited by Alan Soble, 133–57. Savage, Md.: Rowman & Littlefield, 1991.

———. *Pornography, Marxism, Feminism, and the Future of Sexuality*. New Haven: Yale University Press, 1986.

———. "Pornography and the Social Sciences." In *The Philosophy of Sex*, 2d ed., edited by Alan Soble, 317–31. Savage, Md.: Rowman & Littlefield, 1991.

Social Text "Sex Workers and Sex Work" 37 (winter 1993).

Solomon, Robert C. "Love and Feminism." In *Philosophy and Sex*, 2d ed., edited by Robert Baker and Frederick Elliston, 53–70. Buffalo, N.Y.: Prometheus Books, 1984.

———. "Sex and Perversion." In *Philosophy and Sex*, edited by Robert Baker and Frederick Elliston, 268–87. Buffalo, N.Y.: Prometheus Books, 1975.

———. "Sexual Paradigms." In *The Philosophy of Sex*, 2d ed., edited by Alan Soble, 53–62. Savage, Md.: Rowman & Littlefield, 1991.

———. "The Virtue of (Erotic) Love." In *The Philosophy of (Erotic) Love*, edited by Robert C. Solomon and Kathleen M. Higgins, 492–518. Lawrence: University Press of Kansas, 1991.

Sommers, Christina. "Do These Feminists Like Women?" *Journal of Social Philosophy* 21 (fall/winter 1990): 66–74.

———. "Feminist Philosophers Are Oddly Unsympathetic to the Women They Claim to Represent." *Chronicle of Higher Education*, 11 October 1989.

———. "Philosophers against the Family." In *Person to Person*, edited by George Graham and Hugh LaFollette, 82–105. Philadelphia: Temple University Press, 1989.

Sommers, Christina Hoff. *Who Stole Feminism?: How Women Have Betrayed Women*. New York: Simon & Schuster, 1994.

A Southern Women's Writing Collective. "Sex Resistance in Heterosexual Arrangements." In *The Sexual Liberals and the Attack on Feminism*, edited by Dorchen Leidholdt and Janice G. Raymond, 140–47. New York: Teachers College Press, 1990.

Spelman, Elizabeth V. *Inessential Woman: Problems of Exclusion in Feminist Thought*. Boston: Beacon Press, 1988.

———. "On Treating Persons as Persons." *Ethics* 88 (1977): 150–61.

Spivak, Gayatri Chakravorty. *In Other Worlds: Essays in Cultural Politics*. New York: Methuen, 1987.

Sprinkle, Annie. "Beyond Bisexual." In *Bi Any Other Name: Bisexual People Speak Out*, edited by Loraine Hutchins and Lani Kaahumanu, 103–7. Boston: Alyson Publications, 1991.

———. *Post Porn Modernist*. Amsterdam: Torch Books, 1991.

Stanko, Elizabeth A. *Intimate Intrusions: Women's Experience of Male Violence*. London: Routledge & Kegan Paul, 1985.

Steinbock, Bonnie. "Adultery." In *The Philosophy of Sex*, 2d ed., edited by Alan Soble, 187–92. Savage, Md.: Rowman & Littlefield, 1991.

Steinem, Gloria. "Erotica and Pornography: A Clear and Present Difference." In *Pornography: Private Right or Public Menace?*, edited by Robert M. Baird and Stuart E. Rosenbaum, 51–55. Buffalo, N.Y.: Prometheus Books, 1991.

———. "The Real Linda Lovelace." In *Making Violence Sexy: Feminist Views on Pornography*, edited by Diana E. H. Russell, 23–31. Buckingham, U.K.: Open University Press, 1993.

St. James, Margo. "The Reclamation of Whores." In *Good Girls/Bad Girls: Feminists and Sex Trade Workers Face to Face*, edited by Laurie Bell, 81–87. Toronto: Seal Press, 1987.

Stock, Wendy. "Toward a Feminist Praxis of Sexuality." In *The Sexual Liberals and the Attack on Feminism*, edited by Dorchen Leidholdt and Janice G. Raymond, 148–56. New York: Teachers College Press, 1990.

Stoller, Robert J. *Porn: Myths for the Twentieth Century.* New Haven: Yale University Press, 1991.

——. *Sexual Excitement: Dynamics of Erotic Life.* New York: Simon & Schuster, 1980.

Stoltenberg, John. "How Men Have (a) Sex." In *Free Spirits: Feminist Philosophers on Culture,* edited by Kate Mehuron and Gary Percesepe, 410–18, 518. Englewood Cliffs, N.J.: Prentice Hall, 1995.

——. "Pornography and Freedom." In *Making Violence Sexy: Feminist Views on Pornography,* edited by Diana E. H. Russell, 65–77. Buckingham, U.K.: Open University Press, 1993.

——. "You Can't Fight Homophobia and Protect the Pornographers at the Same Time—An Analysis of What Went Wrong in *Hardwick.*" In *The Sexual Liberals and the Attack on Feminism,* edited by Dorchen Leidholdt and Janice G. Raymond, 184–90. New York: Teachers College Press, 1990.

Straayer, Chris. "The Seduction of Boundaries: Feminist Fluidity in Annie Sprinkle's Art/Education/Sex." In *Dirty Looks: Women, Pornography, Power,* edited by Pamela Church Gibson and Roma Gibson, 156–75. London: BFI Publishing, 1994.

Sturdevant, Saundra Pollack, and Brenda Stoltzfus. *Let the Good Times Roll: Prostitution and the U.S. Military in Asia.* New York: New Press, 1993.

Sugarman, David B., and Gerald T. Hotaling. "Dating Violence: A Review of Contextual and Risk Factors." In *Dating Violence: Young Women in Danger,* edited by Barrie Levy, 100–118. Seattle: Seal Press, 1991.

Suppes, Frederick. Commentary on Patrick D. Hopkins, "Rethinking Sadomasochism: Feminism, Interpretation, and Simulation." Paper and commentary presented at a symposium on philosophical perspectives on s/m sex at the Eastern Division meeting of the American Philosophical Association, Atlanta, Georgia, December 1993.

Swanton, Christine, Viviane Robinson, and Jan Crosthwaite. "Treating Women as Sex-Objects." *Journal of Social Philosophy* 20, no. 3 (1989): 5–20.

Tabet, Paola. "Hands, Tools, Weapons." *Feminist Issues* 2 (1982): 3–62.

——. "Imposed Reproduction: Maimed Sexuality." *Feminist Issues* 7 (1987): 3–31.

Tannehill, Reay. *Sex in History.* New York: Stein & Day, 1980.

Teitelbaum, Sheldon. "Cybersex." *Los Angeles Times Magazine,* 15 August 1993.

Tifft, Larry L. *Battering of Women: The Failure of Intervention and the Case for Prevention.* Boulder, Colo.: Westview Press, 1993.

Tong, Rosemarie. "Feminism, Pornography, and Censorship." *Social Theory and Practice* 8, no. 1 (spring 1982): 1–17.

——. *Feminist Thought.* Boulder, Colo.: Westview Press, 1989.

——. "Women, Pornography, and the Law." In *The Philosophy of Sex,* 2d ed., edited by Alan Soble, 301–16. Savage, Md.: Rowman & Littlefield, 1991.

——. *Women, Sex, and the Law.* Savage, Md.: Rowman & Littlefield, 1984.

Trask, Haunani-Kay. *Eros and Power: The Promise of Feminist Theory.* Philadelphia: University of Pennsylvania Press, 1986.

Trebilcot, Joyce. "Taking Responsibility for Sexuality." In *Philosophy and Sex,* 2d ed., edited by Robert Baker and Frederick Elliston, 421–30. Buffalo, N.Y.: Prometheus Books, 1984.

Tronto, Joan. "Beyond Gender Difference to a Theory of Care." In *An Ethic of Care: Feminist and Interdisciplinary Perspectives,* edited by Mary Jeanne Larrabee, 240–57. New York: Routledge, 1993.

——. *Moral Boundaries: A Political Argument for an Ethic of Care.* New York: Routledge, 1993.

Truong, Thanh-Dam. *Sex, Money and Morality: Prostitution and Tourism in South-East Asia.* London: Zed Books, 1990.

Tuana, Nancy. "Sexual Harassment in Academe: Issues of Power and Coercion." In *Sexual Harassment: Confrontations and Decisions*, edited by Edmund Wall, 49–60. Buffalo, N.Y.: Prometheus Books, 1992.

———. *Woman and the History of Philosophy*. New York: Paragon House, 1992.

"Turning Out the Charter for the First World Whores' Congress, Amsterdam, February 14, 1985." In *A Vindication of the Rights of Whores*, edited by Gail Pheterson, 33–42. Seattle: Seal Press, 1989.

Udovicki, Jasminka. "Justice and Care in Close Relationships." *Hypatia* 8 (summer 1993): 48–60.

"Update on HIV Infection and Prostitute Women." In *A Vindication of the Rights of Whores*, edited by Gail Pheterson, 132–40. Seattle: Seal Press, 1989.

Vadas, Melinda. "A First Look at the Pornography/Civil Rights Ordinance: Could Pornography Be the Subordination of Women?" *Journal of Philosophy* 84 (September 1987): 487–511.

———. "Reply to Patrick Hopkins." *Hypatia* 10 (spring 1995): 159–61.

Valentino, Margaret, and Mavis Johnson. "On the Game and On the Move." In *Prostitutes: Our Life*, edited by Claude Jaget, 9–31. Bristol, U.K.: Falling Wall Press, 1980.

Valverde, Mariana. *Sex, Power and Pleasure*. Philadelphia: New Society Publishers, 1987.

———. "Too Much Heat, Not Enough Light." In *Good Girls/Bad Girls: Feminists and Sex Trade Workers Face to Face*, edited by Laurie Bell, 27–32. Toronto: Seal Press, 1987.

Vance, Carole S. "Negotiating Sex and Gender in the Attorney General's Commission on Pornography." In *Sex Exposed: Sexuality and the Pornography Debate*, edited by Lynne Segal and Mary McIntosh, 29–49. New Brunswick, N.J.: Rutgers University Press, 1992.

———. "Pleasure and Danger: Toward a Politics of Sexuality." In *Pleasure and Danger: Exploring Female Sexuality*, edited by Carole S. Vance, 1–27. London: Pandora Press, 1989.

Vannoy, Russell. *Sex without Love*. Buffalo, N.Y.: Prometheus Books, 1980.

Waldby, Catherine. *AIDS and the Body Politic: Biomedicine and Sexual Difference*. New York: Routledge, 1996.

Walker, Alice. "Coming Apart." In *Take Back the Night: Women on Pornography*, edited by Laura Lederer, 95–104. New York: William Morrow, 1980.

Walker, Lenore. *The Battered Woman Syndrome*. New York: Springer Publishing, 1984.

Walkowitz, Judith. "Male Vice and Female Virtue: Feminism and the Politics of Prostitution in Nineteenth-Century Britain." In *Powers of Desire: The Politics of Sexuality*, edited by Ann Snitow, Christine Stansell, and Sharon Thompson, 419–38. New York: Monthly Review Press, 1983.

———. "The Politics of Prostitution." *Signs: Journal of Women in Culture and Society* 6, no. 1 (autumn 1980): 123–35.

———. *Prostitution and Victorian Society: Women, Class, and the State*. New York: Cambridge University Press, 1980.

Wall, Edmund. "The Definition of Sexual Harassment." In *Sexual Harassment: Confrontations and Decisions*, edited by Edmund Wall, 69–85. Buffalo, N.Y.: Prometheus Books, 1992.

Walsh, Kate. "The Hill on Hillary: What a Bright Girl." *Wall Street Journal*, 5 November 1993.

Wardlaw, Grant. "The Problem of Defining Terrorism." In his *Political Terrorism: Theory, Tactics, and Counter-Measures*. Cambridge: Cambridge University Press, 1982.

Wasserstrom, Richard. "Is Adultery Immoral?" In *Philosophy and Sex*, 2d ed., edited by Robert Baker and Frederick Elliston, 93–106. Buffalo, N.Y.: Prometheus Books, 1984.

Webb, Susan L. *Step Forward: Sexual Harassment in the Workplace/What You Need to Know!* New York: MasterMedia Limited, 1991.

Webster, Paula. "The Forbidden: Eroticism and Taboo." In *Pleasure and Danger: Exploring Female Sexuality*, edited by Carole S. Vance, 385–98. London: Pandora Press, 1989.

———. "Pornography and Pleasure." *Heresies* #12 "Sex Issue" 3, no. 4 (1981): 48–51.

Weedon, Chris. *Feminist Practice and Poststructuralist Theory*. Oxford: Basil Blackwell, 1987.

Weene, Seph. "Venus." *Heresies* #12 "Sex Issue" 3, no. 4 (1981): 36–38.

Weinzweig, Marjorie. "Should a Feminist Choose a Marriage-Like Relationship?" *Hypatia* 1 (fall 1986): 139–63.

West, Rachel. "U.S. PROStitutes Collective." In *Sex Work: Writings by Women in the Sex Industry*, edited by Frédérique Delacoste and Priscilla Alexander, 279–89. Pittsburgh: Cleis Press, 1987.

White, Evelyn C. "The Abused Black Woman: Challenging a Legacy of Pain." In *Dating Violence: Young Women in Danger*, edited by Barrie Levy, 84–93. Seattle: Seal Press, 1991.

———. *Chain Chain Change: For Black Women Dealing with Physical and Emotional Abuse*. Seattle: Seal Press, 1985.

Williams, Linda. *Hard Core: Power, Pleasure, and the "Frenzy of the Visible."* Berkeley: University of California Press, 1989.

———. "Pornographies On/scene, or Diff'rent Strokes for Diff'rent Folks." In *Sex Exposed: Sexuality and the Pornography Debate*, edited by Lynne Segal and Mary McIntosh, 184–99. New Brunswick, N.J.: Rutgers University Press, 1992.

———. "A Provoking Agent: The Pornography and Performance Art of Annie Sprinkle." In *Dirty Looks: Women, Pornography, Power*, edited by Pamela Church Gibson and Roma Gibson, 176–91. London: BFI Publishing, 1993.

Willis, Ellen. "Feminism, Moralism, and Pornography." In *Powers of Desire: The Politics of Sexuality*, edited by Ann Snitow, Christine Stansell, and Sharon Thompson, 460–67. New York: Monthly Review Press, 1983.

———. *No More Nice Girls: Countercultural Essays*. Hanover, N.H.: Wesleyan University Press, 1992.

Wittig, Monique. *The Straight Mind and Other Essays*. Boston: Beacon Press, 1992.

Woerner, William L., and Sharon L. Oswald. "Sexual Harassment in the Workplace: A View through the Eyes of the Courts." In *Sexual Harassment: Confrontations and Decisions*, edited by Edmund Wall, 171–81. Buffalo, N.Y.: Prometheus Books, 1992.

Wolf, Naomi. *The Beauty Myth: How Images of Beauty Are Used against Women*. New York: Anchor Books/Doubleday, 1991.

———. *Fire with Fire: The New Female Power and How to Use It*. New York: Ballentine Books, 1994.

Women's AIDS Network. *Lesbians and AIDS: What's the Connection?* San Francisco: S.F. AIDS Foundation and the S.F. Department of Public Health, July 1986. Revised October 1987.

Wreen, Michael J. "What's Really Wrong with Adultery?" In *The Philosophy of Sex*, 2d ed., edited by Alan Soble, 179–86. Savage, Md.: Rowman & Littlefield, 1991.

Wynter, Sarah. "WHISPER: Women Hurt in Systems of Prostitution Engaged in Revolt." In *Sex Work: Writings by Women in the Sex Industry*, edited by Frédérique Delacoste and Priscilla Alexander, 266–70. Pittsburgh: Cleis Press, 1987.

Young, Cathy. "The Sexist Violence against Women Act." *Wall Street Journal*, 23 March 1994.

Zinn, Maxine Baca, Lynn Weber Cannon, Elizabeth Higginbotham, and Bonnie Thornton Dill. "The Costs of Exclusionary Practices in Women's Studies." *Signs: Journal of Culture and Society* 11, no. 2 (1986): 290–303.

Index

Abcarian, Robin, 181
abortion, 62, 64, 75
abstinence, 28, 30, 35, 55, 63, 65
abuse of girls. *See* child abuse; sexual abuse
    of girls
abuse of women. *See* sexual abuse of
    women; violence against women
adult/child sex. *See* cross-generational sex
adultery
    and promiscuity, 28, 35, 36, 39, 40, 43, 44,
        45–46, 50, 54, 55, 58, 61, 145
    and rape, 167
agency of women, sexual
    in producing pornography, 22, 113, 133,
        136, 138, 144
    in promiscuity, 38, 55, 59
    and sexual empowerment, 28, 54–56, 59,
        65, 140, 144, 158, 195–96
    and sexual pleasure, 11, 22–23, 28, 29
    and sexual taboo, 42, 64, 65, 66, 83
    in sex work, 113–17, 130–44, 149, 155
    See also self-definition of women, sexual
AIDS (Acquired Immunodeficiency
    Syndrome)
    and promiscuity, 27, 28, 29–30, 31, 34, 39,
        61–65, 104, 112, 139, 144

and prostitution, 136, 139, 142
    public education about, 136, 139
Alcoff, Linda, 13, 25–26
Allison, Julie, 167, 168–69, 182
androcentrism, 15, 64, 84, 110, 126
    See also sexism
antimale bias. *See* feminism: antimale bias in
antisex bias. *See* feminism: antisex bias in
Aquinas, Thomas, 14
Aristotle, 7, 14
artificial insemination, 80
Astuto, Cynthia, 92–93
Atkinson, Ti-Grace, 68
Attorney General's Commission on
    Pornography (1986), 115
autonomous being for oneself, 106, 211
    and sex work, 151
autonomous relating to others, 54, 55, 102,
    106, 107
    men encouraging women's exercise of,
        211–13
    men's exercise of, 210, 211–13
    and sex work, 149, 151
autonomy, sexual, 96, 99, 100, 113, 150
    resisting abuse, 207
    and romantic love, 48–50